ROGET'S THESAURUS

A Division of Scentex, Inc.
Chicago, Illinois 60651

Published by arrangement with
Thomas Nelson Publishers

ISBN: 0-8407-5634-8

9 10 11 12 13 14 15 16 17 18 19 20-90 89 88 87

Editors' Preface

PETER MARK ROGET (1779–1869) was a British lexicographer and physician. *Roget's Thesaurus*, a standard reference work for over a century, represents his highly personal view of how the English language reflects the structure of the universe. In some ways, that view is dated today; but the complex structure and breadth of the thesaurus still prove surprisingly helpful to the modern user.

For most users, the key to the synonyms in the body of the book lies in the alphabetical listing in the index. The uniqueness of Roget's original plan of classification provides the user with access to related words and requires nothing more than a near-synonym to help locate the word sought. *Roget's Thesaurus* is more than simply a synonym dictionary—both in the lists following individual headwords and in the groupings of headwords under the various sections, it is a diverse collection of associated and related words and phrases.

For example, suppose you are looking for a synonym for *lull*: a check in the index yields the reference number, 403; turning to that entry provides the synonyms *silence, stillness, quiet, hush, peace.*

But, suppose you are trying to find a verb meaning 'to feel very dissatisfied' and the synonyms listed under *discontent* are not "strong" enough for your purpose. A brief check of the related, contiguous headwords will lead you to the entry for *regret* which provides the synonyms *lament, deplore, bemoan, bewail, rue.*

This edition of *Roget's Thesaurus* has a number of other special features. Dictionaries of synonyms, unless they are of considerable size, rarely provide alphabetical listings of all the words in the book. In this *Pocket Roget*, you will find every word listed in the index.

Larger books may provide more synonyms, but the user of a thesaurus is rarely looking for a rare or unusual word: he wants an equivalent word that is part of everyday language. This pocket edition is the only abridged *Roget's Thesaurus* available. While retaining the original structure and all the 1,000 headwords, all antiquated words and phrases have been removed. In addition, the book has been modernized to include the most current usage and the newest developments in language.

It is the Editors' sincere opinion that this *Pocket Roget* will serve the user in a great many situations in which a larger, more comprehensive work would prove confusing or misleading. Certainly, its handy size is sure to prove convenient for any writer who wishes to use the English language more expressively and precisely.

Laurence Urdang
Editor in Chief
Mark Boyer
Managing Editor

In this abridgment, many duplications have been omitted to save space. For maximum usefulness, the user should look through other associated parts of speech for the word he is seeking, for adjectives and verbs can yield nouns and adverbs, and vice versa. For example, adverbs can be formed by adding -*ly* to some adjectives and nouns by adding -*ness* to some adjectives.

Caution: If the word selected is not completely familiar, check its meaning and usage in a good dictionary before risking its use in an incorrect or unidiomatic context.

Plan of Classification
(following the original Roget plan)

1

Tabular Synopsis of Categories

Class I. ABSTRACT RELATIONS

I. EXISTENCE

1. existence	2. nonexistence
3. substantiality	4. unsubstantiality
5. intrinsicality	6. extrinsicality
7. state	8. circumstance

II. RELATION

9. relation	10. nonrelation
11. consanguinity	
12. correlation	
13. identity	14. contrariety

15. difference

16. uniformity	16a. lack of uniformity
17. similarity	18. dissimilarity
19. imitation	20. nonimitation

20a. variation

21. copy	22. prototype
23. agreement	24. disagreement

III. QUANTITY

25. quantity	26. degree
27. equality	28. inequality

29. mean

30. compensation

31. greatness	32. smallness
33. superiority	34. inferiority
35. increase	36. decrease
37. addition	38. deduction
39. adjunct	40. remainder
	40a. decrement
41. mixture	42. simpleness
43. junction	44. disjunction
45. link	
46. coherence	47. incoherence
48. combination	49. decomposition
50. whole	51. part
52. completeness	53. incompleteness
54. composition	55. exclusion
56. component	57. extraneousness

IV. ORDER

58. order	59. disorder
60. arrangement	61. derangement

3

62. precedence	63. sequence
64. precursor	65. sequel
66. beginning	67. end

68. middle

69. continuity	70. discontinuity
71. term	
72. assemblage	73. dispersion
74. focus	
75. class	
76. inclusion	77. exclusion
78. generality	79. specialty
80. regulation	81. multiformity
82. conformity	83. unconformity

V. NUMBER

84. number	
85. numeration	
86. list	
87. unity	88. accompaniment
89. duality	
90. duplication	91. bisection
92. triality	
93. triplication	94. trisection
95. quaternity	
96. quadruplication	97. quadrisection
98. five, etc.	99. quinquesection
100. plurality	100a. fraction
	101. zero
102. multitude	103. fewness
104. repetition	
105. infinity	

VI. TIME

106. time	107. absence of time
108. period	109. course
110. durability	111. transience
112. perpetuity	113. instantaneousness
114. chronometry	115. anachronism
116. antecedence	117. posteriority
118. present time	119. different time
120. contemporaneousness	
121. the future	122. the past
123. newness	124. oldness
125. morning; noon	126. evening; midnight

4

127. youth	128. age
129. infant	130. veteran

131. adolescence

132. earliness	133. lateness
134. opportuneness	135. inopportuneness
136. frequency	137. infrequency
138. regularity	139. irregularity

VII. CHANGE

140. change	141. permanence
142. cessation	143. continuance
144. conversion	
	145. reversion
146. revolution	
147. substitution	148. interchange
149. changeableness	150. stability
151. present events	152. future events

VIII. CAUSATION

153. cause	154. effect
155. attribution	156. chance
157. power	158. impotence
159. strength	160. weakness
161. production	162. destruction
163. reproduction	
164. producer	165. destroyer
166. parentage	167. posterity
168. productiveness	169. unproductiveness
170. agency	
171. energy	172. inertness
173. violence	174. moderation
175. influence	175a. absence of influence
176. tendency	
177. liability	
178. concurrence	179. counteraction

Class II. SPACE
I. SPACE IN GENERAL

180. space (indefinite)	180a. inextension
	181. region (definite)
	182. place
183. situation	
184. location	185. displacement
186. presence	187. absence
188. inhabitant	189. habitation

5

190. contents
191. receptacle

II. DIMENSIONS

192. size
193. littleness
194. expansion
195. contraction
196. distance
197. nearness
198. interval
199. contiguity
200. length
201. shortness
202. breadth, thickness
203. narrowness, thinness
204. layer
205. filament
206. height
207. lowness
208. depth
209. shallowness
210. summit
211. base
212. verticality
213. horizontality
214. suspension
215. support
216. parallelism
217. obliquity
218. inversion
219. crossing
220. exteriority
221. interiority
222. centrality
223. covering
224. lining
225. dress
226. undress
227. environment
228. interspersion
229. circumscription
230. outline
231. edge
232. enclosure
233. limit
234. front
235. rear
236. side
237. opposition
238. right
239. left

III. FORM

240. form
241. formlessness
242. symmetry
243. distortion
244. angularity
245. curvature
246. straightness
247. circularity
248. convolution
249. rotundity
250. convexity
251. flatness
252. concavity
253. sharpness
254. bluntness
255. smoothness
256. roughness
257. notch

6

258. fold
259. furrow
260. opening
262. perforator

261. closure
263. stopper

IV. MOTION

264. motion
266. journey
268. traveler
270. transference
271. carrier
272. vehicle
274. velocity
276. impulse
278. direction
280. precedence
282. progression
284. propulsion
286. approach
288. attraction
290. convergence
292. arrival
294. ingress
296. reception
298. eating
300. insertion
302. passage
303. infringement
305. ascent
307. elevation
309. leap
311. circular motion
312. rotation
314. oscillation
315. agitation

265. rest
267. navigation
269. mariner, flier

273. ship
275. slowness
277. recoil
279. deviation
281. sequence
283. regression
285. traction
287. recession
289. repulsion
291. divergence
293. departure
295. egress
297. ejection
299. excretion
301. extraction

304. shortcoming
306. descent
308. depression
310. plunge

313. evolution

Class III. MATTER
I. MATTER IN GENERAL

316. materiality
318. world
319. gravity

317. immateriality

320. levity

II. INORGANIC MATTER

321. density
323. hardness

322. thinness
324. softness

393. condiment
394. savoriness
396. sweetness
398. odor
400. fragrance
402. sound
404. loudness
406. snap
408. resonance

410. stridency
411. cry
413. melody, concord
415. music
416. musician
417. musical instruments
418. hearing
420. light

395. unsavoriness
397. sourness
399. inodorousness
401. fetor
403. silence
405. faintness
407. roll
408a. nonresonance
409. sibilation

412. ululation
414. discord

419. deafness
421. darkness

422. dimness

423. luminary
425. transparency

424. shade
426. opacity
427. semitransparency

428. color
430. whiteness
432. gray
434. red
436. yellow
438. blue
440. variegation
441. vision

429. colorlessness
431. blackness
433. brown
435. green
437. purple
439. orange

442. blindness
443. dimsightedness

444. spectator
445. optical instruments
446. visibility
448. appearance

447. invisibility
449. disappearance

Class IV. INTELLECT
I. FORMATION OF IDEAS

450. intellect
451. thought
453. idea
455. curiosity
457. attention

450a. absence of intellect
452. absence of thought
454. topic
456. incuriosity
458. inattention

II. COMMUNICATION OF IDEAS

524. interpreter
525. manifestation 526. latency
527. information 528. concealment
529. disclosure 530. ambush
531. publication
532. news 533. secret
534. messenger
535. affirmation 536. negation, denial
537. teaching 538. misteaching
539. learning
540. teacher 541. learner
542. school
543. veracity 544. falsehood
545. deception
546. untruth
547. dupe 548. deceiver
549. exaggeration
550. indication
551. record 552. obliteration
553. recorder
554. representation 555. misrepresentation
556. painting
557. sculpture
558. engraving
559. artist
560. language
561. letter
562. word 563. neology
564. nomenclature 565. misnomer
566. phrase
567. grammar 568. solecism
569. style
570. perspicuity 571. obscurity
572. conciseness 573. diffuseness
574. vigor 575. feebleness
576. plainness 577. ornament
578. elegance 579. inelegance
580. voice 581. muteness
582. speech 583. inarticulateness
584. loquacity 585. taciturnity
586. public address 587. response
588. conversation 589. soliloquy

11

590. writing
591. printing
592. correspondence
593. book
594. description
595. dissertation
596. compendium
597. poetry
598. prose
599. the drama

Class V. VOLITION
I. INDIVIDUAL VOLITION

600. will
601. necessity
602. willingness
603. unwillingness
604. resolution
605. irresolution
604a. perseverance
606. obstinacy
607. recantation
608. caprice
609. choice
609a. neutrality
610. rejection
611. predetermination
612. impulse
613. habit
614. disuse
615. motive
615a. absence of motive
616. dissuasion
617. plea
618. good
619. evil
620. intention
621. chance
622. pursuit
623. avoidance
624. relinquishment
625. business
626. plan
627. method
628. mid-course
629. circuit
630. requirement
631. instrumentality
632. means
633. instrument
634. substitute
635. materials
636. store
637. provision
638. waste
639. sufficiency
640. insufficiency
641. redundance
642. importance
643. unimportance
644. utility
645. inutility

12

646. expedience
647. inexpedience
648. goodness
649. badness
650. perfection
651. imperfection
652. cleanness
653. uncleanness
654. health
655. disease
656. salubrity
657. insalubrity
658. improvement
659. deterioration
660. restoration
661. relapse
662. remedy
663. bane
664. safety
665. danger
666. refuge
667. pitfall
668. warning
669. alarm
670. preservation
671. escape
672. deliverance
673. preparation
674. nonpreparation
675. essay
676. undertaking
677. use
678. disuse
679. misuse

680. action
681. inaction
682. activity
683. inactivity
684. haste
685. leisure
686. exertion
687. repose
688. fatigue
689. refreshment
690. agent
691. workshop
692. conduct
693. direction
694. director
695. advice
696. council
697. precept
698. skill
699. unskillfulness
700. expert
701. bungler
702. cunning
703. artlessness
704. difficulty
705. facility
706. hindrance
707. aid
708. opposition
709. cooperation
710. opponent
711. auxiliary
712. party

713. discord 714. concord
715. defiance
716. attack 717. defense
718. retaliation 719. resistance
720. contention 721. peace
722. warfare 723. pacification
724. mediation
725. submission
726. combatant
727. arms
728. arena
729. completion 730. noncompletion
731. success 732. failure
733. trophy
734. prosperity 735. adversity

736. mediocrity

II. INTERSOCIAL VOLITION

737. authority 738. laxity
739. severity 740. lenience
741. command
742. disobedience 743. obedience
744. compulsion
745. master 746. servant
747. scepter
748. freedom 749. subjection
750. liberation 751. restraint
752. prison
753. keeper 754. prisoner
755. commission 756. abrogation
757. resignation
758. consignee
759. deputy
760. permission 761. prohibition
762. consent
763. offer 764. refusal
765. request 766. deprecation
767. petitioner
768. promise
769. compact
770. conditions
771. security
772. observance 773. nonobservance

14

774. compromise

775. acquisition 776. loss
777. possession 777a. exemption
778. participation
779. possessor
780. property
781. retention 782. relinquishment
783. transfer
784. giving 785. receiving
786. apportionment
787. lending 788. borrowing
789. taking 790. restitution
791. stealing
792. thief
793. booty
794. barter
795. purchase 796. sale
797. merchant
798. merchandise
799. market
800. money
801. treasurer
802. treasury
803. wealth 804. poverty
805. credit 806. debt
807. payment 808. nonpayment
809. expenditure 810. receipt
811. accounts
812. price 813. discount
814. dearness 815. cheapness
816. liberality 817. economy
818. prodigality 819. parsimony

Class VI. AFFECTIONS
I. AFFECTIONS IN GENERAL

820. affections
821. feelings
822. sensibility 823. insensibility
824. excitation
825. excitability 826. inexcitability

II. PERSONAL AFFECTIONS

827. pleasure 828. pain
829. pleasurableness 830. painfulness

15

831. content
832. discontent
833. regret
834. relief
835. aggravation
836. cheerfulness
837. dejection
838. rejoicing
839. lamentation
840. amusement
841. weariness
842. wit
843. dullness
844. humorist
845. beauty
846. ugliness
847. ornament
848. blemish
849. simplicity
850. taste
851. vulgarity
852. fashion

853. ridiculousness
854. fop
855. affectation
856. ridicule
857. laughing-stock
858. hope
859. hopelessness
860. fear
861. courage
862. cowardice
863. rashness
864. caution
865. desire
867. dislike

866. indifference

868. fastidiousness
869. satiety
870. wonder
871. expectance
872. prodigy
873. repute
874. disrepute
875. nobility
876. commonalty
877. title
878. pride
879. humility
880. vanity
881. modesty
882. ostentation
883. celebration
884. boasting
885. insolence
886. servility
887. blusterer

III. SYMPATHETIC AFFECTIONS

888. friendship
889. enmity
890. friend
891. enemy
892. sociality
893. seclusion, exclusion

894. courtesy

896. congratulations

897. love

899. favorite

902. endearment

903. marriage

906. benevolence

910. philanthropy

912. benefactor

914. pity

915. condolence

916. gratitude

918. forgiveness

895. discourtesy

898. hate

900. resentment

901. irascibility

901a. sullenness

904. celibacy

905. divorce

907. malevolence

908. malediction

909. threat

911. misanthropy

913. evildoer

914a. pitilessness

917. ingratitude

919. revenge

920. jealousy

921. envy

IV. MORAL AFFECTIONS

922. right

924. claim

926. duty

928. respect

931. approbation

933. flattery

935. flatterer

937. vindication

939. probity

942. disinterestedness

944. virtue

946. innocence

948. good man

950. penitence

952. atonement

953. temperance

923. wrong

925. unrightfulness

927. dereliction of duty

927a. exemption

929. disrespect

930. contempt

932. disapprobation

934. detraction

936. detractor

938. accusation

940. improbity

941. knave

943. selfishness

945. vice

947. guilt

949. bad man

951. impenitence

954. intemperance

954a. sensualist

955. asceticism
956. fasting
957. gluttony
958. sobriety
959. drunkenness
960. purity
961. impurity
962. libertine
963. legality
964. illegality
965. jurisdiction
966. tribunal
967. judge
968. lawyer
969. lawsuit
970. acquittal
971. condemnation
972. punishment
973. reward
974. penalty
975. scourge

V. RELIGIOUS AFFECTIONS

976. deity
977. angel
978. devil
979. fabulous spirit
980. demon
981. heaven
982. hell
983. theology
983a. orthodoxy
984. heterodoxy
985. revelation
986. religious writings
987. piety
988. impiety
989. irreligion
990. worship
991. idolatry
992. sorcery
993. spell
994. sorcerer
995. churchdom
996. clergy
997. laity
998. rite
999. canonicals
1000. temple

Thesaurus

Class I

Words Expressing Abstract Relations

I. Existence

1 existence *n* being, entity, subsistence, reality, actuality, presence, fact, matter of fact, truth, science of existence: ontology.

v exist, be, subsist, live, breathe; occur, happen, take place; consist in, lie in; endure, remain, abide, survive, last, stay, continue.

adj existent, extant; prevalent, current, afloat; real, actual, true, positive, absolute; substantial, substantive; well founded, well grounded.

adv actually, in fact, in reality.

2 nonexistence *n* inexistence; insubstantiality, nonentity; blank, *tabula rasa*, void, emptiness, nothingness; potential, possibility; annihilation, extinction, obliteration, total destruction.

v not exist; pass away, perish, die, die out, disappear, dissolve; annihilate, destroy, obliterate, wipe off the face of the earth; nullify, void; take away, remove.

adj nonexistent, inexistent; blank, void, empty; unreal, baseless, insubstantial, intangible, ineffable, spiritual, spectral; unborn, uncreated, unbegotten, unconceived; potential, possible; exhausted, gone, lost, departed, extinct, defunct; fabulous, visionary, imaginative, ideal, conceptual, abstract.

3 substantiality *n* materiality, corporality, tangibility, material existence, bodiliness, matter, stuff; creature, being, person, body, flesh and blood, substance; thing, object, article.

adj substantive, substantial, corporeal, material, bodily, physical, concrete, tangible, palpable, corporal, materialistic.

4 unsubstantiality *n* nothingness; nothing, naught, nil, nullity, zero; shadow, phantom, apparition, dream, illusion; fallacy, inanity, frivolity; hollowness, blank, void; flimsiness, thinness, slightness.

v vanish, evaporate, fade, dissolve, melt away, disappear.

adj unsubstantial, baseless, groundless, ungrounded, without foundation, fallacious, erroneous, untenable; insignificant, slight, thin, trifling, frivolous; imaginary, visionary, dreamy, shadowy, ethereal, airy, immaterial, spectral, illusory, incorporeal, intangible, bodiless, abstract; vacant, vacuous, empty, blank, hollow.

5 intrinsicality *n* ego, essence, quintessence, gist, pith, marrow, sap, lifeblood, backbone, heart, soul, core; principle, nature, constitution, construction, character, type, quality; habit, temper, temperament, personality, spirit, humor, grain, moods, features, peculiarities, aspects, idiosyncrasies, tendencies, bents; inhering, inherence, essentiality.

v be intrinsic, be inherent.

adj intrinsic, inherent, implanted, innate, inborn, inbred, ingrained; essential, fundamental, basic, normal; inherited, congenital, hereditary, indigenous, in the blood, in the genes; instinctive, instinctual, internal, personal, subjective; characteristic, peculiar, idiosyncratic; fixed, set in one's ways, invariable, unchangeable, incurable, ineradicable.

adv intrinsically, at bottom, in effect, practically, virtually, substantially.

6 extrinsicality *n* extraneousness, externals.

adj extrinsic, extraneous, external, adventitious; collateral, accidental, incidental, objective.

adv extrinsically.

7 state *n* condition, case, circumstances, situation, status, surroundings, pass, plight, pickle; mood, temper, frame; constitution, structure, form, phase, frame, fabric, stamp, set, fit, mold; mode, style, fashion, light, complexion, character; tone, tenor, turn.

v be in a state.

8 circumstance *n* situation, phase, position, condition, posture, attitude, place, point; footing, standing, status; occasion, happening, event, juncture, conjunction; predicament, exigency, emergency, crisis, pinch, plight, pass; climax, apex, turning point.

adj circumstantial, conditional, provisional; contingent, incidental, adventitious; critical, climactic.

adv under the circumstances,

under the conditions; thus, in such wise; accordingly, that being the case, since, seeing that, as matters stand; conditionally, provided, if, in case; if so, if it so happen, in the event of, provisionally, unless.

II. Absolute Relation

9 relation *n* connection, concern, bearing, reference; correlation, analogy; similarity, affinity, homogeneity, alliance, association, nearness; approximation, relationship; comparison, ratio, proportion; link, tie, bond.

v relate to, refer to; bear upon, regard, concern, touch, affect, have to do with, pertain to, appertain to, belong to; bring into relation with, associate, connect, parallel; link, bind, tie.

adj relative, relative to, relating to, referable to, with reference to; belonging to; related, connected, associated, affiliated, allied; in the same category, relevant.

adv as regards, about, concerning, with relation to, with reference to, with regard to, with respect to, in connection with, under the head of, in the matter of.

10 [absence of relation] **non-relation** *n* irrelation, dissociation, lack of connection; disconnection, disjunction; inconsequence, irreconcilability, disagreement, heterogeneity; independence.

v have no relation to, have no bearing upon, have nothing to do with, have no connection with.

adj unrelated, irrespective, unallied, unconnected, disconnected, heterogeneous, independent; adrift, insular, isolated; extraneous, strange, alien, foreign, outlandish, exotic; irrelevant, inapplicable, not pertinent, beside the mark, off base; remote, farfetched, out-of-the-way, forced, detached, distanced; incidental, parenthetical.

adv parenthetically, by the way, by the by; incidentally.

11 [relations of kindred] **consanguinity** *n* relationship, kindred, blood; parentage, paternity, maternity, lineage, heritage; filiation, affiliation, connection, alliance, tie; family, blood relation, ties of blood, kinsman, kinfolk, kith and kin, relation, relative, one's own, one's own flesh and blood; fraternity, sorority, brotherhood, sisterhood; race, stock, generation.

v be related to, claim relationship with.

adj related, akin, consanguineous, allied, affiliated, connected; kindred, familial.

12 [double or reciprocal relation] **correlation** *n* correspondence, reciprocity, reciprocation, interdependence, mutuality, interchange, exchange.

v reciprocate, alternate, interchange, interact, interdepend; interchange, exchange; correlate, correspond, relate.

adj reciprocal, mutual, correlative, corresponding, analogous, complementary; equivalent, interchangeable, alternate.

adv reciprocally.

13 identity *n* sameness, exactness, equality, correspondence, parallelism, unity, convertibility; resemblance, similarity; self, oneself, name, personality; facsimile, duplicate, replica, copy, reproduction.

v be identical, coincide, coalesce.

adj identical, self, the same, selfsame; coincident, coinciding, coalescent, indistinguishable; one, equal, equivalent.

adv identically.

14 contrariety *n* contrast, foil, antithesis, oppositeness, opposition; contradiction, antipathy, antagonism; the reverse, the inverse, the converse, inversion, subversion, reversal, the opposite, antipodes.

v be contrary, contrast with, differ from, oppose; invert, revert, turn upside down; contradict, contravene; antagonize.

adj contrary, opposite, counter, converse, reverse; opposed, antithetical, contrasted, antipodean, antagonistic, opposing; conflicting, inconsistent, contradictory; negative, hostile.

15 difference *n* discrepancy, disparity, dissimilarity, inconsistency, variance, variation, diversity, imbalance, disagreement, inequality, inequity, divergence, contrast, contrariety; discrimination, distinction, nice distinction, shade, nuance, subtlety.

v differ, vary; diversify, modify, change, alter; contrast, mismatch; discriminate, distinguish.

adj different, diverse, heterogeneous, unlike, divergent, altered, changed, deviant, deviating, variant, varied, modified; diversified, various, divers, miscellaneous, manifold; other, another, not the same, unequal, unmatched, wide apart; distinctive, characteristic, discriminative.

16 uniformity *n* homogeneity, permanence, continuity, consistency, stability, accordance, standardization, conformity, agreement; regularity, constancy, evenness, sameness; monotony, routine, invariability.

v be uniform, accord with; conform to, assimilate; level, smooth, even.

adj uniform, homogeneous, of a piece, consistent; consistent, regular, constant, even, level; invariable, unchanging, unvarying, unvaried, unchanged, constant, regular; undiversified, solid, plain, dreary, monotonous, routine.

adv uniformly; always, invariably, without exception; ever, forever.

16a lack of uniformity *n* diversity, irregularity, unevenness, inconsistency, nonconformity, heterogeneity.

adj diversified, varied, irregular, inconsistent, motley, patchwork, uneven, rough; multifarious, of various kinds.

17 similarity *n* resemblance, likeness, similitude, semblance, affinity, approximation, parallelism; agreement, correspondence, analogy; brotherhood, family likeness; repetition, sameness, uniformity, identity; the like, fellow, match, pair, mate, twin, double, counterpart; alter ego, chip off the old block, birds of a feather, like two peas in a pod; simile, parallel, type, image, representation.

v be similar, resemble, look like, bear a resemblance, take after, approximate, parallel, match, rhyme with.

adj similar, resembling, like, alike; twin; analogous, parallel, of a piece; allied to, akin to, corresponding; approximate, much the same, near, close, something like; imitative, mock, pseudo, simulating, representing, representative; exact, true, lifelike, faithful, true to life, identical.

adv as it, so to speak; as it were, as if it were; quasi, just as.

18 dissimilarity *n* dissimilitude, unlikeness, difference; diversity, disparity, divergence; novelty, originality, uniqueness.

v be unlike, differ from, bear no resemblance; vary, diversify, differentiate.

adj dissimilar, unlike, different, disparate; unique, new, novel, unprecedented, unmatched, unequaled; diversified.

19 imitation *n* copying; copy, duplication, reproduction, replica; mocking, mimicry, aping; simulation, impersonation, representation, semblance, approximation, paraphrase, parody; plagiarism, forgery.

v imitate, copy, mirror, reflect, impersonate, duplicate, reproduce, simulate, counterfeit; mock, take off, mimic, ape, personate, parody, caricature, travesty; follow, emulate,

pattern after, model oneself on, parallel, follow, take after.

adj imitative, modeled after, modeled on, based on; fake, phony, counterfeit, false, imitation, mock; duplicate, second hand.

adv literally, word for word, to the letter.

20 nonimitation *n* originality, uniqueness.

adj unimitated, uncopied; unmatched, unparalleled; inimitable, original, unique, special, one of a kind, rare, exceptional.

20a variation *n* alteration, change, modification; divergency, deviation, aberration, innovation.

v vary, change; deviate, diverge, alternate, modify.

adj varied, modified, diversified, altered, changed.

21 [result of imitation] **copy** *n* facsimile, counterpart, effigy, form, likeness, similitude, semblance, cast, mold, model, representation, image, portrait; reflexion, shadow, echo; transcript, transcription, reproduction, imitation, carbon, ditto, stencil, duplicate, reprint, transfer, replica; parody, caricature, burlesque, travesty, paraphrase; counterfeit, forgery, deception.

adj faithful, lifelike, exact, similar.

22 [thing copied] **prototype** *n* original, model, pattern, precedent, standard; type, archetype, exemplar, paradigm, module, example; text, copy, design; die, mold, matrix, mint, seal, punch, intaglio, negative, plate, stamp.

v be an example, set an example.

23 agreement *n* unanimity, harmony, accord, accordance, concord, union, unity, understanding, settlement, treaty, pact; uniformity, conformity, consistency, congruity, logic, correspondence, parallelism, apposition; consent, assent, concurrence, cooperation.

v agree, accord, harmonize; correspond, tally, (*informal*) jibe; meet, suit, fit, befit, square with, dovetail; match; adapt, fit, accommodate, adjust.

adj agreeing, accordant, correspondent, congenial, harmonious; reconcilable, comfortable, compatible, congruous, consistent, logical, consonant, commensurate; in accordance with, in harmony with, in keeping with; apt, apposite, pat, pertinent; agreeable, happy, felicitous.

24 disagreement *n* discord, dissonance, dissidence, disunion, discrepancy, nonconformity, incongruity, dissension, conflict, opposition, antag-

onism, difference; disparity, disproportion, mismatch, variance, divergence, inequity, inequality.

v disagree, clash, jar, argue, quarrel, dispute.

adj disagreeing, discordant, dissonant, inharmonious; at variance,
hostile, conflicting, antagonistic, clashing, disputing, factious, dissenting,
irreconcilable, incompatible, inconsistent with; incongruous, disproportionate, disparate, divergent; disagreeable, uncongenial, mismatched;
out of joint, out of step, out of tune.

III. Simple Quantity

25 [absolute quantity]   **quantity** *n*
size, mass, volume, amount, measure,
measurement, substance, strength;
mouthful, spoonful, handful; stock,
batch, lot, dose.

adj quantitative, some, any, more
or less.

26 [relative quantity] **degree** *n* grade,
extent, measure, amount, ratio, standard, height, pitch; reach, range, scope,
rate, caliber; gradation, shade, tint;
tenor, tone, compass; sphere, station,
rank, standing; point, mark, stage,
level; intensity, strength.

adj comparative, gradual, shading
off.

adv by degrees, gradually, step by
step, bit by bit, little by little, inch by
inch, drop by drop; in some degree, to
some extent; up to a point.

27 [sameness of quantity or degree]
equality *n* parity, symmetry, balance,
counterbalance; evenness, monotony,
level; equivalence, equipoise, equilibrium; par, even keel, quits; identity,
similarity; tie, dead heat, draw, drawn
game, neck and neck race; match,
peer, equal, mate, fellow, brother;
equivalent.

v equal, match, reach, keep pace
with, run abreast; come up to; balance,
even the score; equalize, level, trim,
adjust; strike a balance; restore
equilibrium.

adj equal, even, level, monotonous, coequal, symmetrical, balanced;
on a par with, on a level with, on an
equal footing with, up to the mark;
equivalent, tantamount, synonymous,
quits, even, much the same, all one,
one and the same; drawn, half and
half, six of one and half a dozen of
another.

adv equally, to all intents and
purposes.

28 [difference of quantity or degree]
inequality *n* disparity, dissimilarity,
difference, odds; unevenness, im-

balance; inferiority, shortcoming, deficiency, imperfection, inadequacy;
mediocrity; superiority.

v be unequal, have the advantage,
turn the scale, turn the tide; topple,
overmatch; not come up to, fall short
of, not come up to snuff.

adj unequal, uneven, imbalanced;
disparate, partial, inferior, insufficient,
deficient, inadequate, mediocre, short.

29 **mean** *n* medium, average, balance,
middle, mid-point, center, median,
golden mean; compromise, neutrality.

v split the difference, take the
average, move to the center.

adj mean, intermediate, middle,
average, standard, normal, neutral;
mediocre, middle class, bourgeois,
commonplace, run of the mill, egalitarian.

adv on the average, in the long
run.

30 **compensation** *n* equation; indem-
nification, requital; compromise, measure for measure, tit for tat, eye for an
eye, retaliation, equalization; setoff,
off-set, counterpoise, ballast; indem-
nity, equivalent, *quid pro quo*, amends,
reparation.

v compensate, indemnify, recompense, remunerate; counterbalance,
counterpoise, countervail, offset, counteract, balance, balance out, make up
for, square, even out, equalize; cover,
neutralize, nullify; redeem, atone,
make amends.

adj compensatory, compensating,
equivalent, equal.

adv but, however, yet, still, notwithstanding, nevertheless, although,
though, nonetheless; howbeit, albeit;
at all events, at any rate, be that as
may, even so, on the other hand, at the
same time.

31 **greatness** *n* magnitude, size, bulk,
dimensions, vastness; multitude; enormousness, immensity, might, strength,
intensity, fullness; importance, distinction, eminence, renown; quantity,
store, volume, mass, bulk, heap; abundance, sufficiency.

v be great, soar, tower, rise above,
transcend; enlarge, increase, expand.

adj great, large, considerable, big,
huge, mammoth, gigantic; ample,
abundant, sufficient; full, intense,
strong; widespread, extensive, wholesale; goodly, noble, precious, mighty;
utter, uttermost, arch, profound,
intense, consummate; extraordinary,
important, unsurpassed, supreme;
complete, total; vast, immense, enormous, extreme, inordinate, excessive,
extravagant, exorbitant, outrageous,
monstrous; towering, stupendous,

prodigious, marvelous; unlimited, infinite; absolute, positive, stark, decided, unequivocal, essential, perfect; remarkable, notable, noteworthy.

adv [in a positive degree] truly; decidedly, unequivocally, absolutely, essentially, fundamentally, downright; [in a complete degree] entirely, completely, totally, wholly; abundantly, fully, amply, widely; [in a great or high degree] greatly, much, indeed, very, very much, most, pretty, pretty well, enough, in a great measure, to a large extent; richly, on a large scale, ever so much; mightily, powerfully; extremely, exceedingly, intensely, exquisitely, consummately, acutely, indefinitely, immeasurably, beyond compare, beyond measure, beyond all bounds, incalculably, infinitely; [in a supreme degree] pre-eminently, superlatively, supremely, incomparably; [in a too great degree] immoderately, inordinately, exorbitantly, excessively, enormously, preposterously, monstrously, out of all proportion, with a vengeance; [in a marked degree] particularly, remarkably, singularly, curiously, uncommonly, unusually, peculiarly, notably, signally, strikingly, pointedly, mainly, chiefly; famously, egregiously, prominently, glaringly, emphatically, strangely, wonderfully, amazingly, surprisingly, astonishingly, incredibly, marvelously, stupendously; [in a violent degree] violently, furiously, severely, desperately, tremendously, extravagantly; [in a painful degree] painfully, sadly, sorely, bitterly, piteously, grievously, miserably, cruelly, woefully, lamentably, shockingly, frightfully, fearfully, dreadfully, terribly, horribly.

32 smallness *n* littleness, tininess, diminutiveness; slenderness, thinness, paltriness, slightness; paucity, fewness, sparseness, scarcity; unimportance, triviality, inconsequentiality, pettiness, insignificance; meanness, sordidness, selfishness narrow-mindedness, small quantity, modicum, atom, particle, molecule, point, speck, dot, dab, mote, jot, iota; minutiae, details, soupçon, scintilla, granule; drop, droplet, drizzle, sprinkling, dash, smack, tinge; dole, scrap, shred, splinter; mite, bit, morsel, crumb, seed; snippet, snatch, slip; chip, sliver; nutshell, thimbleful, spoonful, handful, mouthful; fragment, fraction, drop in the ocean; trifle.

v be small.

adj small, little, tiny, diminutive, petite, miniature, minuscule, minute, microscopic, infinitesimal, fine; unimportant, trivial, minor, secondary, trifling, inconsequential, petty, paltry, insignificant; slender, thin, slight,

scanty, scant, meager, insufficient; few, sparse, scarce; low, so-so, middling, tolerable, inconsiderable, inappreciable; mean, sordid, selfish, narrow, narrow-minded, illiberal, ungenerous; feeble, weak, faint.

adv [in a small degree] to a small extent; a wee bit; slightly, imperceptibly, faintly; miserably, wretchedly; insufficiently, imperfectly; passably, pretty well, well enough; [in a certain or limited degree] partially, in part, to a certain degree; some, rather, to some degree; simply, only, purely, merely, at the least; ever so little; almost, nearly, well nigh, short of, not quite, all but, near the mark; scarcely, hardly, barely, only just, no more than; [in an uncertain degree] about, thereabouts, somewhere about; [in no degree] noway, nowise, not at all, not in the least, not a bit, not a jot, not a whit, in no respect, by no means, on no account.

33 superiority *n* supremacy, pre-eminence, ascendancy, transcendence; excellence, greatness, nobility, eminence, worthiness, preponderance, predominance, prevalence, advantage; majority; quality, high caliber.

v be superior, exceed, excel, transcend, outdo, outweigh, outrival, outrank; pass, surpass; top, cap, outstrip, eclipse, predominate, prevail; take precedence, come first.

adj superior, greater, major, higher, exceeding; supreme, greatest, utmost, paramount, pre-eminent, foremost, crowning; first-rate, important, excellent, unrivaled, matchless, priceless, unparalleled, unequaled, unsurpassed, inimitable, incomparable, superlative, beyond compare, transcendent.

adv beyond, more, over, over and above, at its height; [in a superior or supreme degree] eminently, pre-eminently, prominently, surpassingly, superlatively, supremely, above all, to crown all, par excellence; principally, especially, particularly, peculiarly.

34 inferiority *n* low quality, deficiency, imperfection, shortcoming, inadequacy; mediocrity, commonality, commonness, poorness, meanness; minority, subordination, subjection.

v be inferior, fall short of, come short of, not come up to, not pass muster; want, lack.

adj inferior, minor, less, lesser, deficient; poor, indifferent, mean, base, bad, shabby, paltry, humble, imperfect, mediocre, common, commonplace, second-rate; poorer; secondary, minor, subordinate, lower; diminished, reduced, unimportant.

adv less, subpar; short of, under.

35 increase *n* growth, augmentation, enlargement, extension, expansion, addition, increment, accretion, aggrandizement; development, rise, ascent.

v increase, grow, dilate, enlarge, expand, multiply; augment, add to, enlarge, greaten; extend, spread out, prolong; advance, rise, sprout, ascend; raise, exalt, deepen, heighten, intensify, magnify, redouble; aggrandize.

adj increasing, growing; additional, incremental; developmental.

36 decrease *n* diminution, abatement, decline, reduction, wane, falling-off, contraction, dwindling, shrinking, lessening, ebb, ebbing; subtraction, abridgment, shortening; depreciation, deterioration.

v decrease, lessen, abate, fall off, decline, contract, shrink, dwindle, wane, ebb, subside; diminish, deteriorate, depreciate, languish, decay; abridge, shorten, subtract.

adj decreased, decreasing, on the wane.

37 addition *n* increment, increase, enlargement, aggrandizement, accession; supplement, adjunct, attachment, addendum; annexation, interposition, insertion; uniting, joining.

v add, annex, affix, subjoin, tack on, append, attach, join, supplement, increase, augment, make an addition to; accrue, accumulate, pile up; total, sum, add up; reinforce.

adj additional, supplemental, supplementary; extra, accessory, auxiliary.

adv in addition, more, plus; and, also, likewise, too, further, furthermore, besides, to boot, etc., and so on, and so forth; over and above, moreover; with, as well as, together with, along with, in conjunction with.

38 deduction *n* subtraction, retrenchment, withdrawal, removal; mutilation, amputation, curtailment; shortening, abbreviation; decrease, cutback.

v deduct, subtract, retrench, withdraw, remove; take from, take away; shorten, abbreviate, cut back, pare down, reduce, decrease, diminish, curtail, eliminate, deprive of; mutilate, amputate, cut off, cut away, excise; pare, thin, thin out, prune, scrape, file.

adj subtracted, subtracting; removable, reducible; deductible.

adv less, short of; minus, without, excepting, except; with the exception of, save, exclusive of.

39 [thing added] **adjunct** *n* addition, affix, suffix, appendage, annex, augmentation, increment, reinforcement, accessory, accompaniment, sequel; addendum, complement, supplement,

appendix, attachment; rider, offshoot, episode, corollary.

adj additional.

40 [thing remaining] **remainder** *n* residue, remains, remnant, leftover, excess, superfluity, balance, surplus, rest, relic; leavings, odds and ends, residuum, dregs, refuse, crumbs, stubble, ruins, skeleton, stump.

v remain, survive, be left; be left over.

adj remaining, left, left over, residual; over, odd, spare, unused; superfluous; surviving.

40a [thing deducted] **decrement** *n* discount, defect, loss, deduction.

41 mixture *n* admixture, mix, combination, mingling, amalgamation, junction; infusion, suffusion, transfusion; infiltration, interlarding, interpolation; adulteration. thing mixed: tinge, tincture, touch, dash, sprinkling, spice, seasoning, infusion. compounds: alloy, amalgam, mélange, pastiche, miscellany, medley, patchwork, hotchpotch, gallimaufry, conglomeration, jumble, potpourri, farrago; cross, hybrid, mongrel.

v mix, join; combine, blend, mingle, commingle, confuse, jumble, unite, compound, amalgamate, adulterate; interlard, interlace, intertwine, interweave, interpolate; conjoin, associate, consort, instill, imbue, infuse, suffuse, transfuse, infiltrate, dash, tinge, tincture, season, blend, cross.

adj mixed, composite, half-and-half, hybrid, cross, mongrel, heterogeneous; motley, variegated, miscellaneous, promiscuous, indiscriminate.

adv among, amongst, amid, amidst, with; in the midst of.

42 [freedom from mixture] **simpleness** *n* purity, homogeneity; elimination, sifting, purification.

v simplify; sift, winnow, eliminate, strain, clean, purify; disentangle.

adj simple, uniform, homogeneous, single, pure, clear; unmixed, unadulterated, elemental, elementary, basic.

43 junction *n* joining, union; connection, conjunction, annexation, attachment; coupling, marriage, wedlock; confluence, communication, concatenation; meeting, assemblage, assembly, reunion; joint, joining, juncture, pivot, hinge, articulation; seam, stitch, linkage, link.

v join, unite, connect, link up, link; associate; put together, piece together, bind together; attach, fix, affix, fasten, bind, secure, clinch, twist, tie, string, strap, sew, lace, stitch, hem, knit, button, buckle, hitch, lash, splice, gird, tether, picket, moor, harness, leash; chain; fetter, lock, hook, couple, link, yoke, bracket; marry, wed, bridge over; span; pin, bolt, clasp, clamp, screw, rivet; solder, weld, fuse; entwine, interlace, intertwine, interweave; entangle.

adj joined, joint; corporate, compact; firm, fast, close, tight, taut, secure, set, inseparable, indissoluble.

adv jointly, in conjunction with; fast, firmly; intimately.

44 disjunction *n* disconnection, disunion, disengagement, dissociation, discontinuity; isolation, insularity, insulation, separateness; dispersion; separation, parting; detachment, segregation; divorce; division, subdivision, break, fracture, rupture; dismemberment, dislocation, severance; fissure, breach, rent, split, rift, crack, cut, slit, incision.

v disjoin, disconnect, disengage, disunite, dissociate, divorce, part, detach, separate, disentangle, cut off, rescind, discontinue; segregate, set apart, keep apart, isolate, insulate; cut adrift, loose, set free, liberate; divide, subdivide, sever, dissever, cut, saw, snip, chop, ax, cleave, rive, rend, slit, split, splinter, chip, crack, snap, break, tear, burst, rend; wrench, rupture, shatter; hack, hew, slash, slice, cut up, carve, dissect, tear to pieces; disband, disperse, dislocate, break up, apportion, divide; part, part company, separate, leave.

adj disjoined, discontinuous, disjunctive; isolated, insular; separate, apart, asunder, loose, adrift, free; unattached, unconnected.

adv separately, one by one, severally, apart, adrift, asunder.

45 link *n* connective, connection, vinculum, copula, tie, bond, bridge; junction, bracket.

v link, bond, join, connect, conjoin, fasten, pin, bind, tie; bridge, span.

46 coherence *n* cohesion, cohesiveness, adherence, adhesion, adhesiveness; connection, union, conglomeration, aggregation, consolidation; stickiness, inseparability.

v cohere, adhere, stick, cling, cleave, hold, take hold, clasp, hug; hang together, stay together; glue, cement, paste, solder, weld; consolidate, solidify, agglomerate.

adj cohesive, adhesive, adhering, sticky; tenacious, tough; united, unified, inseparable, inextricable, (*informal*) together, (*informal*) tight.

47 incoherence *n* looseness, laxity, relaxation, nonadhesion; loosening, disjunction, disconnection; disagreement, inconsistency, incongruity.

v loosen, make loose, slacken, relax; detach, disjoin.

adj nonadhesive, noncohesive, detached, loose, slack, lax, relaxed, segregated, unconsolidated; inconsistent, incongruous, illogical, absurd, rambling.

48 combination *n* mixture; junction; union, unification, synthesis, incorporation, amalgamation, coalescence, fusion, blend, blending, mix, centralization; compound, alloy, amalgam, composition, composite.

v combine, unite, incorporate, amalgamate, absorb, blend, mix, merge, fuse, marry, consolidate, coalesce, centralize, cement, harden, solidify.

adj combined, unified.

49 decomposition *n* analysis, dissection, dissolution, breaking down; disjunction; corruption, decay, rot, putrefaction.

v decompose, analyze, dissolve; resolve into its elements, dissect, disperse, crumble; decay, rot, turn.

adj decomposed.

50 [principal part] whole *n* totality, entirety, total, sum, aggregate; unity, completeness, integrity, indivisibility, bulk, mass, lump; body, trunk.

v form a whole, integrate, embody, amass, aggregate, assemble; amount to, come to, add up to.

adj whole, total, full, entire, undiminished, undivided, integral, complete, unimpaired, unbroken, faultless, sound, intact; indivisible, indissoluble.

adv wholly, altogether; totally, completely, entirely, all, all in all, wholesale, in a body, collectively, in the main, on the whole.

51 part *n* division, portion, piece, fragment, fraction, lump, bit, component, constituent, ingredient, element, section, segment, subdivision; member, limb, branch, bough, offshoot, ramification; compartment, department, class.

v part, divide, break, disjoin; partition, apportion, allot.

adj fractional, fragmentary, sectional; divided, split up.

adv partly, in part, partially; piecemeal, bit by bit, by installments, in dribs and drabs, in drips and snatches; in detail.

52 completeness *n* wholeness, entirety, totality, solidarity, fullness, intactness, unity, perfection; thoroughness.

v complete, accomplish, fulfill, finish; fill, charge, load, replenish; fill up, fill in; saturate.

adj complete, entire, whole, full, intact, undivided, one, perfect, fulfilled; full, good, absolute, thorough, solid; exhaustive, radical, sweeping, thoroughgoing; consummate, unmitigated, sheer, unqualified, unconditional; brimming, brimful, chock-full, saturated, crammed, replete, fraught.

adv completely, altogether, outright, wholly, totally, quite, utterly; fully, thoroughly, in all aspects, in every respect, out and out, to all intents and purposes; throughout, from first to last, from beginning to end, from top to bottom, from head to foot, every whit, every inch.

53 incompleteness *n* deficiency, shortcoming, insufficiency, imperfection; immaturity; noncompletion.

[part wanting] defect, deficit, omission, interval, break; discontinuity, missing link.

v be incomplete, fall short of; lack; neglect.

adj incomplete, imperfect, unfinished, uncompleted; defective, deficient, wanting, lacking, failing, short, short of; meager, lame, limp, perfunctory, sketchy, crude, immature; in progress, in preparation, going on, ongoing, proceeding.

adv incompletely.

54 composition *n* constitution, make-up, form; combination, compilation, incorporation, inclusion, synthesis.

v be composed of, be made up of, consist of; include, contain, hold, comprehend, take in, admit, embrace, embody; compose, constitute, form, make.

adj constituting.

55 exclusion *n* omission, exception, rejection, repudiation; exile, seclusion, segregation, separation, elimination, prohibition; restraint, keeping out.

v exclude, bar, leave out, shut out, keep out; reject, repudiate, blackball, throw out; lay aside, put aside, set aside; relegate, segregate, separate, seclude, banish, exile; pass over, omit, eliminate, weed out, winnow.

adj exclusive, not included in; inadmissible.

56 component *n* component part, integral part, element, constituent, ingredient; contents, feature, member, part; personnel.

v enter into, be part of, form part of; merge in, share in, participate; belong to, appertain to; form, make, constitute.

adj inclusive, comprehensive.

57 extraneousness *n* extrinsicality, externality; superfluousness; foreign body, foreign substance; intrusion.

v be extraneous, be unnecessary.

adj extraneous, foreign, alien, extrinsic, external; not germane, nonessential, superfluous; excluded.

IV. Order

58 order *n* regularity, uniformity, arrangement, harmony, symmetry; course, routine, method, methodology; disposition, array, arrangement, system, economy, discipline, orderliness; gradation, progression, series, sequence, continuity; rank, place, grade, class, degree.

v order, regulate, manage, adjust, arrange, systematize, standardize, rank.

adj orderly, regular, systematic, methodical; in order, neat, tidy, well-regulated, well-organized, organized, uniform, symmetrical, businesslike, shipshape.

adv in order, methodically, in turn, in its turn; step by step, at regular intervals, systematically.

59 disorder *n* derangement, disarray, untidiness, irregularity, anomaly; anarchy, anarchism, disunion, discord; confusion, jumble, mess, muddle, hash, hodgepodge, chaos; perplexity, labyrinth, wilderness, jungle; raveling, entanglement, complication, convolution; turmoil, ferment, agitation, trouble, row, disturbance, convulsion, tumult, uproar, riot, rumpus, ruckus, scramble, fracas, melee, pandemonium.

v disorder, put out of order, derange, ruffle, rumble; confuse, jumble, mess up.

adj disorderly, out of order, out of place, irregular, desultory; anomalous, disorganized, straggling, unsystematic, untidy, slovenly, messy; indiscriminate, chaotic, confused, deranged; anarchic, inverted, convoluted, topsy-turvy; complex, complicated, perplexed, involved, raveled, entangled, knotted, tangled; troublesome, problematical; riotous, violent, turbulent, tumultuous.

adv irregularly, helter skelter; at cross purposes, (*informal*), after the flood.

60 [reduction to order] **arrangement** *n* plan, method, organization; preparation, groundwork, planning; sorting, disposal, disposition, distribution, assortment, allotment, apportionment, graduation, groupings; analysis, classification, division, ordering, systematization.

v arrange, dispose, place, form; set out, marshal, range, array, rank, group, parcel out, allot, apportion, assign, dole out, distribute; sort, sift, put into shape; plan, prepare, organize, lay the groundwork; classify, divide, file, register, catalog, record, tabulate, index, graduate, rank; regulate, systematize, coordinate, organize, settle, fix; unravel, disentangle, straighten out.

adj arranged, ordered; methodical, orderly, regular, systematic.

61 [subversion of order] **derangement** *n* disorder, mess, disarray, disorganization; discomposure, disturbance, dislocation, perturbation, interruption.

~ *v* derange, disarrange, discompose, displace, misplace; mislay, disorder, disorganize; embroil, disconcert, convulse, unsettle, disturb, confuse, trouble, perturb, jumble, muddle, fumble; unhinge, dislocate, throw out of gear, throw out of whack; invert, turn upside down, turn topsy-turvy; complicate, confound, tangle, entangle, litter, scatter, mix.

62 precedence *n* coming before, the lead, superiority; precursor, antecedence; importance, consequence; priority, preference.

v precede, come before, forerun, come first; head, lead the way, usher in, introduce; set the fashion, influence, establish; have precedence, take precedence; place before, prefix, preface.

adj preceding, precedent, antecedent, anterior, prior, before; former, foregoing; preliminary, prefatory, introductory; preparatory.

adv before; in advance.

63 sequence *n* coming after, following, succession, order, series; posteriority; continuation; order of succession; outcome, consequence, result, sequel.

v succeed, come after, follow, ensue; replace.

adj succeeding, following; consequent, subsequent; proximate, next; sequential, consecutive.

adv after, subsequently; behind.

64 precursor *n* antecedent, precedent, predecessor, forerunner, pioneer, leader, bellwether; herald, harbinger; prelude, preamble, preface, prolog, proem, prefix, foreword, introduction; heading, frontispiece, groundwork; preparation.

adj prefatory, introductory, preliminary, precursory.

65 sequel *n* continuation, extension, supplement, outgrowth, offshoot, result, consequence, inference, deduction; result, consequence, aftermath, outcome, effect; conclusion, end, culmination, dénouement, finale, finish; appendage, suffix, epilog, postscript, tag, train, trail, wake; afterthought, afterpiece, second thoughts.

66 beginning *n* commencement, opening outset, start, initiation, inauguration; introduction, prelude; outbreak, onset, brunt; initiative, first move; origin, cause, source, bud, germ, genesis, birth, nativity, cradle; starting point, first step, square one; title page, head, heading; rudiments, basics, elements.

v begin, commence, open, start, initiate, inaugurate; conceive; set out, embark, depart; usher in, lead the way, take the lead, take the initiative, head, stand at the head, launch, set in motion, get going, take the first step, break ground; burst forth, break out; begin at the beginning, start again, start over, make a fresh start; originate, conceive, think up.

adj initial, introductory, inaugural; incipient; embryonic, rudimental, primal, essential, natal, nascent; first, foremost, leading; maiden, virgin.

adv first, in the first place, first and foremost; in the bud, n its infancy; from the beginning.

67 end *n* close, termination, conclusion, finale, finish, last word; consummation, climax, apex, dénouement; goal, destination; expiration, death, finality; limit, extreme, extremity; breakup, last stage, final stage, turning point, death blow.

v end, close, finish, terminate, conclude; expire, die, come to a close, draw to a close, run its course, run out, pass away; bring to an end, put an end to, make an end of, wrap up; get through, complete, consummate; stop, desist, call it quits.

adj final, terminal, concluding; conclusive, crowning, definitive, last, ultimate, consummate; ended, settled, decided, over, concluded, played out.

adv finally, at last, once and for all, over and done with.

68 middle *n* center, midpoint, midst; mean, midcourse, middle ground, compromise; core, kernel, heart, nucleus, nub; equidistance, bisection; equator, diaphragm, midriff.

adj middle, medial, mean, mid, median, midmost; intermediate, equidistant, central, halfway.

adv midway, halfway, in the middle.

69 [uninterrupted sequence] **continuity** *n* continuousness, consecutiveness progression, constant flow, succession, train, series, chain, string, scale, gradation; round, suite; procession, column, retinue; pedigree, genealogy, lineage; rank, file, line, row, range, tier.

v follow in a line; arrange in a series, string together, file, thread, graduate, tabulate.

adj continuous, progressive, successive, serial, consecutive, unbroken, uninterrupted, gradual; linear, in a line; perennial, constant.

adv continuously, in succession, consecutively; gradually, step by step, in a column.

70 [interrupted sequence] **discontinuity** *n* disjunction, disconnectedness; interruption, break, fracture, fault, flaw, crack, cut; gap, interval, caesura, pause, (*informal*) breather, rest, intermission, parenthesis, episode.

v alternate; discontinue, break, interrupt, intervene; pause, rest, take a breather, stop; break in upon, interpose; disconnect.

adj discontinuous, disconnected, unconnected, broken, interrupted; fitful, spasmodic, desultory, intermittent, irregular; alternate, recurrent, periodic.

adv at intervals, in snatches, by fits and starts.

71 term *n* rank, station, stage, step, phase; scale, grade, degree, status, position, place, point, mark, period, limit; stand, standing, footing.

72 assemblage *n* collection, levee, gathering, ingathering, muster; concourse, conflux, congregation; meeting, reunion; assembly, congress, convention, conclave, council; miscellany, compilation, menagerie; crowd, throng, mob, flood, rush, rash, deluge, press, crush, horde, body, tribe, crew, gang, squad, band, party, swarm, flock, bevy; company, troop, regiment, squadron, army; host, multitude, populace, clan, brotherhood, sisterhood, association; group, cluster, clump, batch, pack, assortment; accumulation, heap, lump, pile, mass, conglomeration, conglomerate, aggregation, aggregate; quantity.

v assemble, come together, collect, gather, muster; meet, unite, join, rejoin; cluster, flock, swarm, surge, stream, herd, crowd, throng, associate; congregate, concentrate, huddle; bring together, draw together, place together, lump together; convene, invoke; compile, group, assemble, unite; amass, accumulate, store.

adj assembled; closely packed, dense, crowded, teeming, swarming, populous.

73 dispersion *n* divergence, spreading, radiation, dissemination, diffusion, dissipation, distribution, apportionment, division.

v disperse, scatter, sow, disseminate, diffuse, shed, spread, dispense, disband, distribute, apportion, divide; break up, dispel, cast forth, strew, cast, sprinkle; issue, deal out, dole out.

adj dispersed, spread, scattered, strewn, diffuse, diffusive; sparse, widespread, broadcast; adrift, stray, disheveled.

74 [place of meeting] **focus** *n* center, gathering place, haunt, rendezvous, rallying point, headquarters, club, retreat.

v focus, bring to a point, bring to a focus; center on, bring out, clarify, elucidate.

75 class *n* division, subdivision, category, heading, order, section; department, province, domain; type, kind, sort, genus, species, variety, family, race, tribe, cast, clan, breed, sect.

76 inclusion *n* admission, acceptance into, incorporation, comprehension, reception.

v include, comprise, comprehend, contain, admit, embrace, receive, accept; inclose, circumscribe, encircle, encompass, embody, incorporate; number among, count among, fall under.

adj inclusive, comprehensive, extensive, all-embracing, compendious, sweeping; including, incorporating.

77 exclusion *n* (see 55).

78 generality *n* universality, catholicity, miscellany, miscellaneousness; generalization, simplification, oversimplification; prevalence, common run.

v be general, be universal, prevail, be true for everyone; render general, generalize, universalize; make a generalization, abstract, simplify.

adj general, universal, catholic, common, ecumenical, egalitarian, worldwide; prevalent, prevailing, rife, current; generic, collective, all-encompassing, comprehensive, all-inclusive, broad, widespread.

79 specialty *n* speciality, skill, ability, talent; individuality, singularity, distinctive feature, particularity, personality, characteristic, mannerism, idiosyncrasy, nonconformity; particulars, details, items; special feature.

v specify, particularize, individualize, specialize; designate, determine, single out, isolate, differentiate; be specific, come to the point, detail, get down to particulars.

adj special, particular, especial, individual, specific, proper, personal, original, private, respective, definite, certain, endemic, peculiar, characteristic, marked, appropriate, exclusive, singular, exceptional, idiomatic, unique.

adv specially, especially, in particular; each, apiece, severally, respectively, each to each, each to his own; in detail.

80 regulation *n* regularity, uniformity, constancy, clockwork, precision, exactness; routine, custom, formula, rule, form, procedure; standard, model, precedent, prototype; conformity, convention; nature, law, principle; normal state, ordinary condition, normalcy; hard and fast law.

adj regular, uniform, constant, steady; customary, conventional, formal, formulaic, procedural.

81 multiformity *n* variety, diversity.

adj multifold, multifarious, manifold, many-sided; heterogeneous, motley, mosaic; indiscriminate, irregular, diversified, diverse; of every description, all manner of kinds.

82 conformity *n* observance, compliance, assent; conventionality, customariness, agreement; example, instance, specimen, sample, illustration, exemplification, case in point.

v conform to, accommodate oneself to, adapt to; be regular, conform, follow the rules, obey the rules, go by the rules, comply, assent, agree, yield, give in, accept, harmonize; illustrate, stand as an example, embody.

adj conformable to rule, adaptable, agreeable, compliant, malleable; conventional, customary, standard, ordinary, common, habitual, usual, natural, normal, typical; formal, orthodox, strict, rigid, uncompromising; exemplary, illustrative.

adv by rule, in conformity with, in accordance with, in keeping with, consistent with; for the sake of conformity, as a matter of course, for form's sake; invariably, uniformly.

83 unconformity *n* nonconformity, unconventionality, nonobservance, informality; anomaly, variation, inconsistency, irregularity, incongruity, oddity, eccentricity, peculiarity, aberration, abnormality, exception; violation of custom, infraction, infringement; individuality, originality, mannerism, idiosyncrasy, quirk.

v be unconformable.

adj unconformable, unconventional; unnatural, odd, eccentric, peculiar, aberrant, abnormal, exceptional; anomalous, inconsistent, irregular, incongruous, arbitrary, whimsical, wanton; unusual, uncustomary, uncommon, rare, singular, unique, extraordinary; queer, quaint, strange; original, fantastic, newfangled, bizarre, outlandish, exotic, esoteric.

adv unless, except, save, beside.

V. Number

84 number *n* numeral, symbol, figure, cipher, digit, integer, round number, whole number, fraction; sum, total, product.

adj numeral; prime, fractional, decimal; positive, negative.

85 numeration *n* numbering; tallying, enumeration, reckoning, computation, calculation; arithmetic, calculus, algebra; statistics, poll, census, roll call; arithmetic operations.

v number, count, tell, tally, enumerate, add up, sum, reckon, compute, calculate, take account; muster, poll, recite; add, subtract, multiply, divide.

adj numeral, numerical; arithmetical, analytic, algebraic, statistical, numerable, computable, calculable.

86 list *n* catalog, index listing, inventory, schedule, register record, ledger, tally, file, table, calendar; directory, gazette, atlas, dictionary, thesaurus; roll, checklist.

87 unity *n* oneness, singleness, singularity, individuality; unification, unison, uniformity.

v unite, join, combine; isolate, insulate, seclude.

adj one, sole, single, solitary, lone; individual, apart, alone; unaccompanied, unattended, singlehanded, solo; singular, odd, unique; isolated, insular.

adv singly.

88 accompaniment *n* association, partnership, company; accessory, adjunct, concomitant, attachment, complement, attendant, fellow, associate, coexistence.

v accompany, join, escort, convoy, wait on; coexist with, consort with; associate with, couple with.

adj accompanying, fellow, twin, joint; associated with, coupled with; accessory, concomitant, attendant.

adv with, together with, along with, in company with, hand in hand, side by side; therewith, herewith.

89 duality *n* dualism, doubleness, polarity, biformity, duplexity; two, deuce, couple, brace, pair, twins.

v pair, mate, couple, bracket, pair off, yoke.

adj two, twain; dual, twin, two-sided, binary, binomial, duplex; coupled, both.

90 duplication *n* doubling, reduplication; iteration, repetition; renewal.
duplicate, double, copy, carbon, facsimile.
v double; redouble, reduplicate; repeat, renew; duplicate.
adj double; doubled, duplicated; twin, duplicate, second.
adv twice, once more, over again.

91 bisection *n* halving, bifurcation, twofold division, forking, dichotomy, (*informal*) fifty-fifty split.
v bisect, divide in two, halve, divide, split, cut in two, cleave, fork, bifurcate; split down the middle, (*informal*) go halves.
adj bisected, cloven, cleft, halved; bipartite; bifurcated; semi-, demi-, hemi-.

92 triality *n* trinity; three, triad, triplet, trio.
adj three, threefold, triform, tertiary.

93 triplication *n* tripling; triplicity.
v triple, treble, cube.
adj triple, treble; threefold, triplicate; third.
adv three times, thrice; in the third place, thirdly; triply, trebly.

94 trisection *n* tripartition, threefold division, third, third part.
v trisect, divide into three parts.

95 quaternity *n* four, tetrad, quartet, quarter.
v square, reduce to a square.
adj four, fourfold, quadrilateral.

96 quadruplication *n* quadrupling, multiplying by four.
v multiply by four, quadruplicate.
adj four, fourfold, quadruple; fourth.
adv four times, in the fourth place, fourthly.

97 quadrisection *n* quartering, quadripartition, fourfold division; fourth part, quarter.
v quarter, divide into four parts.
adj quartered, quadripartite.

98 five, etc. *n* five; six, half a dozen; seven; eight; nine; ten, decade; eleven; twelve, dozen; thirteen, baker's dozen; twenty, score; twenty-five, quarter of a hundred; fifty, half a hundred; hundred, century, centenary; thousand.

99 quinquesection *n* fivefold division.
adj quinquepartite.

100 [more than one] **plurality** *n* two or more, couple, few, several; majority, multitude.
adj plural, more than one, upwards of, some, several, many, numerous.

100a [less than one] **fraction** *n* fractional part, segment, subdivision, part, portion.

101 zero *n* nothing, naught, (*informal*) zip; none, shutout; nobody.

102 multitude *n* multitudinous, multiplicity, profusion, mass, quantity, volume, abundance, amplitude, enormity; numbers, array, scores, droves, host, throng, collection; mob, crowd, assemblage.
v be numerous, swarm with, teem with, crowd, swarm, outnumber, multiply; people, populate.
adj multitudinous, manifold, profuse, multiple, teeming, populous, crowded, thick; many, several, sundry, various, numerous; endless, infinite.

103 fewness *n* paucity, scarcity, sparseness, scantiness; small number, small quantity; infrequency.
diminution of number: reduction, weeding, elimination.
v render few, reduce, diminish, weed, thin, eliminate, eradicate.
adj few, not many, scanty, scarce, sparse, rare, few and far between, limited, meager; sporadic, occasional, infrequent; reduced, diminished, pared back.

104 repetition *n* iteration, reiteration, recapitulation, restatement; sameness, monotony, harping, recurrence, tautology; redundance; rhythm, beat, echo, reverberation; reappearance, reproduction, duplication.
v repeat, iterate, reiterate, recapitulate, restate, rehash, go over again, harp on, hammer; reproduce, duplicate, echo; recur, revert, return, reappear; resume, return to, go back to; rehearse, go over the same ground.
adj repeated, repetitious, recurrent, recurring, frequent, incessant, never-ending, unceasing; repetitive, redundant, tautological; rhythmic, reverberant, reverberating; monotonous, harping, iterative; habitual.
adv repeatedly, often, again, anew, afresh, over again, once more; over and over, again and again, year after year; ditto, encore.

105 infinity *n* infinitude, infiniteness, perpetuity, endlessness, boundlessness, inexhaustibility, immeasurability, limitlessness, vastness, expanse.
v be infinite, have no limits, know no bounds, go on forever.
adj infinite, countless, numberless, limitless, boundless, measureless, un-

limited, interminable, inexhaustible, incalculable; immense, vast, endless, perpetual; incomprehensible; eternal, perfect, omnipotent, absolute.

adv infinitely, ad *infinitum.*

VI. Time

106 time *n* duration, extent; period, interval, spell, term, space, span, season, stage; course; interim, interlude; interregnum, intermission; respite, break, timeout; era, epoch, season, age, year, date.

v time, measure, pace; continue, last, endure, go on, remain, persist, stand; pass time, spend time, while away the time, waste time, kill time, fill up the time.

adj permanent, lasting, durable; timely.

adv while, whilst, during, in the course of, for the time being, in due time; meantime, meanwhile, in the meantime, in the interim; till, until, up to, yet; the whole time, all the time, throughout, for good, (*informal*) for keeps.

107 absence of time *n* no time; outside time.

adv never, at no time; on no occasion, nevermore.

108 [definite duration or period of time] **period** *n* interval, age, era, eon, epoch, term, time; year, decade, century, millennium; lifetime, generation.

109 [indefinite duration] **course** *n* march of time, course of time, flux, passing time.

v elapse, lapse, flow, run, proceed, advance, pass, flit, fly, slip, slide, drag, creep, crawl; run its course; expire, go by, pass by.

adv in due time, in due course, in due season, in time.

110 [long duration] **durability** *n* permanence, persistence, continuance, lastingness, standing, stability; survival, longevity; protraction, prolongation.

v last, remain, stand, endure, abide, continue, persist; tarry, drag on, drag out, prolong, protract, eke out, draw out, lengthen; outlive, outlast, survive.

adj permanent, durable, lasting, longstanding, stable, immutable, invariable, constant; enduring, abiding, perpetual; lingering, protracted, prolonged, spun-out.

adv long, for a long time, ever so long; long ago; all day long, all the livelong day.

111 [short duration]   **transience** *n* imperma-

nence, evanescence, ephemerality, transitoriness, mortality; suddenness, swiftness, changeableness, vicissitude, uncertainty.

v be transient, flit, pass away, fly, gallop, vanish, fade, evaporate, melt.

adj transient, transitory, evanescent, ephemeral, fleeting, flitting, flying, passing; impermanent, temporal, temporary, provisional, short-lived; perishable, precarious, vulnerable, mortal; brief, quick, brisk; sudden, momentary, instantaneous.

adv temporarily, for the moment, for a time; awhile, soon; briefly.

112 [endless duration] **perpetuity** *n* eternity, timelessness, everlastingness, endlessness, infinity; constancy, endurance, durability, ceaselessness.

v last forever, endure, go on forever; perpetuate, immortalize, eternalize.

adj perpetual, eternal, timeless, everlasting, endless; unceasing, ceaseless, interminable, never ending, continuous, incessant, uninterrupted; unfading, imperishable, unvulnerable, immortal.

adv perpetually, always, ever, evermore, forever; constantly, continuously.

113 [point of time] **instantaneousness** *n* suddenness, abruptness; moment, instant, second, twinkling, trice, flash, crack, burst.

v be instantaneous, twinkle, flash.

adj instantaneous, momentary, sudden, instant, abrupt.

adv instantaneously, in no time, (*informal*) in two shakes (of a lamb's tail), presto, suddenly, like a shot, in a moment, all of a sudden, in a jiffy; immediately, on the spur of the moment, on a moment's notice.

114 [estimation, measurement and record of time] **chronometry** *n* chronology, timetable; almanac, calendar, register, chronicle, log, annal(s), journal, diary; clock, watch, stopwatch, timepiece, chronometer.

v fix the time, mark the time; date, register, chronicle; measure time, mark time, beat time.

adj chronological.

115 [false estimate of time] **anachronism** *n* misdate, misplacement, chronological error; disregard of time.

v misdate, antedate, postdate, anticipate; take no note of time.

adj misdated; undated, overdue; anachronistic, out of place, misplaced.

116 antecedence *n* priority, anteriority, precedence, pre-existence; antecedent, predecessor, precursor, forerunner.

v precede, antedate, come before; go before, lead, forerun; dawn, presage, herald, break the ground.

adj antecedent, prior, previous, anterior, preceding, pre-existent; former, foregoing, aforementioned; precursory, introductory.

adv before, prior to; earlier, previously, ere, already, yet, beforehand.

117 posteriority *n* succession, sequence; subsequence, following, continuance; successor, sequel, follower; future, futurity.

v follow after, come after, go after, succeed, be subsequent to.

adj posterior, subsequent, following, after, later, succeeding, successive, ensuing, resulting; posthumous.

adv subsequently, after, afterwards, since, later; next, close upon, thereafter, thereupon; ultimately.

118 present time *n* the present juncture, the present day; the times, the time being, right now.

adj present, actual, instant, current, existing.

adv at this time, at this moment; at the present time, now, at present, nowadays.

119 different time *n* other time; another time.

adv at that time, at that instant; then, on that occasion; when, whenever, whensoever; at some other time, at a different time, at some time or other.

120 contemporaneousness *n* simultaneousness, synchronism, simultaneity, coincidence, concurrence, coexistence, concomitance.

v coexist, concur, accompany, go side by side, keep pace with; synchronize.

adj simultaneous, coincident, concurrent, concomitant, coexisting; contemporary, contemporaneous, coeval.

adv simultaneously, concurrently, together, at the same time.

121 the future *n* futurity, hereafter, time to come, tomorrow; morrow; millennium, doomsday, day of judgment, crack of doom, flood; advent, eventuality; destiny, fate; heritage, heirs, posterity; prospect, expectation, anticipation.

v look forward, anticipate, expect, foresee; approach, await, threaten, impend, come near, draw near, come on.

adj future, to come; coming, impending, near, close at hand, in prospect; eventual, ulterior.

adv prospectively, hereafter, in future, in course of time, tomorrow; eventually, ultimately, sooner or later; henceforth, from this time; soon, early, on the eve of, on the point of, on the brink of.

122 the past *n* past time, days of old, days of yore, days gone by, yesterday, yesteryear, former times, ancient times; retrospection, memory; antiquity, history, time immemorial, remote past; ancestry, lineage, forbears; heritage.

v run its course, pass away, pass, lapse, blow over.

adj past, gone, gone by, passed away, bygone, elapsed, lapsed, expired, extinct, forgotten, irrecoverable, obsolete; former, pristine, late; foregoing, last, latter, recent; looking back, retrospective; retroactive.

adv formerly, of old, of yore, ago, over; long ago, years ago, a long while back, some time ago; lately, of late; retrospectively, ere now, before now, hitherto, heretofore; already, yet, up to this time.

123 newness *n* novelty, recentness, freshness; immaturity, greenness, youth, juvenility; innovation, uniqueness, originality; renovation, restoration; modernity, modernism, stylishness, fashionableness, newfangledness, fashion, faddishness, the latest thing, futurism, trendiness.

v renew, renovate, restore; modernize.

adj new, novel, recent, fresh; green, immature, unripe, young, youthful, untried, untested, virgin, virginal; modern, late, new, newfangled, stylish, fashionable, faddish, trendy, brand-new, up-to-date; renovated, restored, spick and span.

adv newly, afresh, anew, lately, just now, of late.

124 oldness *n* age, antiquity; maturity, ripeness; decline, decay, old age, senility, superannuation; archaism, antiquarianism, relic, thing of the past; tradition, custom, common law.

v be old, have had its day, have seen its day; become old, age, fade.

adj old, ancient, antique; time-honored, venerable, traditional, vintage, of long standing; elderly, aged, hoary, decayed, senile, decrepit; primeval, primitive, aboriginal, primordial, antediluvian, prehistoric, archaic; traditional, prescriptive, customary, immemorial, inveterate, rooted; antiquated, outdated, outmoded, of other times; out of date, obsolete, out-of-fashion, out-of-style, gone by, stale, old-fashioned, timeworn, crumbling.

ramshackle, run-down, wasted.

125 morning.   noon n morning,
morn, dawn, daybreak, sunrise, sunup,
forenoon, break of day, peep of day,
prime of day, morningtide, matins,
cockcrow, first blush, antemeridian,
A.M.

noon, midday, noonday, noontide,
meridian, prime, height, noontime.

spring, springtime; summer, sum-
mertime, midsummer.

126 evening.   midnight n evening,
eve, eventide, dusk, vespers, nightfall,
sundown, sunset, twilight, curfew,
bedtime; afternoon, post meridian,
P.M.

midnight, end of the day, close of
the day, witching hour, dead of night.

autumn, fall, harvest time; winter.

127 youth n juvenility, infancy childhood, boyhood, girlhood; minority,
tender years, young years, formative
years, next generation, tender age;
cradle, nursery; puberty

adj young, youthful, juvenile,
green, callow, budding, immature,
developing, underage, formative;
younger, junior.

128 age n old age, advanced age,
senility, years, gray hairs, declining
years, golden years, mature years,
decrepitude, anility, superannuation,
longevity, ripe age, ripe old age;
maturity, seniority, eldership.

adj aged, old, advanced, gray,
elderly, senile, decline, failing, waning,
ripe, overripe, mellow, venerable,
wrinkled, wizened; older, elder, eldest.

129 infant n baby, babe, babe in
arms, nursling, little one, to ; toddler,
chick, kid, lamb, cherub, youth,
youngster, child, minor; girl, lass,
maiden, miss, schoolgirl; boy, lad,
stripling, master, schoolboy.

adj infantile, infantlike, puerile,
girlish, boyish, childish, babyish;
newborn, young.

130 veteran n old man, old woman,
patriarch, matriarch, grandmother,
grandfather, grandsire, seer, graybeard,
forefather, elder.

adj aged, old.

131 adolescence n majority, adulthood, manhood, womanhood, maturity, ripeness, fullness, puberty, pubescence; teenage years, prepubescence.

v come of age, grow up, attain
majority

adj adolescent, teenage, pubescent,
of age, grown up, full grown, adult,
womanly, manly, marriageable, nubile.

132 earliness n punctuality, promptitude, speediness, readiness, expedition, alacrity, quickness, haste; suddenness; prematurity, precocity, precipitation, anticipation.

v be early, be beforehand; anticipate, forestall, steal a march on, get
a head start; bespeak, secure, engage,
pre-engage; accelerate, expedite, quicken, hasten, make haste, make time,
hurry.

adj early, timely, punctual, on
time, prompt; premature, precipitate,
precocious, anticipatory; sudden, instantaneous, immediate, expeditious;
unexpected.

adv early, soon, anon, betimes,
before long; punctually, to the minute,
on time, on the dot; beforehand,
prematurely, precipitately, too soon,
hastily, in anticipation, unexpectedly;
suddenly, instantaneously, at short
notice, on the spur of the moment; at
once, on the spot, on the instant, at
sight, straight, offhand, straightway;
forthwith, summarily, immediately,
shortly, quickly, speedily; presently,
by and by, directly.

133 lateness n tardiness, slowness,
sloth, tarrying, dilly-dallying, loitering; delay, procrastination, post-
ponement, adjournment, retardation,
protraction, prolongation; respite,
reprieve, suspension, moratorium,
stop, stay.

v be late, tarry, wait, stay, bide,
take time, linger, loiter, dawdle, shilly-
shally, dilly-dally; put off, defer, delay,
lay over, suspend; retard, postpone,
adjourn; procrastinate, prolong, protract, drag out, draw out, lengthen,
table, shelve, stall.

adj late, tardy, slow, dilatory,
backward, unpunctual; delayed, overdue, belated.

adv late; backward, at the eleventh
hour, at length, at last; ultimately,
behind time; too late; slowly, leisurely,
deliberately, at one's leisure, on one's
own time.

134 opportuneness n timeliness,
opportunity, occasion, suitable time,
proper time, suitability, high time,
crisis, turn, juncture; turning point,
given time; nick of time, golden opportunity; clear stage, open field.

v be opportune, be suitable; seize
the opportunity, seize the time, seize
the day, *carpe diem*, use the occasion;
suit the occasion, be expeditious, strike
while the iron is hot.

adj opportune, timely, well-timed,
seasonable, suitable, appropriate; providential, lucky, fortunate, happy,
favorable, fortuitous, propitious, auspicious.

adv opportunely, in due time, in the nick of time, just in time, now or never; by the way, by the by, speaking of, while on the subject; on the spot, on the spur of the moment, since the occasion presents itself.

135 inopportuneness *n* untimeliness, unseasonableness, improper time, unsuitable time; (*informal*) bad timing; intrusion; anachronism.

v be ill timed, mistime, intrude, break in upon, (*informal*) butt in; lose an opportunity, waste an occasion, (*informal*) blow one's chance, let the opportunity slip by; waste time.

adj inopportune, untimely, unpropitious, unseasonable, unsuitable, inauspicious, unfavorable, unfortunate, unsuited, untoward, unlucky; ill-timed, mistimed, poorly timed; unpunctual, premature.

136 frequency *n* repetition, recurrence, iteration, reiteration.

v recur, repeat, reiterate; keep on, continue; attend regularly, visit often, patronize.

adj frequent, oft-repeated, recurring, incessant, constant, continual, perpetual; habitual, customary.

adv often, oft, oftentimes, frequently, repeatedly, day after day; daily, hourly, every day; perpetually, continually, constantly, incessantly, at all times; commonly, habitually, customarily; sometimes, occasionally, at times, now and then, every once in a while, from time to time.

137 infrequency *n* rarity, rare occurrence; long shot, surprise, (*informal*) mindblower.

v be rare, be infrequent.

adj infrequent, occasional, sporadic, rare, uncommon, unusual, unheard of, unprecedented; few, scant, scarce.

adv infrequently, rarely, seldom, scarcely, hardly; not often, hardly ever.

138 regularity [of recurrence] *n* periodicity, intermittence; beat, pulse, pulsation, rhythm; alternation, oscillation, vibration; bout, round, turn, revolution, rotation, rpm; cycle, period, routine; punctuality, regularity, steadiness.

v recur, revolve, return, come in its turn, come round again; beat, pulsate, alternate.

adj regular, periodic, periodical; serial, recurrent, cyclical, cyclic, recurring, rhythmical, rhythmic; intermittent, alternate, every other; regular, steady, punctual, continual, constant, regular as clockwork.

adv regularly, periodically, serially, cyclically; intermittently, alternately; by turns, in turn, in rotation, off and on, round and round.

139 irregularity [of recurrence] *n* uncertainty, unpredictability, haphazardness, fitfulness, capriciousness.

v be irregular, be haphazard.

adj irregular, uncertain, unpredictable, haphazard, fitful, capricious, flickering; spasmodic, sporadic.

adv irregularly, fitfully, capriciously, by fits and starts.

VII. Change

140 change *n* alteration, modulation, modification, variation, mutation, permutation, qualification, deviation, turn, shift, innovation; diversion, break; transformation, transfiguration, transmutation, metamorphosis; conversion, revolution, inversion, reversal; displacement, transference, transposition; changeableness.

v change, alter, vary, modulate, qualify, diversify, tamper with, play with, experiment with; turn, shift, veer, tack, swerve, warp, deviate, turn aside; turn, take a turn, (*informal*) hang a turn; modify, revamp, transform, transfigure, transmute, metamorphose, convert; innovate, restructure, give a new turn to, recast, redesign, remodel.

adj changed, newfangled; changeable, variable, transformable; innovative.

141 permanence *n* stability, invariability, unalterability, immutability, constancy; endurance, durability, persistence; maintenance, preservation, conservation; obstinacy, immovability, inflexibility, immobility, rigidity.

v endure, bide, abide, stay, remain, last, persist, stand, stand fast; maintain, keep, keep up, preserve; subsist, live, outlive, survive.

adj permanent, lasting, unchanged, unchanging, fixed, stable, invariable, constant; enduring, durable, abiding, everlasting; intact, inviolate; persistent.

adv permanently, for good, for good and all.

142 cessation *n* discontinuation, discontinuance, halt, stoppage, termination, suspension, interruption, stopping; pause, rest, lull, respite, truce, break; interregnum, abeyance; completion, end, finish; stop, death.

v cease, discontinue, terminate, desist, stay; break off, leave off, hold, stop, pull up, stop short, halt, pause, rest; suspend, interrupt, delay, cut short, arrest, bring to a standstill; complete, end, finish, close up shop;

wear away, go out, die out, pass away, die.

143 continuance [in action] *n* continuation, continuity, protraction, prolongation, maintenance, perpetuation; persistence, perseverance, repetition.

v continue, persist, go on, keep on, hold on; abide, keep, pursue, stick to; maintain course, carry on, keep up; sustain, uphold, hold up, keep going, maintain, preserve, perpetuate, prolong.

adj continuing, uninterrupted, unvarying; continuous, persistent, perpetual.

144 conversion *n* transformation, transmutation, reduction, change, changeover, resolution, assimilation; passage, transit, transition, shifting, flux; growth, progress, development; chemistry, alchemy.

v be converted into, become, turn into, lapse, shift; pass into, grow into, ripen into, merge into; melt, grow, ripen, mature, mellow; convert into, resolve into; make, render; mold, form, model, remodel, remake, do over, reform, reorganize; assimilate, bring into, reduce to.

adj convertible, transmutable, changeable.

145 reversion *n* return, revulsion, reverting, returning; alternation, rotation; inversion; recoil, reaction, reflex, repercussion, rebound, boomerang, ricochet, backlash, repulse; retrospection, retrogression, retrogradation, falling back; restoration, going back; turning point, turn of the tide.

v revert, return, turn back, reverse; relapse, regress, fall back; recoil, rebound; retreat; restore, undo, unmake; turn the tide.

146 [sudden or violent change] **revolution** *n* revolt, rebellion, overthrow, overturn, coup, coup d'état, rising, uprising, mutiny, counterrevolution; breakup, destruction, subversion, clean sweep; spasm, convulsion, throe, revulsion.

v revolt, rebel, rise, rise up; revolutionize, remodel, recast, change.

adj revolutionary, rebellious; new.

147 substitution *n* replacement, supplanting, commutation, exchange, change, shift.

v substitute, expedient, makeshift, stopgap, equivalent, double, alternative, representative.

v substitute, put in the place of, change, exchange, interchange; replace, supplant, supersede, take the place of, stand for, represent, pinch hit, substitute for; sub; redeem,

commute, alternate.

adv instead, in place of, in lieu of.

148 [double or mutual change] **interchange** *n* exchange, commutation, permutation, transposition; reciprocation, reciprocity, intercourse; barter, swap, trade; interchangeability; retaliation, reprisal, requital, retort, crossfire.

v interchange, exchange, barter, trade, swap, bandy, transpose, commute, reciprocate; give and take, battle with words; retort, requite, retaliate.

adj interchangeable, all-purpose, multi-purpose; reciprocal; mutual.

adv in exchange, vice versa, turn and turn about.

149 changeableness *n* mutability, inconstancy, volatility, instability; malleability, adaptability, versatility; mobility; vacillation, irresolution, indecision, capriciousness, oscillation, alternation, fluctuation, vicissitude; restlessness, fidgetiness, disquiet, disquietude; unrest, agitation.

v fluctuate, oscillate, vary, waver, flounder, shuffle, hem and haw, vacillate, tremble, alternate.

adj changeable, mutable, variable, malleable, adaptable, adjustable, versatile, mobile, transformable, convertible; inconstant, unsteady, unstable, unreliable, vacillating, oscillating, fluctuating; volatile, fitful, fickle, capricious, mercurial, indecisive, irresolute, flighty, impulsive, fanciful, erratic, wayward, wanton; restless, fidgety, tremulous, agitated; unfixed, unsettled.

150 stability *n* immutability, unchangeableness, constancy, firmness, fixity, solidity, steadiness, soundness, balance, stabilization, equilibrium, quiescence; immobility, immovability, fixedness; steadfastness, reliability, resolution, determination, obstinacy, stubbornness, pertinacity, tenacity, doggedness, will, pluck, resoluteness; permanence, endurance, perseverance, durability; continuity, uniformity, changelessness.

v be firm, stick fast, stand firm; settle, establish, fix, set, stabilize; retain, keep hold; make sure, fasten, make solid.

adj stable, fixed, rigid, firm, steady, established, strong, sturdy, immovable, invariable, unvarying, permanent, unchangeable, unchanging, unalterable, immutable; enduring, constant, durable, lasting, abiding, secure, fast, perpetual; unwavering, steadfast, staunch, reliable, steady, solid, sound, balanced; resolute, obstinate, dogged, willful, stubborn, pertinacious, tenacious.

151 present events *n* event, occurrence, incident, affair, eventuality, happening, proceeding, transaction, fact; phenomenon; circumstance, situation, particular; adventure, episode, thrill; crisis, pass, emergency, contingency, impasse; things, doings, affairs, matters, issues; the world, life, the times.

v happen, occur, take place, come to pass, take place, come about, come round; fall out, turn out, befall, chance, prove, eventuate; turn up, crop up, arise, arrive, issue, ensue, start, hold; take its course, pass off; experience, meet with, meet up with, fall to, be one's lot, be one's fortune, find, encounter, undergo, go through, live through, endure, put up with.

adj happening, going on, doing, current; eventful, stirring, bustling, busy, full of incident.

adv eventually, finally; as things go, in the course of things, as it happens.

152 future events *n* destiny, luck, lot, chance, fortune, karma, doom, end; future, futurity, next world, hereafter; prospects, expectations, tomorrow.

v impend, hang over, hover, threaten, loom, await, come on, approach; foreordain, preordain; destine, predestine, doom, have in store for.

adj impending, destined; coming, in store, to come, at hand, near, close by, imminent, brewing, forthcoming; in the wind, in the cards, in prospect, looming, on the horizon.

adv in time, in the long run, in good time, in its own sweet time, eventually.

VIII. Causation

153 cause *n* origin, source, principle, element; prime mover, first cause; author, producer, creator; mainspring, agent, catalyst; groundwork, foundation, support; spring, fountain, well, fount, font; genesis, descent, remote cause, influence; pivot, hinge, axis, turning point; egg, germ, embryo, root, nucleus, seed; causality, causation, origination, production.

v cause, originate, give rise to, occasion, sow the seeds of, kindle, bring to pass, bring about; produce, create, set up, develop; found, broach, institute; induce, evoke, elicit, draw, provoke; determine, decide; conduce to, contribute, have a hand in, influence, effect.

adj causal, generative, productive, formative, creative; primal, primary, original, embryonic.

adv because.

154 effect *n* consequence, issue, derivation, upshot, outgrowth, development, fruit, crop, harvest, product, outcome, end, conclusion; offspring, offshoot; complications, concomitants, side effects.

v be the effect of, be due to, be owing to; originate in, originate from, rise from, spring from, proceed from, emanate from, come from, grow from, issue from, flow from, result from; depend upon, hinge upon.

adj owing to, resulting from, due to, derivable from, caused by; derived from, evolved from; derivative, hereditary.

adv consequently, as a consequence, necessarily.

155 [assignment of cause] **attribution** *n* theory, ascription, assignment, rationale, reference to, accounting for; imputation, derivation; explanation, interpretation, reason why.

v attribute to, ascribe to, impute to, refer to, point to, trace to, assign to; account for, derive from; theorize, speculate.

adj attributed, attributable, referable, due to, owing to.

adv hence, thence, therefore, *ergo*, for, since, on account of, because; why? wherefore? whence? how come? how so?

156 [absence of assignable cause] **chance** *n* fortune, fate, accident, hap, hazard, luck, fluke, (*informal*) freak; gamble, lottery, tossup, fifty-fifty chance, throw of the dice, heads or tails; probability, possibility, contingency, odds; speculation, gaming, gambling.

v chance, hap, turn up; fall to one's lot; stumble on, light on; take one's chances.

adj chancy, causal, fortuitous, accidental, (*informal*) iffy, adventitious, haphazard, random, indeterminate, flukey, (*informal*) freaky.

adv by chance, by accident; at random; perchance, as chance will have it.

157 power *n* potency, strength, puissance, might, force, energy, vigor; control, command, dominion, authority, rule, sway, ascendancy, sovereignty, omnipotence; ability, capability, capacity, facility, competence, competency, efficacy; validity, cogency.

v be powerful, control, command, rule; confer power, empower, invest, endow; arm, strengthen, authorize; compel, force.

adj powerful, potent, strong, mighty, energetic; able, capable, competent, efficacious, equal to, up to, effective, efficient, adequate; omni-

potent, almighty; influential, forceful.
adv powerfully.
prep by virtue of, by dint of.

158 impotence *n* inability, incapability, incapacity, infirmity, debility, disability; inefficacy, inefficiency, incompetence, ineptitude, feebleness, weakness, frailty, powerlessness; helplessness, prostration, paralysis, collapse, exhaustion; decrepitude, senility; sexual failure, barrenness.

v be impotent; collapse, faint, swoon, drop; render powerless, disable, disarm, incapacitate, disqualify, invalidate; cramp, tie the hands, paralyze, muzzle, cripple, maim, laim, hamstring, throttle, strangle, tie up in knots; unman, unnerve, enervate; shatter, exhaust, weaken; emasculate.

adj impotent, powerless, incapable, unable, incompetent, ineffective, inefficient, ineffectual, inept, unfit, unfitted, unqualified; disabled, incapacitated, crippled, paralyzed, paralytic; decrepit, senile, exhausted, worn out, used up, limp, spent; weak, frail, infirm, feeble, helpless, harmless; sterile, barren, frigid; emasculated, inadequate, inoperative; futile, fruitless, bootless, vain.

159 strength *n* power, force, might, vigor, health, stoutness, hardiness, lustihood, stamina, energy, potency, capacity; spring, bounce, tone, elasticity, tension; virility, vitality, nerve, verve; strengthening, invigoration, refreshment.

v strengthen, invigorate, brace, nerve, fortify, sustain, harden, steel; vivify, revivify, refresh, reinforce, restore.

adj strong, mighty, vigorous, forceful, hard, stout, robust, sturdy, hardy, powerful, potent, puissant; irresistible, invincible, indomitable, unconquerable, impregnable, inextinguishable incontestable; able-bodied, athletic, muscular, sinewy, strapping, gigantic, Herculean.

adv strongly, by force.

160 weakness *n* debility, relaxation, languor, enervation; impotence, infirmity, fragility, flaccidity; frailty, delicacy, softness; senility, decrepitude.

v be weak, drop, crumble, give way, teeter, totter, tremble, shake, halt, limp, fade, languish, decline, flag, fail; weaken, enfeeble, cramp, debilitate, shake, enervate, unnerve; relax; dilute, water down.

adj weak, feeble, infirm, sickly; languid, faint, dull, slack, spent; limp, flaccid, powerless, impotent; relaxed, unstrung, unnerved; frail, fragile, delicate, flimsy; rickety, drooping, teetering, tottering, withered, shaky, shattered; palsied, decrepit, lame; decayed, rotten, worn, seedy, wasted, laid low.

161 production *n* creation, formation, fabrication, construction, manufacture; building, architecture, erection; organization, establishment; workmanship, craftsmanship, performance; achievement, product, end result; flowering, fructification, fruition, fulfillment; gestation, evolution, development, growth; genesis, generation, procreation; authorship, publication, works, *oeuvre*.

v produce, perform, operate, do, make, form, construct, fabricate, frame, contrive, manufacture; build, raise, rear, erect, put up; set up, establish, constitute, compose, organize, institute; achieve, accomplish, fulfill; bud, flower, blossom, bloom, bear fruit, bring forth; propagate, beget, generate, procreate, engender; breed, hatch, develop, bring up; induce, cause.

adj productive, constructive, formative, creative; generative; prolific, blooming.

162 [nonproduction] destruction *n* waste, dissolution, breaking up, disruption; consumption; fall, downfall, ruin, perdition; breakdown, wreck, wrack, havoc, mess, chaos, cataclysm; desolation, extinction, annihilation, demolition; overthrow, subversion, suppression; dilapidation, devastation, road to ruin.

v perish, fall, tumble, topple, fall to pieces, break up, crumble, go to the dogs, go to wrack and ruin; destroy, do away with, demolish, tear up, overturn, overthrow, wipe out, *(informal)* waste; upset, subvert, undo; waste, squander, dissipate, dispel, dissolve; smash, squash, squelch, shatter, crumble, batter, crush, pull to pieces; fell, sink, scuttle, wreck, swamp, ruin, raze, level, expunge, erase, sweep away; lay waste, ravage, gut; disorganize, dismantle, take apart; devour, devastate, desolate, sap, exterminate, extinguish, stamp out, trample out, crush out, eradicate.

adj destructive, subversive, ruinous, incendiary, deadly, lethal, fatal; destroyed, wiped out, extinct.

163 reproduction *n* renovation, restoration, renewal, revival, regeneration, revivification, resuscitation, reanimation, resurrection; reappearance; generation, childbirth.

v reproduce, renovate, restore, renew, revive, regenerate, revivify, resuscitate, breathe new life into, reanimate, refashion, resurrect, bring back to life; give birth to, multiply, people the world.

adj reproductive; - regenerative, restorative; renascent, reappearing, resurgent.

164 producer *n* originator, inventor, author, founder, generator, mover, creator, maker, architect; backer, angel.

165 destroyer *n* spoiler, waster, ravager, wrecker, killer, assassin, executioner; cankerworm, bane; iconoclast, rebel, pessimist, cynic, nihilist, misanthrope.

166 parentage *n* family, ancestry, lineage, genealogy; procreator, progenitor.

paternity: fatherhood, fathership; father, dad, pop, sire, papa, (*informal*) old man; grandfather, grandsire.

maternity: motherhood; mother, mom, ma, mamma, mummy, mum, (*informal*) old lady; grandmother.

adj parental, familial, ancestral, lineal, paternal, maternal; patriarchal, matriarchal.

167 posterity *n* progeny, breed, issue, offspring, brood, litter, family, children, grandchildren, heirs; child, son, daughter; descendant, heir, scion, (*informal*) chip off the old block; heredity.

adj filial.

168 productiveness *n* fecundity, fertility, fruitfulness, productivity; multiplication, propagation, procreation; creativity, inventiveness, originality.

v make productive, fructify, fulfill; procreate, generate, conceive, impregnate, fertilize; teem, multiply, produce, reproduce.

adj productive, prolific, fruitful, copious, teeming, fertile, fecund; procreative, generative, life-giving.

169 unproductiveness *n* infertility, sterility, barrenness, unfruitfulness, impotence; unprofitableness, wastefulness.

v be unproductive, do nothing, produce nothing, come to nothing.

adj unproductive, unfruitful, infertile, barren, sterile, arid; unprofitable, useless.

170 agency *n* operation, force, working, function, office, maintenance, exercise, work, play; causation, instigation, instrumentality, influence.

v operate, work, do; act, perform, play, support, sustain, maintain, take effect, quicken, strike; come into play, have free play; bring to bear upon, influence.

adj operative, efficient, efficacious,

effectual, practical; at work, on foot, in operation, in force, in play, in action.

adv through the agency of, by means of.

171 energy *n* force, power, strength, intensity, vigor, zeal, dynamism, pep, fire, spirit, ebullience, life; activity, agitation, exertion, effervescence, ferment, fermentation, ebullition, bustle.

v give energy, energize, stimulate, kindle, excite, inflame, exert; strengthen, invigorate; sharpen, intensify.

adj energetic, strong, forcible, potent, forceful, active, powerful, intense, vigorous, zealous, dynamic, ebullient, spirited, animated, keen, vivid, sharp, acute, incisive, trenchant, biting; invigorating, rousing, stimulating; energized.

172 inertness *n* inertia, inactivity, torpor, languor, dullness, immobility, passivity, passiveness, lifelessness; quiescence, latency; inexcitability, sloth, indolence, irresolution, indecisiveness, cowardice, spinelessness.

v be inert, be inactive.

adj inert, inactive, immobile, unmoving, motionless, lifeless, passive, dead; sluggish, dull, heavy, flat, slack, tame, slow, blunt, torpid, languid; latent, dormant, sleeping, smoldering, quiescent.

adv in suspense, in abeyance.

173 violence *n* vehemence, fury, ferocity, impetuosity, boisterousness, turbulence, ebullition, effervescence, intensity, severity, acuteness; energy, force, might; fit, paroxysm, orgasm, spasm, convulsion, throe; exacerbation, exasperation, hysterics, excitability, passion; outbreak, outburst, uproar, riot, explosion, blow-up, blast, eruption; turmoil, disorder, ferment, agitation, storm, tempest; destruction, brutality, fighting, combat, warfare, hostilities; injury, wrong, outrage, injustice.

v be violent, ferment, effervesce; romp, rampage, run wild, run riot, rush, tear, run headlong, run amuck, go wild, kick up a row, (*informal*) flip out, go beserk; bluster, rage, roar, riot, storm, boil, boil over, fume, foam; explode, go off, detonate, thunder, blow up, flare, burst; render violent, sharpen, stir up, quicken, excite, incite, urge, lash, whip up, stimulate; irritate, inflame, kindle, accelerate, aggravate, exasperate, exacerbate, convulse, infuriate, madden, fan the fire, whip into a frenzy.

adj violent, vehement, acute, sharp; rough, rude, bluff, boisterous, brusque, abrupt, wild, impetuous, rampant; disorderly, turbulent, blustering, raging, riotous, tumultuous, obstreperous; raving, frenzied, (*informal*) freaked, mad, unhinged, insane; desperate, furious, frantic, hysterical; savage, fierce, ferocious, physical, brutal, combative; uncontrollable, ungovernable, irrepressible, excited; spasmodic, convulsive, orgasmic; explosive, volcanic, stormy.

adv violently; by storm, by force.

174 moderation *n* temperateness, temperance, reasonableness, judiciousness, deliberateness, fairness; gentleness, mildness, calmness, peacefulness; quiet, calm, composure; lenity, lenience; relaxation, assuagement, tranquilization, pacification, mitigation; measure, middle ground, middle of the road.

v moderate, ally, meliorate, calm, pacify, assuage, lull, smooth, compose, still, calm, quiet, hush, sober, mitigate, soften, mollify, temper, qualify, alleviate, appease, lessen, abate, diminish; slake, curb, tame; arbitrate, referee, umpire, regulate.

adj moderate, temperate, reasonable, judicious, deliberate, fair, gentle, mild, calm, cool, sober, measured, unruffled, quiet, tranquil, still, peaceful, pacific; unexciting, even, smooth, bland, palliative; lenient, relaxed, easy going.

adv moderately, in moderation, within reason.

175 influence *n* importance, weight, pressure, preponderance, prevalence, sway; predominance, ascendancy; dominance, reign, rule, authority, power, control, capability; input, (*informal*) say, persuasion, play, leverage, vantage ground; patronage, protection, auspices.

v be influential, have a say, have input, carry weight, affect, sway, impress, bias, direct, control; move, activate, incite, impel, rouse, arouse, induce, persuade; dominate, predominate, outweigh, override, prevail.

adj influential, important, weighty; prevalent, rife, rampant, dominant, predominant; potent, powerful, effective, authoritative.

175a absence of influence *n* impotence, powerlessness; unimportance, irrelevancy.

adj uninfluential, unpersuasive, weak, impotent, (*informal*) wishy-washy.

176 tendency *n* aptness, aptitude, disposition, predisposition, proclivity, proneness, propensity, susceptibility, inclination, leaning, bias, drift, trend, bent, turn; quality, nature, temperament; idiosyncrasy, cast, vein, mood, humor.

v tend, contribute, conduce, lead, dispose, incline, verge, bend to, gravitate toward, lean, drift, tend, affect; promote, influence.

adj tending, leaning; conducive, working toward, in a fair way to; liable, likely; influential, instrumental, useful, subsidiary, subservient.

177 liability *n* susceptibility, penchant, vulnerability, predilection, propensity, tendency; drawback, hindrance, obstacle, difficulty, impediment; responsibility, obligation, debt, debit, indebtedness, pledge.

v be liable, incur, lay oneself open to, run the risk of, stand a chance, expose oneself to.

adj liable, subject, exposed, likely, open, in danger of; obliged, responsible, accountable, answerable; contingent, incidental, possible.

178 concurrence *n* accordance, accord, agreement, consent, assent; cooperation, collaboration, partnership, alliance, concert, union.

v concur, conduce, conspire, contribute; agree, unite, combine, hang together, pull together, cooperate, collaborate; keep pace with, run parallel, go hand in hand with.

adj concurrent, cooperative, collaborative, joint, allied with, of one mind, at one with, in concert with.

179 counteraction *n* opposition, antagonism, contrariety, polarity; clashing, collision, interference, resistance, friction; reaction, response, counterblast, counter maneuver; neutralization, check, curb, hindrance, repression, restraint.

v counteract, run counter to, clash, cross, interfere with, conflict with; jostle, run up against, oppose, antagonize, withstand, resist, hinder, impede, check, curb, repress, restrain; recoil, react; neutralize, nullify, cancel out, undercut, undermine, undo; counterpoise, offset, balance out, compensate.

adj counteracting, antagonistic, conflicting, contrary, reactionary.

adv although.

prep in spite of, against.

Class II
Words Relating to Space
I. Space in General

180 [indefinite space] **space** *n* extension, extent, expanse, span, stretch, scope, range, latitude, spread, proportions, sweep, capacity, play, swing, expansion; elbowroom, room, breathing space, leeway; open space(s), free space, waste, desert, wild, wilderness; unlimited space, wide world, heavens universe, solar system, outer space, abyss, the void, infinity.

adj spacious, roomy, extensive, expansive, capacious, ample; widespread, vast, worldwide, boundless, limitless, unlimited, infinite.

adv extensively, far and wide, right and left, from the four corners of the world, all over, from pole to pole, under the sun, on the face of the earth, from all points of the compass, to the four winds.

180a inextension *n* nonextension, point, atom.

181 [definite space] **region** *n* sphere, ground, soil, area, realm, quarter, orb, hemisphere, circuit, circle; domain, tract, territory, country, county, province; clime, climate, zone, meridian, latitude.

adj regional, provincial, territorial.

182 [limited space] **place** *n* spot, point; niche, nook, hole, pigeonhole; locality; locale, situation.

adv somewhere, in some place, here and there, in various places.

183 situation *n* position, locality, locale, latitude and longitude, location; footing, standing, standpoint; aspect, attitude, posture, perspective, pose; place, site, station, post, predicament, whereabouts; bearings, direction; topography, geography; map, chart.

v be situated, be located, lie, have its seat in; situate, locate.

adj situated, located; local, topical, topographical.

adv here and there, hereabouts, thereabouts, in such and such a place.

184 location *n* place, situation; establishment, settlement, installation; anchorage, mooring, encampment.

v locate, place, situate, put, lay, set, make a place for, seat; station, lodge, quarter, house, post, install; establish, fix, settle, root; graft, plant; inhabit, domesticate, colonize, take root, establish roots, come ·to rest, settle down, take up quarters; locate oneself, relocate; squat, perch, bivouac, burrow, get a footing, encamp.

adj located, placed, ensconced, rooted, settled, moored.

185 displacement *n* dislocation, misplacement, derangement, transposition; ejection, expulsion, banishment, removal, exile.

v displace, dislodge, disestablish; misplace, disturb, disorder, unsettle, derange, confuse; transpose, set aside, transfer, remove, unload, empty, eject, expel, banish, exile; vacate, depart, leave.

adj displaced; unplaced, unhoused, unsettled, unestablished; homeless, out of place, misplaced, out of its element.

186 presence *n* attendance, company; occupancy, occupation; ubiquity, omnipresence, permeation, pervasion, pervasiveness, diffusion, dispersion; nearness, vicinity, proximity, closeness.

v be present; look on, attend, stand by, remain, find oneself; occupy, inhabit, dwell, stay, sojourn, live, abide, lodge, nestle, roost, perch, tenant; fill, pervade, permeate, run through.

adj present, attending; occupying, inhabiting, resident, moored; ubiquitous, omnipresent, pervasive, diffused; near, close, in proximity.

adv here, there, and everywhere; in presence of.

187 absence *n* nonappearance, nonattendance, absenteeism, nonresidence; emptiness, void, vacuum, vacancy, vacuity.

v be absent; keep away, play truant, absent oneself, stay away.

adj absent, not present, away, out, not here, not in, not present, off; wanting, lacking, missing, nonexistent; vacant, empty, void, vacuous, devoid.

adv without, minus, nowhere, sans; elsewhere.

188 inhabitant *n* resident, dweller, occupant; tenant, inmate, boarder, lodger; native, townsman, villager, citizen; population, community, society, state, people, race, nation.

v inhabit, live, reside, dwell.

adj indigenous, native, domestic.

189 habitation *n* abode, residence, domicile, lodging, dwelling, address, habitation, housing, quarters; home, homestead, motherland, fatherland, country; nest, lair, den, cave, hole, hiding place, cell, hive, haunt, habitat, perch, roost, retreat, (*informal*) pad, (*informal*) crashpad.

v inhabit, take up one's abode.

190 [things contained] **contents** *n* stuffing, cargo, lading, freight, shipment, haul, load, bale, burden.

v load, lade, ship, haul, charge, fill, stuff.

191 receptacle *n* container, holder, repository, vessel, receiver, depository, reservoir; storage areas; bulk containers; liquid containers; wrapping.

II. Dimensions

192 size *n* proportions, dimensions,

magnitude, bulk, volume; largeness, greatness; expanse, amplitude, mass; capacity, tonnage; corpulence, obesity, plumpness; hugeness, enormousness, immensity; monstrosity, enormity; giant, monster, mammoth, behemoth, leviathan, elephant; lump, bulk, block, mass, clod, thumper, whopper, strapper, (*informal*) mother, mountain, mound, heap.

v be large; become large, expand.

adj sizable, large, big, great, considerable, bulky, voluminous, ample, massive, massy; capacious, comprehensive, spacious; mighty, towering, magnificent; corpulent; stout, fat, plump, obese, portly; full-grown, stalwart, brawny; hulky, unwieldy, bulky, lumpish, whopping, thundering, thumping; overgrown; huge, immense, enormous, mighty, vast, amplitudinous, stupendous; monstrous, gigantic, colossal.

193 littleness *n* smallness, diminutiveness, tininess; epitome; microcosm; vanishing point.

v be little; become little, decrease.

adj little, small, minute, diminutive, microscopic, submicroscopic; tiny, puny, wee, miniature, pigmy, dwarf, undersized, underdeveloped, dwarfish, stunted, dumpy, squat; imperceptible, invisible, infinitesimal.

194 expansion *n* increase, enlargement, extension, growth, development; augmentation, aggrandizement, increment, amplification; spreading, swelling, distention, puffiness, dropsy.

v expand, widen, enlarge, extend, grow, increase, swell, fill out; dilate, stretch, spread; bud, sprout, shoot, germinate, open, burst forth; outgrow, overrun; spread, extend, aggrandize; distend, develop, amplify, spread out, magnify; inflate, puff up, blow up, stuff, pad, cram, fatten; exaggerate.

adj expanded, larger, swollen, expansive, widespread, overgrown, exaggerated, bloated, fat, turgid, tumid, dropsical; pot-bellied, chubby, corpulent, obese, heavy; full-blown, full-grown.

195 contraction *n* reduction, diminution; decrease, lessening, shrinking; collapse, emancipation, attenuation, atrophy; condensation, compression, compactness, compendium, squeezing.

v contract, become small, lessen, decrease, dwindle, shrink, narrow, shrivel, collapse, wither, wizen, fall away, waste, wane, ebb, decay, deteriorate; diminish, contract, draw in, constrict, condense, compress, squeeze, crush, crumple up, pinch, squash, cramp; pare, reduce, attenuate, scrape, file, grind, chip, shave, shear, cut down; circumscribe, limit, restrain,

confine.

adj contracting, astringent; shrunk, shrunken, contracted; wizened, stunted, waning; compact.

196 distance *n* remoteness, farness, background, offing, far cry to, horizon, elongation; interval, remove, gap, span, reach, range; outpost, outskirts, foreign parts.

v be distant; extend to, stretch to, reach to, spread to; range.

adj distant, far off, far away, remote, far, afar, outlying, removed, at a distance, away, yonder, yon; inaccessible, out of the way, unapproachable.

adv far off, far away, afar, away, a long way off.

197 nearness *n* closeness, propinquity, proximity, proximation; vicinity, neighborhood, contiguity; short distance, earshot, close quarters, stone's throw, gunshot, hair's breadth; approach, access.

v be near, adjoin, neighbor, border upon, touch, stand next to; approximate, come close to, resemble; converge, crowd.

adj near, nigh, close, neighboring, adjoining, adjacent, bordering; proximate, approximate; at hand, handy; intimate.

adv near, nigh, hard by, close to, close upon, within reach, at one's fingertips.

198 interval *n* separation, space, break, gap, caesura, interspace, interstice, distance, hiatus, skip, division, opening; pause, recess, interim, respite, interlude, interregnum, interruption, term, spell, period; cleft, crevice, chink, cranny, crack, slit, fissure, rift, flaw, breach, rent, gash, cut, leak; ditch, dike, gorge, ravine, abyss, gulf.

v gape, open; intervene, interrupt.

199 contiguity *n* contact, contiguousness, proximity, apposition, juxtaposition, touching, abutment, meeting.

v be contiguous, join, adjoin, abut on, border, touch, meet, graze, adhere; coincide, coexist.

adj contiguous, touching, in contact, end to end; close, near.

200 length *n* distance, extent, longitude, span, reach, range; lengthiness, elongation, size; duration, continuance, term, period.

v be long, stretch out, sprawl; extend to, reach to, stretch to; lengthen, stretch, elongate, extend; prolong, protract, draw out, spin out.

adj long, lengthy, extended, outstretched; lengthened, interminable;

linear, lineal, longitudinal; tall, stringy, protracted, lanky.

adv lengthwise, at length, longitudinally.

201 shortness *n* brevity, littleness; shortening, abridgment, abbreviation, conciseness, condensation; retrenchment, curtailment, reduction.

v be short; shorten, abridge, abbreviate, condense, compact, compress, epitomize; retrench, cut short, reduce, pare down, clip back, cut back, prune, shear, shave, crop, chop up, hack up, truncate.

adj short, brief, curt; compendious, compact, compressed, condensed; stubby, stunted, stumpy, squat, dumpy; concise, pointed; curtailed, cut back, reduced, shortened, abbreviated, abridged.

202 breadth. thickness *n* breadth, width, latitude, amplitude, extent, diameter.

thickness, density, denseness, heaviness, bulk, body.

v be broad; expand, widen. be thick; thicken.

adj broad, wide, ample, extended, expansive, large; outspread, outstretched.

thick, dense, heavy, bulky, solid, compact; dumpy, squat, thickset.

203 narrowness. thinness *n* narrowness, slenderness, exiguity, closeness, straitness, scantiness, slightness, slimness.

thinness, slenderness, slimness, leanness, lankness, meagerness, skinniness.

v be narrow; narrow, taper. be thin; thin, slenderize, slim; dilute, water down.

adj narrow, close, slender, thin, fine, threadlike, slim, delicate; restricted, confined, limited; thin, emaciated, lean, skinny, meager, gaunt, spindly, lanky, scrawny, haggard, pinched, skeletal, wasted; frail, unsound, fragile; weak, shrill, faint, feeble; watery, waterish, diluted, unsubstantial.

204 layer *n* stratum, substratum, bed, zone, floor, stage, story, tier, slab, tablet, board, sheet, platter; scale, coat, peel, membrane, film, leaf, slice.

v slice, shave, pare, peel; plate, coat, veneer; cover; layer.

adj layered, stratified, tiered; scaly, filmy, membranous, flaky.

205 filament *n* thread, fiber, strand, hair, cilia, tendril, gossamer, wire, strand, vein.

adj fibrous, threadlike, wiry, stringy, ropy; capillary.

206 height *n* altitude, stature, elevation, tallness; prominence, eminence, pre-eminence, loftiness, sublimity; top, peak, pinnacle, acme, summit, zenith, culmination.

v tower, soar, hover, cap, command; mount, bestride, surmount, overhang; heighten, elevate, raise up, rise up.

adj high, tall, elevated, towering, skyscraping, gigantic, huge, colossal; distinguished, prominent, eminent, pre-eminent, exalted, lofty, sublime; overhanging, overlying.

207 lowness *n* depression, debasement, prostration; flatness, proneness; lowlands, flatlands.

v be low; lie low, lie flat, crouch, slouch, wallow, grovel; underlie; lower, depress.

adj low, flat, level, low-lying; crouched, squat, prone, supine, prostrate, depressed; groveling, abject, sordid, mean, base, lowly, degraded, debased, ignoble, vile.

adv under, beneath, underneath, below, down, downward; underfoot, underground; downstairs, belowstairs.

208 depth *n* deepness, profundity, obscurity; depression, bottom, unfathomable space; pit, hollow, shaft, well, crater, chasm, abyss, bottomless pit; central part, midst, middle, bosom, womb, base, heart, core; soundings, draft, submersion, dive.

v deepen, hollow, plunge, sink, dig, excavate; sound, have the lead, take soundings.

adj deep, deep-seated, profound, mysterious, obscure, unfathomable; sunk, buried, submerged; bottomless, soundless, fathomless, unfathomed, abysmal, yawning, gaping.

adv beyond one's depth, out of one's depth, over one's head.

209 shallowness *n* superficiality, banality, triviality, frivolity, flimsiness, emptiness, vacancy; shallow, shoal, sand bar.

adj shallow, superficial, slight, cursory, trivial, banal, trashy, flimsy, substanceless, empty, vacuous, vacant; skin-deep, ankle-deep, knee-deep.

210 summit *n* top, peak, apex, pinnacle, vertex, acme, culmination, zenith; height, pitch, maximum, climax; crowning point, turning point, watershed.

v culminate, climax, crown, top.

adj highest, top, topmost, uppermost, tiptop; capital, head, polar; supreme, supernal.

211 base *n* bottom, stand, rest, pedestal, dado, understructure, substructure, foot, basis, foundation, ground, groundwork; principle, touchstone, fundamental part, element, ingredient; bottom, nadir, foot, sole, heel.

adj bottom, undermost, nethermost; fundamental, basic, elemental; based on, founded on, grounded on, built on; base, vile, venal.

212 verticality *n* perpendicularity, erectness; wall, precipice, cliff.

v be vertical, stand up straight, stand upright, stand erect, stand straight and tall.

adj vertical, upright, erect, perpendicular, straight, bolt upright, plumb.

adv vertically, on end, endwise.

213 horizontality *n* flatness; level, plane, stratum; horizon; recumbency, lying down, reclination, proneness, supination, prostration.

v be horizontal, lie, recline, lie down, lie flat, sprawl; render horizontal, flatten, level, prostrate, knock down, floor, fell.

adj horizontal, level, even, plane, flat, smooth; prone, supine, prostrate.

adv horizontally, on one's back.

214 suspension *n* hanging down, free swinging; pendant, tail, train, flap, pendulum

v suspend, hang, swing, dangle; flap, trail, flow; depend.

adj suspended, pendent, hanging, swinging, dangling, pendulous; dependent

215 support *n* foundation, base, basis, ground, footing, hold; supporter, prop, brace, stay, rib, truss, stalk, stilts, splint; bar, rod, boom, outrigger; staff, stick, crutch; bracket, ledge, shelf, trestle, buttress

v support, bear, carry, hold, sustain, shoulder, bolster; shore up, hold up, prop up, brace; help, aid, maintain, sustain; base, found, ground.

adj supporting, supported; fundamental.

216 parallelism *n* coextension; comparison, affinity, correspondence, semblance, likeness, resemblance, analogy, equation.

v parallel, compare, relate, associate, connect, correspond to, equate.

adj parallel, coextensive, collateral, aligned, equal; like, similar, allied, corresponding, correlative, analogous, equivalent.

217 obliquity *n* incline, inclination, slope, slant, leaning, tilt, list, bend, curve; acclivity, rise, ascent, grade, rising ground, hill, bank; declivity, decline, downhill, dip, fall; steepness.

v be oblique, slope, slant, lean, incline, stoop, decline, descend; bend, careen, slouch, sidle; render oblique, sway, bias, slant, warp, incline, bend, crook, tilt, distort.

adj oblique, inclined; sloping, tilted; askew, asquint, awry, crooked; uphill, rising, ascending; downhill, falling, descending; declining, declivitous; steep, abrupt, sharp, precipitous; diagonal, transverse.

adv obliquely, on one side; askew, askance, edgewise, at an angle; sidelong, sideways, slantwise.

218 inversion *n* subversion, reversion, contraposition, transposition, transposal, conversion; contrariety, contradiction, opposition, polarity, antithesis; reversal, overturn, somersault, turn of the tide, revulsion, revolution.

v be inverted, turn about, wheel about, go about, turn over, go over, tilt over; invert, subvert, reverse, overturn, upturn, upset, turn topsy-turvy; transpose.

adj inverted, inside out, wrong side out, upside down, topsy-turvy; inverse, reverse, obverse, opposite.

adv inversely.

219 crossing *n* intersection, grade crossing, crossroad, interchange; network, reticulation; net, netting, network, web, mesh, wicker, lace; mat, matting, plait, trellis, lattice, grating, grille, gridiron, tracery, fretwork, filigree; knot, entanglement.

v cross, intersect, interlace, intertwine, interweave, interlink, crisscross; twine, intwine, weave, twist, wreathe; dovetail, splice, link, link up; mat, plait, plat, braid; tangle, entangle, ravel; net, knot, twist

adj crossing; crossed, matted, transverse; weaved, woven, intertwined, interlaced.

220 exteriority *n* outside, exterior; surface, superficies; covering, skin, face, appearance, façade, aspect, facet.

v be exterior, lie around, encircle.

adj exterior, external, outer, outside, outward, superficial; outlying, extraneous, foreign, extrinsic.

adv externally, out, over, outwards.

221 interiority *n* interior, inside, inner part, center, interspace; subsoil, substratum, contents, substance, pith, marrow, backbone, heart, bowels, belly, guts, lap, womb; recesses, innermost recesses, hollows, nook, niche, cave.

v be interior, be inside; inclose, circumscribe, intern; embed, insert.

adj interior, internal, inside, inner,

inward, inmost, innermost; deep-seated, inlaid, embedded, ingrained, innate, inherent, intrinsic, inborn; private, secret, intimate, confidential; home, domestic.

adv internally; inward, within, indoors, withindoors.

222 centrality *n* center, middle, midst; core, kernel, nucleus, heart, pole, axis, pivot, navel, nub, hub; centralization; center of gravity.

v be central; centralize, concentrate; focus on, bring into focus, get to the heart of.

adj central, middle, pivotal, focal, concentric; middlemost.

adv centrally; middle, midst.

223 covering *n* cover; canopy, awning, tent, marquee; umbrella, parasol, sunshade; shade, screen, shield; roof, ceiling, thatch, shed; top, lid; bandage, wrappings; coverlet, blanket, sheet, quilt, tarpaulin; skin, fleece, fur, hide; clothing, mask; peel, crust, bark, rind; veneer, coating, facing, varnish.

v cover, superimpose, overlay, overspread; wrap, encase, face, case, veneer, paper; conceal, cover over.

adj covered, clothed, wrapped; protected.

224 lining *n* inner coating, coating; filling, stuffing, padding, wadding.

v line, stuff, wad, pad, fill; coat, incrust, face, cover.

adj lined.

225 dress *n* clothing, covering, raiment, drapery, costume, attire, garb, apparel, wardrobe, outfit, clothes; equipment, livery, gear, rigging, trappings, togs, accouterments; uniforms, regimentals, suit.

v dress, clothe, drape, robe, array, fit out, deck out, garb, rig out, apparel; equip, harness, outfit, uniform; cover, wrap, wrap up, sheathe, swathe, swaddle.

adj dressed, clothed, clad, invested.

226 undress *n* nudity, nakedness, bareness, dishabille.

v undress, uncover, divest, expose, disrobe, strip, bare, doff, peel, take off, put off, lay open.

adj undressed, nude, naked, bare, stark-naked, exposed, in the buff, *au naturel*, in the altogether, in one's birthday suit; undressed, unclad, undraped, disrobed.

227 environment *n* environs, surroundings, outskirts, suburbs, purlieus, precincts, neighborhood.

v environ, surround, encompass, compass, inclose, enclose, circle, encircle, gird, twine round, hem in.

adj surrounding, circumjacent.

adv around, about; without; on every side, on all sides, right and left, every which way.

228 interspersion *n* interjacence, interlocation, interpenetration, permeation; interjection, interpolation, interlineation, intercalation; intervention, interference, interposition, intrusion; insinuation; insertion.

v intervene, come between, get between, interpenetrate; intersperse, permeate, introduce, throw in, work in, interpose, interject, interpolate, insert; interfere, intrude, obtrude.

adj intervening, interjacent; parenthetical, episodic; intrusive.

adv between, betwixt, among, amid, amongst; in the thick of, betwixt and between; parenthetically.

229 circumscription *n* limitation, enclosure; confinement, restraint.

v circumscribe, limit, bound, confine, inclose; surround, hedge in, fence in, wall in; imprison, restrain; enfold, bury, incase.

adj circumscribed, confined, restrained, imprisoned; buried in, immersed in, embosomed, embedded.

230 outline *n* circumference, perimeter, periphery; circuit, lines, contour, profile, silhouette.

v outline, draw, sketch, trace, profile.

231 edge *n* frame, fringe, trimming, trim, edging, skirting, hem; verge, brink, brim, lip, margin, border, skirt, rim, mouth; threshold, door, porch, portal; coast, shore.

v edge, skirt, border; trim, hem.

232 enclosure *n* envelope, case, wrapper; girdle; pen, fence, fold, cote, corral, stockyard, paddock, yard, pound, compound; fence, pale, paling, balustrade, rail, railing; hedge; wall, barrier, barricade; gate, gateway, door, doorway; boundary, border.

v enclose, circumscribe.

233 limit *n* boundary, bounds, extent, confine, term, pale, verge; termination, terminus; frontier, marches, outer edges, unknown; boundary line, border, edge; turning point, flood gate.

v limit, restrain, restrict, confine, check, hinder, bound, circumscribe, define.

adj limited, definite; terminal.

adv thus far, only so far, thus far and no further.

234 front *n* forefront, foreground, lead; face, frontage, façade, frontispiece, proscenium; vanguard, front rank, first rank, head of the column.

advanced guard.

v front, face, confront; be in front, stand in front; come to the front.

adj fore, foremost; front, frontal, anterior, forward.

adv before, in front, in advance; ahead, right ahead, in the foreground; in the lead.

235 rear *n* back, background, rearguard, rear rank; distance, hinterland; rump, buttocks, posterior, rear, backside, hindquarters; wake, train; reverse, other side of the coin, (*informal*) flipside.

v be behind, bring up the rear; rear, bring up, nurture, raise; elevate, lift, loft, lift up, hold up; build, put up, erect.

adj rear, back, hindmost; posterior.

adv behind, in the rear, in the background, at the heels; after, aft, rearward.

236 side *n* laterality, flank, quarter, lee, hand; cheek, jowl, shoulder; profile, lee side, broadside.

v be on the side; be side by side, be cheek to cheek; flank, skirt, outflank, sidle.

adj sidelong, lateral; flanking, skirting; flanked.

adv sideways, sidelong; broadside, on one side, abreast, alongside, beside, side by side, cheek by jowl; laterally.

237 opposition *n* opposite, contraposition, opposite side, opposite poles, polarity, antithesis, reverse, inverse; counterpart, companion piece, complement.

v be opposite; stand as opposites, oppose.

adj opposite, reverse, inverse, converse; antipodal, antithetical, countering, opposing; fronting, facing, diametrically opposite; complementary.

adv over, over the way, over against; poles apart; face to face.

238 right *n* right hand, right side; offside, starboard.

adj right-handed, dextral.

239 left *n* left hand, left side; near side, port.

adj left-handed, sinistral.

III. Form

240 form *n* shape, outline, mold, appearance, cast, cut, configuration; make, formation, frame, construction, cut, set, build, trim; mold, model, pattern; posture, attitude, convention, rule, formality, formula, ceremony, conformity.

v form, shape, figure, fashion, carve, cut, chisel, hew, cast; shape, model, mold, fashion, cast, construct, build; stamp, cast, type.

adj formal, ceremonial, ceremonious, conventional; regular, set, fixed, stiff, rigid.

241 formlessness *n* shapelessness, amorphism, asymmetry; disorder, chaos; misproportion, deformity, disfigurement, defacement, mutilation, truncation.

v deface, disfigure, deform, mutilate, truncate.

adj formless, shapeless, amorphous, asymmetrical, unformed, unshaped, unfashioned, unshapely, misshapen, out of proportion, disordered, chaotic; rough, rude, coarse, barbarous, rugged.

242 [regularity of form] **symmetry** *n* shapeliness, finish, comeliness, gracefulness, grace, beauty; proportion, uniformity, parallelism; regularity, evenness, balance, order, harmony, agreement.

adj symmetrical, shapely, well set, finished; beautiful, lovely; classic, classical, formal, chaste, severe; regular, uniform, balanced, harmonious, ordered; even, parallel, equal.

243 [irregularity of form] **distortion** *n* contortion, warp, buckle, screw, twist; crookedness, obliquity; deformity, malformation, misproportion, disfigurement, monstrosity, ugliness; asymmetry.

v distort, contort, warp, buckle, screw, twist, wrest; writhe, grimace, make faces; deform, disfigure, misshape.

adj distorted, out of shape, irregular, unsymmetrical, awry, askew, crooked; not true, not straight, uneven; misshapen, ill-made, illfashioned, ill-proportioned, malformed, deformed.

244 angularity *n* bifurcation, bend, fork, crook, notch, angle, elbow, knee, knuckle, crotch; right angle, acute angle, obtuse angle; corner, nook, niche, recess.

v angle, tilt, bend, fork, bifurcate.

adj angular, bent, crooked, jagged, serrated; forked, bifurcate, cornered, V-shaped, hooked; akimbo.

245 curvature *n* curve, incurvature, bend; flexure, bending, crook, hook; deflection, turn, deviation, detour, sweep, curl, winding; curve, arc, arch, arcade, vault, bow, crescent, halfmoon, horse-shoe, loop; parabola, hyperbola.

v be curved, sweep, sag; deviate,

turn; render curved, bend, curve, deflect, inflect, crook; turn, round, arch, arch over, bow, curl, coil, recurve.

adj curved, bowed, vaulted, hooked, arched, arced; circular, nonlinear, semi-circular, rounded, crescent, crescent-shaped, lunar, demi-lune.

246 straightness *n* directness; inflexibility, stiffness; straight line, direct line, bee line.

v be straight, go straight; render straight, straighten, rectify, correct, right; put right, put straight, unbend, unfold, uncurl, unravel.

adj straight, even, true, unbent, direct, rectilinear, linear, not curved, uncurved; square, erect, perpendicular, vertical, upright; candid, forthright, definite, reliable, plain, blunt, frank, sure, positive, irrefutable, certain, unequivocal, inescapable; honest, honorable, fair, just, equitable, impartial, aboveboard, reputable, scrupulous, worthy, lawful, licit, conscientious, decent, ethical; correct, sound, sane, accurate, true; sober, conventional, provincial, (*informal*) unhip, (*informal*) square, (*informal*) not with it.

247 [simple circularity] **circularity** *n* roundness, rotundity; circle, ring, hoop, areola, bracelet, armlet; eye, loop, wheel, cycle, orb, orbit; zone, belt, cord, band, sash, girdle, circuit; wreath, garland, crown, corona, coronet; necklace, collar; ellipse, oval.

v round; go around, encircle, circle.

adj round, rounded, circular, oval, elliptic, elliptical, egg-shaped.

248 [complex circularity] **convolution** *n* involution, winding, wave, undulation, sinuosity, meandering, twist, twirl; coil, roll, curl, buckle, spiral, corkscrew, worm, tendril; serpent, snake, eel; maze, labyrinth.

v wind, twine, entwine, twirl, wave, undulate, meander, turn; twist, coil, roll; wrinkle, curl, frizz, frizzle; wring, contort.

adj convoluted, winding, twisted, wavy, undulating, circling, snaky, serpentine; involved, intricate, complex, complicated, labyrinthine, tortuous, mazy; spiral, coiled.

adv in and out, round and round.

249 rotundity *n* roundness, cylindricality, sphericity, globularity; cylinder, barrel, drum; roll, roller, rolling pin; sphere, globe, ball, spheroid, globule; bulb, pellet, pill, marble, pea, knob, pommel.

v sphere, form into a sphere, roll into a ball, round.

adj rotund, round, circular, ball-shaped; cylindrical, spherical, globular; egg-shaped, pear-shaped, ovoid.

250 convexity *n* prominence, projection, swelling, bulge, protuberance, protrusion; hump, hunch, bunch; knob, node, nodule, bump, clump; pimple, pustule, pock, growth, polyp, blister, boil; nipple, teat, pap, breast; nose, beak, snout, nozzle; peg, button, stud, ridge; cupola, dome, arch; relief, high relief, low relief; hill, mountain, cape, ness, promontory, headland; jetty, ledge, spur.

v project, bulge, protrude, jut out, stand out, stick out, stick up, start up, shoot up, swell up; raise; emboss.

adj convex, prominent, protuberant; bossed, nodular, bunchy, hummocky, bulbous, swollen, swelling, bloated, bowed, arched, bellied; salient, in relief, raised.

251 flatness *n* smoothness, evenness; plane, level; plate, platter, table, tablet, slab.

v flatten, level, even off.

adj flat, plane, even, smooth; level, smooth, horizontal; flat as a pancake.

252 concavity *n* depression, dip, hollow, indentation, dent, cavity, dint, dimple; excavation, pit, trough; cup, basin, crater; valley, vale, dale, dell, glade, grove, glen, cave, cavern.

v render concave, depress, hollow, scoop, scoop out, gouge; dig, delve, excavate, mine, stave in, tunnel.

adj concave, hollow, hollowed out; indented, dented, sunken, cupped; cavernous, rounded inward, incurved.

253 sharpness *n* acuteness, pointedness; point, spike, spine, needle, pin, prick, prickle, spur, barb, thorn; knife edge, cutting edge, razor edge.

v be sharp, taper to a point; sharpen, point, whet, barb, strop, grind, whittle.

adj sharp, keen, acute, trenchant; pointed, peaked, conical, spiked, spiky, tapering; studded, prickly, barbed, spiny, thorny, bristling, thistly; craggy, snaggy; cutting, sharp edged, razor sharp.

254 bluntness *n* dullness; obtuseness, roughness.

v be blunt; render blunt, dull, take off the point, round the edge.

adj blunt, dull, obtuse, dimwitted; rough, gruff; rounded, round, unsharpened, unpointed.

255 smoothness *n* polish, gloss; lubrication, lubricity.

v smooth, plane, file, scrape, shave, sand, sandpaper; level, press, flatten, roll; iron, steam press; polish, burnish, rub, wax, sleek, buff, glaze; lubricate, oil, grease.

adj smooth, polished, glossy, shiny, sleek, silken, silky; even, level, sanded; soft, downy, velvety; slippery, glassy, oily.

256 roughness *n* asperity, irregularity, corrugation, nodulation; grain, texture, pile, nap.

v roughen, rough up, crinkle, ruffle, rumple, crumple.

adj uneven, irregular, rugged, scabrous, knotted, craggy, gnarled; shaggy, coarse, hairy, bristly, hirsute; scraggly, prickly, bushy; unpolished, unsmooth, rough-hewn, textured; downy, velvety, fluffy, woolly.

adv against the grain.

257 notch *n* dent, nick, cut, scratch, indentation; saw, tooth, scallop.

v notch, nick, cut, scratch, indent, jag, scarify, scallop.

adj notched, toothed, serrated.

258 fold *n* plait, ply, crease, pleat, tuck; wrinkle, ripple, rimple, pucker, ruffle.

v fold, double, plait, crumple, crease, pleat, wrinkle, crinkle, ripple, curl, rumple, frizzle, rimple, ruffle, pucker, corrugate; tuck, hem, gather.

adj folded.

259 furrow *n* groove, rut, scratch, streak, cut, crack, score, incision, slit; channel, gutter, trench, gulley, ditch, dike, moat, trough; ravine, valley.

v furrow, dig, plow; channel, flute, groove, incise, cut, engrave, etch, seam, cleave, score; wrinkle, knit, pucker.

adj furrowed, ribbed, striated, fluted.

260 opening *n* hole, gap, aperture, orifice, perforation, pinhole, peephole, keyhole; slot, slit, rift, breach, cleft, chasm, fissure, rent; outlet, inlet, vent; portal, porch, gate, hatch, door, doorway, gateway; way, path, channel, passage.

v open, ope, gape, yawn; perforate, pierce, tap, bore, drill; mine, tunnel, dig to daylight; impale, spike, spear, gore, spit, stab, puncture, lance, stick, prick, riddle; uncover, unclose, lay bare, expose, bare, reveal; lay open, cut open, rip open, throw open.

adj open, unclosed, uncovered, exposed; ajar, wide-open, gaping, yawning; perforated, porous, reticulated, permeable; accessible, available, public.

261 closure *n* blockade, shutting up, obstruction, stoppage, clogging, sealing, plugging; contraction; ,constipation; culmination; cessation, completion, termination, windup; lid, top, cap, stopper, plug, barrier.

v close, plug, block up, stop up, fill up, cork up, cork, button up, stuff up, shut up, dam up; blockade, obstruct, hinder, bar, bolt, stop, seal, choke, throttle, shut.

adj closed, shut, unopened; unpierced, impervious, impermeable; impenetrable, impassable, pathless; tight, snug, airtight, unventilated, watertight, hermetically sealed.

262 perforator *n* piercer, borer, auger, drill, awl, scoop, corkscrew, probe, lancet, scalpel, needle, pin, stiletto, puncher, hole puncher, gouge; knife, spear, bayonet.

263 stopper *n* lid, cap, cover; cork, spike, stopcock, pin, plug, tap, faucet, valve, spigot, rammer, ramrod, wadding, stuffing, padding, stopping, bandage, tourniquet.

IV. Motion

264 motion *n* movement, action, activity, move, going; progress, locomotion; mobilization, mobility, movableness, motive power; unrest, restlessness; stream, flow, flux, run, course, stir; rate, pace, step, tread, stride, gait; velocity, speed.

v move, go, hie, budge, stir, pass, flit; hover around, hover about; shift, slide, glide, roll, roll on; flow, drift, stream, run, sweep along; wander, meander, browse, stroll, walk, perambulate, dodge, keep on one's toes, keep moving, hit the road, *(informal)* truck; move, impel, propel; mobilize.

adj moving, in motion, traveling, on the road; transitional, shifting, mobile, movable; mercurial, restless, unquiet, nomadic, transient.

adv under way; on the move, on the go, on the march.

265 rest *n* quiescence, stillness, quietude, calm, calmness, tranquillity, repose, serenity, peace, silence; pause, lull, cessation, stagnation, immobility, fixity.

v rest, be still, stand still, lie still, stand immobile, keep quiet, repose; remain, stay, pause, wait, mark time, hold, halt, stop short, cease, desist, discontinue, stop; stagnate, be inactive, immobilize; dwell, settle, settle down, establish roots; alight, arrive; stand fast, stand firm, stick fast; quell, becalm, hush, stay, lull, lull to sleep, tranquilize.

adj restful, quiescent, still, calm, tranquil, peaceful, undisturbed, unruffled, serene, silent; motionless, fixed, stationary; unmoved, stable, at rest, at a standstill, stock-still, sleeping, dormant, inactive, stagnant.

266 [locomotion by land] **journey** *n* traveling, travel, excursion, tour, trip, expedition, jaunt, pilgrimage; wayfaring, roving, gadding about, (*informal*) bumming around, nomadism, vagabondism; migration, immigration, moving; walk, promenade, constitutional, stroll, peregrination, perambulation, march, stroll, saunter, jaunt, outing, hike, airing; horsemanship, horseback riding; drive, driving, motoring, ride, spin; cycling, biking; procession, cavalcade, caravan, file, cortege, column.

v journey, travel, tour, take a trip; flit, take wing, (*informal*) hit the road, rove, ramble, roam, prowl, (*informal*) bum, (*informal*) bum around, range, traverse, scour the country, wander, meander, saunter, gad about; move, migrate, immigrate.

adj journeying, traveling, on the road; itinerant, peripatetic, rambling, roving, gadding, flitting, vagrant, nomadic, migratory, wayfaring.

267 [locomotion by water or air] **navigation** *n* voyage, sail, cruise, passage, boat ride; aquatics, boating, yachting, sailing, shipping.

flight, air travel, flying, gliding; aeronautics, aviation.

v navigate; sail, put to sea, embark, shove off, spread the sails, make sail, take oar; go boating, cruise, float, drift, coast; row, paddle, pull, scull, punt, steam; ride the waves.

fly, take off, take wing, take to the skies; aviate, soar, glide, fly over, plane, jet.

adj sailing, nautical, naval, maritime, seagoing, seafaring, ocean-going; afloat; navigable.

flying, jetting; aloft, in flight; aviational, aeronautical, aerial.

268 **traveler** *n* wayfarer, journeyer, rover, rambler, wanderer, free spirit, nomad, vagabond, bohemian, gypsy, itinerant, vagrant, tramp, hobo, straggler, waif; pilgrim, palmer, seeker, quester; voyager, passenger, tourist, sightseer, excursionist, vacationer, globe-trotter, jet-setter; immigrant, emigrant, refugee, fugitive; pedestrian, walker, cyclist, biker, rider, horsewoman, horseman, equestrian, driver.

269 **mariner, flier** *n* mariner, sailor, seaman, seafaring man, sea dog; pilot, skipper, captain, commander, helmsman, steersman; crew, hands, mates; navigator, flier, airman, aviator, avia-

trix, pilot, skipper; astronaut, cosmonaut, spaceman.

270 **transference** *n* transfer, move, shift, transit, transition, passage, transmission, transport, transplantation, transposition; removal, relegation, deportation, extradition.

v transfer, transmit, transport, convey, carry, bear, pass; move, shift, conduct, convey, bring, fetch, reach; send, delegate, consign, turn over, hand over, deliver; transpose, transplant, displace, remove, relegate, deport, extradite; shovel, ladle.

adj transferable, transmittable, transmissible, transportable, movable, portable.

271 **carrier** *n* porter, bearer, messenger, runner, courier; postman, letter carrier; conductor, conveyor, transporter; freighter, ship, barge; train, locomotive; truck, vehicle, carriage; beast of burden.

272 **vehicle** *n* conveyance, carriage, transportation, rig; car, motorcar, automobile, (*informal*) wheels, truck; wagon, cart, coach, chaise, buggy; bicycle, bike, motorcycle, motorscooter; train, sleeping car, cattle car, boxcar.

273 **ship** *n* vessel, boat, liner, freighter, steamer, schooner, sailboat, motorboat, merchant ship, barge, tugboat, tanker, trawler, yacht, cruiser, yawl, ketch, brig, brigantine, square-rigger, sloop, cutter, launch; navy, fleet.

airplane, plane, jet, jumbo jet, aircraft, glider, helicopter, dirigible, blimp, balloon, spaceship, capsule, module, space station.

274 **velocity** *n* rapidity, quickness, swiftness, celerity, speed, alacrity; acceleration, pickup; spurt, rush, dash, race, flying, flight.

v move quickly, speed, hie, hasten, post, scamper, run, race, shoot, tear, whisk, sweep, rush, dash, dash off; bolt, bound, spring, dart, flit; hurry, hasten, haste, accelerate, (*informal*) turn on the juice, quicken, speed up, take off like a shot.

adj fast, speedy, swift, rapid, quick, brisk, fleet; nimble, agile, expeditious, light-footed, fast as a bullet, quick as lightning.

adv swiftly, apace, at full speed, at full gallop, posthaste.

275 **slowness** *n* languor, sluggishness, slackness, sloth, indolence; deliberateness, moderation, leisureliness; tardiness.

v move slowly, creep, crawl, lag, drawl, linger, loiter, saunter, trail, drag, dawdle; plod, trudge, lumber;

grovel, sneak, steal, worm one's way, inch; waddle, wobble, shuffle, hobble, limp, shamble, amble, traipse, slouch, mince, mince steps, halt; flag, totter, teeter, stagger; retard, hinder, impede, obstruct; slacken, check, relax, moderate; brake, curb, slow, put on the brakes.

adj slow, slack, late, tardy; gentle, easy, unhurried, deliberate, gradual, moderate, leisurely; languid, sluggish, indolent, lazy; tedious, humdrum, dull, boring; dense, stupid.

adv slowly, leisurely; at half speed, at a snail's pace; gradually, little by little, step by step, inch by inch, bit by bit, one step at a time.

276 impulse *n* impetus, implosion, push, thrust, shove; propulsion; sudden impulse, yearning, craving; reaction, response, reflex; collision, clash, encounter, shock, bump, crash; impact; blow, stroke, knock, rap, tap, slap, smack, pat, dab; hit, whack, thwack, slam, punch, belt, kick, thump, cut, thrust, lunge.

v impel, push, urge, thrust, shove, heave, prod, shoulder, jostle, hustle, hurtle, jog, jolt; start, make a start to, set going, get going, drive; run against, bump against, butt against; collide with, run into, bang into, butt; strike, knock, bang, hit, thump, beat, slam, dash, punch, thwack, whack; batter, pelt, buffet, butt; hit, rap, slap, tap, pat, dab.

277 recoil *n* reflex, rebound, ricochet, boomerang, backfire, backlash; snap, elasticity; reverberation, resonance; reaction, response, rebuff, repulse, revulsion.

v recoil, rebound, ricochet, boomerang, snap back, spring back, fly back; react, respond, reverberate, echo, quiver.

adj reactionary; elastic, backfiring.

278 direction *n* bearing, course, set, drift, tenor, trend, tendency, inclination; tack, aim, determination, intention; points of the compass, cardinal points; line, path, road, range, line of march; alignment.

v direct, point, aim; tend toward, point toward, conduct to, go to; bend, tend, verge, incline, determine; steer for, make for, aim at, level at, set one's sights on, take aim, hold a course for, be bound for.

adj direct, straight; bound for; undeviating, unswerving.

adv toward, on the road to; hither, thither, whither; directly, straight, straightforward, point-blank, on a line with.

279 deviation *n* diversion, digress-

ion, departure from, aberration; divergence, zigzag, detour, circuit; warp, refraction; swerving.

v deviate, alter one's course, turn, bend, curve, swerve, heel, bear off; divert, deflect, shift, shunt, draw aside, crook, warp; stray, straggle, digress, ramble, rove, drift, go astray, go adrift; wander, wind, twist, meander; veer, turn aside, change direction, steer clear of, dodge.

adj deviating, errant, aberrant; discursive, desultory, loose, rambling, digressive, stray, erratic, undirected; circuitous, indirect, zigzag, roundabout, crooked.

adv astray, roundabout, wide of the mark; circuitously.

280 [going before] **precedence** *n* priority; leading, heading, the lead, van, vanguard; precursor, coming beforehand.

v precede, go before, forerun; usher in, introduce, herald; head, take the lead, lead the way; take precedence, have priority, come first, come before.

adv in advance, before, ahead, in the vanguard, in front.

281 [going after] **sequence** *n* coming after, following, sequel; shadow, dangler, train.

v follow, come in sequence, go after; attend, be attendant on, follow in the steps of, follow in the wake of, trail, shadow; pursue; lag, fall behind.

adj following; sequential.

adv behind, after; in the rear.

282 [motion forward] **progression** *n* progress, improvement proceeding, advance, advancement, headway; growth, rise, increase, development.

v proceed, advance, progress, get on, get along, gain ground, press onward, forge ahead, make headway, make progress, make strides, stride forward; grow, develop, increase, improve.

adj advancing; progressive, advanced.

adv forward, onward; forth, on, ahead.

283 [motion backward] **regression** *n* retrogression, retreat, recession, retirement, withdrawal; reflux, backwater, return, recoil; backsliding; deterioration, decrease, fall.

v regress, recede, return, revert, retreat, back out, back down, turn back, fall back, drop out, retire, withdraw; lose ground, drop off, fall behind; ebb, shrink, shy.

adj retrograde, retrogressive; regressive, refluent, reflex.

adv backwards; aboutface.

284 propulsion *n* propulsive force, impulse, push, projection, thrust, drive, impulsion, impetus; throw, fling, toss, shot, discharge.

v propel, project, throw, fling, cast, pitch, chuck, toss, heave, hurl; drive, sling, push, shove; send off, fire off, discharge, shoot, launch, let fly; put in motion, set in motion, start, get going, impel; expel.

adj propulsive.

285 traction *n* drawing, hauling, pulling, towing, towage; yank, tug, drag, jerk.

v draw, pull, haul, lug, drag, tug, tow, trail, train, take in tow; wrench, jerk, yank.

adj tractile; in tow.

286 [motion towards] **approach** *n* access, advent, advance; nearness, approximation.

v approach, near, draw near, move towards, get close to; gain on, get closer to; pursue, trail.

adj approaching; approximate; impending, imminent.

287 [motion from] **recession** *n* retirement, withdrawal; flight, removal, retreat; regression, return, falling back, regress; reaction, reversal, recoil; departure, leave-taking.

v recede, move back, go back, move away from, retire, withdraw; drift, abate, fade, wane, ebb, subside, drift away, fall back; shrink; react, revert, relapse, recoil, regress; run away, fly, avoid.

288 attraction *n* attractiveness, inclination, affinity; pull, magnetism, gravity.

v attract, draw, drag, pull, magnetize, exert force; interest, invite, engage, fascinate, lure, allure, charm, decoy, bait.

adj attractive, attracting, enticing, seductive, alluring; have pull, magnetic, gravitational.

289 repulsion *n* aversion, antipathy, dislike; repulse, rebuff.

v repel, push back, drive away, chase away, rebuff, beat back; repulse, revolt, offend, sicken, disgust, displease, irritate.

adj repulsive, repellent, averse, repelling.

290 convergence *n* confluence, conflux, concurrence, concourse, congress, coming together, meeting, joining.

v converge, concur, come together, meet, join, unite; gather together, concentrate, center.

adj convergent, confluent, concurrent.

291 divergence *n* division, radiation, spread, severance, separation, refraction, deflection; ramification, furcation, branching, forking, detachment; deviation, aberration, disparity, difference, variance, heterogeneity.

v diverge, ramify, radiate, branch off, fork, spread, swerve, scatter, disperse; divide, separate, part, sever; vary, deviate, dissent, disagree.

adj divergent, radial, radiant, centrifugal.

292 arrival *n* advent, coming; reaching, attainment, landing, debarkation, disembarkation; reception, welcome, welcoming.

v arrive, get to, come to, reach a point, attain, complete; light, alight, dismount; land, disembark, debark, deplane, detrain.

293 departure *n* embarkation; outset, start, starting point, place of departure, point of departure; removal, exit; exodus, flight; leave-taking, valediction, *adieu*, farewell, goodbye.

v depart, go away, take one's leave, start, set out, leave, retire, quit, withdraw, absent, go, (*informal*) split, take off, (*informal*) cut out, move off, move out, ship out, pack it up; vacate, evacuate, abandon; sally, set forth, set forward, go forth; embark, set sail, put out to sea, shove off, get under way, enplane, entrain.

294 [motion into] **ingress** *n* entrance, entry; influx, intrusion, inroad, incursion, invasion, irruption, penetration, infiltration; insinuation, insertion.

v enter, come in, pour in, flow in; burst in, break in, invade, intrude; penetrate, infiltrate, insinuate oneself.

adj incoming, inbound.

295 [motion out of] **egress** *n* exit, issue; emergence, emanation; outbreak, outburst, eruption; evacuation, leakage, percolation, oozing, drainage, drain; outpouring, gush, effluence, effusion, discharge.

v emerge, emanate, issue; pass out of, come out of, pour out of, flow out of; exude, leak, ooze, drain, drip, trickle, dribble; gush, gush out, pour out, spout, flow out, discharge; escape, find vent.

adj outgoing, outward, outbound.

296 [motion into, actively] **reception** *n* admission, admittance, entry, entrée; importation, introduction, initiation, induction, absorption; ingestion, eating, drinking; suction, sucking; insertion, injection.

v give entrance to, admit, introduce, usher, initiate, induct; receive, import, bring in, ingest, absorb, imbibe.

297 [motion out of, actively] **ejection** *n* rejection, expulsion, eviction, dislodgment, banishment, exile; emission, effusion, discharge, evacuation, regurgitation, elimination.

v reject, eject, expel, evict, dislodge, banish, exile; push aside, push away, turn away, brush aside; empty, drain, clear out, clean out, purge, void, evacuate; vomit, spew, regurgitate, throw up, (*informal*) puke, retch, (*informal*) barf, belch out, burp out; discharge, eliminate, discard, get rid of, do away with, cast off, cut adrift, turn out, throw out, oust.

298 eating *n* dining, supping, taking nourishment; ingestion, chewing, mastication; imbibition, drinking. food, nourishment, nutrition, nutriment, sustenance, subsistence, provender, provisions, rations, keep, board, fare; drink, beverage, potion, draught.

v eat, feed, breakfast, lunch, dine, sup, break bread; taste, devour, wolf, swallow, gulp, bolt, gulp down, fall to, dig in; chew, masticate, bite, bite into, chomp, munch, crunch, gnaw, nibble, peck at; live on, live off, fatten, feast on.

drink, drink up, drink one's fill, quaff, (*informal*) down, chug, empty, sip.

adj eatable, edible, digestible; drinkable, potable; nutritious, nutritive.

299 excretion *n* discharge, emanation, exhalation, secretion, effusion, perspiration, sweat; evacuation, elimination, urination; hemorrhage, bleeding.

v excrete; emanate, exhale; secrete, perspire, sweat; eliminate, evacuate; urinate.

300 [forcible ingress] **insertion** *n* implantation, injection, inoculation, infusion, importation, insinuation, interpolation; immersion, submersion, dip, plunge.

v insert, introduce, put in; inject, infuse, instill, inoculate, impregnate, imbue; graft, ingraft, implant, plant, bud; thrust in, stick in, shove in, ram in, stuff in, tuck in, press in, drive in; immerse, merge, dip, plunge.

301 [egress] **extraction** *n* removal, elimination, extrication, eradication, extirpation, extermination, ejection; wrench, squeezing, pulling.

v extract, draw, draw out, take

out, pull out, tear out, rip out, pluck out; wring from, wrench, pull; root out, weed out, rake out, eradicate, uproot, pull up, extirpate; evolve, elicit, draw forth; extricate, remove, eliminate; squeeze out.

302 [motion through] **passage** *n* transmission; permeation, penetration, infiltration; ingress, egress; voyage, trip, tour, excursion, journey; way, route, channel, avenue, road, path, way, thoroughfare, conduit.

v pass, pass through; penetrate, permeate, thread, go through, cut across; ford, traverse, cross; go, move, proceed; leave, go away, depart.

303 [motion beyond] **infringement** *n* transgression, trespass, encroachment, infraction.

v infringe, transgress, trespass, encroach; surpass, go beyond, shoot ahead of, overrun; overstep, overreach, overshoot; outstrip, outrun, outride, outdo; exceed, surmount, transcend, soar.

adv beyond the mark, ahead.

304 [motion short of] **shortcoming** *n* failure, falling short; default, defalcation; incompleteness, imperfection, deficiency, insufficiency, noncompletion.

v fall short, come up short, come short of, not reach; want, lack; fail, break down, collapse, come to nothing; fall through, cave in.

adj deficient, lacking, insufficient; incomplete, imperfect.

305 ascent *n* ascension; rising, rise, upgrowth; leap, jump; acclivity, hill, grade.

v ascend, rise, mount, climb upward, climb, arise; clamber, mount, scale, go up, get up; tower, soar, hover, surmount, scale the heights.

adj ascendant; rising, acclivitous.

306 descent *n* declension, inclination, declination, slope, declivity, grade, decline, drop, cliff, precipice, dip, hill; fall, falling, descending, sinking; downfall, tumble, slip, tilt, trip, lurch.

v descend, go down, drop down, come down, drop, fall, gravitate, slip, slide, settle; decline, set, sink, droop, wilt, slump; dismount, alight, get down; swoop down, stoop; tumble, trip, stumble, lurch, pitch, topple, tilt, sprawl.

adj declivitous, sloping, precipitous, steep; descending.

307 elevation *n* raising; erection, lift; upheaval; sublimation, exaltation; prominence, height.

v elevate, heighten, raise, lift, lift up, erect; set up, tilt up, rear, hoist, heave; uplift, upraise, uprear; exalt, enhance, advance; take up, drag up, fish up, drag, dredge.

adj elevated, stilted, rampant.

308 depression *n* lowering; dip, concavity; upset, overturn, overthrow; prostration, abasement, debasement, degradation; bow, curtsy, genuflection, kowtow, obeisance.

v depress, lower, let down, take down, cast down, let drop, let fall; sink, debase, bring low, abase, degrade, reduce; overthrow, overturn, upset, prostrate, level, fell; bow, curtsy, genuflect, kowtow, kneel, bend over, make obeisance.

adj depressed; at a low ebb; prostrate, horizontal.

309 leap *n* jump, hop, spring, bound, vault; dance, caper, frisk, buck.

v leap, jump, hop, spring, bound, vault, hurtle, hurdle; dance, caper, trip, skip, frisk, bob, flounce, start; trip the light fantastic toe, dance all night.

adj leaping; frisky, lively, springy.

310 plunge *n* dip, dash, rush, dive, leap; ducking, dunking, submersion, immersion.

v plunge, immerse, submerge, douse, souse, dunk, dip; dash, rush, hasten, hurry; dive, leap, jump; descend, drop, fall, hurtle over.

311 circular motion *n* circulation, circularity; turn, excursion; circumvention, circumnavigation, circling; turning; coil, corkscrew, spiral; full circle, full turn, turn, circuit, lap.

v turn, bend, wheel, turn a circle, turn around, make a U-turn, put about, make a complete circle; circle, go around, circuit, circumnavigate; whisk, twirl, twist.

adj circuitous, roundabout; circular.

312 rotation *n* revolution, gyration, circulation, roll; spinning, pirouette, convolution; whir, whirl, eddy, vortex, whirlpool, maelstrom; cyclone, tornado.

v rotate, turn, spin, revolve, wheel, whirl, twirl, spin around; pivot, swivel, circle around.

adj rotating, rotary, gyratory, revolving.

313 evolution *n* evolvement, unfolding, development.

v evolve, unfold, unfurl, unroll, unwind, develop.

adj evolutionary, evolutional.

314 [motion to and fro] oscillation *n* vibration, pulsation, undulation; pulse, beat, (*informal*) vibes, ripple,

wave; alternation, coming and going, ebb and flow, ups and downs, flux and reflux; fluctuation, vacillation, irresolution.

v oscillate, vibrate, vacillate, swing, fluctuate, vary; undulate, wave; pulsate, beat, throb, ripple; reel, quake, quiver, quaver, shake; roll, toss, pitch; flounder, stagger, totter.

adj oscillating; undulatory; pulsating.

adv to and fro, up and down, back and forth, seesaw, zigzag, in and out, from side to side.

315 [irregular motion] agitation *n* stir, ripple, tremor, shake, jog, jolt, jar, jerk, shock, quiver, quaver, twitter, flicker, flutter; disquiet, perturbation, commotion, turbulence, turmoil, tumult; hubbub, bustle, fuss, ado, racket, fits; spasm, throe, throb, palpitation, convulsion, fit; disturbance, disorder, restlessness, hypertension; ferment, fermentation, ebullition, effervescence, hurly-burly; tempest, storm, groundswell, whirlpool, vortex; whirlwind, tornado, cyclone, twister.

v be agitated, shake, tremble, quiver, quaver, quake, shiver, twitter, writhe, toss, shuffle, tumble, stagger, bob, reel, sway; waggle, wriggle, dance, prance, stumble, shamble, flounder, totter, teeter, flounce, flop; throb, pulsate, beat, palpitate, go pit-a-pat; flutter, flicker, bicker, bustle; ferment, effervesce, foam, boil, bubble, simmer; agitate, shake, convulse, toss, tumble, bandy, flap, whisk, jerk, hitch, jolt, joggle, jostle, buffet, hustle, disturb, stir, shake up, churn, jounce, wallop, whip.

adj agitated, shaking, pulsating, tremulous, convulsive, jerky, shaky, throbbing.

adv by fits and starts; in convulsions, in fits.

Class III

Words Relating to Matter

I. Matter in General

316 materiality *n* corporeality, substantiality, flesh and blood, physicality; matter, body, substance, brute matter, physical elements, material; object, article, thing, materials.

science of matter: physics, natural philosophy, physical science, materialism.

materialist, physicist.

v materialize, embody, body in.

adj material, bodily, corporeal, physical, somatic; sensible, tangible, palpable, touchable, substantial, un-spiritual, materialistic.

317 immateriality n incorporeality, insubstantiality, spirituality, ineffability.

   adj immaterial, incorporeal, un-substantial, intangible, ineffable, un-touchable, bodiless, unreal, unearthly, spiritual, psychical, otherworldly.

318 world n creation, nature, uni-verse, solar system, galaxy, globe, earth, wide world, sphere, macrocosm; heavens, firmament, vault, celestial spaces, space, sky; heavenly bodies, planets, asteroids, comets, meteors, constellations.

   adj worldly, mundane, terrestrial, earthly, sublunary; cosmic, celestial, heavenly, astral, solar, lunar.

   adv in all creation, on the face of the earth, under the sun, here below.

319 gravity n gravitation, weight, heaviness, pull, pressure, load, burden.

   v gravitate, weigh, pull, press, encumber, load, be heavy.

   adj weighty, heavy, heavy as lead, ponderous, lumpish, cumbersome, burdensome, cumbrous, massive, un-wieldy, like a ton of bricks.

320 levity n lightness, buoyancy, vol-atility; ferment, leaven, yeast.

   v be light, float, swim, waft; lighten, leaven.

   adj light, subtle, airy, weightless, ethereal, volatile, buoyant, feathery.

II. Inorganic Matter

321 density n solidity, solidness, impenetrability, impermeability; con-densation, solidification, consolida-tion, concretion, coagulation, petri-fication, hardening, crystallization, thickening, solid body, mass, block, knot, lump, conglomerate.

   v be dense; solidify, condense, consolidate, coagulate, congeal, set, cohere, crystallize, petrify, harden; condense, compress, thicken.

   adj dense, solid, compact, close, thick, substantial, massive; impene-trable, impermeable, coherent, co-hesive; indivisible, indissoluble, in-soluble.

322 thinness n rarity, tenuity; rare-faction, expansion, dilation, inflation.

   v thin, rarefy, expand, dilate, inflate.

   adj thin, rare, fine, tenuous, com-pressible, flimsy, slight, light; unsub-stantial.

323 hardness n rigidity, firmness, inflexibility, temper; induration, petri-fication, ossification, crystallization.

   v harden, stiffen, cement, petrify, temper, ossify.

   adj hard, solid, firm, inflexible, rigid, resistant, adamantine, impene-trable, strong, hard as a rock, hard as nails, tough.

324 softness n pliability, flexibility, pliancy, malleability, ductility, trac-tility, plasticity, flaccidity, elasticity; mollification, softening.

   v soften, mollify, mash, knead, temper, bend, yield, give, relent, relax.

   adj soft, tender, supple, pliant, pliable, flexible, limber, plastic, duc-tile, tractile, tractable, plastic, mal-leable, moldable, impressible, elastic; flabby, limp, flimsy, flaccid, doughy, mushy, squishy, waxy, soft as butter.

325 elasticity n springiness, spring, resilience, resiliency, give.

   v be elastic, spring, give, bend, stretch; spring back, recoil.

   adj elastic, tensile, springy, resi-lient, buoyant, rubbery.

326 inelasticity n want of elasticity, flaccidity, limpness, softness, mushi-ness.

   adj inelastic, flaccid, limp.

327 tenacity n toughness, strength, cohesiveness, cohesion; stubbornness, obstinacy, grit.

   adj tenacious, cohesive, tough, strong, resistant, gristly, stringy, gummy, adhesive, sticky, viscous, glutinous; stubborn, obstinate.

328 brittleness n fragility, frailty, breakability.

   v be brittle; break, crack, snap, split, shiver, splinter, crumble, burst, fly, fly to pieces, shatter, give way.

   adj brittle, fragile, breakable, fran-gible, delicate, frail, splintery, crisp.

329 structure n organization, consti-tution, anatomy, frame, framework, mold, form, architecture, construction; texture: tissue, grain, web, surface; coarseness; fineness.

   adj structural, organizational, ana-tomical, anatomic, architectural tex-tural: fine, delicate, subtle, gossamery, filmy; coarse, homespun, rough, wool-ly.

330 granularity n pulverulence, san-diness, graininess, friability; powder, dust, sand, grit, grain, particle, crumb, fine powder.

   reduction to powder: pulverization, granulation, disintegration, abrasion, attenuation, filing.

   tools for pulverization: mill, grater, rasp, file, mortar and pestle, grinder, grindstone.

   v grind, pulverize, granulate, grate,

scrape, file, abrade, rasp, pound, beat, crush, crumble, disintegrate.

adj granular, powdery, mealy, floury, branny, dusty, sandy, arenose, gritty, crumbly.

331 friction *n* attrition, rubbing, abrasion, elbow-grease.

v rub, scratch, scrape, scrub, fray, rasp, curry, scour, polish, rub out, erase, grind.

332 [absence or prevention of friction] **lubrication** *n* anointment, oiling, greasing, coating, lathering.

v lubricate, oil, grease, lather; anoint.

333 fluidity *n* liquidity, liquefaction, solubility, fluency.

v be fluid, flow, run, pour, stream; liquefy.

adj fluid, liquid, watery, serous, sappy, juicy, soluble; fluent, unstable.

334 gaseity *n* gaseousness, vaporousness, volatility.

adj gaseous, vaporous, airy, etheric, voluble, evaporable; flatulent, windy.

335 liquefaction *n* liquefying, deliquescence, melting, thawing, solubleness, dissolution.

v liquefy, melt, thaw, dissolve.

adj deliquescent, soluble, dissolvable, solvent.

336 vaporization *n* atomization, steaming, boiling, distillation, gasification, evaporation.

v vaporize, atomize, distill, evaporate, gasify, boil, steam.

adj vapory, vaporous, volatile, evaporable, gaseous.

337 water *n* liquid, serum, lymph, fluid, aqua.

v add water, water, wet, moisten, dip, immerse, submerge, plunge, douse, dunk, drown, soak, steep, wash, sprinkle, splash, souse, drench; dilute; deluge, inundate.

adj watery, aqueous, liquid, fluid, wet, moist, humid, soggy, sodden, rheumy, thin, weak, tasteless, insipid, vapid, flat, feeble, dull.

338 air *n* atmosphere, stratosphere, the open, open air, blue sky, sky; weather, climate, clime; ventilation, current, breath of air, wind, breeze.

v air, ventilate, fan, aerate, freshen, refresh, cool.

adj airy, open, exposed, breezy, windy; flatulent; effervescent; atmospheric, aerial, ethereal, aeriform.

adv in the open air, out in the

open, out of doors, in the wide open spaces, under the stars.

339 moisture *n* dampness, humidity, dankness, dew, wetness, condensation; perspiration.

v moisten, sponge, damp, bedew, wet, soak, saturate, sodden, sop, drench; perspire.

adj moist, damp, watery, humid, dank, dewy, muggy, juicy, wet; soggy, mushy, marshy, muddy.

340 dryness *n* drought, aridity; dessication, drainage, evaporation.

v dry, dry up, soak up, sponge, swab, wipe; drain, parch, evaporate.

adj dry, arid, parched, juiceless, sapless, dry as a bone.

341 ocean *n* sea, main, deep, brine, salt water, waters, high seas, waves, billows, great waters, tides.

adj oceanic, marine, maritime, seagoing, oceanographic.

342 land *n* earth, ground, dry land, mother earth, *terra firma*; continent, inlands, interior, shore, coast, terrain, dirt, soil, rock, chalk; real estate, lands, grounds, acres, acreage.

v land, alight, arrive, disembark, come ashore, go ashore, tie up, set foot on dry land.

adj earthy, terrestrial, earthly, alluvial, landed, territorial, continental.

adv ashore, on land, on dry land.

343 gulf, lake *n* gulf, bay, inlet, estuary, bayou, arm, fjord, firth, lagoon, cove, mouth, natural harbor, sound, straits.

lake, loch, lough, mere, tarn, basin, reservoir, lagoon, pond, pool.

344 plain *n* plateau, champaign, grassland, pasture, pasturage, meadow, flat, moor, heath, tundra, prairie, lowland, steppe, field, desert, basin, fields, grounds.

345 marsh *n* swamp, morass, moss, fen, bog, quagmire, slough, wash, mud.

adj marshy, swampy, boggy, quaggy, soft, muddy, sloppy, squashy.

346 island *n* isle, islet, atoll, reef, ait, key, bar, holm, ridge, eyot, archipelago.

adj insular, sea-girt.

347 [fluid in motion] **stream** *n* stream, etc. (of water) **348**; (of air) **249.** *v* flow, etc., **348**; blow, etc., **349.**

348 [water in motion] **river** *n* running water, jet, spurt, squirt, spout, splash, rush, gush, torrent; fall, cascade, inundation, deluge; rain, rainfall, storm; trickle, drizzle, shower; stream, course, flux, flow, flowing, current, tide, race;

spring, rill, rivulet, stream, river, tributary; rapids, flood, whirlpool, maelstrom, vortex, eddy; wave, billow, surge, swell, ripple, surf, breaker, white caps, rough seas, rolling seas, choppy seas; irrigation, pump, hose.

v flow, run, gush, pour, spout, roll, jet, well issue; drop, drip, dribble, drizzle, trickle, stream, overflow, inundate, deluge, flow over, splash, swash; gurgle, murmur, babble, bubble, sputter, spurt, regurgitate; ooze, flow out, squeeze; rain, rain hard, rain cats and dogs, rain in torrents, rain in buckets; flow into, open into, drain into; pour, pour out, shower down, irrigate, drench, spill.

adj fluent, tidal, streamy, showery, rainy, trickly, drizzly, bubbly.

349 [air in motion] **wind** *n* draft, air, breath of air, puff, whiff, zephyr, drift, blow; fresh wind, stiff breeze, keen blast, trade wind, gust, blast, breeze, squall, gale, storm, tempest, hurricane, whirlwind, tornado, twister, cyclone, monsoon.

v blow, waft, blow hard, blow great guns, stream, gust, blast, storm; respire, breathe, pant, puff, gasp, wheeze, cough; fan, ventilate, inflate, pump, blow up.

adj windy, drafty, breezy, stormy, tempestuous, cyclonic.

350 [channel for the passage of water] **conduit** *n* channel, duct, aqueduct, canal, trough, gutter, dike, main, gully, moat, ditch, drain, sewer, culvert, sough, siphon, pipe, tube, hose, funnel, tunnel, artery, spout, floodgate, watergate, sluice, lock, valve.

351 [channel for the passage of air] **air-pipe** *n* tube, shaft, flue, chimney, funnel, vent, hole, windpipe, duct.

352 **semiliquidity** *n* viscosity, adhesiveness, stickiness, glutinosity, pastiness.

v thicken, mash, squash, churn, beat up, blend.

adj semiliquid, semifluid; milky, muddy, creamy, slushy, starchy, gummy, gluey, sticky, slimy, oozy, thick, succulent, viscous, viscid, glutinous, adhesive, clammy.

353 [mixture of air and water] **bubble, cloud** *n* bubble, foam, froth, head, lather, suds, spray, surf, yeast; effervescence, fermentation, bubbling, boiling, gurgling, foaming.

cloud, vapor, fog, mist, haze, steam; nebula, nebulosity, cloudiness, opacity, dimness

v bubble, boil, foam, froth, gurgle, lather, effervesce, ferment, fizzle.

cloud, fog, mist, steam, shadow,

darken, cast over, steam up.

adj bubbly, foamy, frothy; effervescent.

cloudy, foggy, misty, hazy, steamy.

354 **pulpiness** *n* pulp, paste, dough, curd; fleshiness, fattiness, sponginess.

v pulp, mash, squeeze, juice, squash.

adj pulpy, pasty, doughy, fleshy, meaty, fatty.

355 **unctuousness** *n* unctuosity, oiliness, greasiness, lubricity; lubrication, ointment, grease, oil, anointment.

v oil, grease, lubricate.

adj unctuous, oily, greasy, oleaginous, slippery, slimy, slick.

356 **oil** *n* fat, butter, cream, grease, tallow, suet, lard, dripping, blubber; soap, wax; petroleum, gasoline, kerosene, propane, naphtha; vegetable oil, salad oil, olive oil, linseed oil; ointment, unguent, liniment, salve, balm.

356a **resin** *n* rosin, gum, wax, amber, ambergris, bitumen, pitch, tar, asphalt; varnish, lacquer, shellac, mastic, sealing wax, putty.

v resin, rosin; varnish, shellac, lacquer, overlay.

adj resinous, gummy, waxy.

III. Organic Matter

357 **animate matter** *n* nature, natural world, animated nature, living beings, organisms, organic remains, animal life, plant life, fauna, flora; protoplasm, cell.

science of living beings: biology, natural history, zoology, botany, anatomy, physiology, organic chemistry.

naturalist, biologist, zoologist, botanist.

adj animate, organic.

358 **inanimate matter** *n* mineral world, mineral kingdom, inorganic matter, brute matter.

science of the mineral kingdom: mineralogy, geology, metallurgy.

adj inanimate, inorganic, mineral.

359 **life** *n* existence, being; animation, vigor, vivacity, vitality, energy, vital spark, vital flame, lifeblood, spirit, soul; respiration, breath, breath of life; nourishment, nutriment, staff of life.

v be alive, live, breathe, respire, exist, subsist; be born, come into the world, see the light; quicken, revive, come to; give birth to, bring to life, vitalize; vivify, reanimate; keep alive, *(informal)* keep going, *(informal)* hang in there.

adj alive, live, vigorous, vivacious, vital, energetic, lively, alive and kicking, active.

360 death *n* decease, demise, expiration, passing, dissolution, departure, release, rest, quietus, fall; end, cessation, loss of life, extinction, dying, mortality, doom, finale, stop; last breath, final gasp, death rattle, death agonies, hand of death, dying day, *rigor mortis*; decay, fatality, natural causes, death blow.

v die, decease, pass away, pass on, perish, expire, depart, dissolve; cease, end, vanish, disappear; fail, subside, fade, sink, fall, decline, wither, decay; be taken, yield, give in, breathe one's last, end one's days, depart this life, be no more, drop off, pop off, drop dead, drop down dead, break one's neck, give up the ghost, shuffle off the mortal coil, go the way of all flesh, turn to dust, *(informal)* kick the bucket, *(informal)* go out like a light, *(informal)* croak.

adj dead, lifeless, extinct, defunct, late, gone, no more, dead and gone, dead as a door nail; deadly, fatal, lethal.

361 [destruction of life; violent death] **killing** *n* murder, homicide, assassination, slaughter, bloodshed, carnage, butchery, massacre, holocaust; suffocation, strangulation, garrote, hanging, electrocution, gassing, drawing and quartering; suicide, regicide, parricide, matricide, fratricide, infanticide; death blow, finishing stroke, *coup de grace*, execution; suicide; slaughtering, hunting, coursing, shooting, fishing; butcher, slayer, murderer, executioner, assassin, cutthroat, thug, guerilla, saboteur, garroter.

v kill, put to death, murder, slaughter, butcher, massacre, execute, behead, decapitate, guillotine, dispatch, *(informal)* waste; *(informal)* wipe out, strangle, garrote, hang, throttle, choke, stifle, suffocate, smother, asphyxiate, drown, gas, electrocute, stab, bayonet, cut, cut to pieces, cut to ribbons, mutilate, run through, put to the sword, shoot, gun down, do away with, *(informal)* blow away; hunt, spear; cut off, nip in the bud, cut down, give no quarter, decimate; commit suicide, destroy oneself, blow one's brains out, put an end to oneself.

adj murderous, homicidal, bloodthirsty, bloody, gory; mortal, fatal, lethal, deadly, deathly; suicidal.

362 corpse *n* body, remains, carcass, corse, cadaver, empty vessel, bones, skeleton, relics, mortal remains, mortal coil, clay, dust, ashes, earth, carrion, fodder, food for worms, shade, ghost.

adj corpselike, cadaverous.

363 interment *n* burial, sepulture, entombment, inhumation; cremation; funeral, funeral rites, obsequies, wake; knell, death bell, dirge, elegy; shroud, winding sheet, grave clothes; coffin, shell, sarcophagous, urn, pall, bier, catafalque, hearse; grave, pit, sepulchre, tomb, vault, crypt, catacomb, mausoleum, cemetery, burial ground, mortuary, graveyard, charnel house, morgue; monument, gravestone, tombstone, headstone, *memento mori*; exhumation, disinterment, autopsy, post mortem examination.

v inter, bury, lay in the grave, lay to rest, lay in the ground, consign to the grave, entomb; lay out, mummify, embalm; cremate; exhume, disinter, unearth.

adj burial, funereal, funeral, mortuary, sepulchral, cinerary.

364 animality *n* corporality, animal life, living being, flesh, flesh and blood; physique, strength, vigor, vitality.

adj animalistic, bodily, corporeal, fleshly.

365 vegetation *n* vegetable life, growth, plant life.

adj vegetative; rank, dense, lush, fecund.

366 animal *n* animal kingdom, brute creation, fauna; beast, brute, creature, living thing, creeping thing, dumb animal; mammal, quadruped, bird, reptile, fish, crustacean, shellfish, mollusk, worm, insect; flocks and herds, wild animals, domestic animals, livestock, game, beasts of the field, fowls of the air.

adj animal, animalistic, zoological.

367 vegetable *n* vegetable kingdom, flora, plant life, flowerage, herbage, shrubbery, foliage, leafage, leaves, foliation, verdure, greens; tree, shrub, bush, creeper, herb, fruit, grass.

v vegetate, germinate, shoot, sprout, shoot up, grow, swell, spring up, develop, increase, flourish, blossom, bloom.

adj vegetable, vegetal, vegetative, leguminous, herbal, herbaceous, botanic, verdant.

368 [science of animals] **zoology** *n* morphology, zoography, embryology, anatomy; comparative anatomy, animal physiology, comparative physiology, anthropology, ornithology, icthyology, paleontology, entomology.

adj zoological.

369 [science of plants] **botany** *n* phytology, vegetable physiology, dendrology; flora, botanic garden.

adj botanical, herbal, horticultural.

370 [management of animals] **ranching** *n* breeding, raising; taming, domestication; veterinary science.

v ranch, raise, breed; tame, domesticate, train, housebreak; cage, bridle, restrain.

adj bred; tame, domestic, domesticated, housebroken.

371 [management of plants] **agriculture** *n* farming, cultivation, husbandry, tillage; agronomy, agrobiology, agrology, agronomics; gardening, horticulture, floriculture, landscaping, arboriculture, forestry.

v cultivate, till, till the soil, work the land, farm, garden, sow, seed, plant; reap, mow, cut; plow, plough, harrow, rake, weed, hoe, lop; garden, landscape.

adj agricultural, agrarian; arable, fertile.

372 **mankind** *n* human race, man, woman, humankind, human species, humanity, mortality, people, human being, person, personage, individual, creature, fellow creature, fellow man, mortal, body, soul, somebody, someone, one, party, head, hand, heart.

people, persons, folk, public, society, community, group, general public, society of men, civilization, commonwealth, commonweal, body politic, human community, population, millions, multitudes.

adj human, mortal, personal, individual, social, national, civic, public; cosmopolitan, humanitarian.

373 **man** *n* make, manhood, masculinity, he, him; gentleman, sir, mister, Mr., master, swain, fellow, chap, boy, male animal; cock, drake, gander, dog, boar, stag, hart, buck, stallion, tomcat, billygoat, ram, bull, ox; gelding, steer.

adj male, masculine, manly.

374 **woman** *n* female, womanhood, femininity, she, her; lady, gentlewoman, madam, madame, miss, (informal) ma'am, Ms., Mrs., matron, girl.

female animal; hen, bitch, sow, doe, roe, mare, nannygoat, ewe, cow.

adj female, feminine, womanly.

375 **sensibility** *n* sensation, sensitiveness, feeling, responsiveness, impressibility; sensation, impression, touch; consciousness.

v be sensible, be sensitive to, feel, touch, perceive; render sensible, sharpen, cultivate, stir, excite, sensitize; cause sensation, impress, excite an impression, stir.

adj sensitive, sensible, sensuous; perceptive, sentient, responsive, susceptible, conscious, aware, alive, acute, sharp, keen, vivid, lively.

adv to the quick.

376 **insensibility** *n* lack of feeling, obtuseness, paralysis, numbness, anesthesia; insusceptibility, unresponsiveness, unconsciousness.

v be insensible; render insensible, blunt, pall, numb, benumb, paralyze, deaden, freeze, anesthetize; cloy, stuff, satiate, drown; stupefy, stun.

adj insensible, senseless, unsusceptible, unresponsive, insensitive, numb, hard, dead; dull, dense, thick, obtuse, unperceptive; anesthetic, paralytic.

377 **pleasure** *n* bodily pleasure, sensuality, sensuousness, physical gratification, sex, sexuality, sensual delight, ecstasy, orgasm, climax; titillation, teasing; comfort, ease, relish, delight, joy, luxury, luxuriousness, pleasure, lap of luxury.

v feel pleasure, receive pleasure, enjoy, relish, revel in, bask in, swim in, luxuriate, feast on, wallow in, gloat over, (informal) dig, (informal) get off on, (informal) be turned on, (informal) get into; give pleasure, (informal) turn on, thrill, excite.

adj pleasurable, sensual, sensuous, sexual, voluptuous, luxurious, ecstatic, orgasmic, climactic; agreeable, comfortable, cordial, delightful, joyful; palatable, sweet, tasty; fragrant; melodious, lovely.

adv in comfort, in ecstasy, on a bed of roses.

378 **pain** *n* suffering, dolor, ache, aching, smart, shoot, shooting, twinge, twitch, gripe, grip, hurt, cut, sore, soreness, tenderness, discomfort, malaise, disease; spasm, cramp, crick, stitch, convulsion, throe, throb, pang; torment, torture, rack, anguish, agony.

v feel pain, suffer, undergo pain, ache, smart, bleed, tingle, shoot, twinge, twitch, writhe, wince, hurt; inflict pain, hurt, chafe, sting, bite, gnaw, gripe, pinch, tweak, grate, gall, fret, prick, pierce, wring, convulse; torment, torture, wrack, agonize.

adj painful, dolorous, sore, tender, raw, uncomfortable; convulsive, torturous.

379 **touch** *n* contact, feeling, tactility, palpability, impact, feel, sensation; manipulation, handling, rubbing, massaging, fondling, fingering, kneading, stroking, brushing, grazing over.

v touch, feel, handle, finger, fondle, thumb, paw, grab, rub, massage, knead, stroke, brush, manipulate, run the fingers over, graze over.

   adj tactual, tactile, palpable.

380 sensations of touch *n* itching, tickling, titillation, scratching, pricking, stinging.

   v itch, tingle, creep, thrill, prick, scratch, sting.

   adj itching; ticklish, scratchy, itchy.

381 numbness *n* physical insensibility, lack of feeling, deadness.

   v benumb, anesthetize, deaden, dull, drug.

   adj numb, dull benumbed, insensible, unfeeling, frozen, drugged, dead, deadened, dulled.

382 heat *n* warmth, caloricity, caloric, temperature; glow, flush, warmth, intensity, ardor, passion, fever, fervor, zeal; fire, spark, flame, blaze.

   v be hot, glow, flush, sweat, swelter, smoke, stew, simmer, seethe, boil, burn, broil, blaze, flame; smolder, parch, fume, pant; heat, warm, thaw, defrost; stimulate, stir, animate, a-rouse.

   adj hot, warm, mild, genial, tepid, lukewarm, unfrozen; heated, torrid, sultry, burning, fiery; sunny, tropical, suffocating, stifling, sweltering, oppressive, reeking, baking; fiery, incandescent, ebullient, glowing, smoking, blazing, on fire, afire, in flames, aflame, ablaze; ardent, fervent, fervid, angry, furious, vehement, intense, excited, excitable, irascible, animated, violent, passionate.

383 cold *n* coldness, iciness, frigidity, chilliness, coolness.

   v be cold, shiver, quake, shake, tremble, shudder, quiver; chill, freeze, refrigerate.

   adj cold, chilly, chill, cool, frigid, gelid, frozen, freezing, bitter, bitter cold, numbing, nipping, cutting, shivering, bleak, raw, frost-bitten, icy, glacial, frosty, wintry, hibernal, arctic, polar; impassionate, unemotional, apathetic, unresponsive, unsympathetic, stoical, unfeeling, indifferent, cold-blooded, heartless, imperturbable; polite, formal, reserved, hostile; deliberate, depressing, dispiriting, disheartening.

   adv coldly, bitterly.

384 calefaction *n* heating, melting, fusion, liquefaction, combustion; cauterization; calcination; incineration; cremation; carbonization.

   v heat, warm, chafe; fire, set fire to, set on fire, kindle, light, ignite, rekindle; melt, thaw, fuse, liquefy; burn, inflame, roast, broil, toast, cook, fry, grill, singe, parch, bake, scorch; brand, cauterize, sear, burn in; boil,

digest, stew, sauté, cook, scald, parboil, simmer; take fire, catch fire.

   adj heated, warmed, fired, burnt, scorched; molten; flammable, combustible, volcanic.

385 refrigeration *n* cooling, congelation, glaciation, icing; solidification, hardening.

   v refrigerate, keep cold, chill, ice, congeal, freeze; cool, fan, refresh; benumb, starve, pinch, nip, cut, pierce, bite; quench, put out, stamp out, extinguish.

   adj cooled, frozen, chilled; incombustible, inflammable, fireproof.

386 furnace *n* oven, stove, range; hearth, heater, kiln, oil burner, space heater, blast furnace, forge, fire place, fiery furnace.

387 refrigerator *n* ice box, fridge, ice chest, frigidaire, cold storage, freezer, ice house.

388 fuel *n* firing, combustible; coal, hard coal, anthracite, bituminous coal, soft coal, carbon, coke, charcoal; wood, firewood, kindling, brushwood, log, cinder, ember, ash; turf, peat, fuel oil, fossil fuel, petroleum, gasoline, kerosene; gas, natural gas, propane; electricity; nuclear power; solar energy; waterpower; windpower.

   v fuel, feed, stoke, fire; power.

   adj carbonaceous; combustible, flammable, burnable.

389 thermometer *n* thermometograph, thermoscope, thermostat, tele-thermometer, pyrometer, calorimeter, glass, mercury.

390 taste *n* flavor, savor, sensation, gusto, relish; smack, smatch, tang, aftertaste; morsel, bit, sip.

   v taste, flavor, savor, smatch, smack; tickle the palate, tickle the tastebuds; smack the lips.

   adj tasty, savory, flavory, flavorful, flavored; palatable, digestible, *(informal)* edible.

391 tastelessness *n* insipidity, blandness, flatness, unsavoriness.

   v be tasteless.

   adj tasteless, insipid, bland, flat, weak, mild, vapid, wishy-washy, *(informal)* plastic, pasty.

392 pungency *n* piquancy, poignancy, tang, bite, nip, sharpness, acridity, bitterness, hotness, sourness, unsavoriness.

   v be pungent; make pungent, season, spice, salt, pepper, ,pickle, brine, devil, smoke, curry.

   adj pungent, strong, full-flavored, seasoned, highly seasoned, spiced; sharp, biting, nippy, acrid, bitter, sour, stinging, spicy, salty, peppery, piquant, hot; unsavory.

393 condiment *n* seasoning, flavoring, sauce, spice, relish; salt, pepper.

    v season.

394 savoriness *n* flavor, flavorfulness, taste, tastiness, relish, piquancy, zest, tang, delectability, palatability.

    v be savory, tickle the palate, taste good, taste great; savor, enjoy, appreciate, relish, like, taste.

    adj savory, good, tasty, palatable, nice, dainty, delectable, flavorful, appetizing, delicate, delicious, exquisite, rich, luscious, full-flavored, pungent, ambrosial.

395 unsavoriness *n* tastelessness, flavorlessness, blandness; acridness, sourness.

    v be unsavory, be unpalatable, taste bad, sicken, disgust, pall, nauseate, turn the stomach, make one sick.

    adj unsavory, tasteless, flavorless, bland, flat; bad tasting, ill-flavored, acrid, bitter, sour, unpalatable, inedible, offensive, repulsive, nasty, vile, sickening, nauseous, loathsome, unpleasant, awful.

396 sweetness *n* sugariness, saccharinity, syrupiness.

    v sweeten, sugar, candy.

    adj sweet, sugary, syrupy, honeyed, saccharine, candied, sticky, gooey, luscious, lush, cloying; sweetened.

397 sourness *n* acridity, tartness, sharpness, vinegariness, acerbity, acidity.

    v sour, acidify, acerbate, curdle, acidulate, ferment, spoil.

    adj sour, acid, bitter, tart, sharp, vinegary, acidulous, astringent, acerbic, acrid; fermented, rancid, bad, spoiled, turned, curdled, gone bad; styptic, hard, rough.

398 odor *n* smell, scent; effluvium; exhalation, emanation; fume, essence, redolence.

    v have an odor, smell, smell of, give out a smell; smell, scent, sniff, snuff, inhale.

    adj odorous, odoriferous, smelly, strong smelling, redolent, pungent.

399 inodorousness *n* absence of smell, odorlessness.

    v be inodorous, not smell, have no odor, be odorless.

    adj odorless, scentless, unsmelling.

400 fragrance *n* aroma, redolence, perfume, sweet smell, sweet scent, smell.

    v be fragrant, smell sweet, have a perfume, scent, perfume.

    adj fragrant, aromatic, redolent, spicy, scented, perfumed, sweet scented, sweet smelling, odoriferous, odorific.

401 fetor *n* bad smell, bad odor, foul smell, offensive smell, stink, stench, fume, foulness, fetidness, rancidity, rankness, fustiness, mustiness.

    v have a bad smell, smell bad, smell rotten, smell, stink, reek.

    adj fetid, strong smelling, bad, strong, fulsome, offensive, rank, rancid, noisome, mephitic, miasmic, musty, fusty, foul, rotten, putrid, reeking, stinking, stinky, suffocating, nauseating, nauseous, *(informal)* gross.

402 sound *n* noise, tone, pitch, sound vibrations, strain, sonority, sonorousness, twang, intonation, cadence; audibility, resonance, echo.

    science of sound: acoustics, phonology, phonetics, electronic sound reproduction.

    v sound, make a noise; give out sound, emit sound; resound, echo.

    adj sounding, sonorous, resonant, audible, distinct.

403 silence *n* stillness, quiet, peace, hush, lull, quiescence, dead silence; muteness, speechlessness, taciturnity.

    v silence, still, hush, stifle, muffle, stop, muzzle, gag; be silent, hold one's tongue, shut up, keep quiet, be still.

    adj silent, quiet, still, calm, noiseless, soundless, hushed, quiescent; mute, speechless, taciturn; solemn, soft, deathlike, awful, silent as the grave.

    adv silently.

404 loudness *n* loud noise, power, resonance, thunderousness, roaring, vociferousness, clamorousness; din, clang, clangor, clamor, noise, roar, uproar, hubbub, boom, racket, outcry; blast, peal, swell, flourish of trumpets, boom; thunder, explosion.

    v be loud, peal, swell, clang, boom, thunder, fulminate, roar, resound, bellow, scream, holler, shout; ring in the ears, pierce the ears, split the eardrums, stun, deafen; shake, awake.

    adj loud, noisy, vociferous, resounding, clamorous, deafening, stentorian, boisterous, tumultuous, sonorous, deep, full, powerful, thundering, ear-splitting, piercing, uproarious, obstreperous, shrill, sharp.

    adv loudly, noisily, at the top of one's voice, at the top of one's lungs, aloud.

405 faintness *n* faint sound, whisper, breath, undertone, murmur, hum; inaudibility; hoarseness.

v whisper, breathe, murmur, hum, mutter, speak softly, speak in low tones.

adj faint, whispered, indistinct, dim, inaudible, barely audible, low, stifled, muffled, murmured, muted; gentle, soft, languid, floating, flowing; hoarse, husky.

406 [sudden and violent sounds] **snap** *n* rap, thud, burst, explosion, detonation, discharge, firing, salvo, pop, bang, blast.

v rap, snap, tap, knock, click, clash, crack, crackle, crash, beat.

407 [repeated and protracted sounds] **roll** *n* drumming, tapping, rumbling, grumbling; dingdong, whirring, droning; ratatat, rubadub, pitapat; quaver, quiver, clutter, racket; peal of bells; reverberation.

v roll, drum, rumble, grumble, rattle, clatter, patter, clack; hum, trill, shake; chime, peal, toll; tick, beat.

408 resonance *n* ring, ringing, chime, clang, clangor, boom, roll, roar, rumble, thunder, vibrato, timbre, twang, vibration, reverberation, tintinnabulation, booming, quaver, dingdong, echoing, sonorousness.

v resound, reverberate, re-echo; ring, jingle, chink, clink; gurgle, echo, ring in the ear.

adj resonant, resounding, reverberant, reverberating; deep-toned, deep-sounding.

408a nonresonance *n* dead sound, thud, thump, muffled drums, cracked bell; damper, mute, muffler.

v sound dead, thud, thump; muffle, dampen, mute.

adj nonresonant, dampened, muted, muffled, deadened; dead.

409 [hissing sounds] **sibilation** *n* hissing, wheezing, buzzing, zipping, whooshing; high note.

v hiss, buzz, whiz, wheeze, whoosh, zip, rustle, whistle, fizzle; squash, sneeze.

adj sibilant; hissing, wheezy.

410 [harsh sounds] **stridency** *n* discord, dissonance, harshness, raucousness, atonality, clashing, grinding, grating, rasping, sharpness, creaking, shrillness.

v creak, grate, jar, jangle, clank, clink, grind, grate; scream, yelp.

adj strident, sharp, high, acute, shrill, atonal, unharmonious, unmusical, dissonant, discordant, cacophonous; piercing, ear-piercing, cracked; creaking, harsh, coarse, hoarse, rough, gruff, grating, jarring, guttural, squawking, acute, scratching, croaking, rasping, sour, clashing.

411 cry *n* shout, scream, yell, shriek, roar, howl, wail; exclamation, outcry, clamor, vociferation; hubbub, hullabaloo, chorus, hue and cry; entreaty, appeal, solicitation, plea, plaint, prayer, crying, weeping, wailing, sobbing, lament, whimper, whimpering, tears, moaning.

v cry, roar, shout, bawl, brawl, hoop, whoop, yell, bellow, howl, scream, screech, shriek, squeak, squeal, whine, whimper, wail, weep, sob, moan, lament; cheer, hoot; grumble, groan, complain; vociferate, raise one's voice, sing out, cry out, yell out, exclaim, holler, shout at the top of one's lungs.

adj crying, clamorous; vociferous; solicitous; stentorian.

412 [animal sounds] **ululation** *n* howling, crying, belling, screeching, singing, growling, purring.

v cry, roar, bellow, bark, yelp, yap, growl, snarl, howl, bay, grunt, snort, neigh, bray, mew, purr, caterwaul, bleat, low, moo, squeak, oink, baa, crow, croak, screech, caw, coo, gobble, quack, cackle, gaggle, chuck, cluck, clack, chirp, chirrup, twitter, cuckoo, hum, buzz, hiss, blatter.

413 melody, concord *n* melodiousness, tunefulness, sweet sounds, mellifluence, musicalness, euphony; timbre, tone color, pitch; tune, song, aria, theme, measure, plainsong, canticle, strain, lay.

harmony, harmoniousness; rhythm, meter; symphony, euphony, consonance, attunement, modulation, syncopation; counterpoint, polyphony; concordance, pleasing combination.

v harmonize, chime, symphonize, blend; tune, accord.

adj melodious, musical, tuneful, melodic, lyrical, euphonious, singing, ringing, sweet-sounding, euphonic, mellifluous, dulcet, mellow, clear, sweet, rich, soft, silvery, agreeable, pleasing.

concordant, harmonious, agreeing, symphonious, suiting, congenial, blending, synchronized, consistent, in rapport, in unison, confluent, conjoined, symmetrical, proportionate, consonant, compatible.

414 discord *n* dissonance, atonality; harshness; racket, noise, inharmoniousness.

v be discordant; jar, grate.

adj discordant, dissonant, atonal, harsh; out of tune, tuneless, unmelodious, inharmonious, unmusical; jarring, grating, cacophonous, screeching.

415 music *n* sweet sounds, pleasing

sounds, harmonious sounds, melody, song, tune, strain, air, harmony; classical music, popular music, folk music, jazz, electronic music; orchestral music, instrumental music, symphonic music, chamber music; ragtime, reggae, swing, bebop, bop, barrelhouse, rock; pop music, vocal music, choral music, solo, duet, duo, sonata, trio, quartet, quintet, sextet, septet, octet.

v make music, perform; compose.

adj musical, lyrical; instrumental, orchestral, symphonic, vocal, choral, operatic.

416 musician [performance of music] *n* artist, performer, concert artist, player, soloist, instrumentalist, vocalist, accompanist, singer, minstrel; symphony orchestra, orchestra, chamber orchestra, band, rock and roll band, group, combo, ensemble, chamber group, quartet, trio; chorus, choir, vocal group.

v make music, play, perform, strike up, concertize, execute, accompany, present the music, solo, improvise, play the notes; sing, croon, warble, vocalize, spin a melody.

adj musical, instrumental, vocal, choral, operatic; lyrical, harmonious, brilliant, sharp, incisive.

417 musical instruments *n* orchestra, band, brass band, marching band, military band, ensemble, group; strings, plucked instruments, bowed instruments, hammered instruments; woodwinds, winds, tubed instruments, reed instruments, brass instruments; percussion; synthesizer.

418 hearing *n* audition, auscultation, listening, perception, audibility, ear; regarding, attending, heeding.

hearer, auditor, listener; eavesdropper.

v hear, listen, attend, lend an ear, bend an ear, *(informal)* tune in, give a hearing to, give audience to, prick up one's ears, be all ears; overhear, eavesdrop; heed, regard.

adj hearing, auditory, auricular.

419 deafness *n* hardness of hearing, inaudibility.

v be deaf, not hear; turn a deaf ear to, plug up one's ears; deafen, stun, split the eardrums.

adj deaf, stone-deaf, hard of hearing; deafened, stunned; unheeding, inattentive.

420 light *n* ray, beam, stream, gleam, streak; sunbeam, moonbeam, aurora, dawn, sunrise, day-break, day, daylight, light of day, sunshine, broad daylight, glow, glint, glimmering; sun, moon; flush, halo, glory, aureole;

spark, scintilla, scintillation, flash, blaze, coruscation; flame, lightening, flare; luster, sheen, shimmer, reflection, refraction; brightness, brilliancy, splendor, effulgence, radiance, illumination, radiation; luminosity, lucidity.

science of light: optics, photography, radioactivity.

v shine, glow, glitter, glisten, gleam, beam, flare, flare up, glare, flash, glimmer, shimmer, flicker, sparkle, scintillate, coruscate, flash, blaze; light, reflect, dazzle, bedazzle, daze, radiate; lighten, enlighten, light, irradiate, shed light upon, cast light upon, illuminate, illumine, kindle, fire.

adj luminous, lucent; light, bright, vivid, splendid, resplendent, lustrous, shiny, radiant; sheeny, glossy, glassy, sunny, burnished; cloudless, clear, unclouded; effulgent, blazing, ablaze, phosphorescent, aglow; iridescent.

421 darkness *n* blackness; obscurity, doom, murkiness, murk; duskiness, dusk, dimness; night, midnight, dead of night; shade, shadow, umbra, penumbra; obscuration, adumbration, extinction, eclipse, total eclipse.

v be dark; darken, obscure, shade, dim, shadow, overcast, cloud, becloud; extinguish, put out, blow out, snuff out.

adj dark, obscure, black, pitch black, nocturnal, overcast, cloudy, darkened; dingy, lurid, murky, gloomy, oppressive; shadowy, shady, umbrageous.

422 dimness *n* duskiness, shadowiness, gloominess, cloudiness, mist, mistiness, haze, haziness, fogginess, paleness, shade, nebulosity, gray, grayness.

v be dim, grow dim, darken, obscure, adumbrate, becloud, cloud, shadow, shade, eclipse, cloud over; blur, dull, fade, pale; glimmer, twinkle, flutter, flicker, waver.

adj dim, dull, dingy, lackluster, darkish, darkened, gray, dark, faint, pale, cloudy, misty, murky, overcast, nebulous, shadowy, umbrageous, blurry, hazy, opaque, foggy, bleary, gloomy, lurid, leaden.

423 [source of light] **luminary** *n* natural light, sun, moon, stars, flame, fire, spark, phosphorescence; artificial light, lamp, gas lamp, oil lamp, kerosene lamp, electric light, lantern, torch, candle, taper, light bulb.

v light, illuminate.

adj self-luminous; phosphorescent, radiant.

424 shade *n* cover, awning, umbrella,

parasol, sunshade; screen, curtain, shutter, blind, gauze, veil, mantle, mask, sunglasses, *(informal)* shades; cloud, mist, fog, shadow.

v shade, veil, cover, screen, curtain, veil, draw a curtain, pull the shade, cast a shadow.

adj shady, shadowy, cloudy.

425 transparency *n* transparence, transluscence, diaphanousness, clearness, lucidity, limpidity, thinness, sheerness, gauziness, flimsiness.

v be transparent, transmit light.

adj transparent, pellucid, lucid, diaphanous, translucent, limpid, clear, crystalline, see-through, sheer, gauzy, flimsy.

426 opacity *n* opaqueness, darkness, cloudiness, filminess, haziness, mistiness, nontransparency.

v be opaque, obstruct the passage of light.

adj opaque, impervious to light, impenetrable to light, dim, filmy, thick, smoky, misty, smoggy, shady, murky, cloudy, hazy, obscure, clouded, foggy, unclear, frosted, nontransparent, nontranslucent.

427 semitransparency *n* opalescence, milkiness, pearliness; film, mist.

v let in partial light.

adj semitransparent, semipellucid, semiopaque, opalescent, pearly, nacreous, milky.

428 color *n* hue, tint, tinge, dye, complexion, shade, tincture, cast, coloration, tone, key; primary color, secondary color, complementary color; coloring; spectrum, prism, spectroscope; pigment, paint, dye, wash, stain.

v color, dye, tinge, stain, tint, paint, wash; illuminate, emblazon.

adj colored, dyed, tinted; prismatic, chromatic; bright, vivid, intense, deep, rich, gorgeous; fresh, unfaded; gaudy, florid, garish, showy, flashy, glaring; mellow, harmonious, pearly, sweet, delicate, tender, refined; dull, gray.

429 [absence of color] **colorlessness** *n* neutral tint, black and white, chiaroscuro, monochrome; etiolation, pallor, paleness, discoloration.

v lose color, fade, turn pale, become colorless, pale; deprive of color, bleach, wash out, blanch, tarnish, etiolate, tone down, whiten.

adj uncolored, colorless, hueless, pale, pallid, faint, dull, dun, wan, sallow, dingy, ashy, gray, ashen, lackluster; discolored; light-colored, fair, blond, white.

430 whiteness *n* milkiness, frostiness, silveriness, pearliness; etiolation, albification, decoloration, colorlessness; albinism.

v whiten, bleach, blanch, etiolate, whitewash.

adj white, snowy, frosted, snow-white, milk-white, milky, chalky, pearly, ivory, silver, silvery, opaline, whitish, albinistic, etiolated, bleached, blanched, fair, light, wan, pallid, pale, lackluster, colorless, anemic, sallow, faint.

431 blackness *n* darkness, swarthiness, lividness; ink, ebony, coal, charcoal, pitch; obscurity.

v black, blacken, darken; blot, smutch, smut, smirch.

adj black, sable, somber, livid, dark, inky, ebony, pitchy, swarthy, sooty, dingy, dusky, murky; jet-black, pitch-black, black as coal, coal-black, kohl-black, black as night.

432 gray *n* grayness, neutral tint, silver, salt and pepper, dove color.

adj gray, iron-gray, silver, silvery, silverish, grayish, dun, drab, ashy, ashen, dove-colored, dapple-gray; grizzly, grizzled, hoary.

433 brown *n* brownness, beige, khaki.

adj brown, bay, dapple, auburn, nutbrown, chocolate, chestnut, cinnamon, russet, tawny, tan, brunette, mahogany, khaki, beige, ochre, sepia, hazel, brownish, coffee, cocoa, rust, roan, sorrel.

434 red *n* redness; blush, color.

v redden, blush, flush, get red in the face, turn color.

adj red, reddish, scarlet, crimson, blood red, bloody, cherry-colored, vermilion, carmine, maroon, pink, hot pink, rosy, ruby, salmon, wine-colored; red-faced, blushing, embarrassed, red as beet, red as a lobster, flushed, burning, fuming, flaming, inflamed; ruddy, glowing, blooming, warm, hot.

435 green *n* greenness, verdure, blue and yellow.

adj green, greenish, verdant, olive, pea-green, emerald, apple, Kelly green, blue-green, aquamarine, sea-green; grassy, verdurous; fresh, new, recent, young, innocent, naive, raw, unseasoned, immature, inexperienced, ignorant; sickly, wan, pale, livid; jealous, envious.

436 yellow *n* yellowness, jaundice.

v yellow, age, turn color, dry up.

adj yellow, yellowish, gold, golden, **ocher**, lemon, citrine, saffron, aureate, creamy, straw-colored, flaxen, blond, tawny, sallow; sordid, cheap; cowardly, *(informal)* chicken, craven, lily-livered, contemptible, despicable, mean, cringing, groveling; jaundiced.

437 purple *n* blue and red.

adj purple, purplish, lavender, lilac, magenta, orchid, violet, plum-colored, mauve.

438 blue *n* blueness.

adj blue, bluish, azure, marine blue, navy, aquamarine, greenish blue, sapphire, turquoise, cobalt, baby blue; depressed, down in the dumps, *(informal)* in the pits, *(informal)* down, low.

439 orange *n* red and yellow; flame.

adj orange, orangy, orangish, brass, copper, apricot, tangerine, gold, flame-colored.

440 variegation *n* striation, spottiness, streakiness, iridescence, play of colors.

v variegate, diversify, streak, stripe, checker, speckle, bespeckle, fleck, dapple; dot, striate, tattoo, inlay; embroider, quilt.

adj variegated, multi-colored, many-colored, kaleidoscopic; iridescent, prismatic, opaline, nacreous, pearly; pied, piebald, mottled; dappled, salt and pepper, marbled, flecked, speckled, spotty, studded, freckled, flecky, spotted, diversified; striped, veined, lined, striated, streaked, brindled, banded, checked, checkered, plaid, mosaic, inlaid.

441 vision *n* sight, optics, eyesight; view, look, glance, ken, glimpse, peep, peek, gaze, stare, leer; contemplation, regard, survey, point of view, outlook, viewpoint, perspective, standpoint; perspicacity, discernment, perception, penetration.

v see, behold, discern, perceive, have in sight, descry, sight, make out, discover, distinguish, recognize, spy, espy, catch a glimpse of, command a view of, witness; envision, contemplate; look, view, eye, survey, scan, inspect, run the eye over, glance around; observe, watch, watch for, peep, peer, peek, pry, take a peep, leer, ogle, glare.

adj visual, ocular, optic; clear-sighted, eagle-eyed, discerning; visionary, farsighted.

adv on sight, at first sight, at a glance.

442 blindness *n* sightlessness; cataract; ignorance.

v be blind, not see; grope in the dark; blind, hoodwink, dazzle; screen,

hide, mask.

adj blind, eyeless, sightless, unseeing, dark, purblind, stone-blind; dim-sighted, undiscerning, ignorant.

adv blindly, blindfold, darkly.

443 [imperfect vision] **dimsightedness** *n* nearsightedness, farsightedness, purblindness, presbyopia, myopia, astigmatism, color blindness, cataract, ophthalmia; squint, cross-eye, strabismus, lazy eye, cockeye, swivel eye, goggle eyes.

fallacies of vision: refraction, distortion, illusion, mirage, phantasm, vision, specter, apparition, ghost, mirror, lens.

v be dimsighted, see double, wink, blink, squint, look askance, screw up the eyes.

adj dimsighted, purblind, myopic, astigmatic, nearsighted, farsighted, colorblind; blear-eyed, goggle-eyed, cockeyed, crosseyed.

444 spectator *n* beholder, observer, looker-on, onlooker, witness, eyewitness, bystander, passerby; sightseer, audience, crowd; spy, sentinel.

v witness, behold, look on.

445 optical instruments *n* lens, magnifying glass, microscope; spectacles, monocle, eyeglasses, glasses, contact lens, goggles, pince-nez; telescope, lorgnette, binoculars, spyglass, opera glasses; mirror, looking glass, reflector; prism, kaleidoscope, stereoscope.

446 visibility *n* perceptibility, discernibleness, distinctness, clearness, clarity, perceivability, conspicuousness, definition, sharp outline; appearance, manifestation.

v be visible, appear, open to the view, present itself, show itself, reveal itself, peep up, show up, turn up, start up, pop up, crop up; glimmer, loom; burst forth, burst upon the view, come into sight, come into view, come forth, come forward, attract attention.

adj visible, perceptible, discernible, perceivable, apparent, obvious, manifest, plain, clear, distinct, definite, well-defined, outlined, well-marked; recognizable, palpable, glaring, conspicuous, in full view, in full sight, in front of one's nose, under one's nose, before one's eyes.

447 invisibility *n* indistinctness, imperceptibility, invisibleness, indefiniteness; mystery, obscurity, delitescence, haziness, cloudiness; concealment; latency.

v be invisible; be hidden; escape notice; render invisible, conceal, hide.

adj invisible, imperceptible; not in sight, out of sight, out of view, unseen;

inconspicuous, covert; dim, faint, mysterious, dark, obscure, confused, indistinct, indistinguishable, shadowy, indefinite, undefined, unmarked, blurry, blurred, unfocused, out of focus, misty, veiled; concealed, hidden.

448 appearance n phenomenon, sight, show, scene, view; prospect, vista, perspective, lookout, outlook, bird's-eye view, scenery, landscape, picture, tableau; display, exposure; pageant, spectacle; aspect, phase, seeming, shape, form, manifestation, guise, look, complexion, color, image, mien, air, cast, carriage, comportment, demeanor; presence; feature, trait, lines, outline, contour, face, countenance, physiognomy, visage, profile, outsides.

v appear, be visible, seem, look, show, present; figure, cut a figure; present to the view.

adj apparent, seeming, ostensible.

adv apparently, to all appearance, ostensibly, seemingly, on the face of it, at first sight, to the eye.

449 disappearance n evanescence, eclipse; departure, exit; loss.

v disappear, vanish, dissolve, melt, melt away, fade, pass, pass out, go, depart, leave no trace, be gone.

adj disappearing, evanescent; departed, left; missing, lost, vanished.

Class IV

Intellectual Faculties

I. Formation of Ideas

450 intellect n rationality, mind, understanding, reason, faculties, judgment, sense, common sense, wits, brains, (informal) smarts; brain, head, pate, (informal) noodle, skull, (informal) upstairs.

v intellectualize, reason, understand, realize, ruminate; note, notice, mark, be aware of, take cognizance of.

adj intellectual, mental, cerebral, rational, sensical, commonsensical.

450a absence of intellect n want of intellect; inanity, imbecility, brutishness, brute instinct.

adj. unintellectual, unintelligent, unrational, nonrational, emptyheaded.

451 thought n abstraction, concept, conception, opinion, judgment, belief, idea, notion, tenet, conviction, speculation, consideration, contemplation; meditation, pondering, reflection, musing, cogitation, thinking; intention, design, purpose, intent; antici-

pation, expectation; consideration, attention, care, regard; trifle, mote.

v think, cogitate, meditate, reflect, muse, ponder, ruminate, contemplate; consider, regard, suppose, look upon, judge, esteem, deem, count, account; bear in mind, recollect, recall, remember; intend, mean, design, purpose; believe, suppose; anticipate, expect.

adj thoughtful, contemplative, meditative, reflective, pensive, deliberate; lost in thought, absorbed, engrossed in; careful, heedful, mindful, regardful, considerate, attentive; discreet, prudent, wary, cautious, circumspect.

452 absence of thought n incogitancy, vacancy of mind, thoughtlessness, fatuity, vacuity, emptiness; inattention.

v not think, make the mind a blank, (informal) turn off the brain, (informal) tune out.

adj vacant, unoccupied, empty; unthinking; inattentive, absent, (informal) turned off, (informal) tuned out; thoughtless, inconsiderate, unmindful, unheedful, imprudent; unreflective.

453 idea n thought, conception, theory, notion; observation, impression, apprehension, perception, brainstorm, brainchild, fancy, (informal) flash; opinion, view, belief, sentiment, judgment, supposition; plan, object, objective, aim.

adj ideational.

454 topic n subject, theme, thesis, subject-matter, food for thought; business, affair, argument.

adj topical, thematic.

adv under consideration, in question.

455 curiosity n interest, inquisitiveness, inquiring mind, thirst for knowledge; spying, prying, meddlesomeness. spy, eavesdropper, gossip.

v be curious, take an interest in, stare, gape, spy, pry.

adj curious, inquisitive, inquiring, prying, spying, peeping, meddlesome, interested.

456 incuriosity n lack of interest, incuriousness, indifference, unconcern.

v have no curiosity, take no interest in.

adj incurious, uninquisitive, uninquiring, uninterested, indifferent, impassive, bored, apathetic.

457 attention n attending to, attentiveness, intentiveness, care, consideration, observation, heed, regard, mindfulness, notice, watchfulness, alertness; study, scrutiny; civility, courtesy, respect, politeness.

v be attentive, attend, observe, look, see, notice, remark, regard, pay attention, heed; examine, study, scrutinize.

adj attentive, observant, mindful, heedful, thoughtful, alive, alert, awake, on the watch, wary, circumspect, watchful, careful; polite, courteous, respectful, deferential.

458 inattention *n* inattentiveness, inconsideration, heedlessness, unmindfulness, disregard, unconcern.

v be inattentive, overlook, disregard, pay no attention to, gloss over.

adj inattentive, unobservant, unmindful, unheeding, thoughtless, blind to, deaf to, napping, asleep, lost.

459 care *n* heed, caution, prudence, pains, anxiety, regard, attention, vigilance, carefulness, solicitude, circumspection, alertness, watchfulness, wakefulness; accuracy, exactness.

v be careful, take care.

adj careful, cautious, circumspect, watchful, vigilant, guarded, wary, prudent, tactful; painstaking, meticulous, discerning, exact, thorough, concerned, scrupulous, particular, finical, conscientious, attentive, heedful, thoughtful.

460 neglect *n* disregard, dereliction, negligence, remissness, carelessness, failure, omission, default, inattention, heedlessness, recklessness.

v neglect, disregard, ignore, slight, overlook, omit, be remiss, be negligent.

adj neglectful, disregardful, remiss, careless, negligent, unmindful, inattentive, indifferent, heedless, inconsiderate, thoughtless, imprudent; unwary, unguarded; neglecting, neglected, unheeded, uncared for, unobserved, unnoticed, unattended to.

461 inquiry *n* investigation, examination, study, scrutiny, exploration, research, search, pursuit; inquiring, questioning, interrogation; query, question.

inquirer, investigator, inquisitor, inspector.

v inquire, ask, question, interrogate, query, investigate, examine, seek, search, look for, study, consider.

adj inquiring, inquisitive, curious, scrutinizing, questioning, exploring; inquisitorial, exploratory, interrogative.

462 answer *n* reply, response, retort, rejoinder; discovery, solution; rationale.

v answer, reply, respond, rebut, retort, rejoin; explain, interpret, discover, solve; satisfy, set at rest, atone for.

adj responsive; answerable, discoverable, soluble.

463 experiment *n* test, trial, examination, proof, assay, procedure; experimentation, research, investigation, analysis.

experimenter, analyzer, adventurer.

v experiment, try, test, examine, analyze, prove, assay, essay.

adj experimental, probative, analytic.

464 comparison *n* collation, association, relating, likening, correlation, comparative relation, setting side by side, juxtaposition.

v compare, collate, confront, place side by side, pit one against another, juxtapose, relate, correlate.

adj comparative, metaphorical, compared with; comparable.

465 discrimination *n* distinction, differentiation, diagnosis; appreciation, estimation, discernment, critique, judgment; nicety, refinement, taste.

v discriminate, distinguish, set apart, differentiate.

adj discriminating, critical, distinguishing, discriminative, discriminatory, choosy, picky; discerning, perceptive; tasteful, refined.

465a indiscrimination *n* indistinction, indistinctness, lack of discernment.

v be indiscriminate, not discriminate, confound, confuse.

adj indiscriminate, miscellaneous, undiscriminating.

466 measurement *n* survey, valuation, appraisal, assessment, estimate, estimation, reckoning, gauging; measure, standard, rule, gauge, scale.

v measure, survey, assess, rate, value, appraise, estimate.

adj measurable.

467 [on one side] **evidence** *n* facts, indication, sign, signal; ground, grounds, proof, testimony; information, deposition, affidavit, exhibit, citation, reference, confirmation, corroboration.

v be evident, evince, show, tell, cite, signal, indicate, imply, argue, bespeak; give evidence, testify, depose, witness.

adj evident, evidential, indicative, inferential, referential, corroborative, confirmatory.

468 counter-evidence *n* disproof, refutation, rebuttal, conflicting evidence, negation.

v rebut, refute, check, weaken, contravene, contradict, deny.

adj countervailing, contradictory, conflicting, unsupportive, uncorroborative.

469 qualification *n* modification, limitation, mitigation, narrowing, restriction, coloring, allowance, consideration, extenuation, extenuating circumstances, condition, proviso, exception.

v qualify, modify, limit, mitigate, restrain, narrow, restrict, color, allow, allow for, make allowance for, consider, extenuate, except, make an exception, take into account, take into consideration.

adj qualified, qualifying, provided, conditional, extenuating, mitigating, admitting, supposing, with the proviso, provided that.

470 possibility *n* feasibility, practicality, likelihood, potentiality; contingency, chance.

v be possible, stand a chance, admit of, (*informal*) could be.

adj possible, imaginable, conceivable, credible, feasible, practical, performable, achievable, within reach, within the bounds of possibility, potential.

adv possibly, perhaps, perchance, peradventure, maybe.

471 impossibility *n* impracticality, unfeasibility, hopelessness.

v be impossible, have no chance.

adj impossible, not possible, inconceivable, incredible, unimaginable, unreasonable, unfeasible, impractical, unobtainable, unperformable, unachievable, beyond the bounds of reason, absurd, (*informal*) fat chance, (*informal*) no way.

472 probability *n* likelihood, likeliness, plausibility, tendency, prospect, good chance, reasonable chance, expectation.

v be probable, point to, tend, imply, bid fair.

adj probable, likely, plausible, reasonable, presumable, well-founded, hopeful.

adv probably, in all probability, in all likelihood, most likely, presumably.

473 improbability *n* unlikelihood, bare possibility, implausibility, doubtfulness, questionableness.

v be improbable, not have much of a chance.

adj improbable, unlikely, implausible, doubtful, questionable, beyond all reasonable expectation.

474 certainty *n* fact, truth; infal-

libility, reliability, unquestionableness, inevitability, certitude, assurance, confidence, conviction.

v be certain, stand to reason, render certain, clinch, make sure; know.

adj certain, confident, sure, assured, convinced, satisfied, indubitable, indisputable, unquestionable, undeniable, incontestable, unimpeachable, irrefutable, unquestioned, incontrovertible, absolute, positive, plain, patent, obvious, clear; sure, inevitable, infallible, unfailing; fixed, agreed upon, settled, prescribed, determined, determinate, constant, stated, given; definite, particular, special, especial; reliable, trustworthy, dependable, trusty.

adv certainly, for certain, no doubt, doubtless, undoubtedly, (*informal*) sure enough.

475 uncertainty *n* insecurity, instability, unreliability, fallibility, danger; incertitude, doubt, doubtfulness, ambiguity, vagueness, questionableness, dubiousness; haziness, fogginess, obscurity; undependability, changeableness, variability, capriciousness, irregularity, fitfulness, chanciness.

v be uncertain, hesitate, flounder, waver; render uncertain, pose, puzzle, perplex, confuse, confound, bewilder; doubt, question.

adj uncertain, insecure, precarious, unsure, doubtful, unpredictable, problematical, unstable, unreliable, unsafe, fallible, perilous, dangerous; unassured, undecided, indeterminate, undetermined, unfixed, unsettled, indefinite, ambiguous, questionable, dubious; doubtful, vague, indistinct; undependable, changeable, variable, capricious, unsteady, irregular, fitful, desultory, chance, (*informal*) chancy.

476 reasoning *n* ratiocination, rationalism, dialectics; discussion, comment, argumentation, debate, disputation.

logic, induction, deduction, chain of thought, analysis, synthesis, syllogistic reasoning.

argument, case, proposition, terms, premises, postulate, data; inference, *argumentum ad hominem, paralipsis, a priori, a posteriori, reductio ad absurdum,* enthymeme, dilemma, on the horns of a dilemma.

reasoner, logician, dialectician, disputant, wrangler, arguer, debater, polemicist, casuist, rationalist.

arguments, reasons, pros and cons.

v to reason, discuss, argue, debate, dispute, wrangle; deduce, induce, infer, analyze, synthesize, postulate, propose, contend, demonstrate.

adj reasoning, rationalistic, dialectical, dialectic, argumentative, disputatious; logical, inductive, deductive, analytical, synthetic, syllogistic, inferential; demonstrable.

477 [the absence of reasoning] **intuition.**

[false reasoning] **sophistry** *n* intuition, instinct, hunch, presentiment; insight, discernment, inspiration.

casuistry, jesuitry, perversion, equivocation, evasion, chicanery, quiddity, speciousness, (*informal*) bull, (*informal*) malarkey, bunk; false statement; fallacy, sophism.

sophist.

v intuit; reason falsely, pervert, quibble, equivocate, evade, mislead, gloss over, cavil, refine, subtilize, misrepresent, fence, beg the question.

adj intuitive, instinctive, instinctual, sophistical, equivocal, evasive, specious, fallacious, illogical, unsound, false, incorrect, untenable; inconsequential, weak, feeble, poor, flimsy, vague, nonsensical, absurd, foolish; frivolous, pettifogging, trifling, quibbling, nit-picking, subtle, over-refined.

adv intuitively, by intuition; illogically.

478 demonstration *n* proof, conclusiveness, example, verification, explanation.

v demonstrate, prove, establish, verify; evince, show, explain.

adj demonstrative, demonstrable, probative, conclusive, convincing; demonstrated, proven, proved, shown

479 confutation *n* refutation, answer, disproof, invalidation exposure.

v confute, refute, disprove, expose the error, overturn, invalidate.

adj confutable, refutable.

480 judgment *n* verdict, decree, decision, determination, conclusion, result, upshot, deduction, inference, assessment, opinion, estimate, criticism, critique; understanding, discrimination, discernment, perspicacity, sagacity, wisdom, intelligence, prudence, brains, taste, penetration, discretion, common sense.

judge, assessor, reviewer, critic, commentator; connoisseur.

v judge, estimate, consider, regard, esteem, appreciate, appraise, reckon, value; decide, determine, conclude, form an opinion, pass judgment; criticize, rate, rank; try, pass sentence upon, rule.

adj judicious, judicial, judgmental, determinate, conclusive; critical, discriminating, penetrating, perspicacious.

480a discovery *n* detection, determination, disclosure, trove, find.

v discover, learn of, ascertain, unearth, uncover, determine, ferret out, flush out, dig up; find out, detect, espy, descry, discern, see, notice, hit upon, stumble onto.

481 misjudgment *n* miscalculation, miscomputation, misconception, misinterpretation, misapprehension.

v misjudge, misconjecture, misconceive, misunderstand, misconstrue, misinterpret; overestimate, underestimate.

adj misjudging, ill-judging, wrongheaded, (*informal*) off base, wrong, in error.

482 overestimation *n* exaggeration, overvaluation, optimism; miscalculation.

v overestimate, overrate, overprize, overpraise, exaggerate, magnify, attach too much importance to, set too high a value on; miscalculate.

adj overestimated, overrated, inflated, pompous, pretentious.

483 underestimation *n* undervaluation, depreciation, detraction; modesty, self-depreciation; pessimism.

v underestimate, undervalue, underrate, depreciate, disparage, detract, slight, minimize, make light of, make little of, disregard.

adj underestimating, depreciating, depreciative, deprecatory; underestimated, depreciated, unvalued, unprized; modest, pessimistic.

484 belief *n* opinion, view, tenet, doctrine, dogma, creed; certainty, conviction, assurance, confidence, persuasion, believing, trust, reliance; credence, credit, acceptance, faith, assent.

v believe, credit, give credence to, accept, have faith in, give assent, accept; know, see, realize, assume, presume; think, opine, hold, conceive, consider; rely on, put one's trust on, have confidence in.

adj certain, sure, assured, positive, cocksure, satisfied, confident, convinced, secure; believing, trusting, confiding, credulous; believed, accredited, trusted, accepted; believable, credible, trustworthy.

485 disbelief, doubt *n* disbelief, incredulity; dissent, change of mind, retraction.

uncertainty, irresolution, hesitation, hesitancy, vacillation, misgiving, suspense; scruple, qualm, mistrust, distrust, suspicion, skepticism.

unbeliever, nonbeliever; skeptic.

v disbelieve, discredit, dissent,

doubt, distrust, mistrust, suspect, have qualms; hesitate, waver, demur.

adj unbelieving, incredulous, doubtful, disputable, questionable, suspicious; uncertain, unsure; doubting, hesitating, hesitant, wavering, irresolute, dubious, skeptical.

486 credulity n credulousness, gullibility, infatuation, superstition, self-deception, self-delusion.

gull, dupe, (informal) sucker.

v be credulous, swallow.

adj credulous, believing, trusting, unsuspecting, gullible; simple, silly, childish, stupid; infatuated, superstitious.

487 incredulity n incredulousness, caution, wariness, suspicion, doubt, skepticism, disbelief.

nonbeliever, skeptic, heretic.

v be incredulous, distrust, doubt, suspect.

adj incredulous, cautious, wary; suspicious, dubious, doubtful, skeptical, unbelieving.

488 assent n acknowledgment, agreement, concurrence, acquiescence, consent, allowance, approval, concord, accord, approbation.

v assent, acquiesce, accede, concur, agree, fall in, acknowledge, admit, yield, allow; own, avow, confess.

adj assenting, agreeing, concurring, consenting, of one accord, of the same mind; agreed, acquiescent.

489 dissent n difference, discordance, dissension, disagreement, dissatisfaction; opposition, protest; nonconformity, separation.

dissenter, protester, rebel, radical, dissident, nonconformist.

v dissent, differ, disagree, protest, contradict; repudiate.

adj dissenting, negative; dissident, contradictory, disagreeing, opposing; nonconformist.

490 knowledge n enlightenment, erudition, wisdom, science, letters, information, learning, scholarship, lore; understanding, discernment, perception, apprehension, comprehension, judgment.

v know, be aware of; understand, discern, perceive, realize, fathom, apprehend, comprehend, (informal) dig; (informal) be hip; learn, discover.

adj knowing, aware of, cognizant of, acquainted with, privy to; discerning, perceptive, (informal) sharp, shrewd; knowledgeable, educated, enlightened, erudite, wise, instructed, learned, well-educated, bookish, well-read; known, recognized, received.

491 ignorance n illiteracy, unenlightenment, unawareness, unlearnedness, unacquaintance, unconsciousness, inexperience, darkness, blindness, incomprehension, simplicity, stupidity.

v be ignorant, know nothing, have no idea, be blind to.

adj ignorant, illiterate, unlettered, uneducated, uninstructed, untaught, untutored, uninformed, unenlightened, nescient; shallow, superficial; stupid, dumb, thick, dull.

492 scholar n savant, wise man, sage, academician, thinker, intellectual, bibliomaniac, bookworm, pedant; student, pupil, disciple, learner.

493 ignoramus n illiterate, know-nothing, blockhead, numskull, dullard, simpleton, dunce, ass, fool, bonehead, duffer, dolt, turkey, twerp, idiot, imbecile, cretin, moron, dimwit, (informal) jerk.

494 truth n fact, reality, verity, veracity; accuracy, precision, exactness.

v be true, be the case, have a true ring.

adj true, factual, actual, real, authentic, genuine, veracious, truthful, veritable; pure, natural; accurate, exact, faithful, correct, precise; agreeing; right, proper; legitimate, rightful; to the point, (informal) right on, (informal) where it's at, (informal) on target.

495 error n fallacy, misconception, misapprehension, misunderstanding, misinterpretation, misjudgment; aberration, inexactness, laxity; mistake, fault, blunder, slip, oversight, flaw, stumble, bungle; delusion, false impression.

v err, be in error, mistake, blunder, slip, go astray, trip up; misconceive, misapprehend, misunderstand, misinterpret, miscalculate, misjudge.

adj erroneous, in error, fallacious, mistaken, incorrect, inaccurate, false, wrong, untrue, (informal) off base, (informal) off the mark.

496 maxim n proverb, aphorism, dictum, saying, adage, apothegm; motto, epigram, mot juste, truism, words of wisdom, axiom.

adj proverbial, aphoristic, axiomatic, truistic, (informal) corny, trite.

adv as they say, as the saying goes.

497 absurdity n nonsense, imbecility, foolishness, silliness, inanity, stupidity; farce, rhapsody, farrago, blunder, bathos; inconsistency, paradox, non sequitur, jargon, extravagance, exaggeration.

v be absurd, talk nonsense, play the fool.

adj absurd, nonsensical, ridiculous, silly, preposterous, foolish, inane, asinine, stupid, senseless, unreasonable, irrational, incongruous, self-contradictory, paradoxical; farcical, rhapsodic, bathetic, extravagant, exaggerated, bombastic, fantastic, meaningless.

498 intelligence, wisdom *n* intelligence, intellect, mind, capacity, understanding, discernment, reason, acumen, aptitude, penetration, brains, (*informal*) smarts; knowledge, news, information, tidings.

discretion, reasonableness, judgment, discernment, insight, sense, common sense, sagacity, insight, understanding, prudence; knowledge, information, learning, sapience, erudition, enlightenment.

v be intelligent; understand, discern, reason; be wise, discriminate.

adj intelligent, understanding, intellectual, quick, bright; astute, clever, sharp, alert, bright, apt, discerning, canny, shrewd, nimble, penetrating, piercing, on the ball.

wise, discerning, judicious, sage, sapient, sensible, sound, penetrating, sagacious, intelligent, perspicacious, profound, rational, prudent, cautious, politic, reasonable, thoughtful, reflective; learned, educated, erudite, schooled.

499 imbecility, folly *n* imbecility, want of intelligence, incompetence, incapacity, vacancy, dull understanding, meanness, simplicity, shallowness, stolidity, hebetude, puerility, fatuity, silliness, foolishness, driveling, stupidity, idiocy.

frivolity, irrationality, trifling, ineptitude, silliness, eccentricity, extravagance; rashness.

v be imbecilic.

be foolish, trifle, drivel, dote, ramble.

adj imbecile, imbecilic, idiotic, fatuous, driveling, vacant, mindless, witless, brainless, weak-headed, addle-brained, muddle-headed, dull-witted, feeble-minded, half-witted, dull, shallow, stolid, dim-witted, thick-skulled; shallow, weak, wanting, soft, sappy, stupid, obtuse, blunt, stolid, doltish, thick as a brick, asinine; childish, childlike, infantile, puerile, simple.

foolish, silly, senseless, irrational, insensate, nonsensical, inept, frivolous, trifling; eccentric, crazed, rash, thoughtless, giddy, obstinate, bigoted, narrow-minded; foolish, unwise, injudicious, improper, unreasonable, ridiculous, stupid, asinine; ill-conceived, ill-advised, ill-judged, inexpedient, extravagant, frivolous, trivial, useless.

500 sage *n* wise man, master mind, thinker, philosopher, oracle, luminary, man of learning, expert, authority.

501 fool *n* simpleton, dolt, dunce, blockhead, nincompoop, ninny, numskull, ignoramus, booby, sap, dunderhead, dunderpate, idiot, natural, oaf, lout, loon, dullard; jester, buffoon, droll, zany, harlequin, clown; imbecile, moron, idiot, cretin.

502 sanity *n* soundness, mental balance, rationality, reason, sense, clearheadedness, lucidity, coherence, normality, sobriety, (*informal*) good head.

v be sane, (*informal*) have one's act together.

adj sane, rational, reasonable, sensible, clearheaded, level-headed, logical, sober, lucid, self-possessed, (*informal*) together.

503 insanity *n* disorder, imbalance, derangement, dementia, lunacy, madness, craziness, aberration; frenzy, raving, incoherence, delirium, delusion; (*informal*) oddity, eccentricity, twist, mania.

v be insane, become insane, lose one's senses, go mad, rave, rant, (*informal*) lose it.

adj insane, deranged, demented, lunatic, crazed, crazy, maniacal, mad, touched, cracked, unhinged, unsettled, daft, frenzied, possessed, delirious, far gone, wild, flighty, distracted, frantic, mad as a hatter, (*informal*) crackers, (*informal*) zonkers, (*informal*) nuts, (*informal*) zonko, (*informal*) weird, (*informal*) bananas, (*informal*) kaput.

504 madman *n* lunatic, maniac, bedlamite, raver, (*informal*) nut, (*informal*) weirdo, (*informal*) crazy; dreamer, romantic, rhapsodist, enthusiast, visionary, seer, fanatic.

505 memory *n* retention, retentiveness, remembrance, recollection, reminiscence, retrospect, recognition; reminder, hint, suggestion, keepsake, souvenir, memento, token, memorial.

v remember, recall, recollect, call up, call to mind, bring to mind, think back upon, haunt one's thoughts, (*informal*) flash on; remind, suggest, hint, prompt, summon up, reminisce; retain, keep in mind, bear in mind, memorize, engrave in the mind, learn by heart; keep the memory alive.

adj reminiscent (of), mindful (of); fresh, alive, vivid; unforgotten, enduring, indelible, memorable, never to be forgotten, unforgettable, stirring, eventful.

506 oblivion n forgetfulness, short memory, slippery memory, untrustworthy memory, obliteration of the past, amnesia.

v forget, be forgetful, have a short memory, lose sight of, sink into oblivion; unlearn, efface from the memory, think no more of, consign to oblivion, banish from one's thoughts.

adj oblivious, forgetful, heedless, deaf to the past, insensible; out of mind, unremembered, forgotten, past recollection, buried, sunk into oblivion.

507 expectation n expectancy, anticipation, prospect, reckoning, calculation; suspense, waiting; hope, trust, assurance, confidence, reliance, presumption.

v expect, look for, look out for, look forward to, anticipate, await, hope for, wait for, foresee, prepare for, count on, rely on; predict, prognosticate, forecast.

adj expectant, watchful, vigilant, open-eyed; on tenterhooks, on one's toes, ready, in readiness, prepared, (informal) all set for; foreseen, long expected, prospective, in view, in sight, on the horizon, impending.

adv expectantly, on the watch, on edge, with bated breath.

508 nonexpectation n unforeseen occurrence, surprise, shock, blow, wonder, bolt out of the blue, astonishment; miscalculation, false expectation.

v not expect, be taken by surprise, catch unawares; burst upon, come out of nowhere, drop from the clouds; surprise, startle, stun, stagger, throw off one's guard, astonish.

adj nonexpectant, surprised, unwarned, unaware, off one's guard; unanticipated, unexpected, unlooked for, unforeseen; unheard of, startling; sudden.

adv unexpectedly, abruptly, suddenly, without warning.

509 [failure of expectation] **disappointment** n failure, defeat, frustration, unfulfillment, blighted hope, vain expectation, disillusion, (informal) come-down.

v be disappointed; disappoint, dash one's hopes, dash one's expectations, balk, jilt, tantalize; dumfound, disillusion, let down.

adj disappointed; disgruntled, disconcerted, aghast.

510 foresight n prudence, forethought, prevision, anticipation, precaution; forecast; prescience, fore-knowledge, prospect.

v foresee; look forward to, look ahead, look beyond; look into the future; see one's future, catch the lay of the land; anticipate, expect, assume, surmise, predict, forewarn.

adj anticipatory, prescient; farsighted, prudent, provident; prospective, expectant.

511 prediction n prophecy, forecast, augury, prognostication, foretoken, portent, divination, soothsaying, presage.

v predict, foretell, prophesy, foresee, forecast, presage, augur, prognosticate, foretoken, portend, divine.

adj prophetic, oracular, portentous, premonitory.

512 omen n portent, foreboding, augury, sign, harbinger; sign of the times, symbol, warning.

513 oracle n prophet, prophetess, seer, soothsayer, augur, fortune-teller, witch, sibyl, necromancer, sorcerer, clairvoyant, interpreter.

514 supposition n assumption, presumption, condition, hypothesis, theory, postulate, proposition, thesis, theorem; conjecture, suggestion, guess, guesswork, suspicion, inkling, speculation.

v suppose, conjecture, surmise, suspect, guess, divine; theorize, speculate, presume, presuppose, assume, predicate; believe, take for granted; propound, put forth, propose, advance, hazard a suggestion, suggest.

adj assumed, given; conjectural, hypothetical, presumptive, theoretical, speculative, suggestive.

515 imagination n imaginativeness, fancy, invention, inspiration, creativity, originality, fiction, vision, fantasy, illusion, ideality, castles in the air, dreaming, dream, golden dreams; mental image, conception, idea, notion, thought, conceit, fancy, whim, figment, romance, vision, dream, chimera, shadow, illusion, phantasm, supposition, delusion; verve, vivacity, liveliness, animation.

v imagine, fancy, conceive, dream, idealize; create, originate, think up, devise, invent, coin, fabricate.

adj imaginative, fanciful, original, inventive, creative, visionary, ideal, unreal, illusory, unsubstantial, dreamy, dreamlike, romantic, fantastic, fabulous, chimerical, fantastical; vivacious, lively, animated; imaginable, conceivable, possible, believable; imagined.

II. Communication of Ideas

516 [idea to be conveyed] **meaning** n
tenor, spirit, gist, trend, idea, purport,
significance, signification, sense, import, denotation, conotation, interpretation; intent, intention, aim,
object, purpose, design.

    thing signified: matter, subject
matter, substance, gist, argument.

    v mean, signify, denote, conote,
express, import, purport; convey,
imply, indicate, point to, allude to,
touch on, drive at, involve; declare,
affirm, state; intend, aim, design,
purpose.

    adj meaning; meaningful, pointed,
poignant, significant, expressive

517 meaninglessness n unmeaningness, absence of meaning, senselessness, emptiness, empty words, rhetoric, platitude, nonsense, jargon,
gibberish, jabber, rant, bombast,
(informal) hot air; inanity, rigmarole,
absurdity, ambiguity.

    v mean nothing, jabber, rant, say
nothing.

    adj meaningless, senseless, non-
sensical, inexpressive, vague, trivial,
insignificant.

518 intelligibility n comprehensibility, clarity, clearness, lucidity, coherence, explicitness, persicuity, precision, plain-speaking.

    v be intelligible; render intel-
ligible, clear up, simplify, elucidate,
explain; understand, comprehend, take
in, catch on, grasp, follow, master.

    adj intelligible, understandable,
comprehensible, clear, clear as day,
lucid, luminous, transparent; plain,
distinct, pointed, clear-cut, obvious,
explicit, precise; graphic, illustrative,
expressive.

519 unintelligibility n incompre-
hensibility, vagueness, obscurity, ambiguity, uncertainty, confusion.

    v be unintelligible; render unin-
telligible, conceal, darken, confuse,
perplex, mystify, bewilder.

    adj unintelligible, incomprehen-
sible, indecipherable, unfathomable,
inexplicable, inscrutable, insoluble,
impenetrable; puzzling, enigmatic,
obscure, muddy, dim, nebulous, mysterious, (informal) strange, (informal)
weird; inexpressible, incommunicable,
ineffable, unutterable.

520 equivocalness n ambiguity, uncertainty, questionableness, dubiousness, indeterminateness; double-meaning, word-play, double entendre, pun,
play on words, conundrum, riddle,
quibble; equivocation, duplicity, prevarication, white lie.

    v be equivocal; have two mean-
ings; equivocate, prevaricate.

    adj equivocal, ambiguous, uncer-
tain, doubtful, questionable, dubious,
indeterminate; duplicitous, enigmatic,
double-edged, deceptive, misleading.

521 figure of speech n phrase, expression, euphemism, manner of
speaking, colloquialism, idiom, image;
metaphor, simile, imagery, poetic
device, poetics, figures of beauty.

    v employ figures of speech; image,
speak prettily.

    adj figurative, idiomatic, collo-
quial, colorful, imagistic, poetic,
expressive, allusive.

522 interpretation n definition, explanation, explication, elucidation,
translation; exegesis, exposition, comment, commentary, gloss; solution,
answer, meaning.

    v interpret, define, explain, expli-
cate, elucidate, translate, shed light
on, cast light on, decipher, decode,
unravel, disentangle, gloss, annotate,
expound, comment upon; construe,
understand.

    adj explanatory, expository, exe-
getical, interpretative, interpretive;
interpretable, explicable, intelligible.

    adv in explanation, that is to say,
namely.

523 misinterpretation n misapprehension, misconception, misunderstanding, misreading, misconstruction,
mistake; misrepresentation, perversion, exaggeration, false coloration,
falsification, travesty.

    v misinterpret, misapprehend, mis-
conceive, misunderstand, misread,
misconstrue, misapply, mistake; misrepresent, pervert, misstate, garble,
falsify, distort, travesty, stretch the
meaning, twist the meaning.

524 interpreter n translator, explainer, expounder, expositor, commentator, annotator, guide, critic; spokesman, speaker, representative.

525 manifestation n indication, expression, exposition, demonstration,
showing, display, exhibition, declaration; materialization; openness, candor.

    v make manifest, show, display,
reveal, disclose, open, exhibit, evince,
evidence, demonstrate, declare, express, make known; appear, be plain,
come to light, materialize; indicate,
point out.

    adj manifest, evident, obvious,
apparent, plain, clear, distinct, patent,
open, palpable, visible, unmistakable,
conspicuous, explicit; unreserved,

downright, frank, plain spoken; bare-faced, bold; manifested.

adv manifestly, openly, plainly, above board, in broad daylight, in plain sight.

526 latency *n* dormancy, latentness, quiescence, obscurity, darkness, hidden meaning, obscure meaning, undercurrent, suggestion, concealment; potentiality.

v be latent, lurk, smolder, underlie.

adj latent, dormant; lurking, secret, cryptic, veiled, hidden; potential; implied, implicit; allusive.

527 information *n* enlightenment, knowledge, news, data, facts, circumstances, situations, intelligence, advice; communication, notification, announcement; record; hint, suggestion, innuendo, inkling, whisper, insinuation.

informant, authority, intelligencer, reporter; informer, eavesdropper, detective, newsmonger; messenger.

guide, guidebook, handbook, manual, map, chart.

v inform, tell, acquaint with, impart to, make acquainted with, apprize, advise, enlighten; communicate, make known, express, mention, let fall, intimate, hint, insinuate, allude to, suggest; announce, report, give an account, disclose; know, learn, find out, get the scent of.

adj informed, communicated, reported, advised, apprized of, acquainted with, enlightened, published, (*informal*) filled in; declarative, expository, communicative.

528 concealment *n* hiding, secretion, ensconcing, sheltering, covering, burying, screening; keeping secret, secrecy, hiding, disguising, veiling, camouflaging, obscuring, dissembling, obfuscation, evasiveness; reticence, reserve, reservation, suppression, silence, secretiveness.

v conceal, hide, secrete, cover, put away, ensconce, bury, screen, shelter, keep out of sight, stow away; keep secret, hide, disguise, veil, cloak, mask, camouflage, obscure, obfuscate, dissemble, be evasive.

adj concealed, hidden, secret, private, privy, confidential, in secret, close, undercover, in hiding, in disguise, covert, mysterious; furtive, stealthy, surreptitious, secretive, evasive, clandestine; reserved, reticent, suppressed, uncommunicative.

adv secretly, in secret, in private, behind closed doors, on the sly; confidentially; stealthily.

529 disclosure *n* revelation, divulgence, exposition, exposure; exposé, uncovering, muckraking; acknowledgment, avowal, confession.

v disclose, discover, uncover, lay open, expose, bring to light, unmask; reveal, make known, divulge, show, tell, unveil, unmask, communicate; let slip, let drop, betray, blurt out; acknowledge, allow, concede, grant, admit, own up, confess.

adj disclosed, revealed.

530 [means of concealment] **ambush** *n* ambuscade, lurking place, trap, snare, pitfall; hiding place, secret place, recess, hole, cubbyhole; screen, cover, shade, blinker, veil, curtain, cloak, cloud; mask, visor, disguise, masquerade.

v ambush, lie in wait for, set a trap for.

531 publication *n* issuance, distribution; announcement, proclamation, promulgation, propagation, pronouncement, declaration, disclosure, divulgence, advertisement, publicity; edition.

v publish, issue, distribute, print; make public, make known, announce, proclaim, promulgate, propagate, circulate, spread, disseminate, declare, disclose, divulge, advertise, publicize, get into print.

adj published; current, public, in circulation, in print, in black and white.

532 news *n* information, intelligence, tidings, report, rumor, scuttlebutt, hearsay, gossip, (*informal*) the word; newsstory, headlines, copy.

reporter, newsmonger, talebearer, gossip, tattler, informer.

v transpire, make news, make headlines; be rumored.

adj in the news, in the headlines, current, in circulation, in print.

533 secret *n* mystery; problem, question, difficulty, a confidence; unintelligibility.

adj secret, hidden, concealed, unrevealed, unknown, mysterious; reticent, secretive; private.

534 messenger *n* envoy, emissary, representative, intermediary, go-between, delegate, courier, runner, errand boy; intelligencer, reporter, newsmonger, spokesman, informant; forerunner, harbinger, herald, precursor.

535 affirmation *n* statement, profession, pronouncement, deposition, assertion, declaration; confirmation, ratification, endorsement; swearing, oath, affidavit; emphasis, dogmatism.

v affirm, state, assert, aver, avow, maintain, declare, swear, asseverate, depose, testify, say, pronounce; establish, confirm, ratify, approve, endorse, assent, acknowledge; swear, emphasize.

adj affirmative, declaratory, declarative, positive, assertive, emphatic, dogmatic; confirmative, corroborative, affirming, acquiescent.

536 negation, denial *n* nullification, invalidation.

disputation, confutation, contradiction, qualification; repudiation, rejection, abjuration, disavowal, disclaimer, recantation, retraction, rebuttal.

v negate, nullify, cancel, invalidate.

deny, dispute, controvert, contravene, oppose, gainsay, contradict, rebut; reject, renounce, abjure, disclaim, disavow; recant, revoke; refuse, repudiate, disown.

adj contradictory; negative.

537 teaching *n* instruction, education, pedagogy, pedagogics, edification, tutelage, tutorship; guidance, direction, preparation, schooling, learning, discipline; lesson, lecture, disquisition, discourse, explanation, harangue, homily, sermon, lore; doctrine, dogma, tenet, principle, rule, maxim, article of faith, creed, credo, belief, opinion.

v teach, instruct, edify, educate, inform, enlighten, prepare, discipline, train, drill, tutor, prime, coach, guide, direct, school, indoctrinate, inculcate, infuse, instill, imbue; expound, interpret, lecture, discourse, hold forth, sermonize, moralize.

adj educational, scholastic, academic, pedagogic, pedagogical, didactic; edifying, instructive.

538 misteaching *n* misinformation, misdirection, misguidance, perversion, sophistry, error.

v misteach, misinform, misinstruct, misdirect, misguide, pervert, mislead, misrepresent, confuse, bewilder, lie.

539 learning *n* acquisition of knowledge, acquirements, attainment, mental cultivation, scholarship, erudition, study, inquiry, questioning, search, pursuit of knowledge.

apprenticeship, tutelage, matriculation.

v learn, acquire, gain knowledge, memorize, master, study, grind, cram, (*informal*) book, read, peruse, pore over, wade through, ingest, burn the midnight oil, (*informal*) pull an allnighter.

adj studious, industrious; scholarly, scholastic, well-read, learned, erudite.

540 teacher *n* instructor, tutor, lecturer, professor, don, -master, schoolmaster, guide, counselor, adviser, mentor; preacher, missionary, propagandist.

541 learner *n* scholar, student, pupil, apprentice, novice, neophyte, beginner; disciple, acolyte, follower.

542 school *n* academy, educational institution, college, university, institute, seminary, place of learning.

schoolbook, textbook, text, primer, grammar, reader, workbook.

adj scholastic, academic, collegiate.

543 veracity *n* truthfulness, frankness, truth, sincerity, candor, honesty, probity, fidelity, accuracy.

v speak the truth, (*informal*) level with, (*informal*) be straight with.

adj veracious, true, truthful, sincere, honest, honorable, candid, frank, open, straightforward, honest, scrupulous, punctilious, trustworthy.

544 falsehood *n* falsification, lie, fib, untruth, distortion, deception, misrepresentation, fabrication, fiction, sham; untruthfulness, lying, prevarication, duplicity, double dealing, deceitfulness, equivocation, dissembling, cunning, guile, insincerity, dishonesty, inaccuracy.

v lie, fib, falsify, prevaricate, misrepresent, deceive, (*informal*) come on to, doctor, feign, pretend, play false, dissemble, counterfeit, fabricate.

adj false, untrue, wrong, mistaken, incorrect, erroneous; untruthful, lying, mendacious, dishonest, deceitful, treacherous, faithless, insincere, hypocritical, disingenuous, unfaithful, cunning, perfidious, two-faced, recreant; deceptive, misleading, fallacious, spurious, fraudulent, bogus, phony, sham, counterfeit.

545 deception *n* deceiving, guiling, falseness, untruthfulness; artifice, sham, cheat, imposture, deceit, treachery, subterfuge, stratagem, ruse, hoax, fraud, trick, wile, snare, trap, illusion, delusion.

v deceive, mislead, lead astray, take in, delude, cheat, cozen, dupe, gull, fool, bamboozle, hoodwink, (*informal*) con, trick, double-cross, defraud, outwit; entrap, ensnare, betray.

adj deceptive, misleading, delusive, illusory, fallacious, specious, untrue, false, deceitful; tricky, cunning, insidious.

546 untruth *n* falsehood, fib, lie, fiction, story, tale, tall tale, fabrication, fable, forgery, invention.

   v make believe, pretend, feign, sham, fib, lie.

   adj untrue, false, trumped up, unfounded, invented, fictitious, fabulous.

547 dupe *n* gull, pigeon, laughing-stock, greenhorn, fool, sucker, puppet, (*informal*) nebbish.

   v be deceived, be the dupe of, fall into a trap, go for the bait, bite, swallow.

   adj credulous, gullible, unsuspecting, trusting.

548 deceiver *n* dissembler, hypocrite, sophist, liar, (*informal*) fast talker, storyteller, (*informal*) faker, (*informal*) phony, fraud, (*informal*) four-flusher, (*informal*) shyster, confidence man, con man, cheat, swindler, imposter, pretender, humbug, adventurer, adventuress, serpent, snake in the grass.

549 exaggeration *n* overstatement, hyperbole, extravagance, coloring, coloration, embroidery; yarn, tale, (*informal*) shaggy dog story, (*informal*) fish story; tempest in a teacup, much ado about nothing, puffery, rant.

   v exaggerate, magnify, amplify, expand, overestimate, overstate; heighten, color, embroider, puff up, fill out.

   adj exaggerated, overwrought, bombastic, magniloquent, hyperbolic, fabulous, extravagant, preposterous.

550 [means of communication] indication *n* symbolism, semiology; sign, symbol, index, indicator, pointer, note, token, symptom; type, mark, figure, emblem, insigne, cipher, device, representation; signal, beacon, alarm; feature, trait, characteristic, peculiarity, quality, earmark, cast; gesture, gesticulation, motion, cue, hint, clue, scent.

   v indicate, denote, betoken, designate, signify, represent, stand for, typify, symbolize; note, mark, stamp; label, ticket; make a sign, signalize, signal, gesture, gesticulate; sign, seal, attest, underline, underscore, call attention to.

   adj indicative, indicatory; connotative, denotative, typical, representative, symbolic, symbolical, characteristic, significant, emblematic.

551 record *n* trace, vestige, relic, remains; monument, achievement; account, chronicles, annals, history, note, register, memorandum, document, diary, log, journal, ledger.

   v record, set down, place in the record, chronicle, enter, register, enter, list, enroll; commemorate, celebrate.

552 [suppression of sign] obliteration *n* erasure, cancelation, deletion, blot, effacement, extinction.

   v obliterate, efface, expunge, erase, cancel, delete, blot out, rub out, strike out, wipe out, leave no trace.

   adj obliterated, erased, blotted out; unrecorded.

553 recorder *n* notary, clerk, registrar, register, secretary, scribe, bookkeeper; annalist, historian, historiographer, chronicler, biographer, journalist, antiquarian, memorialist.

554 representation *n* depiction, imitation, illustration, delineation, expression, imagery, portraiture, figuration.

   v represent, delineate, depict, portray, picture, figure, describe, trace, copy, illustrate, symbolize; personate, personify play, mimic.

   adj representative, imitative, illustrative, figurative, symbolic, descriptive.

555 misrepresentation *n* distortion, exaggeration, misfiguration, falsification, bad likeness, caricature.

   v misrepresent, distort, overdraw, exaggerate, falsify, caricature, daub.

556 painting *n* fine art, picture, depiction, representation, pictorialization, delineation, design, drawing, likeness, copy, imitation, fake, image. art gallery, picture gallery, studio.

   v paint, design, limn, draw, sketch, pencil, color; depict, represent.

   adj pictorial, picturesque.

557 sculpture *n* carving, modeling, statuary; ceramics, potting.

   statue, statuette, bust; cast, mold.

   v sculpt, fashion, cast, mold, model, chisel, carve, cut, shape, form, figure, hew.

558 engraving *n* etching, chiseling, incising, plate engraving, photoengraving.

   v engrave, grave, carve, incise, chisel, hatch, etch, stipple, print.

559 artist *n* painter, drawer, sketcher, designer, draftsman, cartoonist, caricaturist, sculptor, engraver.

560 language *n* speech, phraseology, style, expression, diction, jargon, dialect, terminology, vernacular, lingo, tongue.

   literature, letters, belles lettres, humanities, classics, dead language. linguist.

   v express, say, express by words.

   adj lingual, linguistic; dialectic.

vernacular, current, colloquial, slangy, polyglot, literary.

561 letter *n* character, hieroglyph, symbol, alphabet, consonant, vowel.

   syllable, monosyllable, dissyllable, polysyllable.

   spelling, orthography; phonetics; cipher, code; monogram, anagram.

   v spell.

   adj literal; alphabetical; syllabic; phonetic.

562 word *n* term, symbol, name, part of speech.

   dictionary, vocabulary, lexicon, index, thesaurus, glossary.

   etymology, derivation, philology, terminology, lexicography.

   adj literal, verbal.

563 neology *n* neologism, new-fangled expression, (*informal*) hip expression, barbarism, corruption.

   neologist, word coiner.

   v coin words.

   adj neologic, neological; colloquial, slang, (*informal*) hip, cant, barbarous.

564 nomenclature *n* naming; name, appellation, designation, epithet, nickname, (*informal*) moniker, (*informal*) handle, label, title, head, heading; style, proper name, surname, namesake.

   v name, call, term, designate, denominate, style, entitle, dub, christen, baptize, nickname, characterize, specify, label.

   adj titular, nominal.

565 misnomer *n* misnaming, malapropism; sobriquet, nickname, assumed name, alias, pen name, stage name, pseudonym, nom de plume, nom de guerre.

   v misname, miscall, misterm; take an assumed name.

   adj misnamed, sol-disant, self-styled; so-called.

566 phrase *n* expression, set phrase, turn of speech, idiom, tag phrase, figure of speech, euphemism, motto; phraseology.

   v phrase, express, put into words, find the right words, arrange in words, voice, vocalize.

567 grammar *n* rules of language, usage, forms, style, formal features, constructions, parts of speech; accidence, syntax, inflection, case, declension, conjugation; grammar book, primer, rulebook.

   grammarian.

   adj grammatical, syntactic, syntactical.

568 solecism *n* ungrammatical usage, bad grammar, faulty grammar, error, slip, inconsistency, impropriety.

   v solecize.

   adj ungrammatical, incorrect, inaccurate, faulty, inconsistent, improper.

569 style *n* diction, phraseology, wording; composition, mode of expression, choice of words, command of language, mode, manner, method, approach; kind, form, appearance, character, touch, characteristic, mark, signature, imprint, (*informal*) name.

   v style, compose, express by words; write.

   adj stylistic; characteristic; expressive.

570 perspicuity *n* clearness, clarity, lucidity, plainness, plain-speaking, distinctness, explicitness, exactness, intelligibility.

   adj perspicuous, pellucid, clear, lucid, intelligible, plain, distinct, explicit, exact, definite, unequivocal.

571 obscurity *n* unintelligibility, involution, confusion, indistinctness, indefiniteness, ambiguity, vagueness, inexactness, impenetrability.

   adj obscure, involved, confused, unintelligible, impenetrable, indefinite, vague, inexact, hidden, dark.

572 conciseness *n* brevity, summary, abridgment, terseness, pithiness, compression, tightness.

   v be concise, condense, abridge, abstract, compress, tighten, come to the point.

   adj concise, brief, compendious, short, terse, laconic, pithy, trenchant, succinct, compact, tight.

   adv concisely, briefly, summarily, in short.

573 diffuseness *n* long-windedness, verbosity, wordiness, verbiage, looseness, exuberance, redundancy, profuseness, richness.

   v be diffuse, enlarge, amplify, expand, inflate; meander, digress, ramble, run on and on.

   adj diffuse, profuse, wordy, verbose, copious, exuberant; lengthy, long-winded, protracted, prolix, diffusive, roundabout; digressive, discursive, loose.

574 vigor *n* power, force, boldness, spirit, verve, heart, ardor, enthusiasm, raciness, glow, fire, warmth; loftiness, elevation, gravity, sublimity; eloquence, strong language.

   adj vigorous, nervous, powerful, forcible, forceful, trenchant, biting, incisive, impressive; spirited, lively, glowing, sparkling, racy, bold, pungent, pithy; lofty, elevated, sublime, grand, weighty; eloquent, vehement, impassioned, passionate.

575 feebleness *n* weakness, enervation, frailty, faintness.

adj feeble, tame, weak, meager, vapid, insipid; trashy, poor, dull, dry, languid; prosy, prosaic, slight; careless, loose, slip-shod, wishy-washy, sloppy, slovenly; puerile, childish.

576 plainness *n* simplicity, homeliness, restraint, severity.

v speak plainly, speak directly, come straight to the point, be straightforward, not beat around the bush.

adj plain, simple, homely, homey, unadorned, unvarnished, neat, homespun; severe, chaste, pure.

adv in plain terms, in plain English; point-blank.

577 ornament *n* floridness, ornateness, elegance, grandiloquence, magniloquence, rhetorical flourish, declamation, rhetoric, flourish, fancy talk, (*informal*) big words; pretention, inflation, bombast, fustian, rant, fine writing, fine speaking.

v ornament, overcharge, talk big, talk fancy.

adj ornate, ornamented, beautified, florid, rich, flowery, fancy; euphuistic, euphemistic; sonorous, high sounding, inflated, swelling, turgid, pompous, pedantic, stilted, high-flown, sententious, rhetorical, declamatory, grandiose, grandiloquent, magniloquent, bombastic, flashy.

578 elegance *n* taste, good taste, propriety, correctness; lucidity, purity, grace, ease; gracefulness, euphony, gentility, cultivation, polish, refinement.

purist, classicist.

adj elegant, polished, classic, classical, fine, tasteful, proper, correct; chaste, pure, graceful, easy, readable, fluent, flowing, unaffected, natural, mellifluous, euphonious, felicitous, neat, well put.

579 inelegance *n* tastelessness, vulgarity, impropriety; bad diction, awkwardness, stiffness, turgidity, abruptness; barbarism, solecism, slang, mannerism, affectation, formality.

adj inelegant, graceless, ungraceful, harsh, abrupt, dry, stiff, cramped, formal, forced, labored, awkward, ponderous, turgid; artificial, mannered, affected, euphuistic; tasteless, barbarous, uncouth, rude, crude, vulgar.

580 voice *n* vocality, intonation, articulation, enunciation, distinctness,

clearness, delivery; accent, accentuation, emphasis, stress; utterance, vocalization.

v voice, speak, utter; articulate, enunciate, vocalize, intone, pronounce, accent, accentuate, deliver.

adj vocal, oral; articulate, distinct, euphonious, melodious.

581 muteness *n* dumbness, silence, speechlessness; aphasia.

v be mute, be silent, be dumb; silence, muzzle, muffle, suppress, smother, gag, strike dumb, dumfound.

adj mute, silent, dumb, mum, tongue-tied; voiceless, speechless.

582 speech *n* talk, parlance, locution, conversation, parley, communication, prattle; talk, oration, address, discourse, lecture, recitation, sermon, harangue, tirade; oratory, eloquence, rhetoric, declamation.

speaker, spokesman, mouthpiece, orator, rhetorician.

v speak, utter, talk, voice, converse, communicate, pronounce, say, articulate; declaim, harangue, stump, spout, rant, lecture, sermonize, discourse, expatiate, soliloquize, address.

adj oral; talkative, conversational; declamatory.

583 [imperfect speech] **inarticulateness** *n* stammering, hesitation, muttering, mumbling, stuttering; reticence, taciturnity; speech impediment, aphasia.

v be inarticulate, stammer, hesitate, mutter, mumble, slur one's words, garble, sputter, hem and haw, whisper, croak, crack.

adj inarticulate, tongue-tied, speechless, voiceless, hesitant, reticent, taciturn.

584 loquacity *n* loquaciousness, volubility, talkativeness, verbosity, garrulity, volubility; chatter, jabber, prattle, twaddle.

talker, chatterer, chatterbox, babbler, ranter.

v be loquacious, talk a mile a minute, pour forth, prate, chatter, babble, gab, run off at the mouth, jabber, jaw, gush.

adj loquacious, voluble, talkative, verbose, wordy, garrulous, chatty, chattering, glib, fluent, effusive.

585 taciturnity *n* silence, muteness, reserve, reticence, uncommunicativeness.

v be silent, keep silence, keep quiet, hold one's tongue, say nothing.

adj taciturn, silent, mute, mum, reserved, reticent, guarded, uncommunicative, close-mouthed, quiet.

586 public address *n* allocution, speech, formal speech, address, invocation.

v speak to, address; invoke, hail, salute; lecture, pronounce.

587 response *n*. See answer 462.

588 conversation *n* interlocution, colloquy, confabulation, talk, (*informal*) rap, discourse, verbal interchange, dialog, oral communication; chat, chit, chit-chat, small talk, table talk, idle talk, prattle, gossip; conference, parley, interview, audience, *tête-à-tête*, council, congress; palaver, debate, discussion.

v converse, confabulate, talk together, hold a conversation, carry on a conversation, engage in a discussion; bandy words, chat, chit-chat, gossip, tattle, prate; discourse with, confer with; talk it over, (*informal*) rap, (*informal*) chew the fat.

adj conversational, conversable; chatty, gossipy.

589 soliloquy *n* monolog, apostrophe, aside.

v soliloquize, talk to oneself, think out loud, apostrophize.

590 writing *n* chirography, penmanship, calligraphy, hand, script, longhand, shorthand, stenography; handwriting, signature, mark, hand; manuscript, MS., document, script, writ, author's copy, copy, original; composition, authorship, work, opus, book, volume, tome, publication, article, poetry, verse, literature.

writer, author, scribe, scrivener, clerk, copyist, secretary.

v write, pen, copy, transcribe; print, scribble, scrawl, scratch; compose, draw out, write down, set down, put pen to paper, take up the pen, take pen in hand.

adj written, in writing, in black and white.

591 printing *n* lettering, typography; type; composition, print, letterpress, text, matter; copy, impression, proof.

printer, compositor, reader, proofreader, copyeditor.

v print, compose; go to press, publish, bring out, issue.

adj typographical, printed.

592 correspondence *n* letter, epistle, missive, note, post card; communication, dispatch, bulletin, circular.

v correspond, communicate, write to, send a letter.

adj epistolary; in touch with, in communication with.

593 book *n* booklet; writing, work, volume, tome, opus, tract, treatise, brochure, handbook; novel, story;

script, libretto; publication.

writer, author, essayist, editor; bookseller, publisher; librarian, bibliophile, bookworm.

594 description *n* narration, account, recounting, telling, recital, relation, statement, report, record; delineation, portrayal, characterization, representation, depiction, sketch, vignette.

v describe, set forth, narrate, account, recount, recite, rehearse, tell, relate, detail; picture, delineate, portray, characterize, limn, represent, depict.

595 dissertation *n* treatise, essay, thesis, theme, tract, discourse, disquisition, investigation, study, discussion, exposition; commentary, critique, criticism, review, article, commentator, critic, essayist, reviewer.

v discuss a subject, treat, examine, comment, criticize, explain.

596 compendium *n* abstract, précis, epitome, analysis, digest, compendium, brief, abridgment, abbreviation, condensation, summary; draft, note, synopsis, outline, syllabus, contents, prospectus; compilation, collection, album, anthology; extracts, cuttings, fragments, pieces; list, inventory, survey.

v abridge, abstract, précis, epitomize, summarize; abbreviate, shorten, condense, compress, compile, collect, note; list, inventory, survey.

adj compendious, synoptic, analytic, analytical.

597 poetry *n* poetics; verse, poesy, versification, rhyming, rhymes, making verses, metrics, doggerel.

poet, laureate, bard, troubadour, minstrel, versifier, rhymer, sonneteer, rhapsodist, poetaster.

v poeticize, sing, versify, rhyme, make verses, compose.

adj poetic, poetical, rhythmic, metrical, lyrical, tuneful, musical; beautiful, lovely, tender, sensitive.

598 prose *n* writing, fiction, imaginative writing, narrative prose.

v write prose.

adj prosy, unpoetic, rhymeless; prosaic, dull, flat, matter-of-fact, unimaginative, commonplace, humdrum, pedestrian, trite, hackneyed, mediocre, stock, ordinary; fictional.

599 the drama *n* the stage, the theater; theatricals, dramaturgy, playwriting; play, drama, stage-play, opera.

performance, acting, representation, impersonation, stage business, actor, actress, player, performer, thespian.

theater, playhouse, operahouse, amphitheater.

dramatist, playwriter, playwright.

v dramatize, act, play, perform, personate, act a part, put on the stage, enact.

adj dramatic, theatrical, histrionic, stagy.

Class V

Voluntary Powers

I. Individual Volition

600 will *n* volition, free will, freedom; choice, wish, desire, pleasure, disposition, inclination; intent, purpose, option; determination, resolution, resoluteness, decision, forcefulness; force of will, will power, self-control.

v will, see fit, think fit, decide, decree, determine, direct, command, bid.

adj willful, voluntary, volitional, intentional; free, optional, discretionary; autocratic, obdurate, adamant.

adv willfully, voluntarily, at will; of one's own accord, intentionally, deliberately.

601 necessity *n* obligation, compulsion, subjection; fate, destiny, fatality; inevitability, inevitableness, unavoidability, unavoidableness, irresistibility; requirement, requisite, demand; instinct, impulse.

v be obligated, be obliged, be fated; necessitate, compel, subject; require.

adj necessary, essential, requisite, needful; inevitable, unavoidable, ineluctable, irresistible, inexorable; compulsory, involuntary, instinctive, automatic, blind, mechanical.

adv necessarily, of necessity, willy nilly.

602 willingness *n* disposition, inclination, leaning, propensity, frame of mind, liking, humor, mood, vein, bent, penchant, aptitude; geniality, cordiality, good will; alacrity, readiness, eagerness, enthusiasm; assent, compliance, agreement.

v be willing, incline, lean to, mind, hold to, cling to; desire; acquiesce, assent, comply; find one's way to, give it a shot, *(informal)* take a swing at, *(informal)* lay into.

adj willing, fain, favorable, content, well disposed; ready, earnest, eager, desirous; genial, cordial.

adv willingly, freely, with pleasure, with all one's heart, graciously.

603 unwillingness *n* indisposition, disinclination, reluctance, dislike; aversion, indifference, slowness, lack of readiness, obstinacy; scrupulousness, hesitation, qualm, shrinking, holding back, recoil; averseness, dissent, refusal.

v be unwilling, dislike; demur, hesitate, shrink from, swerve, recoil; dissent, refuse.

adj unwilling, loath, reluctant, averse; laggard, backward, slow, slack, indifferent; scrupulous, hesitant.

adv unwillingly, grudgingly, against one's will, under protest.

604 resolution *n* determination, will, decision, strength of mind, resolve, firmness, energy, manliness, vigor, resoluteness; pluck, zeal, devotion; self-control, self-command, self-possession, self-reliance, self-restraint, self-denial; tenacity, perseverance, obstinacy, *(informal)* gumption.

v be resolute, resolve, will, determine, decide, make a resolution, conclude, fix, bring to a crisis, take a decisive step; stand firm, insist upon, make a point of, not give an inch.

adj resolute, firm, steadfast, resolved, purposeful, fixed, inflexible, bold, game, indomitable, relentless, tenacious, gritty, stern, irrevocable, obstinate.

adv resolutely, in earnest, earnestly, manfully.

604a perseverance *n* persistence, tenacity, resolution, doggedness, determination, steadfastness, indefatigability, pluck, stamina, backbone.

v persevere, persist, continue, keep on, last, stick it out, hang in there.

adj persevering, constant, steady, steadfast, persistent, tenacious, resolute, dogged, indefatigable, indomitable, staunch, true, game, *(informal)* tough.

605 irresolution *n* indecision, indetermination, instability, uncertainty; hesitation, hesitancy, vacillation, oscillation, changeableness, fluctuation, fickleness, weakness, frailty, timidity, cowardice.

v be irresolute, dawdle, dilly-dally, shilly-shally, hesitate, falter, waver, vacillate, change, fluctuate, blow hot and cold.

adj irresolute, indecisive, indeterminate, unstable, uncertain; hesitant, changeable, capricious, fickle, frail, feeble, weak, timid, *(informal)* soft, cowardly.

606 obstinacy *n* doggedness, persistence, pertinacity, resolution, intractability, firmness, immovability, inflexibility, obduracy, willfulness, perversity, stubbornness, mulishness; uncontrollability, wildness.

fixed idea, *idée fixe*, fanaticism,

zealotry, infatuation, monomania; bigotry, intolerance, dogmatism.

bigot, dogmatist, zealot, fanatic.

v be obstinate, persist, die hard, fight, stick to an idea.

adj obstinate, dogged, persistent, pertinacious, resolute, intractable, firm, refractory, headstrong, willful, inflexible, immovable, perverse, stubborn, mulish, pig-headed; wayward, unruly, incorrigible, uncontrollable, wild; fanatic, zealous, monomaniacal; intolerant, dogmatic, arbitrary.

607 recantation *n* tergiversation, renunciation, abjuration, retraction, defection, apostasy, disavowal, revocation, reversal.

turncoat, apostate, renegade, deserter.

v recant, change one's mind, abjure, retract, renounce, disavow, revoke, defect, change sides.

adj changeful, irresolute, slippery, timeserving.

608 caprice *n* fancy, humor, whim, quirk, freak, fad, vagary, prank.

v be capricious.

adj capricious, erratic, eccentric, fitful, inconsistent, fanciful, whimsical, crotchety, freakish, wayward, wanton; contrary, captious, unreasonable, arbitrary, fickle; frivolous.

609 choice *n* selection, decision, pick, choosing, election, option, alternative, preference, predilection, desire.

v choose, select, elect, make a choice, prefer, pick, cull, decide.

adj optional, discretional, preferential.

609a neutrality, absence of choice *n* neutrality, indifference; indecision, irresolution.

no choice, first come first served.

v be neutral, have no preference, waive, abstain.

take what's offered.

adj neutral, indifferent; indecisive, irresolute.

610 rejection *n* refusal, repudiation, renunciation; exclusion, elimination.

v reject, refuse, repudiate, decline, deny, rebuff, repel, renounce; discard, throw away, exclude, eliminate; jettison.

611 predetermination *n* premeditation, predeliberation, foregone conclusion; resolve, intention; fate, predestination, destiny.

v predetermine, predestine, premeditate, resolve beforehand, calculate.

adj aforethought; foregone.

adv advisedly, deliberately, intentionally.

612 impulse *n* sudden thought, flash, spurt, inspiration, improvisation.

v improvise, extemporize; flash on, hit on, come up with, pull out of a hat, pull out of the air; say what comes to mind.

adj impulsive, impromptu, spontaneous; extemporaneous.

adv extempore, extemporaneously; impromptu, offhand, impulsively.

613 habit *n* addiction, disposition, tendency, bent, wont; custom, prescription, practice, way, usage, wont, manner; prevalence, observance; conventionalism, conventionality, mode, fashion, vogue, conformity; rule, precedent, routine, rut, groove.

v habituate, inure, harden, season; accustom, familiarize; acclimate, accommodate; cling to, adhere to, acquire a habit, fall into a rut; be habitual, come into use, become a habit, take root.

adj habitual, customary, prescriptive, usual, general, ordinary, common, frequent, everyday, familiar, trite, commonplace, conventional, regular, set, stock, fixed, permanent; prevalent, current, fashionable; addictive.

adv habitually, as usual, as things go, as the world goes; as a rule, for the most part, generally.

614 disuse *n* desuetude, disusage, lack of practice.

v be unaccustomed, break a habit; disuse.

adj unaccustomed; unusual, original.

615 motive *n* reason, ground, principle, mainspring, purpose, cause, occasion, influence, impulse, instigation, spur, stimulus, incitement, incentive, inducement, consideration, temptation, motivation; intention, ulterior motive.

v motivate, induce, move, inspire, put up to, prompt, stimulate, spur, excite, arouse, rouse, incite, instigate; influence, sway, incline, dispose, lead, persuade, prevail upon, enlist, engage, invite, court, tempt, charm.

adj suasive, persuasive, seductive, attractive, provocative.

615a absence of motive *n* caprice, chance, absence of design.

v have no motive.

adj capricious, without rhyme or reason.

adv capriciously.

616 dissuasion *n* expostulation, remonstrance, deprecation, discouragement, damper, restraint, curb, check.

v dissuade, cry out against, remonstrate, expostulate, warn, disincline, indispose, shake, discourage, dishearten, disenchant; deter, hold back, restrain, repel, turn aside, wean from, damp, cool, chill, blunt.

adj dissuasive.

617 [ostensible motive, ground, or reason] **plea** *n* pretext, allegation, excuse; pretense, shallow excuse, lame excuse, makeshift.

v plead, allege, excuse, make a pretext of, pretend.

adj ostensible, alleged.

adv ostensibly, under the pretense of.

618 good *n* benefit, interest, service, behalf, advantage, improvement, gain, boot, profit, harvest; boon, blessing, good luck, prize, good fortune, windfall, godsend; prosperity, happiness, goodness.

v benefit, serve, profit, advantage.

adj commendable; useful, good, beneficial, advantageous.

619 evil *n* ill, harm, hurt, mischief, nuisance; damage, loss; disadvantage, drawback; disaster, accident, casualty, mishap, misfortune; calamity, catastrophe, tragedy, ruin, destruction, adversity; mental suffering, pain, anguish; outrage, wrong, injury, foul play.

v be in trouble; harm, hurt, injure, ruin, destroy, torture.

adj evil, hurtful, injurious, harmful; disastrous, catastrophic, cataclysmic, tragic, ruinous.

620 intention *n* intent, purpose, project, undertaking, design, ambition, contemplation, view, proposal, meaning; object, aim, end, destination, mark, point, goal, target, prey, quarry, game; decision, determination, resolve, resolution, settled purpose.

v intend, mean, design, purpose, propose, contemplate, plan, expect, mediate, calculate, project, aim for, aim at, aspire at.

adj intentional, advised, express, determinate, bound for, bent upon, in view, in prospect.

adv intentionally, advisedly, wittingly, knowingly, purposely, on purpose, by design, pointedly; deliberately.

621 [absence of design] **chance** *n* destiny, lot, fate, luck, good luck, turn, (*informal*) break, (*informal*) jinx, fortune; speculation, venture, stake, shot in the dark, fluke; wager, gambling, betting.

gambler, gamester, adventurer.

v chance, chance it, tempt fate, speculate, risk, venture, hazard, stake, wager, bet, place a bet, gamble, play for.

adj unintentional, accidental, random; fortuitous, lucky; speculative, venturesome.

adv unintentionally, unwittingly.

622 pursuit *n* pursuance, enterprise, undertaking, business, adventure, essay, quest, search.

v pursue, prosecute, follow, do, engage in, undertake, endeavor, seek, aim at, fish for, press on, go after, chase.

adj in quest of, in pursuit of.

623 avoidance *n* evasion, flight, escape, retreat, recoil, departure; abstention, abstinence, forbearance, inaction.

avoider, shirker, quitter, truant; fugitive, refugee, runaway, deserter.

v avoid, shun, steer clear of, keep clear of, evade, elude, shirk, fly from, turn away from; abstain, refrain, eschew, leave alone, not get involved; shrink, hold back, retire, recoil, flinch, blink, shy, dodge, beat a retreat, turn tail, run for one's life, head for the hills, take flight, beat it out; desert, sneak off, shuffle off, slink away, steal away, slip, sneak, bolt, abscond.

adj elusive, evasive, escapist, fugitive.

624 relinquishment *n* surrender, resignation, yielding, waiver, waiving, abdication, leaving, desertion, withdrawal, secession, abandonment, renunciation.

v relinquish, surrender, give up, resign, yield, cede, waive, forswear, forgo, abdicate, leave, forsake, desert, renounce, quit, abandon, let go, resign, (*informal*) throw in the towel, call it quits, (*informal*) hang it up.

625 business *n* occupation, trade, craft, profession, calling, employment, vocation, pursuit; affair, matter, concern, transaction, undertaking; function, duty, office, position, part, role, capacity.

v employ oneself, undertake, turn one's hand to; be at work on, be engaged in, be occupied with.

adj businesslike; workaday, professional, official, functional; busy.

626 plan *n* scheme, plot, stratagem, policy, procedure, project, formula, method, system, organization, design, contrivance, device; drawing, sketch, draft, map, chart, diagram, representation; intrigue, cabal, conspiracy.

planner, designer, organizer, schemer, strategist, intriguer.

v plan, arrange, frame, scheme,

plot, design, devise, contrive, invent, concoct, hatch; project, forecast; systematize, organize, cast, recast, lay groundwork.

adj procedural, formulaic, methodological, systematic, organizational; conspiratorial; strategic.

627 [path] **method** *n* road, procedure, way, means, manner, fashion, technique, process, course, route, track, beat, tack; door, gateway, channel, passage, avenue, means of access, approach.

adv how, in what way, in what manner; by what mode; one way or another, after this fashion.

628 mid-course *n* middle way, middle course, mean, golden mean; compromise, (*informal*) six of one and half a dozen of another, half measures, neutrality.

v steer a middle course, go straight; compromise, go half way, make a compromise.

adj moderate, midway; neutral, impartial.

629 circuit *n* roundabout way, digression, detour, loop, winding.

v go round about, make a circuit, detour, wind around, circle around; deviate, digress.

adj circuitous, indirect, roundabout; zigzag.

adv in a roundabout way, by an indirect course, indirectly.

630 requirement *n* requisite, requisition, need, necessity, wants, claim, demand, prerequisite; mandate, order, command, directive, injunction, charge, claim, precept.

v require, need, call for, have occasion for, necessitate, obligate, demand, request, need, order, enjoin, direct, ask.

adj requisite, necessary, essential, indispensable, needful; urgent, exigent, instant, crying.

adv of necessity.

631 instrumentality *n* mediation, intervention, medium, intermedium, vehicle, hand; aid; subservience.

go-between, intermediary, minister.

v mediate, minister, intervene; be instrumental, aid.

adj instrumental, useful, serviceable; intermediary, intermediate.

adv through, by, whereby, thereby, by the agency of, by dint of, by means of.

632 means *n* resources, wherewithal, way, ways and means, know how, ability; agency, method, approach; capital, provisions.

v have the means, find the means, possess the means.

adj instrumental.

adv by means of; herewith, therewith; wherewithal.

633 instrument *n* tool, implement, utensil, machinery, equipment.

adj instrumental; mechanical.

634 substitute *n* deputy, alternate, understudy, stand-in, proxy, (*informal*) sub, replacement.

v to substitute for, sub.

635 materials *n* raw materials, resources, stuff, stock, staples, supplies.

636 store *n* stock, fund, mine, supply, reserve, reservoir, (*informal*) stash; accumulation, hoard, storing, storage.

v store, put aside, lay away; store up, put up, hoard away, accumulate, amass, garner; reserve, husband, (*informal*) stash, hold back.

adj in store, in reserve, spare.

637 provision *n* supply, grist, resources, store, provender, stock, food; catering, providing, purveying, purveyance, supplying.

v make provision, provide, lay in, lay in a stock, lay in a store; supply, furnish, purvey, provision, cater, stock, store, replenish.

638 waste *n* consumption, expenditure, dissipation, diminution, decline, emaciation, exhaustion, loss, destruction, decay, impairment; misuse, prodigality, wasting; ruin, devastation, spoliation, desolation.

v waste, consume, spend, throw out, expend, squander, misuse, misspend, dissipate; destroy, wear away, erode, eat away, reduce, wear down, exhaust, enfeeble, wear out.

adj wasteful, prodigal, spendthrift; destructive, wasted, gone to waste.

639 sufficiency *n* adequacy, enough, competence.

v be sufficient, suffice, do, just do, satisfy; have enough.

adj sufficient, enough, adequate, ample, up to the mark, competent, commensurate, satisfactory.

adv sufficiently, amply.

640 insufficiency *n* inadequacy, incompetence, incompleteness, deficiency, imperfection, shortcoming; paucity, scarcity, dearth; dole, pittance, emptiness, poorness, depletion, flaccidity.

v be insufficient, not suffice, not do, fall short of, (*informal*) not cut it; want, lack, need, require, be in want.

adj insufficient, inadequate, too little, not enough, incomplete, deficient, imperfect, wanting, short, scarce, meager, poor, thin, sparse, scant; incompetent, perfunctory.

641 redundance *n* superfluity, super-abundance, too much, too many, exuberance, profuseness, profusion, plenty, repletion, plethora, congestion, surfeit, overdose, overflow; excess, surplus; repetition, verbosity.

v superabound,   overabound, swarm, overflow, run over, run riot, overrun, overdose, overload, overdo, overwhelm; supersaturate, gorge, glut, load, drench, inundate, deluge, flood; choke, cloy, suffocate, pile on, lay on thick, lavish.

adj redundant, exuberant, inor-dinate, superabundant, excessive, over-much, replete, profuse, lavish; exor-bitant, extravagant, overweening, (*in-formal*) much; superfluous, unneces-sary, needless, over and above, spare, duplicate; repetitious, verbose.

adv over and above, over much, out of proportion, beyond bounds, over one's head.

642 importance *n* consequence, sub-stance, weight, moment, prominence, consideration, significance, import, concern, emphasis, interest, momen-tousness, weightiness; gravity, serious-ness, solemnity; pressure, urgency, stress.

v be important, deserve considera-tion, be worthy of notice, merit atten-tion; attach importance, ascribe imp-ortance, value, care for, set store by; import, signify, matter, boot, carry weight; accentuate, emphasize, lay stress on; mark, underline, underscore.

adj important, consequential, wei-ghty, momentous, prominent, con-siderable, significant, notable, salient; grave, serious, earnest, grand, solemn, impressive, commanding, imposing; urgent, pressing, critical, crucial, paramount, essential, vital, prime, primary, principal, all-important, capi-tal, foremost, of vital importance; superior, considerable; significant, telling, trenchant, emphatic.

643 unimportance *n* insignificance, immateriality, triviality, paltriness, indifference, nothing, trifling; trump-ery, trash, rubbish, frippery, chaff, bauble, trifle.

v be unimportant, not matter, matter little, signify little; make light of.

adj unimportant, of little account, of small importance, immaterial, unessential, nonessential, inconse-quential, insignificant, inconsiderable, so-so; commonplace, ordinary, un-eventful, mere, common; trifling, trivi-

al, slight, slender, light, flimsy, shal-low; frivolous, petty, niggling, pid-dling; poor, paltry, pitiful, sorry, mean, meager, shabby, beggarly, worthless, cheap, tawdry, trashy, gimmicky; unworthy of consideration, unworthy of notice; useless, of no account.

644 utility *n* usefulness, efficacy, hel-pfulness, service, use, stead, avail, help, aid; applicability, value, worth, pro-ductiveness.

v be useful, avail, serve, perform, help, aid, benefit; act a part, discharge a function, stand one in good stead.

adj useful, serviceable, functional, advantageous, valuable, productive, profitable, helpful, effectual, effective, efficacious, beneficial, salutary; ap-plicable, available, practical, practi-cable, workable.

645 inutility *n* uselessness, inefficacy, ineptitude, inaptitude, inadequacy, inefficiency, unfruitfulness, futility, worthlessness, hopelessness.

v be useless, be of no help.

adj useless, unavailing, futile, in-utile, fruitless, vain, ineffectual, profit-less, bootless, valueless, worthless, hopeless; unserviceable, unusable, inoperative.

646 expedience *n* expediency, fit-ness, utility, suitability, profitability, advisability, propriety, appropriate-ness, desirability; opportunism, prag-matism, realism.

v be expedient, suit, befit, suit the occasion.

adj expedient, advantageous, op-portune, fit, suitable, convenient, profitable, worthwhile, advisable, meet, proper, becoming, appropriate, desirable.

647 inexpedience *n* inexpediency, impropriety, unfitness, unsuitability, inappropriateness, undesirability; in-convenience, impracticality.

v be inexpedient, be inconvenient, hinder.

adj inexpedient, inopportune, unfit, unsuitable, disadvantageous, discommodious, unadvisable, unseem-ly, improper, unworkable, impractical, inconvenient, unprofitable, useless, worthless.

648 [good qualities] goodness *n* vir-tue, excellence, merit, value, worth; perfection, eminence, superiority, masterpiece, *chef d'oeuvre*, prime, flower, cream, elite, pick, pick of the litter, salt of the earth, *(informal)* A-1, *(informal)* tops, second to none; gem, jewel, treasure, one in a million; be-neficence.

v be good, excel, transcend, stand the test, pass muster, challenge comparison, vie, emulate, rival, (informal) dwarf the competition; be beneficial, do good, profit, benefit, improve, be the making of, do a world of good, produce a good effect, do a good turn.

adj good, excellent, better, superior, above par, fine, genuine, true; best, choice, select, rare, invaluable, priceless, inestimable, superlative, perfect, inimitable, first-rate, first-class, very best, crack, prime, tip-top, capital, (informal) tops; beneficial, valuable, advantageous, profitable, edifying, salutary, serviceable; favorable, propitious.

649 [bad qualities] **badness** n harmfulness, hurtfulness, virulence, painfulness, abomination, pestilence, guilt, depravity, vice, evil, malignity, malevolence; bane, plague, evil star, ill wind, bad omen, (informal) jinx, (informal) whammy; snake in the grass, skeleton in the closet, (informal) ghosts, (informal) demons; ill-treatment, annoyance, molestation, abuse, oppression, persecution, outrage, misusage, injury, damage.

v hurt, harm, injure, damage, pain; wrong, aggrieve, oppress, persecute, trample upon, tread upon, walk over, overburden, weigh down, run down; victimize, maltreat, molest, abuse, illuse, bruise, scratch, maul, smite, do violence, do harm, stab, pierce.

adj hurtful, harmful, baleful, injurious, deleterious, detrimental, noxious, pernicious, mischievous; oppressive, burdensome, onerous, malign, malevolent; virulent, venomous, corrosive, poisonous, deadly, destructive; bad, ill, dreadful, horrid, horrible, dire, rank, foul, rotten, as low as one can go, (informal) the pits; evil, wrong, reprehensible, hateful, abominable, detestable, execrable, damnable, infernal, diabolical, vile, base, villainous, cruel, mean, low; deplorable, wretched, sad, grievous, lamentable, pitiable, pitiful, woeful, painful.

650 perfection n ideal, summit, paragon, model, standard, pattern, mirror; impeccability, faultlessness, excellence; masterpiece, master stroke; transcendence, superiority.

v perfect, bring to perfection, ripen, mature, complete, finish; be perfect, transcend.

adj perfect, faultless, immaculate, spotless, unblemished, impeccable, exquisite, consummate; in perfect condition, sound, intact; best, model, standard, inimitable, beyond all praise.

651 imperfection n deficiency, inadequacy, insufficiency, immaturity; fault, defect, weak point, weak spot,

flaw, taint, blemish, weakness, shortcoming, drawback.

v be imperfect, have a defect, not pass muster, fall short.

adj imperfect, deficient, inadequate, insufficient, immature, defective, faulty, unsound, out of order, out of tune, warped, lame, frail, weak, crude, incomplete, below par, found wanting; indifferent, middling, ordinary, mediocre, average, so-so, tolerable, fair, passable, decent, not bad, bearable, better than nothing; inferior, secondary, second-rate, poor substitute.

652 cleanness n purity, purification, purgation, cleanliness; ablution, lavation; neatness, tidiness, orderliness; cathartic, purgative, laxative; detergent, disinfectant.

v clean, cleanse, purify, purge, expurgate, clarify, refine; wash, launder, scour, scrub, disinfect, fumigate, deodorize, ventilate; root out, clear out, sweep out, make a clean sweep of, start fresh; neaten, tidy up, order, put things in order.

adj clean, pure, immaculate, spotless, stainless, unsullied, sweet; neat, spruce, tidy, trim, kempt.

653 uncleanness n impurity, defilement, contamination, taint; decay, putrefaction, corruption, mold, mildew, rot, dry rot; squalor, slovenliness, filth, dirt, smut, grime, mud, mire, muck, quagmire, slime.

v be unclean, rot, putrefy, fester, rankle, reek, stink, mold, go bad; dirty, soil, tarnish, spot, smear, blot, blur, smudge, smirch; besmear, befoul, splash, stain, sully, pollute, defile, debase, contaminate, taint, corrupt.

adj unclean, dirty, filthy, grimy, soiled; dusty, smutty, sooty, slimy; slovenly, untidy, sluttish, dowdy, unkempt, unscoured, squalid; nasty, coarse, foul, impure, offensive, abominable, beastly, reeky, fetid; moldy, musty, moth-eaten, bad, gone bad, rancid, rotten, corrupt, putrid, carious, fecal; gory, bloody; gross.

654 health n soundness, well-being, vigor, good health, bloom, color, vitality, robust health.

v be in health, be healthy, bloom, flourish, feel fine, feel good.

adj healthy, healthful, in health, well, sound, hearty, hale, strong, hardy, robust, vigorous, fit as a fiddle, in top shape, chipper, (informal) all together.

655 disease n illness, sickness, ill health, ailment, infirmity, indisposition, complaint, disorder, malady;

delicacy, delicate condition, decline, deterioration, decay.

v ail, suffer, be affected with, droop, flag, languish, sicken, pine, gasp, waste away, fail; take sick, fall ill, come down with, contract a disease, catch a bug.

adj ill, sick, indisposed, not well, unwell, in poor health, in bad health, ailing, poorly, laid up, bed-ridden, out of sorts, under the weather, *(informal)* in bad shape; sickly, infirm, unsound, unhealthy, *(informal)* falling apart, weak, lame, decrepit; diseased, morbid, mangy, corrupt, contaminated, leprous.

656 salubrity *n* healthiness, healthfulness, wholesomeness.

v be salubrious, be good for, agree with.

adj salubrious, healthy, healthful, salutary, wholesome, sanitary, bracing, invigorating, benign, nutritious, tonic, hygienic.

657 insalubrity *n* unhealthiness, unsoundness.

v be unhealthy, not be good for, disagree with.

adj insalubrious, unhealthy, unwholesome, noxious, noisome, deleterious, pestilential, bad, harmful, virulent, venomous, poisonous, septic, toxic, deadly.

658 improvement *n* amelioration, amendment, emendation, correction, revision, reformation, restoration, repair, betterment, gain, advancement, elevation, increase, refinement, elaboration; acculturation, cultivation, civilization.

reformer, radical.

v improve, mend, amend, get better; ameliorate, better, amend, emend, correct, right, rectify, revise, reform, restore, repair; advance, progress, ascend, increase, fructify, ripen, mature; refine, enrich, elaborate; promote, cultivate, foster, enhance.

adj better, better off, all for the better; emendatory, corrective, reformative, restorative, improving, progressive, improved.

659 deterioration *n*, debasement, recession, retrogradation, degeneracy, degeneration, degradation, deprivation, depravity, retrogression; detriment, damage, loss, injury, impairment, contamination, spoilage, corruption, adulteration; decline, declension, senility, decrepitude, decadence, decay, dilapidation, falling off, wear and tear, erosion, corrosion, rottenness, blight, atrophy, collapse.

v deteriorate, degenerate, fall off, wane, ebb, decline, droop, go down,

go downhill, sink, go to seed, go to waste, lapse, break down, crack, shrivel, fade, wither, molder, rot, rankle, decay, go bad, rust, crumble, shake, totter, perish, die; taint, infect, contaminate, poison, canker, corrupt, pollute, vitiate, debase, degrade, adulterate; injure, impair, damage, harm, hurt, spoil, mar, despoil, dilapidate, waste, ravage; wound, maim, cripple, scotch, mangle, mutilate, disfigure, blemish, deface, warp; blight, rot, corrode, erode, wear away, wear out, sap, mine, undermine, shake the foundations of, break up, destroy, decimate.

adj deteriorated, unimproved, injured, degenerate, imperfect; battered, weathered, weather-beaten, all the worse for wear, stale, dilapidated, faded, shabby, threadbare, worn, far gone, *(informal)* had it; decayed, motheaten, worm-eaten, mildewed, rusty, moldy, seedy, time-worn, wasted, crumbling, moldering, rotten, blighted, tainted; decrepit, broken down, wornout, used up, out of commission, in a bad way, past cure, past hope, *(informal)* long gone.

660 restoration *n* reestablishment, replacement, reinstatement, renewal, rehabilitation, reconstruction, reproduction, rebuilding, renovation, revival; refreshment, resuscitation, revivification; renaissance, renascence, new birth, regeneration, reconversion; redress, retrieval, reclamation, recovery, resumption; repair, reparation, restitution, relief, deliverance, rectification, cure, healing; redemption.

v restore, recover, rally, revive, come round, pull through, get well, get over; reestablish, replace, rehabilitate, reinstate; reconstruct, rebuild, reproduce, reorganize, reconstitute, renew, renovate; redeem, reclaim, recover, retrieve, rescue, deliver; redress, recure; cure, heal, remedy, doctor, bring round; resuscitate, revive, reanimate, revivify, reinvigorate, refresh; recoup, make good, square, set to rights, correct, put in order; repair, retouch, patch up, fix.

adj restorative, recuperative, curative, remedial; restorable, remediable, retrievable, curable; restored, convalescent, renascent, reborn.

661 relapse *n* lapse, falling back, retrogradation, deterioration, backsliding.

v relapse, lapse, fall back, slip back, sink back, suffer a relapse, fall again.

adj retrograde.

662 remedy *n* help, redress, solution, answer, panacea; cure, relief, medicine, treatment, restorative, specific, medication, ointment, balm; antidote, corrective, antitoxin, counteractive.

doctor, physician, surgeon.

v remedy, cure, heal, set right, put right, doctor, nurse, restore, recondition, repair, redress; counteract, remove, correct, right, solve.

adj remedial, restorative, corrective, palliative; medicinal, therapeutic, curative; soluble.

663 bane *n* curse, evil, plague, scourge, pain, nuisance, thorn in the side, pain in the neck; poison, virus, venom; fungus, mildew, dry rot, canker, cancer; sting, fang, thorn, bramble, briar, nettle.

adj baneful, bad, sinister, pernicious, evil, baleful, poisonous, venomous, ruinous, unwholesome, harmful, deadly.

664 safety *n* security, surety, impregnability, invulnerability; safeguard, safety valve, precaution, custody, safe keeping, preservation, protection.

protector, guardian, warden, preserver, custodian, watchdog, sentinel, scout.

v be safe; protect, take care of, care for, preserve, cover, screen, shelter, shroud, guard, defend, secure, house, garrison; watch, patrol, look out, take precautions.

adj safe, secure, snug, warm, sure, sound, on the safe side, out of danger; dependable, trustworthy, sure, reliable; cautious, wary, careful, defensible, tenable, invulnerable, impregnable, unassailable, safe and sound.

665 danger *n* hazard, insecurity, instability, precariousness, slipperiness, risk, peril, jeopardy, liability, exposure; injury, evil; warning, alarm, apprehension.

v be in danger, run into trouble, lay oneself open to, hang by a thread, totter; endanger, expose to danger, imperil, jeopardize, adventure, venture, risk, hazard threaten.

adj dangerous, hazardous, risky, perilous, precarious, unsafe, insecure, unstable, untrustworthy, unsteady, shaky, slippery, ominous, fearful, explosive, fraught with danger, defenseless, vulnerable, open, liable.

666 refuge *n* sanctuary, retreat, asylum, hiding place, stronghold, fortress, shelter, cover; anchor, mainstay, support, check, last resort, safeguard.

v seek refuge, take refuge, find refuge, take shelter, find safety.

667 pitfall *n* snare, trap, snag, ambush, snake in the grass, wolf in sheep's clothing, menace, complication, danger; slippery ground, weak foundation, rocks, reefs, sunken rocks, sand, quick-

sand, breakers, shoals, shallows, precipice, maelstrom.

668 warning *n* caution, notice, premonition, prediction, admonition, advice, lesson; alarm, omen, sign, signal, augury, portent, presage.

sentinel, sentry, watch, watchman, watchdog, patrol, scout, spy.

v warn, caution, admonish, forewarn; give notice, notify, appraise, inform; menace, threaten, portend.

adj premonitory, cautionary, advisory; ominous, portentous.

669 [indication of danger] **alarm** *n* alarum, alarm bell, tocsin, distress signal, siren, danger signal, hue and cry, SOS, cry, scream.

v alarm, sound the alarm, warn, cry out.

670 preservation *n* safekeeping, conservation; guarding, safeguard, shelter, protection, defense; maintenance, support, sustenance, continuance, retention, salvation.

v preserve, keep, conserve; guard, safeguard, shelter, shield, protect, defend, rescue; keep up, maintain, continue, support, uphold, sustain; retain; store, husband; cure, pickle, bottle, can.

adj preserved, unimpaired, uninjured, unhurt, safe, sound, intact, conservative, preservative.

671 escape *n* flight, evasion, loophole, retreat; reprieve, release, liberation; narrow escape, close call, near miss.

v escape, flee, abscond, fly, steal away, run away, *(informal)* take off, *(informal)* split, shun, fly, elude, evade, avoid.

adj stolen away, fled, *(informal)* cut out.

672 deliverance *n* extrication, disentanglement, rescue, reprieve, respite; liberation, release, emancipation, freedom; redemption, salvation.

v deliver, extricate, disentangle, rescue, reprieve, save, redeem; set free, liberate, release, emancipate, free; come to the rescue.

673 preparation *n* provision, plan, arrangement, anticipation, precaution, forecast, rehearsal; groundwork, homework, foundation, scaffolding; training, education, dissemination; readiness, ripeness, maturity.

v prepare, get ready, make ready, prime, arrange, make preparations, plan, devise, anticipate, lay the foundations, provide, order; mature, ripen, mellow, season, nurture; equip, arm, fit out, furnish; train, teach, prepare for, rehearse, make provision for, take steps, provide against.

adj prepatory, precautionary, provident, preparative, preparatory; provisional, preliminary; prepared, ready, available, all ready, handy; ripe, mature, mellow.

674 nonpreparation *n* unpreparedness, unreadiness; improvidence.

v be unprepared; extemporize, improvise.

adj unprepared, incomplete, premature, rudimental, embryonic, immature, unripe, raw, green, coarse, crude, rough, unhewn, untaught, fallow, unready; out of order, nonfunctional, *(informal)* on the fritz, in disrepair, *(informal)* out of whack; shiftless, improvident, thoughtless, careless, slack, remiss, happy-go-lucky.

675 essay *n* trial, endeavor, effort, attempt, struggle, venture, adventure, speculation, experiment.

v essay, try, experiment; endeavor, strive, strain, attempt, venture, adventure, speculate, tempt fortune, *(informal)* give it a go, *(informal)* take a shot at.

adj experimental, tentative, probationary; venturesome, adventurous, speculative.

adv èxperimentally, on trial.

676 undertaking *n* task, job, venture, engagement, compact, contract, enterprise; pilgrimage, quest.

v undertake, engage in, embark on, launch into, plunge into, volunteer; engage, promise, contract, take upon onself, devote onself to, determine, take up, take in hand; tackle, set about, fall to, begin, broach.

677 use *n* employ, exercise, application, appliance; disposal; consumption; agency, usefulness; benefit, recourse, resort, avail; utilization, utility, service, wear; usage.

v use, make use of, employ, put to use, put into operation, apply, set in motion, set to work; ply, work, wield, handle, manipulate; exert, exercise, practice, avail oneself of, profit by; resort to, have recourse to, recur to, take up, try; utilize, bring into play, press into service; use up, consume, expend, tax, task, wear.

adj useful, instrumental, utilitarian, subservient, employable, applicable, beneficial.

678 disuse *n* forbearance, abstinence; relinquishment, abandonment; desuetude.

v not use, do without, dispense with, let alone, forbear, abstain, spare,

waive, neglect; keep back, reserve; disuse, lay up, shelve, set aside, put aside, leave off, have done with; supersede, discard, throw aside, relinquish, dismantle.

adj not in use, unemployed, unapplied; disused, unused, done with.

679 misuse *n* misusage, misemployment, misapplication, misappropriation; abuse, profanation, prostitution, desecration; waste.

v misuse, misemploy, misapply, misappropriate; abuse, profane, prostitute, desecrate; waste, squander, destroy; overwork, overtask, overtax.

680 action *n* movement, work, labor, performance, moving, working, performing, operation; deed, act, feat, exploit; conduct, behavior, procedure, execution; energetic activity, exercise, exertion, energy, effort; affair, encounter, meeting, engagement, conflict, combat, fight, battle.

actor, doer, worker.

v act, do, perform, execute, achieve, transact, enact; commit, perpetrate, inflict; exercise, prosecute, carry on, work, function, labor, operate, exert energy, be active; behave, conduct oneself, comport oneself; play, feign, fake, imitate.

· *adj* in action, in operation, operative.

681 inaction *n* passivity, inactivity, idleness, slothfulness; waiting; mulling around, killing time; rest, repose.

v not act, not do, be inactive, abstain from doing, do nothing, let alone, let things take their course; stand aloof, refrain, pause, wait, bide one's time, cool one's heels, waste time, lie idle.

adj inactive, passive, idle, slothful; out of work.

682 activity *n* movement, hustle, bustle, stir, fuss, flurry, action, business; industry, assiduity, assiduousness, laboriousness, drudgery; diligence, perseverance, vigilance, wakefulness, restlessness, fidgetiness; briskness, liveliness, animation, life, vivacity, spirit, dash, energy; eagerness, zeal, ardor, vigor, abandon, exertion; earnestness, intentness, devotion.

v be active, busy oneself in, stir about, rouse oneself, speed, hasten, bustle, fuss, *(informal)* raise a ruckus; push, push ahead, *(informal)* step on it, *(informal)* move it, make progress; toil, plod, persist, persevere, hustle, *(informal)* hustle it, *(informal)* push; look sharp, keep moving, seize the opportunity, *carpe diem*, lose no time, dash off, make haste; have a hand in, trouble oneself about.

adj active, brisk, lively, busy as a bee, vivacious, alive, frisky; quick, prompt, ready, alert, spry, sharp, smart, awake, wide awake, eager, zealous; industrious, assiduous, diligent, vigilant; businesslike; restless, fussy, fidgety, busy.

683 inactivity *n* inaction, inertness, lull, quiescence; idleness, remissness, sloth, indolence, dawdling, laziness; dullness, languor, sluggishness, torpor, stupor, lethargy; procrastination.

idler, drone, dawdler, moper, lounger, loafer, sluggard, laggard, slumberer.

v be inactive, do nothing, dawdle, lag, hang back, slouch, loll, lounge, loaf, loiter, take it easy; fritter away time, idle, piddle, putter, dabble, dally, dilly-dally; languish, flag, relax; kill time, waste time.

adj inactive, motionless; indolent, lazy, slothful, idle, remiss, slack, inert, torpid, sluggish, languid, supine, heavy, dull, listless; laggard, slow, rusty, lackadaisical, irresolute; drowsy, lethargic, soporific, dreamy, dreamy-eyed.

684 haste *n* urgency, need, hurry, flurry, bustle, spurt, rush, dash, scramble, bustle, ado, precipitancy, precipitation; swiftness, celerity, alacrity, quickness, rapidity, dispatch, speed, expedition, promptitude, timeliness, promptness.

v haste, hasten, make haste, hurry, dash, push on, press on, press forward, scurry, bustle, scramble, rush, accelerate, urge, expedite, quicken, speed, precipitate, dispatch.

adj hasty, speedy, quick, hurried, swift, rapid, fast, fleet, brisk; precipitate, rash, foolhardy, reckless, indiscreet, thoughtless, headlong; testy, touchy, irascible, petulant, waspish, fretful, fiery, excitable, irritable, peevish.

685 leisure *n* spare time, free time, convenience, liberty, pause, stay, halt, lull, breather, (*informal*) letup, breathing spell, break, (*informal*) time out; interlude, vacation, holiday.

v have leisure, take one's time; rest, relax, repose.

adj leisure, spare, free; leisurely, slow, deliberate, quiet, calm, restful, peaceful, languid, easy, gradual.

686 exertion *n* effort, action, activity, endeavor, struggle, attempt, strain, trial, stress; labor, work, toil, travail; trouble, pain; energy.

v exert, exert oneself, labor, work, toil, sweat, drudge, strive, strain; work hard, rough it, buckle to, take pains, concentrate, spare no effort.

adj laborious, wearisome, burdensome, (*informal*) tough, (*informal*) rough, strenuous, herculean, Sisyphean.

687 repose *n* rest, sleep, slumber; relaxation, breathing spell; halt, pause, respite, cessation; day of rest, Sabbath; holiday, vacation, recess.

v repose, rest; relax, unbend, slacken, catch one's breath, get one's wind, take a breather, pause; recline, lie down, go to bed, take a nap, go to sleep; take a holiday, go on vacation, shut up shop.

adj reposing, resting.

adv at rest.

688 fatigue *n* weariness, lassitude, tiredness, exhaustion, faintness; ennui, boredom, tedium, languor, yawning, drowsiness.

v be fatigued, yawn, droop, sink, flag, (*informal*) give out; gasp, pant, puff, blow, drop, swoon, faint; fatigue, tire, weary, exhaust, wear out; tax, task, strain; bore, tire, irritate, annoy.

adj fatigued, weary, drowsy, haggard, faint, exhausted, spent, tired, tired to death, worn out, (*informal*) gone; breathless.

689 refreshment *n* recovery of strength, restoration, revival, repair, relief.

v refresh, brace, strengthen, reinvigorate, revive, stimulate, freshen, cheer, enliven, reanimate; restore, repair, renew.

adj refreshing, restoring.

690 agent *n* doer, actor, performer, perpetrator, operator; practitioner, executioner, executor, executrix, minister, representative, deputy, servant, worker; participant, party to.

691 workshop *n* laboratory, factory, mill, mint, forge, studio; hive, beehive, seat of activity.

692 conduct *n* behavior, demeanor, action, actions, deportment, bearing, carriage, mien, manners; process, ways, practice, procedure, method; policy, tactics, strategy, plan; direction, management, execution, guidance, leadership, administration.

v conduct, behave, deport, act, bear; transact, execute, dispatch, discharge, proceed with, enact; direct, manage, carry on, supervise, regulate, administer, guide, lead.

adj procedural, practical, methodical, tactical, strategical, businesslike; directive, managerial, administrative, executive.

693 direction *n* guidance, advice, regulation, conduct, management, disposition, supervision, auspices, steerage, stewardship, ministration, administration, control, leadership, government, rule, command; order, command, instruction.

v direct, guide, advise, regulate, conduct, manage, control, dispose, supervise, overlook, steer, steward, pilot, minister, administer, legislate, lead, rule, govern, have charge of, command; order, instruct, prescribe.

adj directing, guiding, supervisory, managing, administering.

694 director *n* manager, governor, controller, superintendent, supervisor, overseer, inspector, foreman, surveyor, taskmaster, master, leader, boss; adviser, guide, pilot, captain, helmsman, driver; head, chief, principal, president, minister, official, functionary.

695 advice *n* counsel, opinion, recommendation, guidance, suggestion, persuasion, urging, exhortation; instruction, charge, injunction; admonition, warning, caution.

adviser, council, counselor, mentor.

v advise, give counsel to, suggest, recommend, prescribe, advocate, exhort, persuade; enjoin, enforce, charge, instruct; admonish, caution, warn; take counsel, confer, deliberate, discuss, consult, refer to; give counsel, offer counsel.

adj advisory, suggestive, persuasive, suasive; admonitory.

696 council *n* committee, court, chamber, cabinet, board, board of directors, advisory board, staff, syndicate, chapter; assembly, caucus, conclave, meeting, conference, session.

697 precept *n* direction, instruction, charge, prescript, prescription; golden rule, maxim, canon, law, code, act, statute, regulation, formula, form, technicality, rubric; order, command.

698 skill *n* skillfulness, dexterity, adroitness, expertness, proficiency, competence, facility, knack, mastery; accomplishment, acquirement, attainment, ability, craft; knowledge, wisdom, *savoir faire*, tact, wit, sagacity, discretion, finesse, craftiness, cunning; management; cleverness, ingenuity, capacity, talent, talents, faculty, endowment, *forte*, turn, gift, genius; intelligence, sharpness, readiness, invention, inventiveness, aptness, aptitude, proclivity, capacity for, genius for; felicity, capability, qualification.

v be skillful, excel in, be master of, have a knack for; take advantage of.

adj skillful, dextrous, adroit, adept, expert, apt, handy, quick, deft, proficient, masterly, crack, first-rate, conversant; skilled, experienced, practiced, competent, efficient, qualified, capable, fit, fit for, trained, prepared, finished; clever, able, ingenious, felicitous, inventive; shrewd, sharp, smart, intelligent, cunning, tactful, discreet, wise, knowledgeable.

adv skillfully, artistically, with consummate skill.

699 unskillfulness *n* want of skill, incompetence, inability, inexpertness, maladroitness, ineptitude, clumsiness, awkwardness, carelessness, bumbling, bungling; indiscretion.

v be unskillful, blunder, bungle, boggle, fumble, botch, stumble.

adj unskillful, unskilled, inexpert, incompetent, unable, inapt, bungling, inept, maladroit, awkward, clumsy, gawky; unfit, ill-qualified, unhandy, not conversant; raw, rusty, out of practice.

700 expert *n* specialist, authority, master, professional, connoisseur, veteran, old hand, old soldier; genius, mastermind, wizard, prodigy, *(informal)* pro.

701 bungler *n* blunderer, blunderhead, fumbler, duffer, clown, *(informal)* turkey, butter-fingers, greenhorn, amateur, rookie, novice, *(informal)* Sunday driver, *(informal)* armchair quarterback.

702 cunning *n* craftiness, skillfulness, shrewdness, artfulness, wiliness, subtlety, finesse, artifice, device, stratagem, intrigue, craft, guile, chicanery, duplicity, subterfuge, deceit, deceitfulness, slyness, deception; ability, skill, adroitness, expertness.

v be cunning, maneuver, contrive, manipulate, intrigue, finesse, surprise.

adj crafty, shrewd, artful, wily, subtle, tricky, foxy, politic, insidious, stealthy, Machiavellian, deceitful, duplicitous, sly, deceptive; canny, astute; ingenious, clever, skillful, sharp.

703 artlessness *n* simplicity, innocence, naivete, unworldliness, inexperience, inexposure, plainness, plain speaking, sincerity, honesty, openness, candor, matter of factness, bluntness.

v be artless, speak one's mind, come to the point, pull no punches.

adj artless, natural, simple, innocent, naive, childlike, unsuspicious, unworldly, unartificial, plain; sincere, frank, open, candid, honest, ingenuous, guileless, straightforward, aboveboard, point-blank, plain spoken, outspoken, blunt, direct, matter of fact.

adv in plain English, in simple words, without mincing words.

704 difficulty *n* dilemma, predicament, quandary, fix, exigency, emergency, crisis, trouble, problem, scrape, entanglement, strait, pass, pinch; reluctance, unwillingness, obstinacy, stubbornness; demur, objection, obstacle; labor, task, hard task, herculean task.

v be difficult, pose, perplex, bother, nonplus, hinder; encumber, embarrass, entangle.

adj difficult, hard, arduous, troublesome, irksome, laborious, formidable; awkward, unwieldy, unmanageable; fastidious, particular, stubborn, intractable, perverse; obscure, complex, intricate, delicate, uncertain, ticklish, critical; unfeasible, impractical, impossible, hopeless; austere, rigid.

705 facility *n* ease, easiness, capability, feasibility, practicability; flexibility, pliancy, smoothness, child's play.

v be easy, run smoothly, work well; facilitate, smooth, ease, lighten, free, clear, disencumber, disentangle, extricate, unravel.

adj easy, facile; feasible, practicable, within reach, accessible; manageable, tractable, pliant, smooth.

adv easily, readily, smoothly.

706 hindrance *n* impediment, deterrent, hitch, encumbrance, obstruction, check, stricture, restraint, hobble, obstacle, stumbling block; interruption, interference; impeding, stopping, stoppage, preventing.

v hinder, interrupt, check, impede, retard, encumber, delay, hamper, obstruct, trammel, cramp, handicap; block, thwart, frustrate, disconcert, prevent.

adj obstructive, intrusive; onerous, burdensome, cumbersome, obtrusive.

707 aid *n* help, support, succor, assistance, service, furtherance; relief, rescue, charity; assistant, helper, supporter, servant; patronage, championship, advocacy, favor, interest.

v aid, support, help, succor, assist, serve, abet, back, second; spell, relieve, rescue; sustain, uphold, prop, hold up, bolster; promote, facilitate, ease, advocate; be of help, give help, give assistance, oblige, accommodate, humor, encourage.

adj aiding, auxiliary, helpful, supportive; charitable; friendly, amicable, well-disposed, neighborly.

708 opposition *n* antagonism, hostility, resistance, counteraction; competition, enemy, foe, adversary, antagonist; opposing, resisting, combating.

v oppose, resist, combat, withstand, thwart, confront, contravene, interfere; hinder, obstruct, prevent, check; contradict, gainsay, deny, refuse, dissent.

adj adverse, antagonistic, contrary, at variance, at odds, anti, at issue, in opposition; unfavorable, unfriendly, hostile, inimical, resistant.

adv against, versus, counter to, in conflict with, at cross purposes; in spite, in defiance.

709 cooperation *n* concert, concurrence, agreement, concord, togetherness, harmony, unanimity; complicity, collusion, participation, combination, union, team-work; association, partnership, alliance, pool, coalition, confederation, fusion, fellowship, fraternity; unanimity, partisanship, spirit, party spirit, *esprit de corps.*

v cooperate, concur, combine, unite, pool, share, band together, pull together; act in concert, join forces, fraternize, conspire, be in league with; side with, go along with, join hands with, throw in one's lot with, rally round; participate, have a hand in.

adj cooperating, cooperative, participatory; in league, party to.

adv cooperatively, unanimously, shoulder to shoulder.

710 opponent *n* adversary, antagonist, competitor, rival, opposition; enemy, foe.

711 auxiliary *n* helper, aid, ally, assistant, confederate, collaborator, colleague, associate, partner, mate, friend.

712 party *n* group, gathering, assembly, assemblage, company, crew, band; clan, family, fellowship, community; body, faction, side, circle, clique, set, gang, claque, coterie, combination, ring, league, alliance, association.

v unite, join, band together, cooperate, assemble.

adj clannish, cliquish, communal, familial, fraternal.

713 discord *n* dissidence, dissonance, disagreement, clash, shock; variance, difference, dissension, misunderstanding, cross-purposes, odds, division, split, rupture, disruption, breach, schism, feud, conflict, struggle, argument, contention, quarrel, dispute, tiff, squabble, altercation, words; strife, outbreak.

v be discordant, disagree, clash, jar, conflict, differ, dissent, fall out, quarrel, dispute, squabble, wrangle, bicker, have words with; split, break, disunite, feud.

adj discordant, dissident, dissonant; divisive, disruptive; contentious, argumentative, quarrelsome, disputatious, fractious; at variance, at cross purposes.

714 concord *n* accord, harmony, sympathy, agreement, union, unison, unity, peace; amity, friendship, alliance, *detente*, understanding, togetherness, conciliation.

v agree, accord, harmonize with, fraternize, understand one another, concur, pull together; side with, sympathize with.

adj concordant, congenial, in accord; harmonious, sympathetic, friendly, fraternal, conciliatory.

adv with one voice, unanimously, in concert with.

715 defiance *n* daring, courage, courageousness, bravery, boldness; assertiveness, aggressiveness; antagonism, insubordination, recalcitrance, rebelliousness, insolence, resistance.

v defy, challenge, resist, dare, brave, flout, scorn, despise.

adj defiant, daring, courageous, brave, bold; resistant, insolent, rebellious, recalcitrant, contumacious, insubordinate, antagonistic.

adv in the face of, under one's very nose.

716 attack *n* onslaught, assault, offense, battery, onset, charge, encounter, aggression, incursion, invasion, sally, sortie, raid, foray; criticism, blame, censure, abuse.

assailant, aggressor, invader, attacker.

v assail, assault, molest, threaten, storm, charge, set upon, invade, bombard, beset, besiege, lay siege, storm; criticize, impugn, blame, censure, abuse; declare war, begin hostilities.

adj aggressive, offensive; critical, abusive.

adv on the offensive.

717 defense *n* guard, garrison, fortification, shield, shelter, screen, preservation, protection, guardianship, safeguard, security; justification, pleading, vindication.

v defend, guard, fortify, shield, shelter, screen, preserve, protect, keep safe, guard against, watch over, safeguard, secure; parry, repel, put to flight; uphold, maintain, justify, vindicate.

adj defensive, protective.

718 retaliation *n* reprisal, requital, retort, counterstroke, counterattack, retribution, reciprocation, reciprocity, recrimination, revenge, vengeance, reaction.

v retaliate, requite, retort, counterattack, revenge, repay, return, avenge.

adj retaliatory, vengeful, revengeful, retributive, reciprocal, reactive.

adv in retaliation.

719 resistance *n* opposition, withstanding, front, stand, oppugnance, reluctance, repulsion; interference, friction; insurrection, insurgence, rebellion.

v resist, withstand, stand up, stand; confront, oppose, grapple with, rise up, revolt, rebel, repel, repulse.

adj resistant, refractory, recalcitrant, repulsive, repellent; stubborn, indomitable, obstinate.

720 contention *n* struggling, struggle, strife, discord, dissention, quarrel, disagreement, squabble, feud; rupture, break, falling out; opposition, belligerency, combat, conflict, competition, rivalry, contest; disagreement, dissension, debate, wrangle, altercation, dispute, argument, controversy.

v contend, struggle, strive, fight, battle, combat, vie, compete, rival; debate, dispute, argue, wrangle; assert, maintain, claim.

adj contentious, combative, belligerent, bellicose, warlike, quarrelsome, pugnacious; competitive.

721 peace *n* treaty, truce, accord, amity, harmony, concord; calm, quiet, tranquillity, peacefulness, calmness; order, security.

v be at peace; keep the peace; make peace.

adj peaceful, tranquil, placid, serene, calm, complacent; mellow, halcyon, pacific; peaceable, amicable, friendly, amiable, mild, gentle.

722 warfare *n* fighting, hostilities, war, combat, battle, ordeal; tactics, strategy, generalship.

v war, make war, wage war, fight, give fight, battle, do battle, combat, contend, cross swords.

adj warlike, contentious, belligerent, combative, bellicose, martial, military, militant.

adv to arms.

723 pacification *n* conciliation, reconciliation, accommodation, arrangement, adjustment, compromise; amnesty, peace offering, truce, armistice, suspension of hostilities.

v pacify, reconcile, propitiate, placate, conciliate, accommodate, appease, make peace; quiet, calm, tranquilize, assuage, still, smooth, moderate, ameliorate, mollify, meliorate, soothe, bury the hatchet.

adj pacific, conciliatory.

724 mediation *n* negotiation, arbitration, parley; intervention, intercession, interposition.

mediator, arbiter, arbitrator, peacemaker, go-between, negotiator, moderator, diplomat.

v mediate, intercede, intervene, interpose, interfere; step in, negotiate, arbitrate.

adj mediatory.

725 submission *n* nonresistance, obedience, compliance, acquiescence, yielding, submissiveness, pliancy; surrender, cessation, capitulation; resignation, passivity, docility.

v succumb, submit, yield, bend, acquiesce, resign, agree, obey, comply, bow, surrender, capitulate.

adj submissive, obedient, compliant, acquiescent, passive, docile, tame, humble.

726 combatant *n* fighter, contestant, disputant, battler, litigant, contender, competitor, militarist, soldier, warrior, polemic, candidate; antagonist, foe, enemy, opponent, rival, adversary, assailant, opposition, assailer, assailant, assaulter, opposer, opponent.

727 arms *n* weapons, weaponry, armaments, armor, ammunition, munitions, deadly weapons.

v arm, outfit, ready for battle, prepare for battle.

728 arena *n* battleground, battlefield, field of battle, theater, ring, lists; playhouse, amphitheater, stage, boards; Colosseum, gymnasium, playing field.

729 completion *n* culmination, finish, conclusion, close, termination, end, finale; upshot, result; final touch, crowning touch; consummation, accomplishment, achievement, fulfillment; performance, execution; perfection, thoroughness.

v complete, finish, end, conclude, close, terminate, finalize; consummate, perfect, accomplish, do, fulfill, achieve, effect, execute, enact, dispatch, discharge.

adj whole, entire, full, intact, unbroken, one, perfect; done, consummate, perfect, thorough, through-and-through.

adv completely, thoroughly; perfectly.

730 noncompletion *n* incompleteness, nonfulfilment, nonperformance; neglect, shortcoming.

v not complete, leave unfinished, leave undone; neglect, let alone, let slip; fall short of.

adj incomplete, unfinished, sketchy.

731 success *n* progress, advance; hit, stroke, trump card; good fortune, good luck, luck, break; prosperity, achievement, fulfillment, accomplishment; ascendancy, mastery, conquest, victory, triumph; proficiency, skill, mastery.

v succeed, attain an end, secure an objective; progress, advance; accomplish, achieve, effect, complete; prosper, find fulfillment, fulfill oneself; master, conquer, triumph, surmount, overcome.

adj successful, prosperous, well-to-do; victorious, triumphant; masterful, proficient.

adv successfully, with flying colors, in triumph.

732 failure *n* unsuccessfulness, miscarriage, abortion, failing; neglect, omission, dereliction, non-performance; deficiency, insufficiency, defectiveness; blunder, mistake, fault, slip, mishap, scrape, mess, fiasco, breakdown; decline, decay, deterioration, loss; bankruptcy, insolvency, bust, dud.

v fail, come short, fall short, disappoint, miss the mark, miscarry, abort, blunder, botch, make a mess of, *(informal)* blow it, founder, flounder, sink, go amiss, go wrong, go hard with; fall off, dwindle, decline, fade, weaken, wane, give out, cease; desert, forsake.

adj unsuccessful, abortive, stillborn, fruitless, bootless, ineffectual, inefficient, insufficient, useless, lost, undone, bankrupt; wide of the mark, erroneous; frustrated, thwarted, foiled, defeated; defective, faulty.

adv unsuccessfully, in vain, to little purpose.

733 trophy *n* medal, prize, palm, laurel, honor, accolade, decoration, reward, recognition, triumph, celebration.

734 prosperity *n* well-being, success, fortune, wealth, affluence.

v prosper, thrive, flourish, rise, make one's way, flower, grow, blossom, bloom, fructify, succeed, *(informal)* make it.

adj prosperous, successful, wealthy, rich, well-to-do, well-off; favorable, propitious, fortunate, lucky, auspicious, golden, bright.

735 adversity *n* calamity, distress, catastrophe, crisis, disaster, failure; bad luck, hard times, misfortune, *(informal)* downers, *(informal)* bummers, trouble, hardship, pressure, affliction, wretchedness.

v go downhill, go to the dogs, decay, sink, decline, come to grief, *(informal)* hit the pits, fall on evil days.

adj adverse, unfavorable, unlucky, unfortunate; calamitous, disastrous, critical, dire, catastrophic; unprosperous, hapless, in a bad way, under a cloud, in adverse circumstances, down in the mouth.

adv adversely; if worst comes to worst.

736 mediocrity *n* average capacity, ordinariness, commonplaceness, insignificance, passableness, tolerableness, indifference, inferiority, paltriness, triviality; moderation, golden mean.

v jog on, get along.

adj mediocre, average, normal, ordinary, commonplace, run-of-the-mill, insignificant, tolerable, unimportant, indifferent, inferior, poor, slight, paltry; moderate, reasonable, temperate, respectable.

II. Intersocial Volition

737 authority *n* control, influence, jurisdiction, command, rule, sway, power, dominion, supremacy; expert, adjudicator, arbiter, judge, sovereign, ruler; warrant, justification, permit, permission, sanction, liberty, authorization.

v authorize, empower, commission, allow, permit, sanction, approve; warrant, justify, legalize, support, back; rule, sway, control, administer, govern.

adj authoritative, peremptory, magisterial, imperative, dogmatic, masterful; executive, administrative, sovereign, regnant, supreme, dominant, paramount, predominant, preponderant, influential, official, decisive, valid, absolute.

738 [absence of authority] **laxity** *n* laxness, looseness, slackness, lenience, toleration, relaxation, loosening, licence, freedom.

v be lax, tolerate, relax, give a free rein.

adj lax, loose, slack, remiss, lenient, negligent, careless, weak.

739 severity *n* seriousness, gravity, sternness, harshness, austerity, rigidity, rigorousness, strictness, stringency, relentlessness, abruptness, curtness; arbitrariness, absolutism, despotism, dictatorship, autocracy, tyranny, oppression; strength, force, brute force, coercion.

tyrant, disciplinarian, despot, taskmaster, oppressor, inquisitor.

v be severe, tyrannize, domineer, dominate, bully, inflict, wreak, be hard on, ill-treat, maltreat, oppress, trample on, crush, coerce.

adj severe, serious, grave, stern, harsh, austere, rigid, stiff, dour, rigorous, strict, strait-laced, stringent, relentless, hard, inexorable, abrupt, peremptory, curt, short; arbitrary, absolute, despotic, dictatorial, autocratic, tyrannical, oppressive, coercive, inquisitorial, ruthless, cruel, malevolent, arrogant.

adv severely, with a high hand, with a heavy hand.

740 lenience *n* leniency, tolerance, toleration, moderation, mildness, gentleness, favor, indulgence, forbearance, quarter, compassion, clemency, mercy.

v be lenient, tolerate, bear with, favor, indulge, allow.

adj lenient, tolerant, mild, easy, easy-going, gentle, tender, indulgent, compassionate, sympathetic, merciful.

741 command *n* order, ordinance, direction, bidding, injunction, charge, mandate, behest, ukase, commandment, requisition, requirement, instruction, dictum, act, fiat; demand, exaction, claim, request; control, mastery, disposal, rule, sway, power, domination.

v command, order, direct, bid, demand, charge, instruct, enjoin, require, impose; decree, enact, ordain, dictate, prescribe, appoint; claim, lay claim to.

adj commanding, authoritative.

742 disobedience *n* noncompliance, nonobservance, insubordination, contumacy, infraction, infringement, defiance, unruliness, rebelliousness, obstinacy, stubbornness, resistance, mutinousness, mutiny, rebellion.

insurgent, mutineer, rebel, revolutionary, rioter, traitor, (*informal*) radical.

v disobey, transgress, violate, disregard, defy, infringe, shirk, resist, mutiny, rebel, revolt.

adj disobedient, insubordinate, contumacious, defiant, refractory, unruly, fractious, rebellious, mutinous, obstinate, stubborn, unsubmissive, uncompliant, recalcitrant, insurgent, riotous.

743 obedience *n* observance, compliance, docility, tractability, deference, respect, duty, subservience, submissiveness, obsequiousness; allegiance, loyalty, fealty, homage, devotion.

v obey, comply, submit, follow, attend to, serve.

adj obedient, submissive, compliant, tractable, docile, deferential, respectful, dutiful, loyal, subservient.

adv obediently, in compliance with, in obedience to.

744 compulsion n coercion, constraint, duress, enforcement, conscription, force; impulse, necessity.

v compel, force, make, drive, coerce, constrain, enforce, impel, require, necessitate, oblige, motivate; subdue, subject, bend, bow, overpower.

adj compelling, compulsory, coercive, forcible, constraining; obligatory, necessary, unavoidable, inescapable, ineluctable, irresistible, inexorable.

adv by force, forcibly, on compulsion.

745 master n lord, commander, commandant, chief, head, leader, director, ruler, boss, authority.

746 servant n subject, retainer, follower, henchman, domestic, menial, help, helper, employee, worker, laborer.

v serve, function, answer, assist, help, aid, provide, cater, satisfy; wait on, attend.

747 [insignia of authority] **scepter** n regalia, staff, symbol, emblem, flag, badge; title.

748 freedom n liberty, independence, autonomy, noninterference; immunity, franchisement, franchise, privilege, latitude, scope; ease, facility; frankness, openness; familiarity, license, looseness, laxity.

v be free, have scope, do as one likes, do what one wants; free, liberate, permit, allow, set free.

adj free, independent, at large, loose, scot free; unconstrained, unconfined, unchecked, unhindered, unobstructed, unbound, uncontrolled, ungoverned, unchained, unfettered, unshackled, uncurbed, unbridled, unmuzzled; unrestricted, unlimited, unconditional; absolute; discretionary; wanton, rampant, irrepressible, unvanquished; immune, exempt, freed; autonomous.

adv freely.

749 subjection n dependence, subordination, thrall, thralldom, subjugation, bondage, serfdom, slavery, servitude, enslavement; service, employ, tutelage, constraint, yoke, submission, obedience.

v be subject, be at the mercy of, depend upon, fall prey to, play second fiddle to, serve, submit; subject, subjugate, master, tame, tread down, weigh down, enslave, enthrall, rule.

adj subject, dependent, subordinate; under control, in harness.

750 liberation n disengagement, release, enlargement, emancipation, enfranchisement, deliverance, extrica-

tion, discharge, dismissal, acquittal, absolution.

v liberate, set free, free, disengage, release, emancipate, enfranchise, deliver, extricate, discharge, dismiss, unfetter, disenthrall, set loose, loose, let out, acquit, absolve.

adj liberated, freed.

751 restraint n restriction, circumscription, limitation, control, confinement, curb, check, suppression, constraint, repression.

v restrain, check, keep down, repress, curb, bridle, suppress, compel, hold, keep, constrain; restrict, circumscribe, confine, hinder.

adj restrained, constrained, restrictive, suppressive, repressive; imprisoned, pent up, under restraint.

752 prison n jail, gaol, cage, coop, pen, penitentiary, jailhouse, cell, block, dungeon, lock up, stir, irons, (informal) calaboose, (informal) hoosegow, (informal) the joint, (informal) the big house.

753 keeper n custodian, guard (informal) screw, jailer, gaoler, warder, escort, body-guard; protector, guardian, governor, governess, teacher, tutor, nurse.

754 prisoner n captive, convict, con, jailbird.

v be imprisoned, stand convicted.

adj in prison, in custody, in chains, under wraps, in stir.

755 [vicarious authority] **commission** n delegation, consignment, assignment, deputation, legation, mission, embassy, agency, special committee; errand, charge, permit; appointment, nomination, charter.

v commission, delegate, consign, assign, charge, entrust, authorize; appoint, name, nominate, ordain; install, induct, invest, employ, empower.

756 abrogation n abolition, cancelation, annulment, repeal, retraction, revocation, remission, recision, nullification, invalidation.

v abrogate, abolish, cancel, annul, repeal, retract, revoke, rescind, nullify, void, invalidate.

adj null and void.

757 resignation n abjuration, renunciation, abdication, abandonment, desertion, relinquishment, retirement.

v resign, quit, give up, abjure, renounce, forgo, disclaim, abrogate, abandon, desert, relinquish, retire.

758 consignee n trustee, nominee, committee, delegation, delegate, commission; functionary, **agent**, representative, messenger.

759 deputy n substitute, proxy, delegate, representative, surrogate, alternate, second, assistant.

    v stand for, represent, answer for.

760 permission n authorization, warrant, sanction, liberty, license, enfranchisement, franchise, leave, permit, liberty, freedom, allowance, consent, concession, tolerance, sufferance, indulgence, favor.

    v permit, allow, let, tolerate, bear with, agree to, suffer, concede, accord, favor, humor, indulge; grant, empower, franchise, charter, confer, license, authorize, warrant, sanction.

    adj permitted, permissive, indulgent, libertarian, tolerant; permissible, allowable, legal, legalized, lawful, legitimate.

761 prohibition n interdiction, injunction, prevention, embargo, ban, restriction, disallowance.

    v prohibit, forbid, interdict, veto, disallow, bar, restrict, limit; prevent; hinder, preclude, obstruct.

    adj prohibitive, proscriptive, restrictive; preventive.

762 consent n assent, acquiescence, acceptance, acknowledgment, permission, compliance, concurrence, agreement, approval; accord, concord, consensus, settlement, ratification, confirmation.

    v consent, assent, agree, concur, permit, allow, let, yield, grant, comply, accede, acquiesce.

    adj compliant, agreeable, amenable.

763 offer n proposal, proposition, overture, tender, bid; offering, gift.

    v offer, present, proffer, tender; propose, give, move, put forward, advance, invite, hold out, make a motion; hawk, merchandise, offer for sale.

    adj for sale, in the open market.

764 refusal n rejection, spurning, denial, rebuff, repulse, repudiation; abnegation, protest, renunciation, disclaimer.

    v refuse, decline, reject, spurn, turn down, deny, rebuff, repulse, repudiate; resist, repel, repudiate, renounce, disclaim, rescind, revoke.

    adj noncompliant, dissident, recalcitrant, reluctant.

765 request n claim, demand, application, appeal, solicitation, petition, suit, entreaty, supplication, prayer.

    v request, ask, ask for, beg, sue,

petition, entreat, supplicate, solicit, beseech, plead, implore, require, demand, importune, clamor for.

    adj importunate, clamorous, solicitous.

766 [negative request] **deprecation** n expostulation, intercession, mediation, protest, disapproval, remonstrance.

    v deprecate, protest, expostulate, enter a protest, disapprove, remonstrate.

    adj deprecatory, expostulatory, remonstrative; unsought.

767 petitioner n claimant, aspirant, postulant, seeker, solicitor, suitor, applicant, suppliant, supplicant; competitor, bidder; beggar, mendicant, panhandler, (informal) bum, (informal) streetwalker.

768 promise n undertaking, word, covenant, commitment, pledge, assurance, profession, vow, oath, guarantee, warranty, obligation, contract.

    v promise, undertake, engage, enter into, bind oneself, commit oneself, pledge, agree, assure, warrant, guarantee, covenant, swear, give one's word; secure, give security, underwrite.

    adj promissory, upon one's oath, on one's honor; promised, pledged, committed, bound, sworn.

769 compact n covenant, pact, contract, treaty, agreement, negotiation, bargain, arrangement, (informal) deal.

    v contract, negotiate, bargain, stipulate, make terms; agree, engage, promise; complete, settle, confirm, subscribe, endorse.

    adj compactual, contractual, promissory.

770 conditions n terms, articles, clauses, provisions, provisos, stipulations, promises, obligations, covenants.

    v condition, stipulate, insist upon, contract, provide, bind, tie, oblige.

    adj conditional, provisional.

    adv conditionally, provisionally, on condition.

771 security n guarantee, warranty, bond, tie, pledge, promise, contract; mortgage, lien, pawn; stake, deposit, collateral, (informal) IOU, (informal) mark, promissory note; deed, bill of sale, receipt, certificate, title; sponsorship, surety, bail.

    v give security, post bail, pawn, mortgage; guarantee, warrant, assure, promise; accept, endorse, underwrite, sponsor, stand for.

772 observance n performance, compliance, obedience, execution, discharge, acquittance, fulfillment, satisfaction; adhesion, acknowledgment, fidelity, faithfulness.

v observe, comply with, respect, abide by, acknowledge, adhere to, be faithful to, obey, act up to; meet, fulfill; carry out, execute, perform, satisfy, discharge.

adj observant, compliant, faithful, obedient, true, honorable; punctilious, scrupulous, as good as one's word.

adv faithfully.

773 nonobservance *n* evasion, failure, omission, noncompliance, neglect, negligence, laxity, laxness, carelessness, irresponsibility, disobedience; infringement, infraction, violation, transgression.

v fail, neglect, evade, omit, elude, ignore, disregard, discard, set at naught; infringe, transgress, violate, break.

adj nonobservant, lax, loose, disdainful, evasive, elusive, negligent, irresponsible, disobedient.

774 compromise *n* adjustment, negotiation, concession; compensation.

v compromise, bend, give and take, split the differences, come to an agreement, opt for the mean, adjust, arrange, settle.

775 acquisition *n* procurement, appropriation, gain, attainment, purchase, gift, find; profit, earnings, wages, winnings, income, proceeds, produce, crop, harvest, benefit.

v acquire, appropriate, gain, win, earn, attain, gather, collect; take over, take possession of, procure, secure, obtain, get, come into, receive, get hold of; profit, turn to profit.

adj profitable, advantageous, gainful, remunerative.

776 loss *n* damage, injury, privation, lapse, forfeiture, deprivation.

v lose, incur a loss, miss, mislay, let slip, forfeit; waste, get rid of.

adj lost, bereft, minus, deprived of, cut off, rid of; long lost, irretrievable.

777 possession *n* ownership, occupancy, holding, proprietorship, tenure, tenancy, control, custody; belonging.

v possess, own, have, hold, occupy, control, command, have to oneself, have in hand, belong to.

adj possessing, possessed of, in possession of, master of, in hand, at one's disposal; possessive, custodial.

777a exemption *n* exception, immunity, impunity, release.

v exempt, excuse, release; not have, be without.

adj exempt from, immune from, devoid of, without.

778 [joint possession] **participation** *n* partnership, co-ownership, joint tenancy, common holding, communion, community of possessions; communism, socialism, collectivism; cooperation.

participant, sharer, partner, co-partner, shareholder; communist, socialist.

v participate, partake, share, share in, go halves, split up, divide, have in common, own in common.

adj participatory, joint, common, collective, communal, communist, communistic, socialist, socialistic.

779 possessor *n* holder, occupant, tenant, lessee; proprietor, proprietress, master, mistress, owner.

780 property *n* possession, possessions, goods, effects, chattels, estate, belongings, assets, means, resources, land, real estate, acreage; ownership, right; attribute, quality, characteristic, feature.

781 retention *n* keeping, holding, detention, custody, preservation, maintenance.

v retain, keep, hold, hold fast, secure, withhold, preserve, detain, reserve, maintain.

adj retentive.

782 relinquishment *n* renunciation, surrender, resignation, yielding, waiver, abdication, desertion, abandonment, quitting.

v relinquish, renounce, surrender, give up, resign, yield, cede, waive, forswear, forgo, abdicate, leave, forsake, desert, quit, abandon, let go, discard, cast off, dismiss, divest oneself.

adj cast off, done away with, left, forsworn, given up, left behind.

783 transfer *n* sale, lease, release, exchange, interchange; transference, transmission, changing hands.

v transfer, convey, assign, grant, consign, make over, hand over, pass, transmit, change, exchange, interchange, change hands; devolve, succeed.

adj transferable, conveyable, transmissive, exchangeable.

784 giving *n* bestowal, presentation, concession, delivery, consignment, dispensation, endowment, investiture, award; charity, almsgiving, liberality, generosity, philanthropy; gift, donation, present, boon, favor, grant, offering; allowance, contribution, donation, bequest, legacy, alms, largesse, bounty, help, gratuity; bribe, bait.

giver, granter, donor.

v give, bestow, confer, grant, accord, award, assign, entrust, consign; invest, allow, settle upon, donate, bequeath, leave; furnish, supply, help; afford, spare, favor with, lavish; deliver, hand, pass, turn over, present, give away, dispense, dispose of, give out, deal out, dole out, mete out, fork out; pay, render, impart.

adj charitable, beneficent, tributary, liberal, generous, philanthropic.

785 receiving *n* acquisition, reception, acceptance, admission, recipient, receiver, legatee, grantee, donee, beneficiary, pensioner.

v receive, take, acquire, admit, take in, accept; come into, fall to one, accrue.

adj receiving; received.

786 apportionment *n* allotment, consignment, assignment, allocation, distribution, dispensation, division, partition; portion, lot, share, measure, dose, dole, ration, ratio, proportion, quota, allowance.

v apportion, divide, distribute, dispense, allot, share, mete, portion out, parcel out, dole out, deal, carve, administer; partition, assign, appropriate, appoint.

adj distributive; respective.

787 lending *n* loan, advance, accommodation, mortgage, investment.

v lend, loan, advance, accommodate, lend on security, pawn; let, lease.

788 borrowing *n* pledging, pawning; appropriating, stealing, theft.

v borrow, pledge, pawn, borrow money; hire, rent, lease; appropriate, use, steal from, imitate.

789 taking *n* appropriation, capture, apprehension, seizure, abduction, dispossession, deprivation, expropriation, divestment, confiscation, eviction; extortion, theft; reprisal, recovery.

v take, catch, hook, nab, bag, pocket, receive, accept; reap, cull, pluck, gather; appropriate. assume, possess oneself of, help oneself to, commandeer, make free with; take away, abduct, steal, seize, snatch, snap up, capture, get hold of, take from, take away from, dispossess, expropriate, oust, eject, divest, confiscate, usurp, strip, fleece; retake, resume, recover.

adj predatory, rapacious, parasitic, greedy, ravenous.

790 restitution *n* return, restoration, reinvestment, rehabilitation, reparation, atonement, compensation, recovery.

v return, restore, give back, render, give up, let go; recoup, reimburse, compensate, reinvest, remit, rehabilitate, repair, make good, settle up; recover, get back, redeem, take back again.

adj compensatory, redemptive, recouperative.

791 stealing *n* theft, thievery, robbery, swindling, fraud, appropriation.

v steal, take, thieve, rob, pilfer, purloin, *(informal)* swipe, filch, embezzle, swindle, appropriate, fleece, defraud, *(informal)* rip off, *(informal)* screw.

adj thievish, light-fingered, piratical, predatory.

792 thief *n* robber, pilferer, filcher, rifler, crook, *(informal)* rip-off artist, cheat; burglar, house-breaker, second-story man, safecracker.

793 booty *n* spoils, plunder, prize, loot, catch, pickings, stolen goods, *(informal)* haul.

794 barter *n* exchange, trade, traffic, commerce, business, bargain; dealing, transaction, negotiation.

v barter, trade, exchange, traffic, bargain, swap, buy and sell, give and take, deal, haggle, negotiate, drive a bargain, transact.

adj commercial, mercantile; interchangeable, in trade, for sale, marketable.

795 purchase *n* buying, purchasing, acquisition; bargain, buy.

buyer, purchaser, shopper, customer, client, patron, clientele.

v purchase, buy, acquire, get, obtain, procure; shop, market, go shopping.

796 sale *n* selling, vendition, commerce, mercantilism, transaction, exchange, auction, trade.

seller, vendor, merchant.

v sell, trade, barter, vend, exchange, deal in, dispose, merchandise, hawk.

adj salable, marketable, vendible, for sale.

797 merchant *n* trader, dealer, seller, salesman, saleswoman, tradesman, shopkeeper, retailer, hawker, huckster, peddler, broker.

798 merchandise *n* goods, wares, commodity, articles, stock, produce, product, staple commodity, store, cargo.

v merchandise, sell.

799 market *n* mart, marketplace, fair, bazaar, business district, mall, shopping center, store, department store, establishment, place of business, office.

800 money *n* finance, accounts, funds, assets, wealth, supplies, ways and means, wherewithal, capital, almighty dollar, cash, currency, hard cash, *(informal)* bucks, change, small change, *(informal)* green, greenbacks; sum, amount, balance.

adj monetary, pecuniary, financial, fiscal.

801 treasurer *n* bursar, banker, purser, receiver, steward, trustee, accountant, paymaster, cashier, teller, financier.

802 treasury *n* bank, exchequer, strongbox, stronghold, coffer, chest, depository, purse, moneybag, safe, vault, cash box, cash register, till; securities, stocks, bonds, notes.

803 wealth *n* riches, fortune, opulence, affluence, easy circumstance, *(informal)* silver spoon, independence, competence, sufficiency, solvency; provision, livelihood, maintenance, means, resources, substance; income, capital, money.

v be wealthy, be rich.

adj wealthy, rich, affluent, well-off, well-to-do, comfortable.

804 poverty *n* indigence, penury, pauperism, destitution, want, need, neediness, lack, privation, distress, difficulties, straits, bad straits.

v be poor, want, lack, starve, live from hand to mouth, go to the dogs.

adj poor, indigent, destitute, poverty-stricken, needy, penniless, broke, *(informal)* bust, hard up, insolvent, seedy, beggarly.

805 credit *n* trust, score, tally, account, *(informal)* tab, bill.

creditor, lender, usurer.

v credit, accredit entrust, keep an account with.

806 debt *n* obligation, liability, debit, score, duty, due.

debtor, borrower.

adj liable, answerable for, in debt; unpaid, in arrear.

807 payment *n* discharge, settlement, clearance, liquidation, satisfaction, reckoning, arrangement; acknowledgment, release, receipt, voucher; installment, remittance.

v pay, settle, liquidate, discharge, quit, acquit oneself of, reckon up, satisfy, compensate, reimburse, remunerate, recompense, make payment, square accounts, balance accounts, pay in full.

adj out of debt, solvent; straight, clear.

808 nonpayment *n* default, protest, repudiation; insolvency, bankruptcy, failure.

v not pay, default, fail, stop payment; run up bills.

adj in debt.

809 expenditure *n* outlay, expenses, disbursement, payment, costs, fees.

v expend, spend, pay out, disburse, *(informal)* fork out, lay out.

810 receipt *n* value received, acknowledgment of payment.

v receive, take, get, bring in.

adj profitable, remunerative.

811 accounts *n* money matters, finance, budget, bill, score, reckoning, account; statement, ledger, inventory, register, book, books, sheet; balance.

accountant, auditor, bookkeeper, financier.

v keep accounts, enter, post, book, credit, debit, balance.

812 price *n* amount, cost, expense, charge, figure, demand, damage, fare, hire, wages; worth, rate, value, valuation, appraisal; market price, quotation; bill, invoice.

v price, set a price, fix a price, appraise, assess, charge, demand, ask, require, exact; fetch, sell for, bring in, yield, accord.

813 discount *n* abatement, reduction, depreciation, allowance, qualification, rebate, sale.

v discount, put on sale, reduce, take off, allow, deduct, abate, rebate.

814 dearness *n* expensiveness, costliness, high price; overcharge, extravagance, exorbitance

v be expensive, cost a lot; overcharge, bleed, fleece, extort.

adj dear, expensive, costly, precious; extravagant, exorbitant, unreasonable; priceless.

815 cheapness *n* low price, depreciation, bargain, value, *(informal)* steal, *(informal)* great buy.

v be cheap, cost little.

adj cheap, moderate, reasonable, inexpensive, dirt cheap.

816 liberality *n* generosity, munificence, bounty, bounteousness, hospitality, charity.

v be liberal, spend freely, give, spare no expense.

adj liberal, free, generous, bountiful, hospitable, munificent, beneficient, princely, charitable.

817 economy *n* frugality, thrift, thriftiness, saving, care, husbandry, retrenchment, parsimony.

v economize, save, retrench, husband.

adj economical, frugal, careful, thrifty, chary, parsimonious.

818 prodigality *n* unthriftiness, waste, wastefulness, profusion, profuseness, extravagance, profligacy, lavishness, squandering.

prodigal, spendthrift, squanderer.

v be prodigal, squander, lavish, misspend, waste, dissipate, fritter one's money.

adj prodigal, profuse, unthrifty, improvident, wasteful, profligate, extravagant, lavish.

819 parsimony *n* stinginess, illiberality, avarice, rapidity, rapacity, venality, cupidity, selfishness.

miser, niggard, churl, skinflint, codger, scrimp, *(informal)* tightwad, usurer, Scrooge.

v be parsimonious, grudge, begrudge, stint, pinch, hold back, withhold, starve, famish.

adj parsimonious, penurious, stingy, cheap, miserly, mean, pennywise, niggardly, tight, ungenerous, churlish, mercenary, venal, covetous, usurious, avaricious, greedy, rapacious, selfish.

Class VI

Words relating to the Sentient and Moral Powers

I. Affections in General

820 affections *n* character, qualities, disposition, nature, spirit, temper, temperament, idiosyncracy, habit, bent, bias, predisposition, proclivity, propensity, humor, mood, sympathy; soul, heart, inner man, essence; passion, driving spirit, ruling passion.

adj affected, characterized, formed, cast, molded, tempered, predisposed, prone, inclined, imbued; inborn, ingrained, deep-rooted.

adv at heart.

821 feeling *n* consciousness, impression; emotion, passion, sentiment, sensibility; sympathy, empathy; fervor, ardor, zeal, warmth, tenderness, sensitivity, sentimentality, susceptibility, pity; sentiment, opinion.

v feel, receive an impression, respond to.

adj feeling, emotional, sensitive, tender; sympathetic; emotional, impassioned, passionate, fervent, tender, sensitive, heart-felt, thrilling, rapturous, soul-stirring; moved, touched, affected.

adv heart and soul, from the bottom of one's heart.

822 sensibility *n* responsiveness, sensitiveness, awareness, susceptibility, impressibility, tenderness, sentimentality, sentimentalism; excitability; appreciation, understanding, moral sensibility.

v be sensitive, have a soft spot in one's heart.

adj sensitive, impressionable, susceptible, tender, warm-hearted, sentimental; excitable; aware, understanding, appreciative.

823 insensibility *n* insensitiveness, impassivity, apathy, coldness, callousness; imperturbable; dullness, boorishness.

v be insensitive, not care, be unaffected, have no interest in.

adj insensitive, unconscious, unaware; inattentive, indifferent, lukewarm; apathetic, impassive, unimpressionable; cold-blooded, cold-hearted, unmoved, unaffected, callous, thick-skinned, uncaring.

adv in cold blood.

824 excitation *n* excitation of feeling; mental excitation; galvanism, stimulation, provocation, inspiration, infection; animation, agitation, perturbation; fascination, intoxication, ravishment; irritation, anger, passion, thrill.

v excite, affect, touch, move, impress, interest, animate, inspire, infect, awake; evoke, provoke; stir up, wake up, light up; rouse, arouse, stir, fire, kindle, inflame; stimulate, quicken, sharpen, whet, wet the appetite, fan the fire, raise to a fervor; absorb, rivet, intoxicate, fascinate, enrapture; agitate, perturb, ruffle, fluster, disturb, startle, shock, stagger, astound, electrify, galvanize; irritate.

adj excited, excitable, wrought up, overwrought, upset, hysterical, hot, red-hot, flushed, feverish, boiling, ebullient, seething, fuming, raging, raving, frantic, mad, distracted, beside oneself; exciting, warm, glowing, fervid, soul-stirring, thrilling, overwhelming, overpowering, sensational.

825 [excess of sensitiveness] **excitability** *n* impetuosity, vehemence, boisterousness, impatience, intolerance, irritability, restlessness, agitation; passion, excitement, fever, tumult, ebullition, tempest, fit, paroxysm, explosion, outburst, agony; violence, rage, fury, furor, desperation, madness, distraction, delirium, frenzy, hysterics.

v be impatient, lose patience, fuss, fidget; lose one's temper, flare up, burn, boil over, foam, fume, rage, rant, run wild, go mad, go into hysterics.

adj excitable, high-strung, nervous, irritable, impatient, intolerant; feverish, hysterical, delirious, mad; hurried, restless, fidgety, fussy; vehement, violent, wild, furious, fierce, fiery, hotheaded; overzealous, enthusiastic, impassioned, fanatical; rabid, clamorous, turbulent, tumultuous, boisterous; impulsive, impetuous, passionate, uncontrolled, uncontrollable, ungovernable, irrepressible, volcanic.

826 inexcitability *n* imperturbability, even temper, dispassion, patience, impassivity; coolness, calmness, composure, placidity, serenity, quietude; self-possession, self-restraint, stoicism; resignation, submission, sufferance, endurance, forbearance, fortitude, moderation, restraint.

v bear, endure, tolerate, suffer, put up with, reconcile oneself to, resign oneself to, brook, swallow, make the best of; stomach; compose, appease, propitiate, repress, calm down, cool down.

adj inexcitable, imperturbable, unsusceptible, dispassionate, enduring, stoical, staid, sober, sedate; easygoing, peaceful, placid, calm, cool; composed, collected, unruffled, content, resigned, subdued.

II. Personal Affections

827 pleasure *n* happiness, gladness, delectation, enjoyment, delight, joy, glee, cheer, cheerfulness, well-being, satisfaction, gratification, comfort, ease; felicity, bliss, enchantment, transport, rapture, ravishment, ecstasy, luxury, sensuality, voluptuousness.

v be pleased, joy, enjoy oneself, have one's head in the clouds, fall into raptures; be pleased with, derive pleasure from, take pleasure in, *(informal)* get into, delight in, rejoice in, indulge in, luxuriate in, relish, love, enjoy, like, *(informal)* dig, take a fancy to, take a shine to.

adj happy, blissful, joyful, gladsome, cheerful, comfortable, at ease, content; ecstatic.

adv happily, with pleasure.

828 pain *n* suffering, distress, torture, misery, dolor, anguish, agony, torment, throe, pang, ache, smart, twinge, stitch; displeasure, dissatisfaction, discomfort, discomposure, disquiet, malaise, inquietude, uneasiness, vexation, discontent, dejection, weariness; annoyance, irritation, worry, affliction, bore, bother, mortification, plague; care, solicitude, trouble, trial, ordeal,

burden, load, fret; prostration, desolation, despair.

v suffer, afflict, torture, torment, distress, despair; hurt, harm, injure, trouble, grieve, disquiet, discomfort, discompose, worry, irritate, vex, mortify, plague. ·

adj uncomfortable, uneasy, weary; unhappy, infelicitous, poor, wretched, miserable, woebegone, careworn, cheerless, sorry, sorrowful, stricken, in tears, in despair.

829 pleasurableness *n* pleasantness, agreeableness, delectability, delight, congeniality; sprightliness, cheer, cheerfulness, liveliness; attraction, attractiveness, charm, fascination, enchantment, witchery, seduction, winning ways, amenity, amiability, loveliness, beauty, brightness; goodness.

v be pleasurable, afford pleasure, offer pleasure, please, charm, delight, gladden, cheer; attract, invite, allure, stimulate, interest, captivate, fascinate, enchant, entrance, enrapture, bewitch, ravish, enravish, transport; agree with, satisfy, gratify; slake, satiate, quench; regale, refresh, treat, amuse.

adj pleasurable, pleasant, agreeable, enjoyable, delightful, congenial, amiable; comfortable, cordial, genial, gladsome, sweet, delectable, nice, dainty, delicate, delicious, luscious, luxurious, voluptuous, sensual; attractive, lovely, beautiful, seductive, rapturous, ecstatic, beatific, heavenly; fair, sunny, bright; gay, sprightly, merry, cheery, cheerful, lively, vivacious.

830 painfulness *n* trouble, care, trial, affliction, blow, burden, curse, mishap, misfortune, adversity; annoyance, nuisance, grievance, bore, bother, vexation, mortification; wound, sore, sore subject, thorn in the side, skeleton in the closet, sorry sight, heavy news, bad news; affront, insult, offense.

v pain, hurt, wound, sadden, displease, annoy, trouble, disturb, cross, perplex, irk, vex, mortify, worry, plague, bother, pester, harass, badger, bait, heckle, irritate, anger, persecute, provoke; harrow, torment, torture; affront, insult, give offense, offend, maltreat, mistreat; sicken, disgust, revolt, nauseate, repel, shock, horrify, appal.

adj painful, hurtful, dolorous; unpleasant, disagreeable, unpalatable, bitter, distasteful; unwelcome, undesirable, obnoxious; dismal, dreary, melancholy, grievous, piteous, woeful, rueful, mournful, deplorable, pitiable, lamentable, pathetic; invidious, vexatious, troublesome, irksome, wearisome, worrisome; intolerable, insufferable, unsupportable, unbearable, unendurable, grim, dreadful, fearful, frightful, dire, odious, hateful, repulsive, repellant, abhorrent, horrid, horrible, offensive, nauseous, loathsome, vile, hideous; sore, severe, grave, hard, harsh, cruel; ruinous, disastrous, calamitous, tragic; burdensome, onerous, oppressive, cumbersome.

adv painfully.

831 content *n* contentment, complacency, satisfaction, ease, serenity, comfort; conciliation, resignation.

v gratify, satisfy, set at ease, comfort, appease, conciliate, reconcile.

adj contented, complacent, satisfied, sanguine, comfortable; assenting, acceding, resigned, willing, agreeable.

adv to one's heart's content.

832 discontent *n* discontentment, dissatisfaction, uneasiness, disquietude, restlessness, displeasure.

v be discontented, repine, regret, fret, chafe, grumble; dissatisfy, disappoint, disconcert.

adj discontented, dissatisfied, displeased, uneasy, restless, dejected, malcontent, regretful, down in the dumps.

833 regret *n* sorrow, lamentation, grief; remorse, penitence, contrition, repentance.

v regret, deplore, lament, feel sorry about, grieve at, bemoan, bewail, rue, mourn for, repent.

adj regretful, sorry, lamentable, rueful; penitent, contrite.

834 relief *n* deliverance, alleviation, ease, assuagement, mitigation, comfort, solace, consolation; help, assistance, aid.

v relieve, ease, alleviate, assuage, mitigate, allay, comfort, soothe, lessen, abate, diminish; cheer, comfort, console; aid, help, assist, succor, refresh, remedy, support.

adj soothing, consoling, assuaging, comforting, palliative, curative.

835 aggravation *n* worsening, heightening, intensification, exaggeration; (*informal*) annoyance, irritation, vexation.

v aggravate, worsen, intensify, heighten, increase, make serious, make grave.

adj worse, intensified, irritated.

adv from bad to worse, out of the frying pan and into the fire.

836 cheerfulness *n* geniality, high spirits, liveliness, vivacity, joviality, jocularity, mirth, merriment, exhilaration.

v cheer, gladden, enliven, inspirit,

delight, rejoice, exhilarate, animate, encourage; shout, applaud, acclaim, salute.

adj cheery, gay, blithe, happy, lively, spirited, sprightly, joyful, joyous, mirthful, buoyant, sparkling, vivacious, gleeful, sunny, jolly; pleasant, bright, gay, winsome, gladdening, cheery, cheering, inspiring, animating, hearty, robust.

adv cheerfully.

837 dejection *n* depression, heaviness, heavy heart, melancholy, sadness, dumps, doldrums, despondency, gloom, weariness, disgust, despair, hopelessness.

v be dejected, lose heart, frown, mope, droop, despond, brood over, sink, despair.

adj unhappy, depressed, dispirited, disheartened, discouraged, despondent, (*informal*) down, downhearted, sad, melancholy, lugubrious, heartsick, dismal, gloomy, miserable, desolate, pessimistic, cynical.

adv with a long face, with tears in one's eyes.

838 rejoicing *n* exaltation, triumph, jubilation, reveling, merrymaking, celebration, paean; smile, smirk, grin, giggle, titter, laughter, guffaw, shout, peal of laughter.

v rejoice, congratulate oneself, clap one's hands, dance, skip, sing, hurrah, cry for joy, leap with joy, exalt, triumph; smile, smirk, grin, giggle, titter, chuckle, cackle, laugh, crow, burst out, shout, split, roar, shake one's sides, split one's sides.

adj jubilant, exultant, triumphant, flushed, (*informal*) high, elated, laughing, convulsed with laughter.

839 lamentation *n* lament, howl, wail, wailing, complaint, moan, moaning, groan, sob, sigh; dirge, elegy, monody, threnody.

v lament, bewail, bemoan, deplore, grieve, scream, sob, cry, weep, mourn over, sorrow over.

adj lamenting, in mourning, sorrowful, mournful, lamentable, tearful, plaintive.

840 amusement *n* enjoyment, entertainment, recreation, diversion, relaxation, pastime, pleasure, playing, festivity.

v amuse, entertain, cheer, divert, enliven, interest; amuse oneself, play, sport, make merry.

adj amusing, entertaining, diverting, relaxing, pleasant, witty, jovial, jolly, playful.

841 weariness *n* ennui, lassitude, fatigue, exhaustion, boredom; tedium, monotony, dullness.

v weary, tire, fatigue, bore, exhaust.

adj wearisome, tiresome, boring, tedious, irksome, monotonous, humdrum, dull, prosaic, trying; weary, drowsy, exhausted, tired, wearied, fatigued; uninterested, impatient, dissatisfied.

842 wit *n* drollery, facetiousness, pleasantry, repartee, cleverness, humor, fun; understanding, intelligence, sagacity, wisdom, intellect, mind, sense.

v joke, jest, banter, pun.

adj witty, quick, quick-witted, nimble, sharp, clever, facetious, whimsical, pleasant, humorous, playful, sparkling, scintillating; intelligent, sagacious, wise, perceptive, insightful.

843 dullness *n* heaviness, flatness, stupidity, obtuseness, lack of originality, banality.

v be dull, blunt, deaden, benumb.

adj dull, uninteresting, unimaginative, dry, prosaic, matter-of-fact, commonplace, boring, tedious, dreary, vapid; stupid, stolid, slow, flat.

844 humorist *n* wit, wag, comedian, comedienne, joker, jester, wisecracker, epigrammatist, punster, buffoon, clown, fool, satirist, lampooner, cutup, funnyman.

845 beauty *n* loveliness, pulchritude, elegance, grace, gracefulness, comeliness, seemliness, fairness, attractiveness, brilliance, radiance, splendor, gorgeousness, magnificence, sublimity.

v beautify.

adj beautiful, handsome, comely, seemly, attractive, lovely, pretty, fair, fine, elegant, beauteous, graceful, pulchritudinous, brilliant, radiant, gorgeous, magnificent; artistic, aesthetic, picturesque.

846 ugliness *n* homeliness, inelegance, unsightliness, distortion, disfigurement, deformity, frightfulness.

v deface, disfigure, distort.

adj ugly, displeasing, hard-featured, unlovely, unsightly, unseemly, homely; hideous, gruesome, repulsive, offensive, revolting, terrible, base, vile, squalid, gross, monstrous, heinous; disagreeable, unpleasant, objectionable.

847 ornament *n* ornamentation, adornment, decoration, embellishment, frills, finery.

v ornament, embellish, adorn, decorate, beautify.

adj ornamental, decorative; ornamented, ornate, embellished, beautified.

848 blemish *n* disfigurement, deformity, defect, flaw, fault, taint, blot, spot, speck.

v stain, sully, spot, taint, tarnish, injur, mar, damage, deface, impair.

adj disfigured, injured, imperfect, discolored, freckled, pitted.

849 simplicity *n* plainness, homeliness; clarity, chasteness, restraint, severity, lack of adornment, lack of affectation.

v simplify, uncomplicate, clarify, strip to essentials, get back to basics.

adj simple, plain, homely, natural, unadorned, unaffected, unembellished, neat, unassuming, unpretentious; chaste, severe; clear, straightforward, lucid.

850 [good taste] **taste** *n* good taste, delicacy, refinement, polish, elegance, grace, discrimination, culture, cultivation.

v show taste, appreciate, judge, criticize, discriminate.

adj tasteful, in good taste, decorous, attractive, cultivated, cultured, refined, discriminative, polished, felicitous, appropriate, suitable, apt, becoming, pleasing.

adv tastefully, elegantly.

851 [bad taste] **vulgarity** *n* bad taste, barbarism, coarseness, lack of decorum, ill-breeding, boorishness; gaudiness, tawdriness, finery, frippery, tinsel.

v be vulgar; vulgarize.

adj vulgar, in bad taste, unrefined, boorish, common, coarse, ill-bred, ill-mannered, ignoble, mean, plebeian, crude, rude, shabby; gaudy, tawdry, flashy, garish, crass, showy, (*informal*) tacky.

852 fashion *n* custom, style, vogue, mode, rage, craze; conventionality, conformity; society, polite society, beau monde; manners, breeding, air, demeanor, *savoir-faire*, gentility, decorum, propriety, etiquette.

v be fashionable, be the rage; fashion, adapt, suit, fit, adjust; make, shape, frame, form, mold.

adj fashionable, in vogue, à la mode, all the rage; modish, stylish, conventional, customary; well-bred, well-mannered, civil, polite, courteous, polished, refined, genteel, decorous.

853 ridiculousness *n* outrageousness, silliness, absurdity.

v be ridiculous, make a fool of oneself, play the fool.

adj absurd, preposterous, extravagant, asinine, laughable, nonsensical, silly, funny, ludicrous, droll, comical, farcical, outlandish, outrageous, fantastic.

854 fop n fine gentleman, dandy, (*informal*) dude, coxcomb, beau, man about town, prig, jackanapes.

855 affectation n affectedness, pretense, pretention, airs, mannerisms, unnaturalness, display, show, sham, feigning, simulation, foppery.

v affect, act a part, put on airs, pretend, assume, feign, counterfeit, simulate, pose, attitudinize.

adj affected, pretentious, ostentatious, feigned, artificial, stilted, mannered, stagey, theatrical, modish, unnatural.

856 ridicule n derision, scoffing, mockery, gibes, jeers, taunts, raillery; satire, burlesque, sneer, banter, wit, irony.

v ridicule, deride, banter, chaff, twit, mock, taunt, make fun of, sneer at, burlesque, satirize, rail at, lampoon, jeer at, scoff at, (*informal*) put down.

adj derisory, derisive, sarcastic, ironic, ironical, burlesque, mocking.

857 [object and cause of ridicule] **laughing-stock** n butt, game, fair game, fool, dupe, original, oddity, queer fish, square, straight, buffoon.

858 hope n confidence, trust, reliance, faith, assurance; expectation, expectancy, anticipation, aspiration, longing, desire, dream, wish.

v hope, trust, rely on, lean on, have faith in; hope for, expect, presume, anticipate; long for, desire.

adj hopeful, expectant, sanguine, optimistic, confident; probable, promising, propitious, reassuring, encouraging, cheering, inspiriting.

859 hopelessness n despair, desperation, despondency, dejection, pessimism.

v despair, give up hope, despond.

adj hopeless, despairing, desperate, despondent, forlorn, disconsolate; irremediable, remediless, unremedial, incurable.

860 fear n apprehension, consternation, dismay, alarm, trepidation, dread, terror, fright, horror, panic; anxiety, solicitude, suspicion, misgiving, concern; awe, reverence, veneration.

v fear, be afraid of, apprehend, distrust, dread; revere, venerate, reverence.

adj fearful, afraid, apprehensive, dismayed, alarmed, frightened, terrified, horrified, aghast, terror-stricken, horror-stricken, panic-stricken; anxious, concerned, solicitous, suspicious;

fearful, awesome, awe-inspiring; awful, dreadful, terrible.

861 courage n fearlessness, dauntlessness, intrepidity, guts, fortitude, pluck, spirit, nerve, heroism, daring, audacity, bravery, mettle, valor, hardihood, bravado, gallantry.

v dare, venture, look danger in the face, take heart, take the bull by the horns.

adj courageous, fearless, dauntless, intrepid, (*informal*) gutsy, spirited, stout-hearted, resolute, bold, heroic, daring, audacious, brave, valorous, enterprising, adventurous, gallant.

862 cowardice n fear, poltroonery, dastardliness, faint-heartedness, yellow streak, dread, timidity, baseness, abject fear.

coward, poltroon, craven, sneak, lily-liver, (*informal*) chicken.

v be cowardly, cower, skulk, quail, hide.

adj cowardly, fearful, craven, dastardly, pusillanimous, recreant, timid, timorous, faint-hearted, lily-livered, chicken-hearted, fearful, afraid, scared, spineless, (*informal*) chicken.

863 rashness n haste, impetuosity, recklessness, impulsiveness, heedlessness, thoughtlessness, imprudence, indiscretion, audacity, carelessness, foolhardiness.

v be rash, plunge.

adj rash, hasty, impetuous, reckless, headlong, precipitate, impulsive, thoughtless, heedless, imprudent, indiscreet, careless, unwary, foolhardy, presumptuous, audacious.

864 caution n prudence, discretion, circumspection, heed, care, wariness, heedfulness, vigilance, forethought; warning, admonition, advice, injunction, counsel.

v be cautious, take care; warn, admonish, advise, counsel.

adj cautious, prudent, heedful, careful, watchful, discreet, wary, vigilant, alert, provident, chary, circumspect, guarded.

865 desire n longing, fancy, craving, yearning, wish, want, need, hunger, appetite, thirst; request, wish, ambition, aspiration; love, passion, lust.

v desire, wish for, long for, crave, want, wish, covet, fancy; ask, request, solicit; lust for.

adj desirous, desiring, craving, wishful, hungry, thirsty, covetous, fervent, ardent, lustful.

866 indifference n unconcern, listlessness, apathy, insensibility, coolness, insensitiveness, inattention.

v be indifferent, take no interest in, have no heart for, spurn, disdain.

adj indifferent, unconcerned, listless, apathetic, cool, cold, lukewarm, insensitive, inattentive.

867 dislike *n* disinclination, disrelish, distaste, disgust, repugnance, antipathy, antagonism, aversion, hatred, horror, loathing.

v dislike, disrelish, be averse to, be disinclined, be reluctant, have no taste for; disgust, repel, nauseate, hate, loathe.

adj disliking, disinclined, averse, loath; dislikable, distasteful, disagreeable, offensive, repulsive, repugnant, repellent, abhorrent, nauseating, disgusting, loathsome.

868 fastidiousness *n* nicety; hypercriticism; discernment, discrimination, judiciousness, keenness, perspicacity.

v be fastidious, split hairs.

adj fastidious, nice, dainty, delicate; hard to please, finicky, hypercritical, fussy, querulous, meticulous, exacting, scrupulous, proper, priggish, prim; discerning, discriminative, judicious, keen, sharp, perspicacious, sagacious.

869 satiety *n* repletion, saturation, glut, surfeit; disgust, weariness.

v sate, satiate, saturate, cloy, glut, stuff, gorge, surfeit; gall, disgust, bore, tire, weary.

adj satiated, glutted, stuffed, gorged, surfeited; disgusted, bored, tired, weary.

870 wonder *n* surprise, marvel, astonishment, stupefaction, amazement, awe, admiration, bewilderment, puzzlement.

v wonder, think, speculate, conjecture, meditate, ponder, question; marvel, admire, be surprised, start, stare, startle, astonish, amaze, astound, stagger, stupefy, bewilder, dumfound.

adj marvelous, wonderful, extraordinary, remarkable, awesome, startling, wondrous, miraculous, astonishing, amazing, astounding, unique, curious, strange, odd, peculiar; astonished, surprised, aghast, agog, startled, breathless, awe-struck, spell-bound, lost in wonder, amazed, fascinated, bewildered.

871 expectance *n* expectancy, expectation.

v expect, foresee, assume, not be surprised, make nothing of.

adj expecting, expectant, relied on, expected, figured on, foreseen.

872 prodigy *n* phenomenon, wonder,

marvel, miracle; freak, monstrosity, spectacle, curiosity; genius, intellectual giant, wizard, mastermind, expert, sage, child genius, wunderkind.

873 repute *n* estimation, reputation, account, regard, report; name, standing, distinction, credit, respect, respectability, dignity, greatness, eminence, honor, renown.

v consider, esteem, account, hold, regard, deem, reckon; be held in high repute, be distinguished.

adj reputed, regarded, accounted; reputable, respected, respectable, esteemed, celebrated, distinguished, dignified, honored, renowned, eminent.

874 disrepute *n* disgrace, dishonor, disfavor, discredit, ill repute, low repute, bad name, shame, degradation, obloquy, debasement, ignominy, infamy, stain, spot, blot, tarnish, taint.

v disgrace oneself, have a bad name, shame, disgrace, dishonor, tarnish, stain, taint, blot.

adj disreputable, base, low, unsavory, shady, unworthy, disgraced, vile, ignominious, dishonorable, opprobrious, shameful, disgraceful, infamous, tainted, tarnished.

875 nobility *n* distinction, eminence, stateliness, majesty, grandeur, dignity, loftiness, profundity, highmindedness; rank, condition, high birth, gentility, quality, royalty, aristocracy, lord, lady.

v be noble; ennoble.

adj noble, exalted, honorable, dignified, imposing, stately, titled, aristocratic, patrician, high-born.

876 commonalty *n* the common people, the lower classes, commoners, multitude, proletariat, populace, rank and file, bourgeoisie, general public, citizenry, peasantry, crowd, herd, rabble.

adj common, mean, low, base, ignoble, vulgar, homely, plebeian, proletarian, low-born, obscure, rustic, boorish, uncivilized.

877 title *n* honor, name, designation, decoration.

adj titled.

878 pride *n* self-respect, self-assurance, self-esteem, conceit, vanity, egotism, arrogance, vainglory, self-importance; insolence, haughtiness, superciliousness, presumption.

v be proud, presume, swagger, give oneself airs.

adj proud, high-minded, dignified, stately, noble, imposing, honorable, creditable; self-assured, self-satisfied, contented, egotistical, vain, conceited, arrogant, haughty, smug, overbearing, over-confident, snobbish, supercilious, presumptuous.

879 humility *n* modesty, humbleness, meekness, lowliness, submissiveness.

v lower, abase, debase, degrade, humiliate, mortify, shame, subdue, crush, break.

adj humble, low, lowly, unassuming, plain, common, poor, meek, modest, submissive, unpretentious; respectful, polite, courteous.

adv with downcast eyes, on bended knee.

880 vanity *n* pride, conceit, self-esteem, self-complacency, egotism, self-admiration, self-love, self-glorification; hollowness, emptiness, sham, triviality.

v be vain, have too high an opinion of oneself, inflate, puff up.

adj vain, conceited, egotistical, self-complacent, proud, vainglorious, arrogant, overweening, inflated; useless, hollow, trifling, trivial.

881 modesty *n* humility, diffidence, timidity, bashfulness; moderation, decency, propriety, simplicity, chastity, prudery, prudishness.

v be modest, retire, give way to, stay in the background.

adj modest, humble, diffident, timid, timorous, bashful, sheepish, shy; moderate, humble, unpretentious, decent, becoming, proper, inextravagant, unostentatious, retiring, unassuming, unobtrusive; demure, prudish, chaste, pure, virtuous.

adv modestly, humbly, quietly, privately, without ceremony.

882 ostentation *n* pretention, pretentiousness, semblance, show, showiness, pretense, display, pageantry, pomp, pompousness, flourish; splendor.

v show off, parade, display, exhibit, blazon forth, emblazon, flaunt.

adj ostentatious, pretentious, showy, flashy, grand, pompous, garish, gaudy, flaunting, high-sounding, sumptuous, theatrical, dramatic, solemn, majestic, ceremonious, punctilious, over-blown.

adv with a flourish.

883 celebration *n* ceremony, ceremonial, commemoration, solemnization, observance, memorialization, festival, festivity.

v celebrate, commemorate, observe, keep; proclaim, announce; praise, extol, laud, glorify, honor, applaud, commend; solemnize, ritualize.

adj celebrational, commemorative,

honorific, commendatory; celebrated, famous, renowned, illustrious, eminent, famed.

adv in honor of, in commemoration of, in celebration of.

884 boasting *n* bragging, swaggering, braggadocio, bravado.

boaster, braggart, blusterer, (*informal*) windbag.

v exaggerate, brag, vaunt, swagger, crow, strut, talk big.

adj boasting, boastful, pretentious, vainglorious, elated, exultant, jubilant, triumphant.

885 [undue assumption of superiority]
insolence *n* boldness, rudeness, disrespect, impertinence, impudence, haughtiness, arrogance, audacity, abusiveness, contemptuousness.

v be insolent, swagger, assume, presume, take liberties, ride roughshod over.

adj insolent, bold, rude, disrespectful, impertinent, impudent, brazen, brassy, haughty, arrogant, audacious, presumptuous, overbearing, abusive, contemptuous, insulting.

886 servility *n* submissiveness, obsequiousness, abasement, slavishness, cringing, fawning, meanness, baseness, groveling, sycophancy, slavery.

toady, sycophant, boot-licker, (*informal*) apple-polisher, (*informal*) brown-noser.

v be servile, cringe, bow, stoop, kneel, toady, fawn, lick the boots of; sneak, crawl, crouch, cower.

adj servile, obsequious, slavish, cringing, fawning, sycophantic, groveling, sniveling, mealy-mouthed, abject, base, mean.

887 blusterer *n* swaggerer, braggart, boaster, windbag, bully, ruffian, rowdy, redneck.

III. Sympathetic Affections

888 friendship *n* amity, friendliness, harmony, concord, fellow-feeling, sympathy, good will, affection; companionship, comradeship, fellowship, fraternity, intimacy.

v be friendly, have an acquaintance with, keep company with, know, sympathize with, befriend, make friends with.

adj friendly, kind, kindly, amiable, neighborly, brotherly, cordial, genial, well-disposed, benevolent, kind-hearted, affectionate; helpful, advantageous, propitious; acquainted, familiar, intimate.

adv amicably, with open arms.

889 enmity *n* unfriendliness, dislike,

discord, ill will, antagonism, animosity, hostility, malevolence, hatred.

v be at odds with.

adj inimical, unfriendly, alienated, estranged, hostile.

890 friend *n* companion, acquaintance, crony, chum, pal, mate, fellow, bosom buddy, intimate, confidant; well-wisher, patron, supporter, backer, advocate, partisan, defender, sympathizer; ally, associate.

891 enemy *n* foe, adversary, opponent, antagonist, attacker.

892 sociality *n* sociableness, gregariousness, social interaction, social intercourse, comradeship, camaraderie, companionship, cordiality, good fellowship, conviviality.

v be sociable, consort with, fraternize, welcome.

adj sociable, gregarious, social, warm, genial, cordial, friendly, convivial, amicable, clubbish, chummy, neighborly, hospitable.

893 seclusion, exclusion *n* privacy, retirement, withdrawal, solitude, sequestration, retreat, isolation, hiding, secrecy, elimination, prohibition, exception, omission, preclusion, rejection, ejection, expulsion, banishment, ostracism, exile.

recluse, hermit, cenobite, outcast, castaway, pariah, wastrel, foundling.

v seclude oneself, retire, withdraw, retreat, sequester, isolate, hide, exclude, eliminate, prohibit, reject, eject, expel.

adj secluded, retired, withdrawn, sequestered, private, isolated, solitary, excluded, eliminated, prohibited, omitted, precluded, rejected, ejected, repulsed, banished, ostracized, exiled.

894 courtesy *n* civility, sociability, politeness, good manners, good behavior, affability, gentility, graciousness, courtliness, respect.

v be courteous, behave well.

adj courteous, civil, polite, well-mannered, well-bred, gentlemanly, gallant, urbane, debonair, affable, gracious, courtly, respectful, obliging.

895 discourtesy *n* disrespect, ill-breeding, bad manners, tactlessness, rudeness, impudence, vulgarity.

v be discourteous.

adj discourteous, ill-bred, ill-mannered, ill-behaved, ungentlemanly, uncivil, impolite, ungracious, vulgar, crude, disrespectful, rude.

896 congratulations *n* felicitation, compliment, salute, salutation.

v congratulate, offer congratulations, salute.

adj congratulatory; complimentary.

897 love *n* affection, liking, regard, friendliness, kindness, kindliness, tenderness, fondness, devotion, warmth, attachment, yearning, passion, rapture, adoration, idolatry.

lover, admirer, suitor, adorer, wooer; beau, sweetheart, flame, love, truelove, paramour, boyfriend, girlfriend, ladylove, idol, darling, angel, beloved.

v love, like, be fond of, have affection for, be enamored of, be in love with, cherish, adore, revere, adulate, idolize.

adj loving, smitten, affectionate, tender, fond, attached, enamored, devoted, amorous, passionate, adoring; lovable, adorable, winning, enchanting, bewitching.

898 hate *n* dislike, aversion, animosity, hatred, antipathy, detestation, loathing, abhorrence, odium, horror, repugnance.

v hate, dislike, detest, abhor, loathe, despise, execrate, abominate.

adj hateful, detestable, odious, abominable, loathsome, abhorrent, repugnant, invidious, obnoxious, offensive, disgusting, nauseating, revolting, vile, repulsive; hating, averse from, set against, bitter, spiteful, malicious.

899 favorite *n* pet, minion, idol, jewel, spoiled child, apple of one's eye, man after one's own heart; love, dear, darling, honey, sweetheart.

900 resentment *n* displeasure, pique, umbrage, animosity, bitterness, envy, jealousy, anger, wrath, indignation.

v resent, take offense, bristle over, chafe, fume, frown, pout, snarl, gnash, growl, scowl, glower, grouch, bear a grudge.

adj resentful, offended, bitter, worked up, angry, wrathful, irate, indignant; envious, jealous.

901 irascibility *n* irritability, excitability, sensitivity.

v be irascible, quick to fly off the handle, have a temper.

adj irascible, testy, short-tempered, hot-tempered, quick-tempered, touchy, temperamental, irritable, snappish, petulant, overly sensitive, choleric.

901a sullenness *n* moodiness, moroseness, churlishness, sluggishness.

v be sullen, frown, scowl, sulk, pout.

adj silent, reserved, sulky, morose, moody, ill-humored, sour, vexatious, bad-tempered, surly, cross, grumpy, peevish, perverse; gloomy, dismal, cheerless, overcast, somber, mournful, dark; slow, sluggish, dull, stagnant.

902 [expression of affection or love] **endearment** n embrace, caress, hug, kiss, blandishment, dalliance, love token.

v endear, embrace, caress, blandish, hirt, dally.

adj endearing.

903 marriage n wedding, nuptials, matrimony, wedlock; union, alliance, association, confederation.

married man, married woman, husband, wife, spouse, mate, partner, consort, better half, (informal) old man, (informal) old lady.

v marry, tie the knot, take to the altar, wive, couple.

adj married, wed, united.

904 celibacy n sexual abstinence; bachelorhood.

celibate, unmarried man, bachelor, unmarried woman, spinster, old maid, virgin, maiden; priest.

adj celibate, unmarried.

905 divorce n marital separation, legal separation; separation, disunion, isolation.

v divorce, (informal) split up, separate, isolate.

adj divorced, separated, (informal) split up.

906 benevolence n kindness, kindliness, humanity, tenderness, kindheartedness, unselfishness, generosity, liberality, charity, philanthropy, altruism.

good Samaritan, sympathizer, altruist.

v wish well, take an interest in, treat well, comfort, benefit, assist, aid.

adj benevolent, kind, kindly, well-disposed, kind-hearted, humane, tender, tender-hearted, unselfish, generous, liberal, benevolent, obliging, charitable, philanthropic, altruistic.

907 malevolence n ill will, enmity, rancor, resentment, malice, maliciousness, spite, spitefulness, grudge, hate, hatred, venom.

v bear ill will.

adj malevolent, malicious, resentful, spiteful, begrudging, hateful, venomous, vicious, hostile, ill-natured, evil-minded, rancorous.

908 malediction n curse, swear, imprecation, denunciation, cursing, damning, damnation, execration; slander.

v curse, swear, imprecate, denounce, damn, execrate; slander.

909 threat n menace, danger, indication, portent, foreboding, prognosti-

cation; intimidation.

v threaten, menace, endanger, indicate, presage, impend, portend, augur, forebode, foreshadow, prognosticate; frighten, denounce, intimidate, cow, badger.

adj threatening, menacing, endangering, impending, auguring, foreshadowing, foreboding, ominous, inauspicious, sinister, frightening, intimidating.

910 philanthropy n humaneness, compassion, humanitarianism, benevolence, helpfulness, munificence, public spirit, charity.

philanthropist, humanitarian, patriot.

adj philanthropic, humanitarian, benevolent, munificent, altruistic, public spirited, civic minded, charitable.

911 misanthropy n hatred of mankind, incivism.

misanthrope, man-hater; misogynist, woman-hater.

adj misanthropic, antisocial, uncivil.

912 benefactor n succorer, patron, supporter, contributor, friend.

913 evildoer n wrongdoer, troublemaker, subversive, oppressor, destroyer.

914 pity n sympathy, compassion, commiseration, condolence, mercy.

v pity, commiserate, feel sorry for, be sorry for, sympathize with, feel for.

adj pitying, compassionate, sympathetic, touched, moved, affected, feeling.

914a pitilessness n cruelty, meanness, ruthlessness, hard-heartedness.

v have no pity for.

adj pitiless, merciless, cruel, mean, unmerciful, ruthless, implacable, relentless, inexorable, hard-hearted, stony.

915 condolence n lamentation, sympathy, consolation.

v condole with, console, sympathize, lament.

916 gratitude n thanks, thankfulness, appreciation, indebtedness.

v be grateful, thank, appreciate.

adj grateful, appreciative, thankful, obliged, beholding, indebted, in one's debt.

917 ingratitude n thanklessness, unthankfulness.

ingrate.

v be ungrateful.

adj ungrateful, unthankful, unmindful, thankless.

918 forgiveness n pardon, excuse, indulgence, remission, reprieve, amnesty, grace, absolution.

v forgive, pardon, excuse, absolve, reprieve, acquit.

adj forgiving.

919 revenge n vengeance, retaliation, requital, reprisal, retribution, vindictiveness, vengefulness.

avenger, vindicator, nemesis.

v revenge, avenge, retaliate, requite, vindicate.

adj revengeful, vengeful, vindictive, spiteful, malevolent, resentful, malicious, malignant, unforgiving, implacable.

920 jealousy n envy, resentment; suspicion; watchfulness, vigilance.

v be jealous.

adj jealous, envious, resentful; suspicious; solicitous, watchful, vigilant.

921 envy n jealousy, enviousness, grudge, covetousness.

v envy, covet, begrudge, resent.

adj envious, covetous, jealous, begrudging.

IV. Moral Affections

922 right n virtue, justice, fairness, integrity, equity, equitableness, uprightness, rectitude, morality, morals, goodness, honor, lawfulness; accuracy, truth.

v be right; do right.

adj right, just, good, equitable, moral, fair, upright, honest, lawful; correct, proper, suitable, fit; correct, true, accurate, genuine, legitimate, rightful.

adv righteously, rightfully, lawfully, rightly, justly, fairly, equitably.

923 wrong n evil, wickedness, misdeed, sin, vice, immorality, iniquity, inequity, injustice, unlawfulness.

v wrong, injure, harm, maltreat, abuse, oppress, cheat, defraud, dishonor.

adj wrong, bad, evil, wicked, sinful, immoral, iniquitous, reprehensible, unjust, crooked, dishonest; erroneous, inaccurate, incorrect, false, untrue, mistaken; improper, unappropriate, unfit; awry, amiss, out of order.

adv wrongly, wickedly, sinfully.

924 claim n due, right, privilege, prerogative, prescription, demand, sanction, warrant, license.

claimant, appellant.

v claim, deserve, have the right, be entitled.

adj claiming, having a right to,

privileged, prescribed, sanctioned, allowed, licensed, authorized, due.

925 [absence of right] **unrightfulness** n impropriety, illegitimacy, presumption.

usurper, pretender.

v be unentitled.

adj unrightful, having no right to, unentitled, unauthorized, unwarranted, illegitimate, not licensed.

926 duty n obligation, function, responsibility, onus, burden, business; conscience, moral imperative, sense of duty; homage, respect, reverence.

v do one's duty, behoove, become, befit, beseem; observe, perform, fulfill, discharge.

adj obligatory, binding, imperative, incumbent, under obligation, obliged, bound, tied, duty bound; dutiful, respectful, docile, submissive, deferential, reverential, obedient.

927 dereliction of duty n nonobservance, nonperformance, neglect, failure, carelessness, fault, infraction, violation, transgression.

v neglect, slight, fail, violate.

adj undutiful, negligent, careless, at fault, failing, in violation.

927a exemption n immunity, impunity, privilege, freedom, exception, excuse, dispensation.

v exempt, excuse, release, acquit, discharge, free.

adj exempt, immune, privileged, freed, excepted, excused, unbound.

928 respect n esteem, deference, regard, consideration, estimation, veneration, reverence, homage, honor, admiration, approbation, approval, affection, feeling; respects, regards, duty; regard, consideration, attention, devotion.

v honor, revere, reverence, esteem, venerate, regard, consider, defer to, admire, adulate, adore, love; regard, heed, attend, notice, consider.

adj respectful, courteous, polite, well-mannered, well-bred, civil, deferential; respected, estimable, venerable, admirable; respecting, heeding, considering, regarding, attending.

929 disrespect n discourtesy, impoliteness, rudeness, crudeness, incivility, impudence, impertinence, irreverence, derision.

v hold in disrespect, be disrespectful, insult, deride, scoff, mock, sneer, jeer, deride, ridicule, scorn.

adj disrespectful, discourteous, impolite, rude, crude, uncivil, impudent, impertinent, irreverent, insulting, derisive, scornful.

930 contempt n scorn, disdain, derision, contumely; dishonor, disgrace, shame.

v feel contempt for, contemn, scorn, disdain, deride, despise.

adj contemptible, despicable, mean, low, miserable, abject, base, vile; contemptuous, scornful, disdainful, derisive; dishonorable, disgraceful, shameful.

931 approbation n approval, sanction, esteem, admiration, commendation.

v approbate, approve, esteem, value, honor, admire, appreciate, sanction, endorse, commend, praise.

adj commendatory, complimentary, laudatory; approved, praised, in high esteem, in favour; praiseworthy, commendable, good, meritorious, estimable, creditable.

932 disapprobation n disapproval, dislike, disesteem, odium, disparagement, deprecation, denunciation, censure.

v disapprove, dislike, object to, frown upon, censure, blame, reproach, reprove, admonish, berate.

adj disapproving, disparaging, reproachful, defamatory, denunciatory, condemnatory.

933 flattery n adulation, charming, lip-service, (informal) brown-nosing, fawning, flunkeyism, sycophancy.

v flatter, curry favor, slobber over, (informal) lay it on thick, wheedle, fawn, court, (informal) brown-nose, pander to, overpraise.

adj flattering, adulatory, honeymouthed, smooth-tongued, servile, sycophantic.

934 detraction n detracting, disparagement, belittling, defamation, vilification, calumny, abuse, slander, aspersion, deprecation.

v detract, run down, criticize, decry, disparage, blacken, belittle, depreciate, cast aspersions, defame, malign, abuse, slander, vilify.

adj detracting, disparaging, belittling, derogatory, depreciating, calumnious, abusive, slanderous, vilifying, scurrilous.

935 flatterer n adulator, toady, flunkey, (informal) apple-polisher, fawner, sycophant, (informal) brown-noser, bootlicker, opportunist, courtier.

936 detractor n reprover, critic, carper, slanderer, (informal) hatchet man, backbiter, defamer, castigator, satirist, cynic, reviler.

937 vindication n exoneration, exculpation, acquittal; justification, war-

rant, support, defense.

apologist, vindicator, defender.

v vindicate, exonerate, acquit, clear; uphold, justify, maintain, defend; support.

adj -vindicating, vindicated, exonerated, exonerating, exculpatory, acquitted; justified, warranted, supported.

938 accusation n arraignment, indictment, charge, incrimination, impeachment; accusal, blaming, inculpation, charging, imputation.

accuser, prosecutor, plaintiff; relator, informer; appellant.

v charge; arraign, indict, charge, incriminate, impeach; blame, inculpate, charge, involve, point to, impute.

adj accused, accusing, accusatory, accusative, incriminatory, imputative.

939 probity n honesty, uprightness, virtue, rectitude, integrity.

v be honorable.

adj honest, honorable, virtuous, upright, scrupulous, high-principled.

940 improbity n dishonesty, wickedness, immorality, evil.

v be dishonest, play false.

adj dishonest, dishonorable, unscrupulous, immoral, wicked, evil.

941 knave n rogue, rascal, blackguard, sneak, villain, scoundrel.

942 disinterestedness n impartiality, fairness, lack of bias, unselfishness, generosity, liberality.

v be disinterested.

adj disinterested, unbiased, unprejudiced, unselfish, impartial, fair, generous, liberal.

943 selfishness n self-interest, self-seeking, self-love, egoism, egotism, solipsism, illiberality, parsimony, stinginess, meanness.

v be selfish, cultivate one's own garden, look after oneself, feather one's own nest.

adj selfish, self-centered, self-indulgent, self-interested, self-seeking, egotistical, solipsistic, illiberal, parsimonious, stingy, cheap, mean.

944 virtue n virtuousness, goodness, uprightness, morality, ethics, probity, rectitude, integrity; excellence, merit, quality, asset; innocence, chastity, purity.

v be virtuous, have the virtue of.

adj virtuous, right, upright, moral, righteous, good, chaste, pure.

945 vice n fault, sin, depravity, iniquity, immorality, wickedness; blemish, blot, imperfection, defect.

v sin, err, transgress, trespass.

adj vicious, immoral, depraved, profligate, wicked, sinful, sinning, corrupt, bad, iniquitous; reprehensible, blameworthy, censurable, wrong, improper; spiteful, malignant, malicious, malevolent; faulty, defective; ill-tempered, bad-tempered, refractory.

946 innocence *n* purity, virtue, virtuousness, faultlessness, spotlessness; guiltlessness, blamelessness; uprightness, honesty; naïveté, simplicity, artlessness, guilelessness, ingenuousness.

v be innocent.

adj innocent, pure, untainted, sinless, virtuous, virginal, blameless, faultless, impeccable, spotless, immaculate; guiltless, blameless; upright, honest, forthright; naïve, simple, unsophisticated, artless, guileless, ingenuous.

947 guilt *n* guiltiness, culpability, criminality; sinfulness.

v be guilty.

adj guilty, culpable, to blame, in fault.

948 good man *n* model, paragon, hero, soldier, saint, salt of the earth, (*informal*) ace.

949 bad man *n* wrong-doer, evildoer, sinner, scoundrel, miscreant, villain, wretch, monster, devil, demon, scum of the earth.

950 penitence *n* contrition, atonement, compunction, repentance, remorse, regret.

penitent, prodigal son.

v be penitent, repent, rue, regret.

adj penitent, sorry, contrite, repenting; repentant, atoning, amending, remorseful, regretful; penitential.

951 impenitence *n* irrepentance, obduracy, hardness of heart.

v be impenitent, show no remorse.

adj impenitent, uncontrite, not sorry, obdurate, unrepentant, remorseless; unrepenting, unrepented, unatoned; irreclaimable.

952 atonement *n* satisfaction, reparation, compensation, amends, quittance; redemption, expiation, reclamation, conciliation, propitiation.

v atone, atone for; give satisfaction, satisfy, make amends; expiate, propitiate, reclaim, redeem, repair, absolve, purge, shrive, do penance, repent.

adj atoning, propitiating, propitiatory, redemptive, expiating, expiatory.

953 temperance *n* moderation, self-restraint, self-control, continence; sobriety, even-temperedness, calmness, coolness, detachment, dispassion.

vegetarian; teetotaler; abstainer.

v be temperate, abstain, forbear, restrain.

adj temperate, moderate, self-controlled, self-restrained, frugal, sparing; sober, calm, cool, detached, dispassionate.

954 intemperance *n* excess, exorbitance, inordinateness, extravagance; indulgence, high living, self-indulgence, epicurism, epicureanism, sybaritism; inabstinence, alcoholism.

v be intemperate, indulge, wallow in.

adj intemperate, excessive, exorbitant, inordinate, extravagant; indulgent, self-indulgent, epicurean.

954a sensualist *n* sybarite, voluptuary, pleasure-seeker, epicure, epicurean, libertine, hedonist.

955 asceticism *n* puritanism, austerity, abstemiousness, self-abnegation, self-denial, total abstinence, self-motification.

ascetic, anchorite, puritan, martyr; hermit, recluse.

v abstain, deny oneself, fast, starve.

adj ascetic, puritanical, austere, abstemious, rigorous, rigid, stern, severe, harsh, strict, self-denying, self-mortifying.

956 fasting *n* day of fasting; going hungry, starving oneself, starvation.

v fast, starve, famish.

adj fasting, starving, unfed; starved, half-starved, hungry.

957 gluttony *n* greed, greediness, voracity; epicurism, gormandizing, gulosity, crapulence, over-eating, (*informal*) piggishness.

glutton, epicure, cormorant, hog, (*informal*) pig.

v be gluttonous, hog; overeat, gorge, stuff oneself, make a pig of oneself, guzzle, bolt, devour, engorge, gobble up.

adj gluttonous, greedy, voracious; epicurean, gormandizing, crapulent, swinish, (*informal*) piggish.

958 sobriety *n* abstinence, teetotalism.

teetotaler, abstainer.

v be sober, abstain, take the pledge.

adj sober, unintoxicated, on the wagon, (*informal*) straight, (*informal*) dry, dry as a bone.

959 drunkenness *n* intemperance, drinking, inebriety, insobriety, intoxication, alcoholism.

drunkard, sot, tippler, drinker, inebriate, dipsomaniac, alcoholic, (*informal*) boozer, (*informal*) lush, (*informal*) juicer.

v be drunk, drink, imbibe, booze, guzzle, swill, soak, sot, lush, drink like a fish, hit the bottle.

adj drunk, drunken, sotted, intoxicated, inebriated, tipsy, tight, (*informal*) potted, (*informal*) stewed, (*informal*) stewed to the gills, dead drunk, (*informal*) plowed, (*informal*) plastered, (*informal*) tanked, (*informal*) wasted, (*informal*) juiced, (*informal*) blown away, (*informal*) high, (*informal*) flying, (*informal*) feeling no pain.

960 purity *n* cleanness; decency, decorum, delicacy; continence, chastity, innocence, modesty, virtue, virginity; simplicity, genuineness, faultlessness, perfection; guiltlessness, honesty, uprightness.

virgin, vestal virgin.

v be pure.

adj pure, decent, delicate; innocent, continent, chaste, viginal, modest, virtuous, undefiled, unsullied, unstained, untainted, uncorrupted, clean, spotless, immaculate; simple, genuine, faultless, perfect; honest, upright; unmixed, unadulterated, uncontaminated.

961 impurity *n* indecency, indelicacy; incontinence, immodesty, lewdness, concupiscence, prurience, lechery; grossness, obscenity, ribaldry, smut, bawdry; uncleanness, adulteration, contamination, defilement; fault, flaw, imperfection; guilt, sin, sinfulness.

v be impure.

adj impure, indecent, indelicate; incontinent, immodest, unchaste, concupiscent, lewd, prurient, lecherous; gross, obscene, ribald, dirty, smutty, bawdy; unclean, sullied, defiled, contaminated, adulterated, tainted, stained, corrupted, jaded; faulty, flawed, imperfect; guilty, sinning, sinful, wicked.

962 libertine *n* rake, roué, debauchee, lecher, sensualist, voluptuary, profligate, seducer, deceiver, courtesan, prostitute, strumpet, harlot, whore, street-walker, trollop, hussy, bitch, slut, minx.

963 legality *n* legitimacy, legitimateness, lawfulness; duty, obligation.

law, code, constitution, charter, statute, regulation, decree, order.

v legalize; legislate, enact, ordain, decree, codify, formulate, pass a law.

adj legal, legitimate, authorized, licit, lawful, legalized, legislated; constitutional.

964 illegality *n* illegitimacy, unlawfulness, illicitness, lawlessness.

v be illegal, offend against the law, violate the law.

adj illegal, unlawful, illegitimate, illicit, contraband, unconstitutional, unchartered, unwarranted, unauthorized, unlicensed, proscribed, prohibited, outlawed, criminal; lawless, arbitrary, despotic, unanswerable, unaccountable.

965 [executive] **jurisdiction** *n* judicature, authority, power, right, control; territory, range, magistracy.

v judge, sit in judgment; administer.

adj jurisdictive, judicial, administrative; inquisitorial.

966 tribunal *n* court, courtroom, board, bench, court of law, court of justice, bar of justice, judgment seat, dock, forum, witness-chair.

967 judge *n* justice, judiciary, magistrate, judicator, adjudicator, jurist, juror; moderator, arbiter, arbitrator, umpire, referee.

v judge, adjudge, determine, hear a cause, try a case, pass sentence.

adj judicial, judicious, juridical, legal, juristic, judicatory, jurisdictive.

968 lawyer *n* attorney, attorney-at-law, counselor, barrister, solicitor, pleader, counsel, advocate, counselor-at-law, legal adviser; prosecutor, prosecuting attorney, district attorney, public prosecutor, attorney general.

bar, legal profession.

v practice law, be called to the bar, plead, read the law.

adj learned in the law.

969 lawsuit *n* suit, action, cause, dispute, contention; case, debate, litigation, legal proceedings, legal action, legal process, trial, debate, pleadings, argument, argumentation, disputation, prosecution; writ, summons, subpoena, affidavit, suitor, party to a suit, litigant, verdict, decision; precedent.

v go to the law, sue, file a claim, bring to trial, put on trial, serve, serve with a writ, cite, arraign, prosecute, bring an action against, indict, impeach, attach, summon.

adj litigious.

970 acquittal *n* clearance, exculpation, exoneration, absolution, discharge, pardon; impunity, immunity.

v acquit, exculpate, exonerate, clear, absolve, pardon; discharge, release, liberate, set free.

adj acquitted, cleared, exculpated, exonerated; discharged, released, set free.

971 **condemnation** n conviction, guilty verdict, proscription.

v condemn, convict, find guilty, damn, doom, proscribe; stand condemned.

adj condemned, condemnatory, convicted.

972 **punishment** n sentence, judgment, penalty, retribution, discipline, chastisement, castigation, reproof, correction.

v punish, inflict punishment, correct, discipline, penalize, reprove, castigate, chasten, administer correction. scold, berate, jail, incarcerate, execute, torture, banish, flog, whip, lash, scourge.

adj punishing, punitive, castigatory, penalized, penalizing; punished, castigated.

973 **reward** n recompense, prize, desert, compensation, pay, remuneration, requital, merit; bounty, premium, bonus; reparation, redress; retribution, reckoning, amends.

v reward, recompense, requite, compensate, pay, remunerate.

adj rewarding, remunerative, compensatory, retributive, reparatory; rewarded.

974 **penalty** n punishment, retribution, pain, pains, penance; fine, forfeit, damages, sequestration, incarceration, confiscation.

v penalize, punish; fine, confiscate, sequester; penalized, punished.

975 **scourge** n punishment, flogging; affliction, calamity, plague, bane, pest, nuisance; whip, lash, strap, throng, rod, cane, stick; prison, house of correction.

gaoler, jailer, executioner, hangman.

976 **deity** n divinity, god, godhead, omnipotence, providence, lord, the almighty, supreme being, first cause, prime mover, author, creator, the infinite, the eternal, the all-powerful, the all-merciful, omnipresence.

adj divine, godly, almighty, holy, hallowed, sacred, heavenly, celestial, sacrosanct; superhuman, supernatural, spiritual, ghostly, unearthly.

977 **angel** n glorified spirit, beneficent spirit, ministering spirit, heavenly spirit, winged being, seraph, cherub, archangel, helper, spirit, guardian; (informal) friend, patron, protector, guardian angel, love.

adj angelic, seraphic, cherubic, spiritual, ethereal; pure, good, righteous, ideal, beautiful; (informal) adorable, entrancing, transporting, rapturous, lovely, enrapturing.

978 **devil** n Satan, Lucifer, Beelzebub; tempter, evil one, evil spirit, serpent, prince of darkness, demon, evil incarnate.

diabolism, satanism.

adj devilish, satanic, diabolic, infernal, hellish.

979 **fabulous spirit** n god, goddess, fairy, fay, sylph, faun, nymph, nereid, dryad, sea-maid, oread, naiad, mermaid, kelpie, nixie, sprite, pixie, elf.

adj fabulous, mythological, imaginary, sylphic.

980 **demon** n demonology;   devil, fiend, evil spirit, incubus, monster, succubus, succuba, fury, harpy, ghoul, vampire, ogre, gnome, imp, kobold, dwarf, urchin, troll, sprite, bad fairy, leprechaun; ghost, specter, apparition, spirit, shade, shadow, vision, hobgoblin, wraith, spook, banshee, siren, satyr.

adj demonic, supernatural, weird, uncanny, unearthly, spectral, ghostly, ghostlike, elfin, fiendish, impish, haunted.

981 **heaven** n kingdom of heaven, kingdom of god, heavenly kingdom, paradise, nirvana; celestial bliss, glory.

adj heavenly, celestial, supernal, unearthly, paradisaic, paradisical, beatific, elysian, blissful, beautiful, divine, blessed, beatified, glorified.

982 **hell** n Gehenna, inferno, Hades, Erebus, pandemonium, abyss, limbo; [informal] torment, torture, pain, agony, suffering.

adj hellish, infernal, stygian, satanic, diabolic, devilish; [informal] painful, agonizing, excruciating, horrifying, unendurable.

983 **theology** n theosophy, divinity, hagiography, theologics, theism, monotheism, religion, religious persuasion, dogma, creed, credo, doctrine, tenet, articles of faith.

theologian, theologue, divine.

adj theological, religious, theosophical, hagiological.

983a **orthodoxy** n soundness; strictness, faithfulness, adherence, observance; truth, true faith, religious truth.

adj orthodox, sound, strict, faithful, catholic, doctrinal, authoritative, official, traditional; scriptural, divine, Christian; conventional, established, approved, prescriptive, prevailing, customary.

984 **heterodoxy** n unorthodoxy, nonconformity, iconoclasm, doubt, skepticism, recusancy, dissent, misbelief, error, heresy, schism, apostasy.

pagan, heathen, dissenter, nonconformist, skeptic, heretic, atheist.

adj heterodox, nonconformist, nonconforming, iconoclastic, doubting, skeptical, unscriptural, unorthodox, uncanonical, recusant, dissenting, misbelieving, heretical, schismatic.

985 revelation *n* disclosure, discovery, expression, declaration, expression, utterance, publication, admission, convession, acknowledgment; enlightenment, proclamation, announcement; Christian Revelation, Scriptures, Word of God.

adj revelatory; instructive; confessional.

986 religious writings *n* Scriptures, *Bible*, Old Testament, New Testament, The Vedas, Upanishads, Bhagavad Gita, Koran, Alcoran, Avesta.

987 piety *n* godliness, devoutness, devotion, humility, veneration, sanctity, grace, holiness; reverence, regard, respect.

believer, devotee, pietist, righteous man.

v be pious, have faith; believe, revere, venerate, sanctify, consecrate.

adj pious, devout, godly, reverent, religious, holy, sacred, pietistic, saintly; devoted, humble, reverential.

988 impiety *n* irreverence, irreligion, scoffing, profaneness, profanity, blasphemy, desecration, sacrilege, sin, sinfulness; hypocrisy, cant, sanctimony, sanctimoniousness.

sinner, scoffer, blasphemer, sacrilegist, hypocrite.

v be impious, scoff, swear, profane, blaspheme, desecrate, revile, commit sacrilege.

989 irreligion *n* ungodliness, laxity, impiety, indifference, apathy, skepticism, doubt, disbelief, incredulity, agnosticism, freethinking, atheism, infidelity.

skeptic, doubter, nonbeliever, agnostic, cynic, freethinker, atheist, infidel, heathen.

v be irreligious, doubt, disbelieve, lack faith, question.

adj irreligious, godless, ungodly, unholy, unhallowed, undevout; skeptical, doubting, unbelieving, indifferent, apathetic, incredulous, freethinking, agnostic, atheistic, faithless; worldly, earthly, unspiritual.

990 worship *n* reverence, homage, adoration, honor; regard, idolizing, idolatry, deification; prayer, supplication, petition; service, celebration, rites.

worshiper, congregation, suppliant, communicant, celebrant.

v worship, adore, adulate, idolize, deify, love, like; pray, kneel, bow, fall on one's knees; invoke, supplicate, offer prayers, petition; praise, bless, laud, glorify, magnify, sing praises.

adj worshiping, revering, adoring, honoring; worshipful, reverential, honorific, celebrational.

991 idolatry *n* idolism, idolatrousness, idolization, fetishism, idol-worship, deification, demonology; blind adoration, extravagant love, fervor, ardency, enchantment, hero worship.

idol, image, icon, symbol, statue, false god, pagan deity.

v idolize, worship idols, idolatrize, worship, glorify, put on a pedestal, canonize, deify, apotheosize; dote upon, treasure, prize.

adj idolatrous, idol-worshiping, pagan, fetishistic; adoring, impassioned, lovesick.

992 sorcery *n* occultism, magic, witchery, enchantment, witchcraft, spell, necromancy, divination, charm, conjuration, bewitchery, spiritualism.

v practice sorcery, conjure, charm, enchant, bewitch, divine, entrance, mesmerize, cast a spell, call up spirits, raise spirits.

adj magic, magical, bewitching, enchanting, charming, incantory, weird, cabalistic, talismanic; charmed, bewitched, enchanted.

993 spell *n* charm, incantation, exorcism, voodoo, trance, rapture, suggestion, jinx, hocus-pocus, mumbo-jumbo, abracadabra.

994 sorcerer *n* magician, conjuror, necromancer, wizard, witch, exorcist, charmer, medicine man, shaman, medium, clairvoyant, mesmerist, soothsayer, guru.

995 churchdom *n* church, ministry, priesthood, sisterhood, prelacy, hierarchy.

v call, ordain, consecrate, bestow, elect.

adj ecclesiastical, clerical, priestly, pastoral, ministerial, hierarchical.

996 clergy *n* clerical, ministry, priesthood, the cloth, clergyman, divine, ecclesiastic, churchman, pastor, shepherd, minister, preacher, parson, father, reverend, priest, rabbi.

v receive the call, take orders.

adj clerical; ordained.

997 laity *n* fold, flock, congregation, assembly, brethren, people; layman, parishioner.

v secularize.

adj lay, laical, secular, civil, temporal.

998 rite *n* ceremony, observance, function, service, procedure, form, usage.

　　v perform a rite.

　　adj ritualistic, ceremonial.

999 canonicals *n* religious garments, vestments, robe, gown, surplice.

1000 temple *n* place of worship, house of god, cathedral, church, chapel, meetinghouse, synagogue, tabernacle, mosque, shrine, pantheon; monastery, priory, abbey, friary, convent, nunnery, cloister; parsonage, rectory, vicarage.

　　adj churchly, cloistered, monastic.

Index

A

acumen n 498
acute adj 171, 173, 253, 375, 410, 410
acute angle n 244
acutely adv 31
acuteness n 173, 253
adage n 496
adamant adj 600
adamantine adj 323
adapt v 23, 852
adaptability n 149
adaptable adj 82, 149
adapt to v 82
add v 37, 85
addendum n 37, 39
addiction n 613
addictive adj 613
addition n 37
addition n 35, 39
additional adj 35, 37, 39
addle-brained adj 499
address n 189, 582, 586; v 582, 586
add to v 35
add up v 37, 85
add up to v 50
add water v 337
adept adj 698
adequacy n 639
adequate adj 157, 639
adhere v 46, 199
adherence n 46, 983a
adhere to v 613, 772
adhering adj 46
adhesion n 46, 772
adhesive adj 46, 327, 352
adhesiveness n 46, 352
adieu n 293
ad infinitum adv 104
adjacent adj 197
adjoin v 197, 199
adjoining adj 197
adjourn v 133
adjournment n 133
adjudge v 967
adjudicator n 737, 967
adjunct n 39
adjunct n 37, 88
adjust v 23, 27, 58, 774, 852
adjustable adj 149
adjustment n 723, 774
administer n 965; v 692, 693, 737, 786, 965

administer correction v 972
administering adj 693
administration n 692, 693
administrative adj 692, 737, 965
admirable adj 928
admiration n 870, 928, 931
admire v 870, 928, 931
admirer n 897
admission n 76, 296, 785, 985
admit v 54, 76, 296, 488, 529, 785
admit of v 470
admittance n 296
admitting adj 469
admixture n 41
admonish v 668, 695, 864, 932
admonition n 668, 695, 864
admonitory adj 695
ado n 315, 684
adolescence n 131
adolescent adj 131
adorable adj 897, 977
adoration n 897, 990
adore v 897, 928, 990
adorer n 897
adoring adj 897, 990, 991
adorn v 847
adornment n 847
adrift adj 10, 44, 73; adv 44
adroit adj 698
adroitness n 698, 702
adulate v 897, 928, 990
adulation n 933
adulator n 935
adulatory adj 933
adult adj 131
adulterate v 41, 659
adulterated adj 337, 961
adulteration n 41, 659, 961
adulthood n 131
adumbrate v 422
adumbration n 421
advance n 282, 286, 731, 787; v 35, 109, 282, 307, 514, 658, 731, 763, 787

advanced adj 128, 282
advanced age n 128
advanced guard n 234
advancement n 282, 658
advancing adj 282
advantage n 33, 618; v 618
advantageous adj 618, 644, 646, 648, 775, 888
advent n 121, 286, 292
adventitious adj 6, 8, 156
adventure n 151, 622, 675; v 665, 675
adventurer n 463, 548, 621
adventuress n 548
adventurous adj 675, 861
adversary n 708, 710, 726, 891
adverse adj 708, 735
adversely adv 735
adversity n 735
adversity n 619, 830
advertise v 531
advertisement n 531
advice n 695
advice n 527, 668, 693, 864
advisability n 646
advisable adj 646
advise v 527, 693, 695, 864
advised adj 527, 620
advisedly adv 611, 620
adviser n 540, 694, 695
advisory adj 668, 695
advisory board n 696
advocacy n 707
advocate n 890, 968; v 695, 707
aerate v 338
aerial adj 267, 338
aeriform adj 338
aeronautical n 267
aeronautics n 267
aesthetic adj 845
afar adj 196; adv 196
affability n 894
affable adj 894
affair n 151, 454, 625, 680
affairs n 151
affect v 9, 175, 176,

824, 855
affectation n 855
affectation n 579
affected adj 579, 820,
 821, 855, 914
affectedness n 855
affection n 888, 897,
 928
affectionate adj 888,
 897
affections n 820
affidavit n 467, 535,
 969
affiliated adj 9, 11
affiliation n 11
affinity n 9, 17, 216,
 288
affirm v 516, 535
affirmation n 535
affirmative adj 535
affirming adj 535
affix n 39; v 37, 43
afflict v 828
affliction n 735, 828,
 830, 975
affluence n 734, 803
affluent adj 803
afford v 784
afford pleasure v 829
affront n 830; v 830
afire adj 382
aflame adj 382
afloat adj 1, 267
aforementioned adj
 116
aforethought adj 611
afraid adj 860, 862
afresh adv 104, 123
aft adv 235
after adj 117; adv 63,
 117, 235, 281
aftermath n 65
afternoon n 126
afterpiece n 65
aftertaste n 390
after the flood adv 59
after this fashion adv
 627
afterthought n 65
afterwards adv 117
again adv 104
again and again adv
 104
against adv 708, prep
 179
against one's will adv
 603

against the grain adv
 256
age n 128
age n 106, 108, 124; v
 124, 435
aged adj 124, 128, 130
agency n 170
agency n 632, 677, 755
agent n 690
agent n 153, 758
agglomerate v 46
aggrandize v 35, 194
aggrandizement n 35,
 37, 194
aggravate v 173, 835
aggravation n 835
aggregate n 50, 72; v
 50
aggregation n 46, 72
aggression n 716
aggressive adj 716
aggressiveness n 715
aggressor n 716
aggrieve v 649
aghast adj 509, 860,
 870
agile adj 274
agitate v 315, 824
agitated adj 149, 315
agitation n 315
agitation n 59, 149,
 171, 173, 824, 825
aglow adj 420
agnostic adj 989
agnosticism n 989
ago adv 122
agog adj 870
agonize v 378
agonizing adj 982
agony n 378, 825, 828,
 982
agrarian adj 371
agree v 23, 82, 178,
 488, 714, 725, 762,
 768, 769
agreeable adj 23, 82,
 377, 413, 762, 829,
 831
agreeableness n 829
agreed adj 488
agreed upon adj 474
agreeing adj 23, 413,
 488, 494
agreement n 23
agreement n 16, 17, 82,
 178, 242, 488, 602,

709, 714, 762, 769
agree to v 760
agree with v 656, 829
agricultural adj 371
agriculture n 371
agrobiology n 371
agrology n 371
agronomics n 371
agronomy n 371
ahead adv 234, 280,
 282, 303
aid n 707
aid n 631, 644, 711,
 834; v 215, 631, 644,
 707, 746, 834, 906
aiding adj 707
ail v 655
ailing adj 655
ailment n 655
aim n 278, 453, 516,
 620; v 278, 516
aim at v 278, 620, 622
aim for v 620
air n 338
air n 349, 415, 448,
 852; v 338
aircraft n 273
airing n 266
airman n 269
air-pipe n 351
airplane n 273
airs n 855
airtight adj 261
air travel n 267
airy adj 4, 320, 334,
 338
ait n 346
ajar adj 260
akimbo adj 244
akin adj 11
akin to adj 17
alacrity n 132, 274,
 602, 684
à la mode adj 852
alarm n 669
alarm n 550, 665, 668,
 860; v 669
alarm bell n 669
alarmed adj 860
alarum n 669
albeit adv 30
albification n 430
albinism n 430
albinistic adj 430
album n 596
alchemy n 144
alcoholic n 959

alcoholism n 954, 959,
Alcoran n 986
alert adj 457, 498, 682,
864
alertness n 457, 459
algebra n 85
algebraic adj 85
alias n 565
alien adj 10, 57
alienated adj 889
alight v 265, 292, 306,
342
aligned adj 216
alignment n 278
alike adj 17
alive adj 359, 375, 457,
505, 682
alive and kicking adj
359
all adv 50
allay v 834
all but adv 32
all day long adv 110
allegation n 617
allege v 617
alleged adj 617
allegiance n 743
all-embracing adj 76
all-encompassing adj
78
alleviate v 174, 834
alleviation n 834
all for the better adj
658
alliance n 9, 11, 178,
709, 712, 714, 903
allied adj 9, 11, 216
allied to adj 17
allied with adj 178
all-important adj 642
nll in all adv 50
all-inclusive adj 78
all manner of kinds adj
81
allocation n 786
allocution n 586
all of a sudden adv 113
all one adj 27
allot v 51, 60, 786
allotment n 60, 786
all over adv 180
allow v 469, 488, 529,
737, 740, 748, 760,
762, 784, 813
allowable adj 760
allowance n 469, 488,

760, 784, 786, 813
allowed adj 924
allow for v 469
alloy n 41, 48
all-purpose adj 148
all ready adj 673
all set for adj 507
all the livelong day
adv 110
all the rage adj 852
all the time adv 106
all the worse for wear
adj 659
allude to v 516, 527
allure v 288, 829
alluring adj 288
allusive adj 521, 526
alluvial adj 342
ally n 711, 890; v 174
almanac n 114
almighty adj 157, 976
almighty dollar n 800
almost adv 32
alms n 784
almsgiving n 784
aloft n 267
alone adj 87
alongside adv 236
a long way off adv 196
a long while back adv
122
along with adv 37, 88
aloud adv 404
alphabet n 561
alphabetical adj 561
already adv 116, 122
also adv 37
alter v 15, 140
alteration n 20a, 140
altercation n 713, 720
altered adj 15, 20a
alter ego n 17
alternate adj 634, 759; v
12, 20a, 70, 138, 147,
149 adj 12, 70, 138
alternately adv 138
alternation n 138, 145.
149, 314
alternative n 147, 609
alter one's course v
279
although adv 30, 179
altitude n 206
altogether adv 50, 52
altruism n 906
altruist n 906

altruistic adj 906, 910
always adv 16, 112
amalgam n 41, 48
amalgamate v 41, 48
amalgamation n 41, 48
amass v 50, 72, 636
amateur n 701
amaze v 870
amazed adj 870
amazement n 870
amazing adj 870
amazingly adv 31
amber n 356a
ambergris n 356a
ambiguity n 475, 517,
519, 520, 571
ambiguous adj 475,
520
ambition n 620, 865
amble v 275
ambrosial adj 394
ambuscade n 530
ambush n 530
ambush n 667; v 530
ameliorate v 658, 723
amelioration n 658
amenable adj 762
amend v 658
amending adj 950
amendment n 658
amends n 30, 952, 973
amenity n 829
amiability n 829
amiable adj 721, 829,
888
amicable adj 707, 721,
892
amicably adv 888
amid adv 41, 228
amidst adv 41
amiss adj 923
amity n 714, 721, 888
ammunition n 727
amnesia n 506
amnesty n 723, 918
among adv 41, 228
amongst adv 41, 228
amorous adj 897
amorphism n 241
amorphous adj 241
amount n 25, 26, 800,
812
amount to v 50
amphitheater n 599,
728
ample adj 31, 180, 192,
202, 639

amplification n 194
amplify v 194, 549, 573
amplitude n 102, 192, 202
amplitudinous adj 192
amply adv 31, 639
amputate v 38
amputation n 38
amuse v 829, 840
amusement n 840
amuse oneself v 840
amusing adj 840
anachronism n 115
anachronism n 135
anachronistic adj 115
anagram n 561
analogous adj 12, 17, 216
analogy n 9, 17, 216
analysis n 49, 60, 463, 476, 596
analytic adj 85, 463, 596
analytical adj 476, 596
analyze v 49, 463, 476
analyzer n 463
anarchic adj 59
anarchism n 59
anarchy n 59
anatomic adj 329
anatomical adj 329
anatomy n 329, 357, 368
ancestral adj 166
ancestry n 122, 166
anchor n 666
anchorage n 184
anchorite n 955
ancient adj 124
ancient times n 122
and adv 37
and everywhere adv 186
and so forth adv 37
anemic adj 430
anesthesia n 376
anesthetic adj 376
anesthetize v 376, 381
anew adv 104, 123
angel n 977
angel n 164, 897
angelic adj 977
anger n 824, 900; v 830
angle n 244; v 244
angry adj 382, 900
anguish n 378, 619, 828

angular adj 244
angularity n 244
anility n 128
animal n 366
animal adj 366
animalistic adj 364, 366
animality n 364
animal kingdom n 366
animal life n 357, 364
animal physiology n 368
animate v 382, 824, 836; adj 357
animated adj 171, 382, 515
animated nature.n 357
animate matter n 357
animating adj 836
animation n 359, 515, 682, 824
animosity n 889, 898, 900
ankle-deep adj 209
annalist n 553
annal(s) n 114
annals n 551
annex n 39; v 37
annexation n 37, 43
annihilate v 2
annihilation n 2, 162
annotate v 522
annotator n 524
announce v 527, 531, 883
announcement n 527, 531, 985
annoy v 688, 830
annoyance n 649, 828, 830, 835
annul v 756
annulment n 756
anoint v 332
anointment n 332, 355
anomalous adj 59, 83
anomaly n 59, 83
anon adv 132
another adj 15
another time n 119
answer n 462
answer n 479, 522, 662; v 462, 746
answerable adj 177, 462
answerable for adj 806
answer for v 759

antagonism n 14, 24, 179, 708, 715, 867, 889
antagonist n 708, 710, 726, 891
antagonistic adj 14, 24, 179, 708, 715
antagonize v 14, 179
antecedence n 116
antecedence n 62
antecedent n 64, 116; adj 62, 116
antedate v 115, 116
antediluvian adj 124
antemeridian n 125
anterior adj 62, 116, 234
anteriority n 116
anthology n 596
anthracite n 388
anthropology n 368
anti adj 708
anticipate v 115, 121, 132, 451, 507, 510, 673, 858
anticipation n 121, 132, 451, 507, 510, 673, 858
anticipatory adj 132, 510
antidote n 662
antipathy n 14, 289, 867, 898
antipodal adj 237
antipodean adj 14
antipodes n 14
antiquarian n 553
antiquarianism n 124
antiquated adj 124
antique adj 124
antiquity n 122, 124
antisocial adj 911
antithesis n 14, 218, 237
antithetical adj 14, 237
antitoxin n 662
anxiety n 459, 860
anxious adj 860
any adj 25
apace adv 274
apart adj 44, 87; adv 44
apathetic adj 383, 456, 823, 866, 989
apathy n 823, 866, 989
ape v 19
aperture n 260

apex n 8, 67, 210
aphasia n 581, 583
aphorism n 496
aphoristic adj 496
apiece adv 79
aping n 19
apologist n 937
apostasy n 607, 984
apostate n 607
a posteriori n 476
apostrophe n 589
apostrophize v 589
apothegm n 496
apotheosize v 991
appal v 830
apparel n 225; v 225
apparent adj 446, 448, 525
apparently adv 448
apparition n 4, 443, 980
appeal n 411, 763
appear v 446, 448, 525
appearance n 448
appearance n 220, 240, 446, 569
appease v 174, 723, 826, 831
appellant n 924, 938
appellation n 564
append v 37
appendage n 39, 65
appendix n 39
appertain to v 9, 56
appetite n 865
appetizing adj 394
applaud v 836, 883
apple adj 435
apple of one's eye n 899
apple-polisher n 886, 935
appliance n 677
applicability n 644
applicable adj 644, 677
applicant n 767
application n 677, 765
apply v 677
appoint v 741, 755, 786
appointment n 755
apportion v 44, 51, 60, 73, 786
apportionment n 786
apportionment n 60, 73
apposite adj 23
apposition n 23, 199

appraisal n 812
appraise v 466, 480, 668, 812
appraisement n 466
appreciate v 394, 480, 850, 916, 931
appreciation n 465, 822, 916
appreciative adj 822, 916
apprehend v 490, 860
apprehension n 453, 490, 665, 789, 860
apprehensive adj 860
apprentice n 541
apprenticeship n 539
apprize v 527
apprized of adj 527
approach n 286
approach n 197, 569, 627, 632; v 121, 152, 286
approaching adj 286
approbate v 931
approbation n 931
approbation n 488, 928
appropriate v 775, 786, 788, 789, 791; adj 79, 134, 646, 850
appropriateness n 646
appropriating n 788
appropriation n 775, 789, 791
approval n 488, 762, 928, 931
approve v 535, 737, 931
approved adj 931, 983a
approximate v 17, 197; adj 17, 197, 286
approximation n 9, 17, 19, 286
apricot adj 439
a priori n 476
apt adj 23, 498, 698, 850
aptitude n 176, 498, 602, 698
aptness n 176, 698
aqua n 337
aquamarine adj 435, 438
aquatics n 267
aqueduct n 350
aqueous adj 337

arable adj 371
arbiter n 724, 737, 967
arbitrariness n 739
arbitrary adj 83, 606, 608, 739, 964
arbitrate v 174, 724
arbitration n 724
arbitrator n 724, 967
arc n 245
arcade n 245
arced adj 245
arch n 245, 250; v 245; adj 31
archaic adj 124
archaism n 124
archangel n 977
arched adj 245, 250
archetype n 22
archipelago n 346
architect n 164
architecture n 161, 329
arch over v 245
arctic adj 383
ardency n 991
ardent adj 382, 865
ardor n 382, 574, 682, 821
arduous adj 704
area n 181
arena n 728
arenose adj 330
areola n 247
argue v 24, 467, 476, 720
arguer n 476
argument n 454, 476, 516, 713, 720, 969
argumentation n 476, 969
argumentative adj 476, 713
arguments n 476
argumentum ad hominem n 476
aria n 413
arid adj 169, 340
aridity n 340
arise v 151, 305
aristocracy n 875
aristocratic adj 875
arithmetic n 85
arithmetical adj 85
arithmetic operations n 85
arm n 343; v 157, 673, 727
armaments n 727

armistice *n* 723
armlet *n* 247
armor *n* 727
arms *n* 727
army *n* 72
aroma *n* 400
aromatic *adj* 400
around *adv* 227
arouse *v* 175, 382, 615, 824
arraign *v* 938, 969
arraignment *n* 938
arrange *v* 58, 60, 626, 673, 774
arranged *adj* 60
arrange in a series *v* 69
arrange in words *v* 566
arrangement *n* 60
arrangement *n* 58, 673, 723, 769
arrangment *n* 807
array *n* 58, 102; *v* 60, 225
arrest *v* 142
arrival *n* 292
arrive *v* 151, 265, 292, 342
arrogance *n* 878, 885
arrogant *adj* 739, 878, 885, 880
artery *n* 350
artful *adj* 702
artfulness *n* 702
art gallery *n* 556
article *n* 3, 316, 590, 595
article of faith *n* 537
articles *n* 770, 798
articles of faith *n* 983
articulate *v* 580, 582; *adj* 580
articulation *n* 43, 580
artifice *n* 545, 702
artificial *adj* 579, 855
artificial light *n* 423
artist *n* 559
artist *n* 416
artistic *adj* 845
artistically *adv* 698
artless *adj* 703, 946
artlessness *n* 703
artlessness *n* 946
as a consequence *adv* 154
as a matter of course *adv* 82

as a rule *adv* 613
ascend *v* 35, 305, 658
ascendancy *n* 33, 157, 175, 731
ascendant *adj* 305
ascending *adj* 217
ascension *n* 305
ascent *n* 305
ascent *n* 35, 217
ascertain *v* 480a
ascetic *n* 955; *adj* 955
asceticism *n* 955
as chance will have it *adv* 156
ascribe importance *v* 642
ascribe to *v* 155
ascription *n* 155
as good as one's word *adj* 772
ash *n* 388
ashen *adj* 429, 432
ashes *n* 362
ashore *adv* 342
ashy *adj* 429, 432
aside *n* 589
as if *adv* 17
as if it were *adv* 17
asinine *adj* 497, 499, 853
as it happens *adv* 151
as it were *adv* 17
ask *v* 461, 630, 765, 812, 865
askance *adv* 217
askew *adj* 217, 243; *adv* 217
ask for *v* 765
asleep *adj* 458
as low as one can go *adj* 649
as matters stand *adv* 8
aspect *n* 183, 220, 448
aspects *n* 5
asperity *n* 256
aspersion *n* 934
asphalt *n* 356a
asphyxiate *v* 361
aspirant *n* 767
aspiration *n* 858, 865
aspire at *v* 620
asquint *adj* 217
as regards *adv* 9
ass *n* 493
assail *v* 716
assailant *n* 716, 726
assailer *n* 726

assassin *n* 165, 361
assassination *n* 361
assault *n* 716; *v* 716
assaulter *n* 726
assay *n* 463; *v* 463
assemblage *n* 72
assemblage *n* 43, 102, 712
assemble *v* 50, 72, 72, 712
assembled *adj* 72
assembly *n* 43, 72, 696, 712, 997
assent *n* 488
assent *n* 23, 82, 178, 484, 602, 762; *v* 82, 488, 535, 602, 762
assenting *adj* 488, 831
assert *v* 535, 720
assertion *n* 535
assertive *adj* 535
assertiveness *n* 715
assess *v* 466, 812
assessment *n* 466, 480
assessor *n* 480
asset *n* 944
assets *n* 780, 800
asseverate *v* 535
assiduity *n* 682
assiduous *adj* 682
assiduousness *n* 682
assign *v* 60, 755, 783, 784, 786
assignment *n* 155, 755, 786
assign to *v* 155
assimilate *v* 16, 144
assimilation *n* 144
assist *v* 707, 746, 834, 906
assistance *n* 707, 834
assistant *n* 707, 711, 759
associate *n* 88, 711, 890; *v* 9, 41, 43, 72, 216
associated *adj* 9
associated with *adj* 88
associate with *v* 88
association *n* 9, 72, 88, 464, 709, 712, 903
assortment *n* 60, 72
assuage *v* 174, 723, 834
assuagement *n* 174, 834
assuaging *adj* 834
assume *v* 484, 510,

514, 789, 855, 871, 885
assumed *adj* 514
assumed name *n* 565
assumption *n* 514
assurance *n* 474, 484, 507, 768, 858
assure *v* 768, 771
assured *adj* 474, 484
asteroids *n* 318
as the saying goes *adv* 496
as the world goes *adv* 613
as they say *adv* 496
as things go *adv* 151, 613
astigmatic *adj* 443
astigmatism *n* 443
astonish *v* 508, 870
astonished *adj* 870
astonishing *adj* 870
astonishingly *adv* 31
astonishment *n* 508, 870
astound *v* 824, 870
astounding *adj* 870
astral *adj* 318
astray *adv* 279
astringent *adj* 195, 397
astronaut *n* 269
astute *adj* 498, 702
asunder *adj* 44; *adv* 44
as usual *adv* 613
as well as *adv* 37
asylum *n* 666
asymmetrical *adj* 241
asymmetry *n* 241, 243
at a different time *adv* 119
at a distance *adj* 196
at a glance *adv* 441
at all events *adv* 30
at all times *adv* 136
at a low ebb *adj* 308
at an angle *adv* 217
at any rate *adv* 30
at a snail's pace *adv* 275
at a standstill *adj* 265
at bottom *adv* 5
at cross purposes *adj* 713; *adv* 59, 708
at ease *adj* 827
at fault *adj* 927
at first sight *adv* 441, 448

at full gallop *adv* 274
at full speed *adv* 274
at half speed *adv* 275
at hand *adj* 152, 197
at heart *adv* 820
atheism *n* 989
atheist *n* 984, 989
atheistic *adj* 989
athletic *adj* 159
at intervals *adv* 70
at issue *adj* 708
at its height *adv* 33
at large *adj* 748
atlas *n* 86
at last *adv* 67, 133
at length *adv* 133, 200
atmosphere *n* 338
atmospheric *adj* 338
at no time *adv* 107
at odds *adj* 708
atoll *n* 346
atom *n* 32, 180a
atomization *n* 336
atomize *v* 336
atonal *adj* 410, 414
atonality *n* 410, 414
at once *adv* 132
atone *v* 30, 952
atone for *v* 462, 952
atonement *n* 952
atonement *n* 790, 950
at one's disposal *adj* 777
at one's fingertips *adv* 197
at one's leisure *adv* 133
at one with *adj* 178
atoning *adj* 950, 952
at present *adv* 118
at random *adv* 156
at regular intervals *adv* 58
at rest *adj* 265; *adv* 687
atrophy *n* 195, 659
at short notice *adv* 132
at sight *adv* 132
at some other time *adv* 119
at some time or other *adv* 119
attach *v* 37, 43, 969
attached *adj* 897
attach importance *v* 642
attachment *n* 37, 39,

43, 88, 897
attach too much importance to *v* 482
attack *n* 716
attacker *n* 716, 891
attain *v* 292, 775
attain an end *v* 731
attain majority *v* 131
attainment *n* 292, 539, 698, 775
attempt *n* 675, 686; *v* 675
attend *v* 186, 281, 418, 457, 746, 928
attendance *n* 186
attendant *n* 88; *adj* 88
attending *n* 418; *adj* 186, 928
attending to *n* 457
attend regularly *v* 136
attend to *v* 743
attention *n* 457
attention *n* 451, 459, 928
attentive *adj* 451, 457, 459
attentiveness *n* 457
attenuate *v* 195
attenuation *n* 195, 330
attest *v* 550
at that instant *adv* 119
at that time *adv* 119
at the eleventh hour *adv* 133
at the heels *adv* 235
at the least *adv* 32
at the present time *adv* 118
at the same time *adv* 30, 120
at the top of one's lungs *adv* 404
at the top of one's voice *adv* 404
at this moment *adv* 118
at this time *adv* 118
at times *adv* 136
attire *n* 225
attitude *n* 8, 183, 240
attitudinize *v* 855
attorney *n* 968
attorney-at-law *n* 968
attorney general *n* 968
attract *v* 288, 829
attract attention *v* 446
attracting *adj* 288

attraction *n* 288
attraction *n* 829
attractive *adj* 288, 615,
 829, 845, 850
attractiveness *n* 288,
 829, 845
attributable *adj* 155
attribute *n* 780
attributed *adj* 155
attribute to *v* 155
attribution *n* 155
attrition *n* 331
attunement *n* 413
at variance *adj* 24, 708,
 713
at will *adv* 600
at work *adj* 170
auburn *adj* 433
auction *n* 796
audacious *adj* 861,
 863, 885
audacity *n* 861, 863,
 885
audibility *n* 402, 418
audible *adj* 402
audience *n* 444, 588
audition *n* 418
auditor *n* 418, 811
auditory *adj* 418
auger *n* 262
augment *v* 35, 37
augmentation *n* 35, 39,
 194
augur *n* 513; *v* 511, 909
auguring *adj* 909
augury *n* 511, 512, 668
au naturel *adj* 226
aureate *adj* 435
aureole *n* 420
auricular *adj* 418
aurora *n* 420
auscultation *n* 418
auspices *n* 175, 693
auspicious *adj* 134,
 734
austere *adj* 704, 739,
 955
austerity *n* 739, 955
authentic *adj* 494
author *n* 153, 164, 590,
 593, 976
authoritative *adj* 175,
 737, 741, 983a
authority *n* 737
authority *n* 157, 175,
 500, 527, 700, 745,
 965

authorization *n* 737,
 760
authorize *v* 157, 737,
 755, 760
authorized *adj* 924,
 963
author's copy *n* 590
authorship *n* 161, 590
autocracy *n* 739
autocratic *adj* 600, 739
automatic *adj* 601
automobile *n* 272
autonomous *adj* 748
autonomy *n* 748
autopsy *n* 363
autumn *n* 126
auxiliary *n* 711
auxiliary *adj* 37, 707
avail *n* 644, 677; *v* 644
available *adj* 260, 644,
 673
avail oneself of *v* 677
avarice *n* 819
avaricious *adj* 819
avenge *v* 718, 919
avenger *n* 919
avenue *n* 302, 627
aver *v* 535
average *n* 29; *adj* 29,
 651, 736
average capacity *n* 736
averse *adj* 289, 603,
 867
averse from *adj* 898
averseness *n* 603
aversion *n* 289, 603,
 867, 898
Avesta *n* 986
aviate *v* 267
aviation *n* 267
aviational *adj* 267
aviator *n* 269
aviatrix *n* 269
avoid *v* 287, 623, 671
avoidance *n* 623
avoider *n* 623
avow *v* 488, 535
avowal *n* 529
await *v* 121, 152, 507
awake *v* 404, 824; *adj*
 457, 682
award *n* 784; *v* 784
aware *adj* 375, 822
awareness *n* 822
aware of *adj* 490
away *adj* 187, 196; *adv*

196
awe *n* 860, 870
a wee bit *adv* 32
awe-inspiring *adj* 860
awesome *adj* 860, 870
awe-struck *adj* 870
awful *adj* 395, 403, 860
awhile *adv* 111
awkward *adj* 579, 699,
 704
awkwardness *n* 579,
 699
awl *n* 262
awning *n* 223, 424
awry *adj* 217, 243, 923
ax *v* 44
axiom *n* 496
axiomatic *adj* 496
axis *n* 153, 222

B

baa *v* 412
babble *v* 348, 584
babbler *n* 584
babe *n* 129
babe in arms *n* 129
baby *n* 129
baby blue *adj* 438
babyish *adj* 129
bachelor *n* 904
bachelorhood *n* 904
back *n* 235; *v* 707, 737;
 adj 235
back and forth *adv* 314
backbiter *n* 936
backbone *n* 5, 221,
 604a
back down *v* 283
backer *n* 164, 890
backfire *n* 277
backfiring *adj* 277
background *n* 196, 235
backlash *n* 145, 277
back out *v* 283
backside *n* 235
backsliding *n* 283, 661
backward *adj* 133,
 603; *adv* 133
backwards *adv* 283
backwater *n* 283
bad *adj* 34, 397, 401,
 649, 653, 657, 663,
 923, 945
bad diction *n* 579
bad fairy *n* 980
badge *n* 747

bear off v 279
be artless v 703
bear upon v 9
bear with v 740, 760
beast n 366
beastly adj 653
beast of burden n 271
beasts of the field n 366
beat n 104, 138, 314, 627; v 138, 276, 314, 315, 330, 406, 407
beat a retreat v 623
beat back v 289
beatific adj 829, 981
beatified adj 981
beat it out v 623
be at odds with v 889
be at peace v 721
be attendant on v 281
be attentive v 457
be at the mercy of v 749
beat time v 114
beat up v 352
be at work on v 625
beau n 897, 854
beau monde n 852
beauteous adj 845
beautified adj 577, 847
beautiful adj 242, 597, 829, 845, 977, 981
beautify v 845, 847
beauty n 845
beauty n 242, 829
be averse to v 867
be aware of v 450, 490
be beforehand v 132
be behind v 235
be beneficial v 648
be blind v 442
be blind to v 491
be blunt v 254
bebop n 415
be born v 359
be bound for v 278
be brittle v 328
be broad v 202
be called to the bar v 968
becalm v 265
be capricious v 608
be careful v 459
~~cause~~ adv 153, 155
~~ous~~ v 864
~~222~~
~~474~~

be cheap v 815
be cheek to cheek v 236
becloud v 421, 422
be cold v 383
become v 144, 926
become a habit v 613
become colorless v 429
become insane v 503
become large v 192
become little v 193
become old v 124
become small v 195
becoming adj 646, 850, 881
be composed of v 54
be concise v 572
be contiguous v 199
be contrary v 14
be converted into v 144
be courteous v 894
be cowardly v 862
be credulous v 486
be cunning v 702
be curious v 455
be curved v 245
bed n 204
be dark v 421
bedazzle v 420
be deaf v 419
be deceived v 547
be degrees adv 26
be dejected v 837
be dense v 321
bedew v 339
be difficult v 704
be diffuse v 573
be dim v 422
be dimsighted v 443
be disappointed v 509
be discontented v 832
be discordant v 414, 713
be discourteous v 895
be dishonest v 940
be disinclined v 867
be disinterested v 942
be disrespectful v 929
be distant v 196
be distinguished v 873
bedlamite n 504
bed-ridden adj 655
be drunk v 959
bedtime n 126
be due to v 154

be dull v 843
be dumb v 581
be early v 132
be easy v 705
beehive n 691
be elastic v 325
bee line n 246
Beelzebub n 978
be enamored of v 897
be engaged in v 625
be entitled v 924
be equivocal v 520
be evasive v 528
be evident v 467
be expedient v 646
be expeditious v 134
be expensive v 814
be exterior v 220
be extraneous v 57
be faithful to v 772
befall v 151
be fashionable v 852
be fastidious v 868
be fated v 601
be fatigued v 688
be firm v 150
befit v 23, 646, 926
be fluid v 333
be fond of v 897
be foolish v 499
before adj 62; adv 62, 116, 234, 280
beforehand adv 116, 132
before long adv 132
before now adv 122
before one's eyes adj 446
be forgetful v 506
befoul v 653
be fragrant v 400
be free v 748
befriend v 888
be friendly v 888
beg v 765
be general v 78
beget v 161
beggar n 541
beggarly adj 643, 804
begin v 66; 676
begin at the beginning v 66
begin hostilities v 716
beginner n 541
beginning n 66
be gluttonous v 957
be gone v 449

B

beneficent *adj* 784
beneficent spirit *n* 977
beneficial *adj* 618, 644, 648, 677
beneficiary *n* 785
beneficient *adj* 816
benefit *n* 618, 677, 775; *v* 618, 644, 648, 906
be negligent *v* 460
be neutral *v* 609a
benevolence *n* 906
benevolence *n* 910
benevolent *adj* 888, 906, 906, 910
benign *adj* 656
be noble *v* 875
be no more *v* 360
bent *n* 176, 602, 613, 820; *adj* 244
bents *n* 5
bent upon *adj* 620
benumb *v* 376, 381, 385, 843
benumbed *adj* 381
be numerous *v* 102
be obligated *v* 601
be obliged *v* 601
be oblique *v* 217
be obstinate *v* 606
be occupied with *v* 625
be odorless *v* 399
be of help *v* 707
be of no help *v* 645
be old *v* 124
be one's fortune *v* 151
be one's lot *v* 151
be on the side *v* 236
be opaque *v* 426
be opportune *v* 134
be opposite *v* 237
be owing to *v* 154
be parsimonious *v* 819
be part of *v* 56
be penitent *v* 950
be perfect *v* 650
be pious *v* 987
be plain *v* 525
be pleased *v* 827
be pleased with *v* 827
be pleasurable *v* 829
be poor *v* 804
be possible *v* 470
be powerful *v* 157
be present *v* 186
be probable *v* 472
be prodigal *v* 818

be proud *v* 878
be pungent *v* 392
be pure *v* 960
bequeath *v* 784
bequest *n* 784
be rare *v* 137
be rash *v* 863
berate *v* 932, 972
bereft *adj* 776
be regular *v* 82
be related to *v* 11
be reluctant *v* 867
be remiss *v* 460
be resolute *v* 604
be rich *v* 803
be ridiculous *v* 853
be right *v* 922
be rumored *v* 532
be safe *v* 664
be salubrious *v* 656
be sane *v* 502
be savory *v* 394
beseech *v* 765
beseem *v* 926
be selfish *v* 943
be sensible *v* 375
be sensitive *v* 822
be sensitive to *v* 375
be servile *v* 886
beset *v* 716
be severe *v* 739
be sharp *v* 253
be short *v* 201
beside *adv* 83, 236
be side by side *v* 236
beside oneself *adj* 824
besides *adv* 37
beside the mark *adj* 10
besiege *v* 716
be silent *v* 403, 581, 585
be similar *v* 17
be situated *v* 183
be skillful *v* 698
be small *v* 32
besmear *v* 653
be sober *v* 958
be sociable *v* 892
be sorry for *v* 914
be specific *v* 79
bespeak *v* 132, 467
bespeckle *v* 440
best *adj* 648, 650
be still *v* 265, 403
bestow *v* 784, 995
bestowal *n* 784
be straight *v* 246

be straightforward *v* 576
be straight with *v* 543
bestride *v* 206
be subject *v* 749
be subsequent to *v* 117
be sufficient *v* 639
be suitable *v* 134
be sullen *v* 901a
be superior *v* 33
be surprised *v* 870
bet *v* 621
be taken *v* 360
be taken by surprise *v* 508
be tasteless *v* 391
be temperate *v* 953
be that as may *adv* 30
be the case *v* 494
be the dupe of *v* 547
be the effect of *v* 154
be the making of *v* 648
be the rage *v* 852
be thick *v* 202
be thin *v* 203
betimes *adv* 132
betoken *v* 550
be transient *v* 111
be transparent *v* 425
betray *v* 529, 545
be true *v* 494
be true for everyone *v* 78
better *v* 658; *adj* 648, 658
better half *n* 903
betterment *n* 658
better off *adj* 658
better than nothing *adj* 651
betting *n* 621
between *adv* 228
betwixt *adv* 228
betwixt and between *adv* 228
be unaccustomed *v* 614
be unaffected *v* 823
be uncertain *v* 475
be unclean *v* 653
be unconformable *v* 83
be unentitled *v* 925
be unequal *v* 28
be ungrateful *v* 917
be unhealthy *v* 657
be uniform *v* 16

bleeding n 299
blemish n 848
blemish n 651, 945; v 659
blend n 48; v 41, 41, 48, 352, 413
blending n 48, 413
bless v 990
blessed adj 981
blessing n 618
blight n 659; v 659
blighted adj 659
blighted hope n 509
blimp n 273
blind n 424; v 442; adj 442, 601
blind adoration n 991
blindfold adv 442
blindly adv 442
blindness n 442
blindness n 491
blind to adj 458
blink v 443, 623
blinker n 530
bliss n 827
blissful adj 827, 981
blister n 250
blithe adj 836
bloated adj 194, 250
block n 192, 321, 752; v 706
blockade n 261; v 261
blockhead n 493, 501
block up v 261
blond adj 429, 435
blood n 11
blood red adj 434
blood relation n 11
bloodshed n 361
bloodthirsty adj 361
bloody adj 361, 434, 653
bloom n 654; v 161, 367, 654, 734
blooming adj 161, 434
blossom v 161, 367, 734
blot n 552, 848, 874, 945; v 431, 653, 874
blot out v 552
blotted out adj 552
blow n 276, 349, 508, 830; v 347, 349, 688
blow great guns v 349
blow hard v 349
blow hot and cold v 605

blown away adj 959
blow one's brains out v 361
blow one's chance v 135
blow out v 421
blow over v 122
blow-up n 173; v 173, 194, 349
blubber n 356
blue n 438
blue adj 438
blue and red n 437
blue and yellow n 435
blue-green adj 435
blueness n 438
blue sky n 338
bluff adj 173
bluish adj 438
blunder n 495, 497, 732; v 495, 699, 732
blunderer n 701
blunderhead n 701
blunt v 376, 616, 843; adj 172, 246, 254, 499, 703
bluntness n 254
bluntness n 703
blur v 422, 653
blurred adj 447
blurry adj 422, 447
blurt out v 529
blush n 434; v 434
blushing adj 434
bluster v 173
blusterer n 887
blusterer n 884
blustering adj 173
boar n 373
board n 204, 298, 696, 966
boarder n 188
board of directors n 696
boards n 728
boaster n 884, 887
boastful adj 884
boasting n 884
boasting adj 884
boat n 273
boating n 267
boat ride n 267
bob v 309, 315
bodiless adj 4, 317
bodiliness n 3
bodily adj 3, 316, 364
bodily pleasure n 377

body n 3, 50, 72, 202, 316, 362, 372, 712
body-guard n 753
body in v 316
body politic n 372
bog n 345
boggle v 699
boggy adj 345
bogus adj 544
bohemian n 268
boil n 250; v 173, 315, 336, 353, 382, 384
boiling n 336, 353; adj 824
boil over v 173, 825
boisterous adj 173, 404, 825
boisterousness n 173, 825
bold adj 525, 574, 604, 715, 861, 885
boldness n 574, 715, 885
bolster v 215, 707
bolt v 43, 261, 274, 298, 623, 957
bolt out of the blue n 508
bolt upright adj 212
bombard v 716
bombast n 517, 577
bombastic adj 497, 549, 577
bond n 9, 45, 771; v 45
bondage n 749
bonds n 802
bonehead n 493
bones n 362
bonus n 973
booby n 501
book n 593
book n 590, 811; v 539, 811
bookish adj 490
bookkeeper n 553, 811
booklet n 593
books n 811
bookseller n 593
bookworm n 492, 593
boom n 215, 404, 408; v 404
boomerang n 145, 277; v 277
booming n 408
boon n 618, 784
boorish adj 851, 876
boorishness n 823, 851

B

201, 572
briefly *adv* 111, 572
brig *n* 273
brigantine *n* 273
bright *adj* 420, 428, 498, 734, 829, 836
brightness *n* 420, 829
brilliance *n* 845
brilliancy *n* 420
brilliant *adj* 416, 845
brim *n* 231
brimful *adj* 52
brimming *adj* 52
brindled *adj* 440
brine *n* 341; *v* 392
bring *v* 270
bring about *v* 153
bring an action against *v* 969
bring back to life *v* 163
bring forth *v* 161
bring in *v* 296, 810, 812
bring into *v* 144
bring into focus *v* 222
bring into play *v* 677
bring into relation with *v* 9
bring low *v* 308
bring out *v* 74, 591
bring round *v* 660
bring to a crisis *v* 604
bring to a focus *v* 74
bring to an end *v* 67
bring to a point *v* 74
bring to a standstill *v* 142
bring to bear upon *v* 170
bring together *v* 72
bring to life *v* 359
bring to light *v* 529
bring to mind *v* 505
bring to pass *v* 153
bring to perfection *v* 650
bring to trial *v* 969
bring up *v* 161, 235
bring up the rear *v* 235
brink *n* 231
brisk *adj* 111, 274, 682, 684
briskness *n* 682
bristle over *v* 900
bristling *adj* 253
bristly *adj* 256
brittle *adj* 328
brittleness *n* 328

broach *v* 153, 676
broad *adj* 78, 202
broadcast *adj* 73
broad daylight *n* 420
broadside *n* 236; *adv* 236
brochure *n* 593
broil *v* 382, 384
broke *adj* 804
broken *adj* 70
broken down *adj* 659
broker *n* 797
brood *n* 167
brood over *v* 837
brook *v* 826
brother *n* 27
brotherhood *n* 11, 17, 72
brotherly *adj* 888
brown *n* 433
brown *adj* 433
brownish *adj* 433
brownness *n* 433
brown-nose *v* 933
brown-noser *n* 886, 935
brown-nosing *n* 933
browse *v* 264
bruise *v* 649
brunette *adj* 433
brunt *n* 66
brush *v* 379
brush aside *v* 297
brushing *n* 379
brushwood *n* 388
brusque *adj* 173
brutal *adj* 173
brutality *n* 173
brute *n* 366
brute creation *n* 366
brute force *n* 739
brute instinct *n* 450a
brute matter *n* 316, 358
brutishness *n* 450a
bubble *n* 353
bubble *n* 353; *v* 315, 348, 353
bubbling *n* 353
bubbly *adj* 348, 353
buck *n* 309, 373
buckle *n* 243, 248; *v* 43, 243
buckle to *v* 686
bud *n* 66; *v* 161, 194, 300
budding *adj* 127

budge *v* 264
budget *n* 811
buff *v* 255
buffet *v* 276, 315
buffoon *n* 501, 844, 857
buggy *n* 272
build *n* 240; *v* 161, 235, 240
building *n* 161
built on *adj* 211
bulb *n* 249
bulbous *adj* 250
bulge *n* 250; *v* 250
bulk *n* 31, 50, 202
bulk containers *n* 191
bulky *adj* 192, 202
bull *n* 373, 477
bulletin *n* 592
bully *n* 887; *v* 739
bum *v* 266
bum around *v* 266
bumbling *n* 699
bumming around *n* 266
bump *n* 250, 276
bump against *v* 276
bunch *n* 250
bunchy *adj* 250
bungle *v* 495; *v* 699
bungler *n* 701
bungling *n* 699; *adj* 699
bunk *n* 477
buoyancy *n* 320
buoyant *adj* 320, 325, 836
burden *n* 190, 319, 828, 830, 926
burdensome *adj* 319, 649, 686, 706, 830
burglar *n* 792
burial *n* 363; *adj* 363
burial ground *n* 363
buried *adj* 208, 506
buried in *adj* 229
burlesque *n* 21, 856; *v* 856; *adj* 856
burn *v* 382, 384, 825
burnable *adj* 388
burn in *v* 384
burning *adj* 382, 434
burnish *v* 255
burnished *adj* 420
burnt *adj* 384
burn the midnight oil *v* 539

burp out v 297
burrow v 184
bursar n 801
burst n 113, 406; v 44, 173, 328
burst forth v 66, 194, 446
burst in v 294
burst out v 838
burst upon v 508
burst upon the view v 446
bury v 229, 363, 528
burying n 528
bury the hatchet v 723
bush n 367
bushy adj 256
business n 625
business n 454, 622, 682, 794, 926
business district n 799
businesslike adj 58, 625, 682, 692
bust n 557, 732
bustle n 171, 315, 682, 684; v 315, 682, 684
bustling adj 151
busy adj 151, 625, 682
busy as a bee adj 682
busy oneself in v 682
but adj 30
butcher n 361; v 361
butchery n 361
butt n 857; v 276
butt against v 276
butter n 356
butter-fingers n 701
butt in v 135
buttocks n 235
button n 250; v 43
button up v 261
buttress n 215
buy n 795; v 795
buy and sell v 794
buyer n 795
buying n 795
buzz v 409, 412
buzzing n 409
by adv 631
by accident adv 156
by and by adv 132
by an indirect course adv 629
by chance adv 156
by design adv 620
by dint of adv 631; prep 157

by fits and starts adv 70, 139, 315
by force adv 159, i 73. 744
bygone adj 122
by installments adv 51
by intuition adv 477
by means of adv 170, 631, 632
by no means adv 32
by rule adv 82
bystander n 444
by storm adv 173
by the agency of adv 631
by the by adv 10, 134
by the way adv 10, 134
by turns adv 138
by virtue of prep 157

C

cabal n 626
cabalistic adj 992
cabinet n 696
cackle v 412, 838
cacophonous adj 410, 414
cadaver n 362
cadaverous adj 362
cadence n 402
caesura n 70, 198
cage n 752; v 370
calamitous adj 735, 830
calamity n 619, 735, 975
calcination n 384
calculable adj 85
calculate v 85, 611, 620
calculation n 85, 507
calculus n 85
calefaction n 384
calendar n 86, 114
caliber n 26
call v 564, 995
call attention to v 550
call for v 630
calligraphy n 590
calling n 625
call it quits v 67, 624
callous adj 823
callousness n 823
callow adj 127
call to mind v 505
call up v 505
call up spirits v 992
calm n 174, 265, 721; v

174, 723; adj 174, 265, 403, 685, 721, 826, 953
calm down v 826
calmness n 174, 265, 721, 826, 953
caloric n 382
caloricity n 382
calorimeter n 389
calumnious adj 934
calumny n 934
camaraderie n 892
camouflage v 528
camouflaging n 528
can v 670
canal n 350
cancel v 536, 552, 756
cancelation n 552, 756
cancel out v 179
cancer n 663
candid adj 246, 543, 703
candidate n 726
candied adj 396
candle n 423
candor n 525, 543, 703
candy v 396
cane n 975
canker n 663; v 659
cankerworm n 165
canny adj 498, 702
canon n 697
canonicals n 999
canonize v 991
canopy n 223
cant n 988; adj 563
canticle n 413
cap n 261, 263; v 33, 206
capability n 157, 175, 698, 705
capable adj 157, 698
capacious adj 180, 192
capacity n 157, 159, 180, 192, 498, 625, 698
capacity for n 698
cape n 250
caper n 309; v 309
capillary adj 205
capital n 632, 800, 803; adj 210, 642, 648
capitulate v 725
capitulation n 725
caprice n 608
caprice n 615a

cenobite n 893

censurable adj 945

censure n 716, 932; v 716, 932

census n 85

centenary n 98

center n 29, 68, 74, 221, 222; v 290

center of gravity n 222

center on v 74

central adj 68, 222

centrality n 222

centralization n 48, 222

centralize v 48, 222

centrally adv 222

central part n 208

centrifugal adj 291

century n 98, 108

ceramics n 557

cerebral adj 450

ceremonial n 883; adj 240, 998

ceremonious adj 240, 882

ceremony n 240, 883, 998

certain adj 79, 246, 474, 484

certainly adv 474

certainty n 474

certainty n 484

certificate n 771

certitude n 474

cessation n 142

cessation n 261, 265, 360, 687, 725

chafe v 378, 384, 832, 900

chaff n 643; v 856

chain n 69; v 43

chain of thought n 476

chaise n 272

chalk n 342

chalky adj 430

challenge v 715

challenge comparison v 648

chamber n 696

chamber group n 416

chamber music n 415

chamber orchestra n 416

champaign n 344

championship n 707

chance n 156, 621

chance n 152, 470,

615a; v 151, 156, 621; adj 475

chance it v 621

chanciness n 475

chancy adj 156, 475

change n 140

change n 20a, 144, 147, 800; v 15, 20a, 140, 146, 147, 605, 783

changeable adj 140, 144, 149, 475, 605

changeableness n 149

changeableness n 111, 140, 475, 605

changed adj 15, 20a, 140

change direction v 279

changeful adj 607

change hands v 783

changelessness n 150

change of mind n 485

change one's mind v 607

changeover n 144

change sides v 607

changing hands n 783

channel n 260, 302, 350, 627; v 259

chaos n 59, 162, 241

chaotic adj 59, 241

chap n 373

chapel n 1000

chapter n 696

character n 5, 7, 561, 569, 820

characteristic n 79, 550, 569, 780; adj 5, 15, 79, 550, 569

characterization n 594

characterize v 564, 594

characterized adj 820

charcoal n 388, 431

charge n 630, 695, 697, 716, 741, 755, 812, 938; v 52, 190, 695, 716, 741, 755, 812, 938, 938, 938

charging n 938

charitable adj 707, 784, 816, 906, 910

charity n 707, 784, 816, 906, 910

charm n 829, 992, 993; v 288, 615, 829, 992

charmed adj 992

charmer n 994

charming n 933; adj

992

charnel house n 363

chart n 183, 527, 626

charter n 755, 963; v 760

chary adj 817, 864

chase v 622

chase away v 289

chasm n 208, 260

chaste adj 242, 576, 578, 849, 881, 944, 960

chasten v 972

chasteness n 849

chastisement n 972

chastity n 881, 944, 960

chat n 588; v 588

chattels n 780

chatter n 584; v 584

chatterbox n 584

chatterer n 584

chattering adj 584

chatty adj 584, 588

cheap adj 435, 643, 815, 819, 943

cheapness n 815

cheat n 545, 548, 792; v 545, 923

check n 179, 616, 666, 706, 751; v 179, 233, 275, 468, 706, 708, 751

checked adj 440

checker v 440

checkered adj 440

checklist n 86

cheek n 236

cheek by jowl adv 236

cheer n 827, 829; v 411, 689, 829, 834, 836, 840

cheerful adj 827, 829

cheerfully adv 836

cheerfulness n 836

cheerfulness n 827, 829

cheering adj 836, 858

cheerless adj 828, 901a

cheery adj 829, 836, 836

chemistry n 144

cherish v 897

cherry-colored adj 434

cherub n 129, 977

cherubic adj 977

chest n 802

chestnut *adj* 433
chew *v* 298
chewing *n* 298
chew the fat *v* 588
chiaroscuro *n* 429
chicanery *n* 477, 702
chick *n* 129
chicken *n* 862; *adj* 862
chicken-hearted *adj* 862
chief *n* 694, 745
chiefly *adv* 31
child *n* 129, 167
childbirth *n* 163
child genius *n* 872
childhood *n* 127
childish *adj* 129, 486, 499, 575
childlike *adj* 499, 703
children *n* 167
child's play *n* 705
chill *v* 383, 385, 616; *adj* 383
chilled *adj* 385
chilliness *n* 383
chilly *adj* 383
chime *n* 408; *v* 407, 413
chimera *n* 515
chimerical *adj* 515
chimney *n* 351
chink *n* 198; *v* 408
chip *n* 32; *v* 44, 195
chip off the old block *n* 17, 167
chipper *adj* 654
chirography *n* 590
chirp *v* 412
chirrup *v* 412
chisel *v* 240, 557, 558
chiseling *n* 558
chit *n* 588
chit-chat *n* 588; *v* 588
chock-full *adj* 52
chocolate *adj* 433
choice *n* 609
choice of *n* 600; *adj* 648
choice of words *n* 569
choir *n* 416
choke *v* 261, 361, 641
choleric *adj* 901
chomp *v* 298
choose *v* 609
choosing *n* 609
choosy *adj* 465
chop *v* 44

choppy seas *n* 348
chop up *v* 201
choral *adj* 415, 416
choral music *n* 415
chorus *n* 411, 416
christen *v* 564
Christian *adj* 983a
Christian Revelation *n* 985
chromatic *adj* 428
chronicle *n* 114; *v* 114, 551
chronicler *n* 553
chronicles *n* 551
chronological *adj* 114
chronological error *n* 115
chronology *n* 114
chronometer *n* 114
chronometry *n* 114
chubby *adj* 194
chuck *n* 284, 412
chuckle *v* 838
chug *v* 298
chum *n* 890
chummy *adj* 892
church *n* 995, 1000
churchdom *n* 995
churchman *n* 996
churl *n* 819
churlish *adj* 819
churlishness *n* 901a
churn *v* 315, 352
cilia *n* 205
cinder *n* 388
cinerary *adj* 363
cinnamon *adj* 433
cipher *n* 84, 550, 561
circle *n* 181, 247, 712; *v* 227, 247, 311
circle around *v* 312, 629
circling *n* 311; *adj* 248
circuit *n* 629
circuit *n* 181, 230, 247, 279, 311; *v* 311
circuitous *adj* 279, 311, 629
circuitously *adv* 279
circular *n* 592; *adj* 245, 247, 249, 311
circularity *n* 247
circularity *n* 311
circular motion *n* 311
circulate *v* 531
circulation *n* 311, 312

circumference *n* 230
circumjacent *adj* 227
circumnavigate *v* 311
circumnavigation *n* 311
circumscribe *v* 76, 195, 221, 229, 232, 233, 751
circumscribed *adj* 229
circumscription *n* 229
circumscription *n* 751
circumspect *adj* 451, 459, 864
circumspectful *adj* 457
circumspection *n* 459, 864
circumstance *n* 8
circumstance *n* 151
circumstances *n* 7, 527
circumstantial *adj* 8
circumvention *n* 311
citation *n* 467
cite *v* 467, 969
citizen *n* 188
citizenry *n* 876
citrine *adj* 435
civic *adj* 372
civic minded *adj* 910
civil *adj* 852, 894, 928, 997
civility *n* 457, 894
civilization *n* 372, 658
clack *v* 407, 412
clad *adj* 225
claim *n* 924
claim *n* 630, 741, 765; *v* 720, 741, 924
claimant *n* 767, 924
claiming *adj* 924
claim relationship with *v* 11
clairvoyant *n* 513, 994
clamber *v* 305
clammy *adj* 352
clamor *n* 404, 411
clamor for *v* 765
clamorous *adj* 404, 411, 765, 825
clamorousness *n* 404
clamp *v* 43
clan *n* 72, 75, 712
clandestine *adj* 528
clang *n* 404, 408; *v* 404
clangor *n* 404, 408
clank *v* 410

C

cognizant of *adj* 490
cohere *v* 46, 321
coherence *n* 46
coherence *n* 502, 518
coherent *adj* 321
cohesion *n* 46, 327
cohesive *adj* 46, 321, 327
cohesiveness *n* 46, 327
coil *n* 248, 311; *v* 245, 248
coiled *adj* 248
coin *v* 515
coincide *v* 13, 199
coincidence *n* 120
coincident *adj* 13, 120
coinciding *adj* 13
coin words *v* 563
coke *n* 388
cold *n* 383
cold *adj* 383, 866
cold-blooded *adj* 383, 823
cold-hearted *adj* 823
coldly *adv* 383
coldness *n* 383, 823
cold storage *n* 387
collaborate *v* 178
collaboration *n* 178
collaborative *adj* 178
collaborator *n* 711
collapse *n* 158, 195, 659; *v* 158, 195, 304
collar *n* 247
collate *v* 464
collateral *n* 771; *adj* 6, 216
collation *n* 464
colleague *n* 711
collect *v* 72, 596, 775
collected *adj* 826
collection *n* 72, 102, 596
collective *adj* 78, 778
collectively *adv* 50
collectivism *n* 778
college *n* 542
collegiate *adj* 542
collide with *v* 276
collision *n* 179, 276
colloquial *adj* 521, 560, 563
colloquialism *n* 521
colloquy *n* 588
collusion *n* 709
colonize *v* 184
color *n* 428

color *n* 434, 448, 654; *v* 428, 469, 549, 556
coloration *n* 428, 549
colorblind *adj* 443
color blindness *n* 443
colored *adj* 428
colorful *adj* 521
coloring *n* 428, 469, 549
colorless *adj* 429, 430
colorlessness *n* 429
colorlessness *n* 430
colossal *adj* 192, 206
Colosseum *n* 728
column *n* 69, 266
combat *n* 173, 680, 720, 722; *v* 708, 720, 722
combatant *n* 726
combating *n* 708
combative *adj* 173, 720, 722
combination *n* 48
combination *n* 41, 54, 709, 712
combine *v* 41, 48, 87, 178, 709
combined *adj* 48
combo *n* 416
combustible *n* 388; *adj* 384, 388
combustion *n* 384
come about *v* 151
come after *v* 63, 117
come ashore *v* 342
come before *v* 62, 116, 280
come between *v* 228
come close to *v* 197
comedian *n* 844
comedienne *n* 844
come-down *n* 509; *v* 306
come down with *v* 655
come first *v* 33, 62, 280
come forth *v* 446
come forward *v* 446
come from *v* 154
come in *v* 294
come in its turn *v* 138
come in sequence *v* 281
come into *v* 775, 785
come into play *v* 170
come into sight *v* 446
come into the world *v* 359

come into use *v* 613
come into view *v* 446
comeliness *n* 242, 845
comely *adj* 845
come near *v* 121
come of age *v* 131
come on *v* 121, 152
come on to *v* 544
come out of *v* 295
come out of nowhere *v* 508
come round *v* 151, 660
come round again *v* 138
come short *v* 732
come short of *v* 34, 304
come straight to the point *v* 576
come to *v* 50, 292, 359
come to a close *v* 67
come to an agreement *v* 774
come together *v* 72, 290
come to grief *v* 735
come to light *v* 525
come to nothing *v* 169, 304
come to pass *v* 151
come to rest *v* 184
come to the front *v* 234
come to the point *v* 79, 572, 703
come to the rescue *v* 672
comets *n* 318
come up short *v* 304
come up to *v* 27
come up with *v* 612
comfort *n* 377, 827, 831, 834; *v* 831, 834, 834, 906
comfortable *adj* 23, 377, 803, 827, 829, 831
comforting *adj* 834
comical *adj* 853
coming *n* 292; *adj* 121, 152
coming after *n* 63, 281
coming and going *n* 314
coming before *n* 62
coming beforehand *n* 280
coming together *n* 290

C

complaint n 655, 839
complement n 39, 88, 237
complementary adj 12, 237
complementary color n 428
complete v 52, 67, 142, 292, 650, 729, 731, 769; adj 31, 50, 52
completely adv 31, 50, 52, 729
completeness n 52
completeness n 50
completion n 729
completion n 142, 261
complex adj 59, 248, 704
complexion n 7, 428, 448
compliance n 82, 602, 725, 743, 762, 772
compliant adj 82, 725, 743, 762, 772
complicate v 61
complicated adj 59, 248
complication n 59, 667
complications n 154
complicity n 709
compliment n 896
complimentary adj 896, 931
comply v 82, 602, 725, 743, 762
comply with v 772
component n 56
component n 51
component part n 56
comportment n 448
comport oneself v 680
compose v 54, 161, 174, 415, 569, 590, 591, 597, 826
composed adj 826
composite n 48; adj 41
composition n 54
composition n 48, 569, 590, 591
compositor n 591
composure n 174, 826
compound n 48, 232; v 41
comprehend v 54, 76, 490, 518
comprehensibility n

518
comprehensible adj 518
comprehension n 76, 490
comprehensive adj 56, 76, 78, 192
compress v 195, 201, 321, 572, 596
compressed adj 201
compressible adj 322
compression n 195, 572
comprise v 76
compromise n 774
compromise n 29, 30, 68, 628, 723; v 628, 774
compulsion n 744
compulsion n 601
compulsory adj 601, 744
compunction n 950
computable adj 85
computation n 85
compute v 85
comradeship n 888, 892
con n 754; v 545
concatenation n 43
concave adj 252
concavity n 252
concavity n 308
conceal v 223, 447, 519, 528
concealed adj 447, 528, 533
concealment n 528
concealment n 447, 526
concede v 529, 760
conceit n 515, 878, 880
conceited adj 878, 880
conceivable adj 470, 515
conceive v 66, 168, 484, 515
concentrate v 72, 222, 290, 686
concentric adj 222
concept n 451
conception n 451, 453, 515
conceptual adj 2
concern n 9, 625, 642, 860; v 9
concerned adj 459, 860

concerning adv 9
concert n 178, 709
concert artist n 416
concertize v 416
concession n 760, 774, 784
concilatory adj 723
conciliate v 723, 831
conciliation n 714, 723, 831, 952
conciliatory adj 714
concise adj 201, 572
concisely adv 572
conciseness n 572
conciseness n 201
conclave n 72, 696
conclude v 67, 480, 604, 729
concluded adj 67
concluding adj 67
conclusion n 65, 67, 154, 480, 729
conclusive adj 67, 478, 480
conclusiveness n 478
concoct v 626
concomitance n 120
concomitant n 88; adj 88, 120
concomitants n 154
concord n 413, 714
concord n 23, 413, 488, 709, 721, 762, 888
concordance n 413
concordant adj 413, 714
concourse n 72, 290
concrete adj 3
concretion n 321
concupiscence n 961
concupiscent adj 961
concur v 120, 178, 290, 488, 709, 714, 762
concurrence n 178
concurrence n 23, 120, 290, 488, 709, 762
concurrent adj 120, 178, 290
concurrently adv 120
concurring adj 488
condemn v 971
condemnation n 971
condemnatory adj 932, 971
condemned adj 971
condensation n 195,

928
considerable adj 31, 192, 642
considerate adj 451
consideration n 451, 457, 469, 615, 642, 928
considering adj 928
consign v 270, 755, 783, 784
consignee n 758
consignment n 755, 784, 786
consign to oblivion v 506
consign to the grave v 363
consistency n 16, 23
consistent adj 16, 23, 413
consistent with adv 82
consist in v 1
consist of v 54
consolation n 834, 915
console v 834, 915
consolidate v 46, 48, 321
consolidation n 46, 321
consoling adj 834
consonance n 413
consonant n 561; adj 23, 413
consort n 903; v 41
consort with v 88, 892
conspicuous adj 446, 525
conspicuousness n 446
conspiracy n 626
conspiratorial adj 626
conspire v 178, 709
constancy n 16, 80, 112, 141, 150
constant adj 16, 69, 80, 110, 136, 138, 141, 150, 474, 604a
constant flow n 69
constantly adv 112, 136
constellations n 318
consternation n 860
constipation n 261
constituent n 51, 56
constitute v 54, 56, 161
constituting adj 54
constitution n 5, 7, 54,

329, 963
constitutional n 266; adj 963
constrain v 744, 751
constrained adj 751
constraining adj 744
constraint n 744, 749, 751
constrict v 195
construct v 161, 240
construction n 5, 161, 240, 329
constructions n 567
constructive adj 161
construe v 522
consult v 695
consume v 638, 677
consummate v 67, 729; adj 31, 52, 67, 650, 729
consummately adv 31
consummation n 67, 729
consumption n 162, 638, 677
contact n 199, 379
contact lens n 445
contain v 54, 76
container n 191
contaminate v 653, 659
contaminated adj 655, 961
contamination n 653, 659, 961
contemn v 930
contemplate v 441, 451, 620
contemplation n 441, 451, 620
contemplative adj 451
contemporaneousness n 120
contemporaneous adj 120
contemporary adj 120
contempt n 930
contemptible adj 435, 930
contemptuous adj 885, 930
contemptuousness n 885
contend v 476, 720, 722
contender n 726

content n 831
content adj 602, 826, 827
contented adj 831, 878
contention n 720
contention n 713, 969
contentious adj 713, 720, 722
contentment n 831
contents n 190
contents n 56, 221, 596
contest n 720
contestant n 726
contiguity n 199
contiguity n 197
contiguous adj 199
contiguousness n 199
continence n 953, 960
continent n 342; adj 960
continental adj 342
contingency n 151, 156, 470
contingent adj 8, 177
continual adj 136, 138
continually adv 136
continuance n 143
continuance n 110, 117, 200, 670
continuation n 63, 65, 143
continue v 1, 106, 110, 136, 143, 604a, 670
continuing adj 143
continuity n 69
continuity n 16, 58, 143, 150
continuous adj 69, 112, 143
continuously adv 69, 112
continuousness n 69
contort v 243, 248
contortion n 243
contour n 230, 448
contraband adj 964
contract n 676, 768, 769, 771; v 36, 195, 676, 769, 770
contract a disease v 655
contracted adj 195
contracting adj 195
contraction n 195
contraction n 36, 261
contractual adj 769
contradict v 14, 468,

489, 536, 708
contradiction n 14, -
218, 536
contradictory adj 14,
468, 489, 536
contraposition n 218,
237
contrariety n 14
contrariety n 15, 179,
218
contrary adj 14, 179,
608, 708
contrast n 14, 15; v 15
contrasted adj 14
contrast with v 14
contravene v 14, 468,
536, 708
contribute v 153, 176,
178
contribution n 784
contributor n 912
contrite adj 833, 930
contrition n 833, 950
contrivance n 626
contrive v 161, 626,
702
control n 157, 175,
693, 737, 741, 751,
777, 965; v 157, 175,
693, 737, 777
controller n 694
controversy n 720
controvert v 536
contumacious adj 715,
742
contumacy n 742
contumely n 930
conundrum n 520
convalescent adj 660
convene v 72
convenience n 685
convenient adj 646
convention n 72, 80,
240
conventional adj 80,
82, 240, 246, 613,
852, 983a
conventionalism n 613
conventionality n 82,
613, 852
converge v 197, 290
convergence n 290
convergent adj 290
conversable adj 588
conversant adj 698
conversation n 588
conversation n 582

conversational adj
582, 588
converse v 582, 588;
adj 14; 237
conversion n 144
conversion n 140, 218
convert v 140
convertibility n 13
convertible adj 144,
149
convert into v 144
convex adj 250
convexity n 250
convey v 270, 516, 783
conveyable adj 783
conveyance n 272
conveyor n 271
convict n 754; v 971
convicted adj 971
conviction n 451, 474,
484, 971
convinced adj 474, 484
convincing adj 478
convivial adj 892
conviviality n 892
convoluted adj 59, 248
convolution n 248
convolution n 59, 312
convoy v 88
convulse v 61, 173,
315, 378
convulsed with
laughter adj 838
convulsion n 59, 146,
173, 315, 378
convulsive adj 173,
315, 378
coo v 412
cook v 384, 384
cool v 338, 385, 616;
adj 174, 383, 826,
866, 953
cool down v 826
cooled adj 385
cooling n 385
coolness n 383, 826,
866, 953
cool one's heels v 681
coop n 752
cooperate v 178, 709,
712
cooperating adj 709
cooperation n 709
cooperation n 23, 178,
778
cooperative adj 178,
709

cooperatively adv 709
coordinate v 60
co-ownership n 778
co-partner n 778
copious adj 168, 573
copper adj 439
copula n 45
copy n 21
copy n 13, 19, 22, 90,
532, 556, 590, 591; v
19, 554, 590
copyeditor n 591
copying n 19
copyist n 590
cord n 247
cordial adj 377, 602,
829, 888, 892
cordiality n 602, 892
core n 5, 68, 208, 222
cork n 263; v 261
corkscrew n 248, 262,
311
cork up v 261
cormorant n 957
corner n 244
cornered adj 244
corny adj 496
corollary n 39
corona n 247
coronet n 247
corporal adj 3
corporality n 3, 364
corporate adj 43
corporeal adj 3, 316,
364
corporeality n 316
corpse n 362
corpselike adj 362
corpulence n 192
corpulent adj 192, 194
corral n 232
correct v 246, 658, 660,
662, 972; adj 246,
494, 578, 922, 922
correction n 658, 972
corrective n 662; adj
658, 662
correctness n 578
correlate v 12, 464
correlation n 12
correlation n 9, 464
correlative adj 12, 216
correspond v 12, 23,
592
correspondence n 592

correspondence *n* 12,
13, 17, 23, 216
correspondent *adj* 23
corresponding *adj* 12,
17, 216
correspond to *v* 216
corroboration *n* 467
corroborative *adj* 467,
535
corrode *v* 659
corrosion *n* 659
corrosive *adj* 649
corrugate *v* 258
corrugation *n* 256
corrupt *v* 653, 659; *adj*
653, 655, 945
corrupted *adj* 961
corruption *n* 49, 563,
653, 659
corse *n* 362
cortege *n* 266
coruscate *v* 420
coruscation *n* 420
cosmic *adj* 318
cosmonaut *n* 269
cosmopolitan *adj* 372
cost *n* 812
cost a lot *v* 814
costliness *n* 814
cost little *v* 815
costly *adj* 814
costs *n* 809
costume *n* 225
cote *n* 232
coterie *n* 712
cough *v* 349
could be *v* 470
council *n* 696
council *n* 72, 588, 695
counsel *n* 695, 864,
968; *v* 864
counselor *n* 540, 695,
968
counselor-at-law *n*
968
count *v* 85, 451
count among *v* 76
countenance *n* 448
counter *adj* 14
counteract *v* 30, 179,
662
counteracting *adj* 179
counteraction *n* 179
counteraction *n* 708
counteractive *n* 662
counterattack *n* 718; *v*
718

counterbalance *n* 27; *v*
30
counterblast *n* 179
counter-evidence *n*
468
counterfeit *n* 21; *v* 19,
544, 855; *adj* 19, 544
countering *adj* 237
counter maneuver *n*
179
counterpart *n* 17, 21,
237
counterpoint *n* 413
counterpoise *n* 30; *v*
30, 179
counterrevolution *n*
146
counterstroke *n* 718
counter to *adv* 708
countervail *v* 30
countervailing *adj* 468
countless *adj* 104
count on *v* 507
country *n* 181, 189
county *n* 181
coup *n* 146
coup d'état n 146
coup de grace n 361
couple *n* 89, 100; *v* 43,
89, 903
coupled *adj* 89
coupled with *adj* 88
couple with *v* 88
coupling *n* 43
courage *n* 861
courage *n* 715
courageous *adj* 715,
861
courageousness *n* 715
courier *n* 271, 534
course *n* 109
course *n* 58, 106, 264,
278, 348, 627
course of time *n* 109
coursing *n* 361
court *n* 696, 966; *v*
615, 933
courteous *adj* 457,
852, 879, 894, 928
courtesan *n* 962
courtesy *n* 894
courtesy *n* 457
courtier *n* 935
courtliness *n* 894
courtly *adj* 894
court of justice *n* 966
court of law *n* 966

courtroom *n* 966
cove *n* 343
covenant *n* 768, 769; *v*
768
covenants *n* 770
cover *n* 223, 263, 424,
530, 666; *v* 30, 204,
223, 224, 225, 424,
528, 664
covered *adj* 223
covering *n* 223
covering *n* 220, 225,
528
coverlet *n* 223
cover over *v* 223
covert *adj* 447, 528
covet *v* 865, 921
covetous *adj* 819, 865,
921
covetousness *n* 921
cow *n* 374; *v* 909
coward *n* 862
cowardice *n* 862
cowardice *n* 172, 605
cowardly *adj* 435, 605,
862
cower *v* 862, 886
coxcomb *n* 854
cozen *v* 545
crack *n* 44, 70, 113,
198, 259; *v* 44, 328,
406, 583, 659; *adj*
648, 698
cracked *adj* 410, 503
cracked bell *n* 408a
crackers *adj* 503
crackle *v* 406
crack of doom *n* 121
cradle *n* 66, 127
craft *n* 625, 698, 702
craftiness *n* 698, 702
craftsmanship *n* 161
crafty *adj* 702
craggy *adj* 253, 256
cram *v* 194, 539
crammed *adj* 52
cramp *n* 378; *v* 158,
160, 195, 706
cramped *adj* 579
cranny *n* 198
crapulence *n* 957
crapulent *adj* 957
crash *n* 276; *v* 406
crashpad *n* 189
crass *adj* 851
crater *n* 208, 252
crave *v* 865

craven n 862; adj 435,
862
craving n 276, 865; adj
865
crawl v 109, 275, 886
craze n 852
crazed adj 499, 503
craziness n 503
crazy n 504; adj 503
creak v 410
creaking n 410; adj
410
cream n 356, 648
creamy adj 352, 435
crease n 258; v 258
create v 153, 515
creation n 161, 318
creative adj 153, 161,
515
creativity n 168, 515
creator n 153, 164, 976
creature n 3, 366, 372
credence n 484
credible adj 470, 484
credit n 805
credit n 484, 873; v
484, 805, 811
creditable adj 878, 931
credo n 537, 983
credulity n 486
credulous adj 484, 486,
547
credulousness n 486
creed n 484, 537, 983
creep v 109, 275, 380
creeper n 367
creeping thing n 366
cremate v 363
cremation n 363, 384
crescent n 245; adj 245
crescent-shaped adj
245
cretin n 493, 501
crevice n 198
crew n 72, 269, 712
crick n 378
criminal adj 964
criminality n 947
crimson adj 434
cringe v 886
cringing n 886; adj
435, 886
crinkle v 256, 258
cripple v 158, 659
crippled adj 158
crisis n 8, 134, 151,
704, 735

crisp adj 328
criss-cross v 219
critic n 480, 524, 595,
936
critical adj 8, 465, 480,
642, 704, 716, 735
criticism n 480, 595,
716
criticize v 480, 595,
716, 850, 934
critique n 465, 480,
595
croak v 412, 583
croaking adj 410
crony n 890
crook n 244, 245, 792;
v 217, 245, 279
crooked adj 217, 243,
244, 279, 923
crookedness n 243
croon v 416
crop n 154, 775; v 201
crop up v 151, 446
cross n 41; v 41, 179,
219, 302, 830; adj
41, 901a
crossed adj 219
cross-eye n 443
crosseyed adj 443
cross-fire n 148
crossing n 219
crossing adj 219
cross-purposes n 713
crossroad n 219
cross swords v 722
crotch n 244
crotchety adj 608
crouch v 207, 886
crouched adj 207
crow v 412, 838, 884
crowd n 72, 102, 444,
876; v 72, 102, 197
crowded adj 72, 102
crown n 247; v 210
crowning adj 33, 67
crowning point n 210
crowning touch n 729
crucial adj 642
crude adj 53, 579, 651,
674, 851, 895, 929
crudeness n 929
cruel adj 649, 739, 830,
914a
cruelly adv 31
cruelty n 914a
cruise n 267; v 267
cruiser n 273

crumb n 32, 330
crumble v 49, 160, 162,
328, 330, 659
crumbling adj 124, 659
crumbly adj 330
crumbs n 40
crumple v 256, 258
crumple up v 195
crunch v 298
crush n 72; v 162, 195,
330, 739, 879
crush out v 162
crust n 223
crustacean n 366
crutch n 215
cry n 411
cry n 669; v 411, 412,
839
cry for joy v 838
crying n 411, 412; adj
411, 630
cry out v 411, 669
cry out against v 616
crypt n 363
cryptic adj 526
crystalline adj 425
crystallization n 321,
323
crystallize v 323
cubbyhole n 530
cube v 93
cuckoo v 412
cue n 550
cull v 609, 789
culminate v 210
culmination n 65, 206,
210, 261, 729
culpability n 947
culpable adj 947
cultivate v 371, 375,
658
cultivated adj 850
cultivate one's own
garden v 943
cultivation n 371, 578,
658, 850
culture n 850
cultured adj 850
culvert n 350
cumbersome adj 319,
706, 830
cumbrous adj 319
cunning n 702
cunning n 544, 698;
adj 544, 545, 698
cup n 252
cupidity n 819

CD

dawdling *n* 683
dawn *n* 125, 420; *v* 116
day *n* 420
day after day *adv* 136
daybreak *n* 125, 420
daylight *n* 420
day of fasting *n* 956
day of judgment *n* 121
day of rest *n* 687
days gone by *n* 122
days of old *n* 122
days of yore *n* 122
daze *v* 420
dazzle *v* 420, 442
de *n* 220, 234
dead *adj* 172, 360, 376, 381, 408a
dead and gone *adj* 360
dead as a door nail *adj* 360
dead drunk *adj* 959
deaden *v* 376, 381, 843
deadened *adj* 381, 408a
dead heat *n* 27
dead language *n* 560
deadly *adj* 162, 360, 361, 649, 657, 663
deadly weapons *n* 727
deadness *n* 381
dead of night *n* 126, 421
dead silence *n* 403
dead sound *n* 408a
deaf *adj* 419
deafen *v* 404, 419
deafened *adj* 419
deafening *adj* 404
deafness *n* 419
deaf to *adj* 458
deaf to the past *adj* 506
deal *v* 786, 794
dealer *n* 797
deal in *v* 796
dealing *n* 794
deal out *v* 73, 784
dear *n* 899; *adj* 814
dearness *n* 814
dearth *n* 640
death *n* 360
death *n* 67, 142
death agonies *n* 360
death bell *n* 363
death blow *n* 67, 360, 361
deathlike *adj* 403

deathly *adj* 361
death rattle *n* 360
debark *v* 292
debarkation *n* 292
debase *v* 308, 653, 659, 879
debased *adj* 207
debasement *n* 207, 308, 659, 874
debate *n* 476, 588, 720, 969; *v* 476, 720
debater *n* 476
debauchee *n* 962
debilitate *v* 160
debility *n* 158, 160
debit *n* 177, 806; *v* 811
debonair *adj* 894
debt *n* 806
debt *n* 177
debtor *n* 806
decade *n* 98, 108
decadence *n* 659
decapitate *v* 361
decay *n* 49, 124, 360, 638, 653, 655, 659, 732; *v* 36, 49, 195, 360, 659, 735
decayed *adj* 124, 160, 659
decease *n* 360; *v* 360
deceit *n* 545, 702
deceitful *adj* 544, 545, 702
deceitfulness *n* 544, 702
deceive *v* 544, 545
deceiver *n* 548
deceiver *n* 962
deceiving *n* 545
decency *n* 881, 960
decent *adj* 246, 651, 881, 960
deception *n* 545
deception *n* 21, 544, 702
deceptive *adj* 520, 544, 545, 702
decide *v* 153, 480, 600, 604, 609
decided *adj* 31, 67
decidedly *adv* 31
decimal *adj* 84
decimate *v* 361, 659
decipher *v* 522
decision *n* 480, 600, 604, 609, 620, 969

decisive *adj* 737
deck out *v* 225
declaim *v* 582
declamation *n* 577, 582
declamatory *adj* 577, 582
declaration *n* 525, 531, 535, 985
declarative *adj* 527, 535
declaratory *adj* 535
declare *v* 516, 525, 531, 535
declare war *v* 716
declension *n* 306, 567, 659
declination *n* 306
decline *n* 36, 124, 217, 306, 638, 655, 659, 732; *v* 36, 160, 217, 306, 360, 610, 659, 732, 735, 764; *adj* 128
declining *adj* 217
declining years *n* 128
declivitous *adj* 217, 306
declivity *n* 217, 306
decode *v* 522
decoloration *n* 430
decompose *v* 49
decomposed *adj* 49
decomposition *n* 49
decorate *v* 847
decoration *n* 733, 847, 877
decorative *adj* 847
decorous *adj* 850, 852
decorum *n* 852, 960
decoy *v* 288
decrease *n* 36
decrease *n* 38, 195, 283; *v* 36, 38, 193, 195
decreased *adj* 36
decreasing *adj* 36
decree *n* 480, 963; *v* 600, 741, 963
decrement *n* 40a
decrepit *adj* 124, 158, 160, 655, 659
decrepitude *n* 128, 158, 160, 659
decry *v* 934
deduce *v* 476
deduct *v* 38, 813

deductible adj 38
deduction n 38
deduction n 40a, 65,
476, 480
deductive adj 476
deed n 680, 771
deem v 451, 873
deep n 341; adj 208,
404, 428
deepen v 35, 208
deepness n 208
deep-rooted adj 820
deep-seated adj 208,
221
deep-sounding adj 408
deep-toned adj 408
deface v 241, 659, 846,
848
defacement n 241
defalcation n 304
defamation n 934
defamatory adj 932
defame v 934
defamer n 936
default n 304, 460,
808; v 808
defeat n 509
defeated adj 732
defect n 40a, 53, 651,
848, 945; v 607
defection n 607
defective adj 53, 651,
732, 945
defectiveness n 732
defend v 664, 670, 717,
937
defender n 890, 937
defense n 717
defense n 670, 937
defenseless adj 665
defensible adj 664
defensive adj 717
defer v 133
deference n 743, 928
deferential adj 457,
743, 926, 928
defer to v 928
defiance n 715
defiance n 742
defiant adj 715, 742
deficiency n 28, 34, 53,
304, 640, 651, 732
deficient adj 28, 34, 53,
304, 640, 651
deficit n 53
defile v 653
defiled adj 961

defilement n 653, 961
define v 233, 522
definite adj 79, 233,
246, 446, 474, 570
definition n 446, 522
definitive adj 67
deflect v 245, 279
deflection n 245, 291
deform v 241, 243
deformed adj 243
deformity n 241, 243,
846, 848
defraud v 545, 791, 923
defrost v 382
deft adj 698
defunct adj 2, 360
defy v 715, 742
degeneracy n 659
degenerate v 659; adj
659
degeneration n 659
degradation n 308,
659, 874
degrade v 308, 659,
879
degraded adj 207
degree n 26
degree n 58, 71
deification n 990, 991
deify v 990, 991
deity n 976
dejected adj 832
dejection n 837
dejection n 828, 859
delay n 133; v 133,
142, 706
delayed adj 133
delectability n 394,
829
delectable adj 394, 829
delectation n 827
delegate v 534, 758,
759; n 270, 755
delegation n 755, 758
delete v 552
deleterious adj 649,
657
deletion n 552
deliberate v 695; adj
174, 275, 383, 451,
685
deliberately adv 133,
600, 611, 620
deliberateness n 174,
275
delicacy n 160, 655,

850, 960
delicate adj 160, 203,
328, 329, 394, 428,
704, 829, 868 960
delicate condition n
655
delicious adj 394, 829
delight n 377, 827,
829; v 829, 836
delightful adj 377, 829
delight in v 827
delineate v 554, 594
delineation n 554, 556,
594
deliquescence n 335
deliquescent adj 335
delirious adj 503, 825
delirium n 503, 825
delitescence n 447
deliver v 270, 580, 660,
672, 750, 784
deliverance n 672
deliverance n 660, 750,
834
delivery n 580, 784
dell n 252
delude v 545
deluge n 72, 348; v
337, 348, 641
delusion n 495, 503,
515, 545
delusive adj 545
delve v 252
demand n 601, 630,
741, 765, 812, 924; v
630, 741, 765, 812
demeanor n 448, 692,
852
demented adj 503
dementia n 503
demi- adj 91
demi-lune adj 245
demise n 360
demolish v 162
demolition n 162
demon n 980
demon n 949, 978
demonic adj 980
demonology n 980,
991
demonstrable adj 476,
478
demonstrate v 476,
478, 525
demonstrated adj 478
demonstration n 478

D

D

digestible adj 299, 390
dig in v 298
digit n 84
dignified adj 873, 875, 878
dignity n 873, 875
digress v 279, 573, 629
digression n 279, 629
digressive adj 279, 573
dig to daylight v 260
dig up v 480a
dike n 198, 259, 350
dilapidate v 659
dilapidated adj 659
dilapidation n 162, 659
dilate v 35, 194, 322
dilation n 322
dilatory adj 133
dilemma n 476, 704
diligence n 682
diligent adj 682
dilly-dally v 133, 605, 683
dilly-dallying n 133
dilute v 160, 203, 337
diluted adj 203
dim v 421; adj 405, 422, 426, 447, 519
dimensions n 31, 192
diminish v 36, 38, 103, 174, 195, 834
diminished adj 34, 103
diminution n 36, 195, 638
diminution of number n 103
diminutive adj 32, 193
diminutiveness n 32, 193
dimness n 422
dimness n 353, 421
dimple n 252
dim-sighted adj 442, 443
dimsightedness n 443
dimwit n 493
dimwitted adj 254, 499
din n 404
dine v 298
dingdong n 407, 408
dingy adj 421, 422, 429, 431
dining n 298
dint n 252
dip n 217, 252, 300, 306, 308, 310; v 300, 310, 337

diplomat n 724
dipsomaniac n 959
dire adj 649, 735, 830
direct v 175, 278, 537, 600, 630, 692, 693, 741; adj 246, 278, 703
directing adj 693
direction n 278, 693
direction n 183, 537, 692, 697, 741
directive n 630; adj 692
direct line n 246
directly adv 132, 278
directness n 246
director n 694
director n 745
directory n 86
dirge n 363, 839
dirigible n 273
dirt n 342, 653
dirt cheap adj 815
dirty v 653; adj 653, 961
disability n 158
disable v 158
disabled adj 158
disadvantage n 619
disadvantageous adj 647
disagree v 24, 291, 489, 713
disagreeable adj 24, 830, 846, 867
disagreeing adj 24, 489
disagreement n 24
disagreement n 10, 15, 47, 489, 713, 720
disagree with v 657
disallow v 761
disallowance n 761
disappear v 2, 4, 360, 449
disappearance n 449
disappearing adj 449
disappoint v 509, 732, 832
disappointed adj 509
disappointment n 509
disapprobation n 932
disapproval n 766, 932
disapprove v 766, 932
disapproving adj 932
disarm v 158
disarrange v 61

disarray n 59, 61
disaster n 619, 735
disastrous adj 619, 735, 830
disavow v 536; v 607
disavowal n 536, 607
disband v 44, 73
disbelief n 485
disbelief n 485, 487, 989
disbelieve v 485, 989
disburse v 809
disbursement n 809
discard v 297, 610, 678, 773, 782
discern v 441, 480a, 490, 498
discernible adj 446
discernibleness n 446
discerning adj 441, 459, 465, 490, 498, 868
discernment n 441, 465, 477, 480, 490, 498, 868
discharge n 284, 295, 297, 299, 406, 750, 772, 807, 970; v 284, 295, 297, 692, 729, 750, 772, 807, 926, 927a, 970
discharge a function v 644
discharged adj 970
disciple n 492, 541
disciplinarian n 739
discipline n 58, 537, 972; v 537, 972
disclaim n 536; v 757, 764
disclaimer n 536, 764
disclose v 525, 527, 529, 531
disclosed adj 529
disclosure n 529
disclosure n 480a, 531, 985
discoloration n 429
discolored adj 429, 848
discomfort n 378, 828; v 828
discommodious adj 647
discompose v 61, 828
discomposure n 61, 828
disconcert v 61, 706,

disorderly adj 59, 173
disorganization n 61
disorganize v 61, 162
disorganized adj 59
disown v 536
disparage v 483, 934
disparagement n 932, 934
disparaging adj 932, 934
disparate adj 18, 24, 28
disparity n 15, 18, 24, 28, 291
dispassion n 826, 953
dispassionate adj 826, 953
dispatch n 592, 684; v 361, 684, 692, 729
dispel v 73, 162
dispensation n 784, 786, 927a
dispense v 73, 784, 786
dispense with v 678
disperse v 44, 49, 73, 291
dispersed adj 73
dispersion n 73
dispersion n 44, 186
dispirited adj 837
dispiriting adj 383
displace v 61, 185, 270
displaced adj 185
displacement n 185
displacement n 140
display n 448, 525, 855, 882; v 525, 882
displease v 289, 830
displeased adj 832
displeasing adj 846
displeasure n 828, 832, 900
disposal n 60, 677, 741
dispose v 60, 176, 615, 693, 796
dispose of v 784
disposition n 58, 60, 176, 600, 602, 613, 693, 820
dispossess v 789
dispossession n 789
disproof n 468, 479
disproportion n 24
disproportionate adj 24
disprove v 479
disputable adj 485

disputant n 476, 726
disputation n 476, 536, 969
disputatious adj 476, 713
dispute n 536, 713, 720, 969; v 24, 476, 713, 720
disputing adj 24
disqualify v 158
disquiet n 149, 315, 828; v 828
disquietude n 149, 832
disquisition n 537, 595
disregard n 458, 460; v 458, 460, 483, 742, 773
disregardful adj 460
disregard of time n 115
disrelish n 867; v 867
disreputable adj 874
disrepute n 874
disrespect n 929
disrespect n 885, 895
disrespectful adj 885, 895, 929
disrobe v 226
disrobed adj 226
disruption n 162, 713
disruptive adj 713
dissatisfaction n 489, 828, 832
dissatisfied adj 832, 841
dissatisfy v 832
dissect v 44, 49
dissection n 49
dissemble v 528, 544
dissembler n 548
dissembling n 528, 544
disseminate v 73, 531
dissemination n 73, 673
dissension n 24, 489, 713, 720
dissent n 489
dissent n 485, 603, 984; v 291, 485, 489, 603, 708, 713
dissenter n 489, 984
dissenting adj 24, 489, 984
dissention n 720
dissertation n 595
dissever v 44
dissidence n 24, 713

dissident n 489; adj 489, 713, 764
dissimilar adj 18
dissimilarity n 18
dissimilarity n 15, 28
dissimilitude n 18
dissipate v 162, 638, 818
dissipation n 73, 638
dissociate v 44
dissociation n 10, 44
dissolution n 49, 162, 335, 360
dissolvable adj 335
dissolve v 2, 4, 49, 162, 335, 360, 449
dissonance n 24, 410, 414, 713
dissonant adj 24, 410, 414, 713
dissuade v 616
dissuasion n 616
dissuasive adj 616
dissyllable n 561
distance n 196
distance n 198, 200, 235
distanced adj 10
distant adj 196
distaste n 867
distasteful adj 830, 867
distend v 194
distention n 194
distill v 336
distillation n 336
distinct adj 402, 446, 518, 525, 570, 580
distinction n 15, 31, 465, 873, 875
distinctive adj 15
distinctive feature n 79
distinctness n 446, 570, 580
distinguish v 15, 441, 465
distinguished adj 206, 873
distinguishing adj 465
distort v 217, 243, 523, 555, 846
distorted adj 243
distortion n 243
distortion n 443, 544, 555, 846
distracted adj 503, 824
distraction n 825
distress n 735, 804,

828; v 828
distress signal n 669
distribute v 60, 73,
531, 786
distribution n 60, 73,
531, 786
distributive adj 786
district attorney n 968
distrust n 485; v 485,
487, 860
disturb v 61, 185; 315,
824, 830
disturbance n 59, 61,
315
disunion n 24, 44, 59,
905
disunite v 44, 713
disusage n 614
disuse n 614, 678
disuse v 614, 678
disused adj 678
ditch n 198, 259, 350
ditto n 21; adv 104
dive n 208, 310; v 310
diverge v 20a, 291
divergence n 291
divergence n 15, 18,
24, 73, 279
divergency n 20a
divergent adj 15, 24,
291
divers adj 15
diverse adj 15, 81
diversified adj 15, 16a,
18, 20a, 81, 440
diversify v 15, 18, 140,
440
diversion n 140, 279,
840
diversity n 15, 16a, 18,
81
divert v 279, 840
diverting adj 840
divest v 226, 789
divestment n 789
divest oneself v 782
divide v 44, 44, 51, 60,
73, 85, 91, 291, 778,
786
divided adj 51
divide into four parts v
97
divide into three parts
v 94
divide in two v 91
divination n 511, 992
divine n 996; v 511,

514, 992; adj 976,
981, 983a
divinity n 976, 983
division n 44, 51, 60,
73, 75, 198, 291, 713,
786
divisive adj 713
divorce n 905
divorce n 44; v 44, 905
divorced adj 905
divulge v 529, 531
divulgence n 529, 531
do v 161, 170, 622, 639,
680, 729
do a good turn v 648
do as one likes v 748
do away with v 162,
297, 361
do a world of good v
648
do battle v 722
docile adj 725, 743,
926
docility n 725, 743
dock n 966
doctor n 662; v 544,
660, 662
doctrinal adj 983a
doctrine n 484, 537,
983
document n 551
dodge v 264, 279, 623
doe n 374
doer n 680, 690
doff v 226
dog n 373
dogged adj 150, 604a,
606
doggedness n 150,
604a, 606
doggerel n 597
dogma n 484, 537, 983
dogmatic adj 535, 606,
737
dogmatism n 535, 606
dogmatist n 606
do good v 648
do harm v 649
doing adj 151
doings n 151
doldrums n 837
dole n 32, 640, 786
dole out v 60, 73, 784,
786
dolor n 378, 828
dolorous adj 378, 830

dolt n 493, 501
doltish adj 499
domain n 75, 181
dome n 250
domestic n 746; adj
188, 221, 370
domestic animals n
366
domesticate v 184, 370
domesticated adj 370
domestication n 370
domicile n 189
dominance n 175
dominant adj 175, 737
dominate v 175, 739
domination n 741
domineer v 739
dominion n 157, 737
don n 540
donate v 784
donation n 784
done adj 729
done away with adj
782
donee n 785
done with adj 678
donor n 784
do nothing v 169, 681,
683
doom n 152, 360, 421;
v 152, 971
doomsday n 121
do one's duty v 926
door n 231, 232, 260,
627
doorway n 232, 260
do over v 144
do penance v 952
do right v 922
dormancy n 526
dormant adj 172, 265,
526
dose n 25, 786
dot n 32; v 440
dote v 499
dote upon v 991
double n 17, 90, 147; v
90, 258; adj 90, 147
double-cross v 545
doubled adj 90
double dealing n 544
double-edged adj 520
double entendre n 520
double-meaning n 520
doubleness n 89
doubling n 90
doubt n 485

D

economical *adj* 817
economize *v* 817
economy *n* 817
economy *n* 58
ecstasy *n* 377, 827
ecstatic *adj* 377, 827,
  829
ecumenical *adj* 78
eddy *n* 312, 348
edge *n* 231
edge *n* 233; *v* 231
edgewise *adv* 217
edging *n* 231
edible *adj* 299
edification *n* 537
edify *v* 537
edifying *adj* 537, 648
edition *n* 531
editor *n* 593, 805
educate *v* 537
educated *adj* 490, 498
education *n* 537, 673
educational *adj* 537
educational
  institution *n* 542
eel *n* 248
efface *v* 552
efface from the
  memory *v* 506
effacement *n* 552
effect *n* 154
effect *n* 65; *v* 153, 729,
  731
effective *adj* 157, 175,
  644
effects *n* 780
effectual *adj* 170, 644
effervesce *v* 173, 315,
  353
effervescence *n* 171,
  173, 315, 353
effervescent *adj* 338,
  353
efficacious *adj* 157,
  170, 644
efficacy *n* 157, 644
efficient *adj* 157, 170,
  698
effigy *n* 21
effluence *n* 295
effluvium *n* 398
effort *n* 675, 680, 686
effulgence *n* 420
effulgent *adj* 420
effusion *n* 295, 297,
  299

effusive *adj* 584
egalitarian *adj* 29, 78
egg *n* 153
egg-shaped *adj* 247,
  249
ego *n* 5
egoism *n* 943
egotism *n* 878, 880,
  943
egotistical *adj* 878,
  880, 943
egregiously *adv* 31
egress *n* 295
egress *n* 302
eight *n* 98
eject *v* 185, 297, 789,
  893
ejected *adj* 893
ejection *n* 297
ejection *n* 185, 301,
  893
eke out *v* 110
elaborate *v* 658
elaboration *n* 658
elapse *v* 109
elapsed *adj* 122
elastic *adj* 277, 324,
  325
elasticity *n* 325
elasticity *n* 159, 277,
  324
elated *adj* 838, 884
elbow *n* 244
elbow-grease *n* 331
elbowroom *n* 180
elder *n* 130; *adj* 128
elderly *adj* 124, 128
eldership *n* 128
eldest *adj* 128
elect *v* 609, 995
election *n* 609
electricity *n* 388
electric light *n* 423
electrify *v* 824
electrocute *v* 361
electrocution *n* 361
electronic music *n* 415
electronic sound
  reproduction *n* 402
elegance *n* 578
elegance *n* 577, 845,
  850
elegant *adj* 578, 845
elegantly *adv* 850
elegy *n* 363, 839
element *n* 51, 56, 153,
  211

elemental *adj* 42, 211
elementary *adj* 42
elements *n* 66
elephant *n* 192
elevate *v* 206, 235, 307
elevated *adj* 206, 307,
  574
elevation *n* 307
elevation *n* 206, 574,
  658
eleven *n* 98
elf *n* 979
elfin *adj* 980
elicit *v* 153, 301
eliminate *v* 38, 42, 55,
  103, 297, 299, 301,
  610, 893
eliminated *adj* 893
elimination *n* 42, 55,
  103, 297, 299, 301,
  610, 893
elite *n* 648
ellipse *n* 247
elliptic *adj* 247
elliptical *adj* 247
elongate *v* 200
elongation *n* 196, 200
eloquence *n* 574, 582
eloquent *adj* 574
elsewhere *adv* 187
elucidate *v* 74, 518,
  522
elucidation *n* 522
elude *v* 623, 671, 773
elusive *adj* 623, 773
elysian *adj* 981
emaciated *adj* 203
emaciation *n* 638
emanate *v* 295, 299
emanate from *v* 154
emanation *n* 295, 299,
  398
emancipate *v* 672, 750
emancipation *n* 195,
  672, 750
emasculate *v* 158
emasculated *adj* 158
embalm *v* 363
embargo *n* 761
embark *v* 66, 267, 293
embarkation *n* 293
embark on *v* 676
embarrass *v* 704
embarrassed *adj* 434
embassy *n* 755
embed *v* 221
embedded *adj* 221, 229

embellish *v* 847
embellished *adj* 847
embellishment *n* 847
ember *n* 388
embezzle *v* 791
emblazon *v* 428, 882
emblem *n* 550, 747
emblematic *adj* 550
embody *v* 50, 54, 76, 82, 316
embosomed *adj* 229
emboss *v* 250
embrace *n* 902; *v* 54, 76, 902
embroider *v* 440, 549
embroidery *n* 549
embroil *v* 61
embryo *n* 153
embryology *n* 368
embryonic *adj* 66, 153, 674
emend *v* 658
emendation *n* 658
emendatory *adj* 658
emerald *adj* 435
emerge *v* 295
emergence *n* 295
emergency *n* 8, 151, 704
emigrant *n* 268
eminence *n* 31, 33, 206, 648, 873, 875
eminent *adj* 206, 873, 883
eminently *adv.* 33
emissary *n* 534
emission *n* 297
emit sound *v* 402
emotion *n* 821
emotional *adj* 821
empathy *n* 821
emphasis *n* 535, 580, 642
emphasize *v* 535, 642
emphatic *adj* 535, 642
emphatically *adv* 31
employ *n* 677, 749; *v* 677, 755
employable *adj* 677
employee *n* 746
employ figures of speech *v* 521
employment *n* 625
employ oneself *v* 625
empower *v* 157, 737, 755, 760

emptiness *n* 2, 187, 209, 452, 517, 640, 880
empty *v* 185, 297; *adj* 2, 4, 187, 209, 298, 452
empty-headed *adj* 450a
empty vessel *n* 362
empty words *n* 517
emulate *v* 19, 648
enact *v* 599, 680, 692, 729, 741, 963
enamored *adj* 897
encamp *v* 184
encampment *n* 184
encase *v* 223
enchant *v* 829, 992
enchanted *adj* 992
enchanting *adj* 897, 992
enchantment *n* 827, 829, 991, 992
encircle *v* 76, 220, 227, 247
enclose *v* 227, 232
enclosure *n* 232
enclosure *n* 229
encompass *v* 76, 227
encore *adv* 104
encounter *n* 276, 680, 716; *v* 151
encourage *v* 707, 836
encouraging *adj* 858
encroach *v* 303
encroachment *n* 303
encumber *v* 319, 704, 706
encumbrance *n* 706
end *n* 67
end *n* 65, 142, 152, 154, 360, 620, 729; *v* 67, 142, 360, 729
endanger *v* 665, 909
endangering *adj* 909
endear *v* 902
endearing *adj* 902
endearment *n* 902
endeavor *n* 675, 686; *v* 622, 675
ended *adj* 67
endemic *adj* 79
endless *adj* 102, 104, 112
endlessness *n* 105, 112
end of the day *n* 126

end one's days *v* 360
endorse *v* 535, 769, 771, 931
endorsement *n* 535
endow *v.* 157
endowment *n* 698, 784
end result *n* 161
end to end *adj* 199
endurance *n* 112, 141, 150, 826
endure *v* 1, 106, 110, 112, 141, 151, 826
enduring *adj* 110, 141, 150, 505, 826
endwise *adv* 212
enemy *n* 891
enemy *n* 708, 710, 726
energetic *adj* 157, 171, 359
energetic activity *n* 680
energize *v* 171
energized *adj* 171
energy *n* 171
energy *n* 157, 159, 173, 359, 604, 680, 682, 686
enervate *v* 158, 160
enervation *n* 575
enfeeble *v* 160, 638
enfold *v* 229
enforce *v* 695, 744
enforcement *n* 744
enfranchise *v* 750
enfranchisement *n* 750, 760
engage *v* 132, 288, 615, 676, 768, 769
engage in *v* 622, 676
engage in a discussion *v* 588
engagement *n* 676, 680
engender *v* 161
engorge *v* 957
engrave *v* 259, 558
engrave in the mind *v* 505
engraver *n* 559
engraving *n* 558
engrossed in *adj* 451
enhance *v* 307, 658
enigmatic *adj* 519, 520
enjoin *v* 630, 695, 741
enjoy *v* 377, 394, 827
enjoyable *adj* 829
enjoyment *n* 827, 840
enjoy oneself *v* 827

E

exaggeration *n* 482, 497, 523, 555, 835
exalt *v* 35, 307, 838
exaltation *n* 307, 838
exalted *adj* 206, 875
examination *n* 461, 463
examine *v* 457, 461, 463, 595
example *n* 22, 82, 478
exasperate *v* 173
exasperation *n* 173
excavate *v* 208, 252
excavation *n* 252
exceed *v* 33, 303
exceeding *adj* 33
exceedingly *adv* 31
excel *v* 33, 648
excel in *v* 698
excellence *n* 33, 648, 650, 944
excellent *adj* 33, 648
except *v* 469; *adv* 38, 83
excepted *adj* 927a
excepting *adv* 38
exception *n* 55, 83, 469, 777a, 893, 927a
exceptional *adj* 20, 79, 83
excess *n* 40, 641, 954
excessive *adj* 31, 641, 954
excessively *adv* 31
exchange *n* 12, 147, 148, 783, 794, 796; *v* 12, 147, 148, 783, 794, 796
exchangeable *adj* 783
exchequer *n* 802
excise *v* 38
excitability *n* 825
excitability *n* 173, 822, 901
excitable *adj* 382, 684, 822, 824, 825
excitation *n* 824
excitation of feeling *n* 824
excite *v* 171, 173, 375, 377, 615, 824
excite an impression *v* 375
excited *adj* 173, 382, 824
excitement *n* 825
exciting *adj* 824

exclaim *v* 411
exclamation *n* 411
exclude *v* 55, 610, 893
excluded *adj* 57, 893
exclusion *n* 5, 77, 893
exclusion *n* 610
exclusive *adj* 55, 79
exclusive of *adv* 38
excrete *v* 299
excretion *n* 299
excruciating *adj* 982
exculpate *v* 970
exculpated *adj* 970
exculpation *n* 937, 970
exculpatory *adj* 937
excursion *n* 226, 302, 311
excursionist *n* 268
excuse *n* 617, 918, 927a; *v* 617, 777a, 918, 927a
excused *adj* 927a
execrable *adj* 649
execrate *v* 898, 908
execration *n* 908
execute *v* 361, 416, 680, 692, 729, 772, 972
execution *n* 361, 680, 692, 729, 772
executioner *n* 165, 361, 690; 975
executive *adj* 692, 737
executor *n* 690
executrix *n* 690
exegesis *n* 522
exegetical *adj* 522
exemplar *n* 22
exemplary *adj* 82
exemplification *n* 82
exempt *v* 777a, 927a; *adj* 748, 927a
exempt from *adj* 777a
exemption *n* 777a, 927a
exercise *n* 170, 677, 680; *v* 677, 680
exert *v* 171, 677, 686
exert energy *v* 680
exert force *v* 288
exertion *n* 686
exertion *n* 171, 680, 682
exert oneself *v* 686
exhalation *n* 299, 398
exhale *v* 299

exhaust *v* 158, 638, 688, 841
exhausted *adj* 2, 158, 688, 841
exhaustion *n* 158, 638, 688, 841
exhaustive *adj* 52
exhibit *n* 467; *v* 525, 882
exhibition *n* 525
exhilarate *v* 836
exhilaration *n* 836
exhort *v* 695
exhortation *n* 695
exhumation *n* 363
exhume *v* 363
exigency *n* 8, 704
exigent *adj* 630
exiguity *n* 203
exile *n* 55, 185, 297, 893; *v* 55, 185, 297
exiled *adj* 893
exist *v* 1, 359
existence *n* 1
existence *n* 1, 359
existent *adj* 1
existing *adj* 118
exit *n* 293, 295, 449
exodus *n* 293
exonerate *v* 937, 970
exonerated *adj* 937, 970
exonerating *adj* 937
exoneration *n* 937, 970
exorbitance *n* 814, 954
exorbitant *adj* 31, 641, 814, 954
exorbitantly *adv* 31
exorcism *n* 993
exorcist *n* 994
exotic *adj* 10, 83
expand *v* 31, 35, 192, 194, 202, 322, 549, 573
expanded *adj* 194
expanse *n* 105, 180, 192
expansion *n* 194
expansion *n* 35, 180, 322
expansive *adj* 180, 194, 202
expatiate *v* 582
expect *v* 121, 451, 507, 510, 620, 858, 871
expectance *n* 871
expectancy *n* 507, 858,

E

871
expectant *adj* 507, 510,
　858, 871
expectantly *adv* 507
expectation *n* 507
expectation *n* 121,
　451, 472, 858, 871
expectations *n* 152
expected *adj* 871
expecting *adj* 871
expedience *n* 646
expediency *n* 646
expedient *n* 147; *adj*
　646
expedite *v* 132, 684
expedition *n* 132, 266,
　684
expeditious *adj* 132,
　274
expel *v* 185, 284, 297,
　893
expend *v* 638, 677, 809
expenditure *n* 809
expenditure *n* 638
expense *n* 812
expenses *n* 809
expensive *adj* 814
expensiveness *n* 814
experience *v* 151
experienced *adj* 698
experiment *n* 463
experiment *n* 675; *v*
　463, 675
experimental *adj* 463,
　675
experimentally *adv*
　675
experimentation *n* 463
experimenter *n* 463
experiment with *v* 140
expert *n* 700
expert *n* 500, 737, 872;
　adj 698
expertness *n* 698, 702
expiate *v* 952
expiating *adj* 952
expiation *n* 952
expiatory *adj* 952
expiration *n* 67, 360
expire *v* 67, 109, 360
expired *adj* 122
explain *v* 462, 478,
　518, 522, 595
explainer *n* 524
explanation *n* 155,
　478, 522, 537

explanatory *adj* 522
explicable *adj* 522
explicate *v* 522
explication *n* 522
explicit *adj* 518, 525,
　570
explicitness *n* 518, 570
explode *v* 173
exploit *n* 680
exploration *n* 461
exploratory *adj* 461
exploring *adj* 461
explosion *n* 173, 404,
　406, 825
explosive *adj* 173, 665
exposé *n* 529; *v* 226,
　260, 529
exposed *adj* 177, 226,
　260, 338
expose oneself to *v*
　177
expose the error *v* 479
expose to danger *v* 665
exposition *n* 522, 525,
　529, 595
expositor *n* 524
expository *adj* 522,
　527
expostulate *v* 616, 766
expostulation *n* 616,
　766
expostulatory *adj* 766
exposure *n* 448, 479,
　529, 665
expound *v* 522, 537
expounder *n* 524
express *v* 516, 525,
　527, 560, 566; *adj*
　620
express by words *v*
　560, 569
expression *n* 521, 525,
　554, 560, 566, 985,
　985
expressive *adj* 516,
　518, 521, 569
expropriate *v* 789
expropriation *n* 789
expulsion *n* 185, 297,
　893
expunge *v* 162, 552
expurgate *v* 652
exquisite *adj* 394, 650
exquisitely *adv* 31
extant *adj* 1
extemporaneous *adj*
　612

extemporaneously *adv*
　612
extempore *adv* 612
extemporize *v* 612,
　674
extend *v* 35, 194, 200
extended *adj* 200, 202
extend to *v* 196, 200
extension *n* 35, 65,
　180, 194
extensive *adj* 31, 76,
　180
extensively *adv* 180
extent *n* 26, 106, 180,
　200, 202, 233
extenuate *v* 469
extenuating *adj* 469
extenuating
　circumstances *n* 469
extenuation *n* 469
exterior *n* 220; *adj* 220
exteriority *n* 220
exterminate *v* 162
extermination *n* 301
external *adj* 6, 57, 220
externality *n* 57
externally *adv* 220
externals *n* 6
extinct *adj* 2, 122, 162,
　360
extinction *n* 2, 162,
　360, 421, 552
extinguish *v* 162, 385,
　421
extirpate *v* 301
extirpation *n* 301
extol *v* 883
extort *v* 814
extortion *n* 789
extra *adj* 37
extract *v* 301
extraction *n* 301
extracts *n* 596
extradite *v* 270
extradition *n* 270
extraneous *adj* 6, 10,
　57, 220
extraneousness *n* 57
extraneousness *n* 6
extraordinary *adj* 31,
　83, 870
extravagance *n* 497,
　499, 549, 814, 818,
　954
extravagant *adj* 31,
　497, 499, 549, 641,
　814, 818, 853, 954

162

extravagant love n 991
extravagantly adv 31
extreme n 67; adj 31
extremely adv 31
extremity n 67
extricate v 301, 672, 705, 750
extrication n 301, 672, 750
extrinsic adj 6, 57, 220
extrinsicality n 6
extrinsicality n 57
extrinsically adv 6
exuberance n 573, 641
exuberant adj 573, 641
exude v 295
exultant adj 838, 884
eye n 247; v 441
eye for an eye n 30
eyeglasses n 445
eyeless adj 442
eyesight n 441
eyewitness n 444
eyot n 346

F

fable n 546
fabric n 7
fabricate v 161, 515, 544
fabrication n 161, 544, 546
fabulous adj 2, 515, 546, 549, 979
fabulous spirit n 979
façade n 220, 234
face n 220, 234, 448; v 223, 224, 234
facet n 220
facetious adj 842
facetiousness n 842
face to face adv 237
facile adj 705
facilitate v 705, 707
facility n 705
facility n 157, 698, 748
facing n 223; adj 237
facsimile n 13, 21, 90
fact n 1, 151, 474, 494
faction n 712
factious adj 24
factory n 691
facts n 467, 527
factual adj 494
faculties n 450
faculty n 698

fad n 608
faddish adj 123
faddishness n 123
fade v 4, 111, 124, 160, 287, 360, 422, 429, 449, 659, 732
faded adj 659
fail v 160, 304, 360, 655, 732, 773, 808, 927
failing n 732; adj 53, 128, 927
failure n 732
failure n 304, 460, 509, 735, 773, 808, 927
fain adj 602
faint v 158, 688; adj 32, 160, 203, 405, 422, 429, 430, 447, 688
faint-hearted adj 862
faint-heartedness n 862
faintly adv 32
faintness n 405
faintness n 575, 688
faint sound n 405
fair n 799; adj 174, 246, 429, 430, 651, 829, 845, 922, 942
fair game n 857
fairly adv 922
fairness n 174, 845, 922, 942
fairy n 979
faith n 484, 858
faithful adj 17, 21, 494, 772, 983a
faithfully adv 772
faithfulness n 772, 983a
fake n 556; v 680; adj 19
fake god n 991
faker n 548
fall n 126, 162, 217, 283, 306, 348, 360; v 162, 306, 310, 360
fallacious adj 4, 477, 495, 544, 545
fallacy n 4, 477, 495
fall again v 661
fall away v 195
fall back v 145, 283, 287, 661
fall behind v 281, 283
fallibility n 475

fallible adj 475
fall in v 488
falling n 306; adj 217
falling back n 145, 287, 661
falling-off n 36, 659
falling out v 720
falling short n 304
fall into a rut v 613
fall into a trap v 547
fall into raptures v 827
fall off v 36, 659, 732
fall on evil days v 735
fall on one's knees v 990
fall out v 151, 713
fallow adj 674
fall prey to v 749
fall short v 304, 651, 732
fall short of v 28, 34, 53, 640, 730
fall through v 304
fall to v 151, 298, 676
fall to one v 785
fall to one's lot v 156
fall to pieces v 162
fall under v 76
false adj 19, 477, 495, 544, 545, 546, 923
false coloration n 523
false expectation n 508
false god n 991
falsehood n 544
falsehood n 546
false impression n 495
falseness n 545
false statement n 477
falsification n 523, 544, 555
falsify v 523, 544, 555
falter v 605
famed adj 883
familial adj 11, 166, 712
familiar adj 613, 888
familiarity n 748
familiarize v 613
family n 11, 75, 166, 167, 712
family likeness n 17
famish v 819, 956
famous adj 883
famously adv 31
fan v 338, 349, 385
fanatic n 504, 606; adj 606

fanatical *adj* 825
fanaticism *n* 606
fanciful *adj* 149, 515, 608
fancy *n* 453, 515, 608, 865; *v* 515, 865; *adj* 577
fancy talk *n* 577
fang *n* 663
fantastic *adj* 83, 497, 515, 853
fantastical *adj* 515
fantasy *n* 515
fan the fire *v* 173, 824
far *adj* 196
far and wide *adv* 180
far away *adj* 196; *adv* 196
farce *n* 497
farcical *adj* 497, 853
far cry to *n* 196
fare *n* 298, 812
farewell *n* 293
farfetched *adj* 10
far gone *adj* 503, 659
farm *v* 371
farming *n* 371
farness *n* 196
far off *adj* 196; *adv* 196
farrago *n* 41, 497
farsighted *adj* 441, 443, 510
farsightedness *n* 443
fascinate *v* 288, 824, 829
fascinated *adj* 870
fascination *n* 824, 829
fashion *n* 852
fashion *n* 7, 123, 613, 627; *v* 240, 557, 852
fashionable *adj* 123, 613, 852
fashionableness *n* 123
fast *v* 955, 956; *adj* 43, 150, 274, 684; *adv* 43
fast as a bullet *adj* 274
fasten *v* 43, 45, 150
fastidious *adj* 704, 868
fastidiousness *n* 868
fasting *n* 956
fasting *adj* 956
fast talker *n* 548
fat *n* 356; *adj* 192, 194
fatal *adj* 162, 360, 361
fatality *n* 360, 601

fat chance *adj* 471
fate *n* 121, 156, 601, 611, 621
father *n* 166, 996
fatherhood *n* 166
fatherland *n* 189
fathership *n* 166
fathom *v* 490
fathomless *adj* 208
fatigue *n* 688
fatigue *n* 841; *v* 688, 841
fatigued *adj* 688, 841
fatten *v* 194, 298
fattiness *n* 354
fatty *adj* 354
fatuity *n* 452, 499
fatuous *adj* 499
faucet *n* 263
fault *n* 70, 495, 651, 732, 848, 927, 945, 961
faultless *adj* 50, 650, 946, 960
faultlessness *n* 650, 946, 960
faulty *adj* 568, 651, 732, 945, 961
faulty grammar *n* 568
faun *n* 979
fauna *n* 357, 366
favor *n* 707, 740, 760, 784; *v* 740, 760
favorable *adj* 134, 602, 648, 734
favorite *n* 899
favor with *v* 784
fawn *v* 886, 933
fawner *n* 935
fawning *adj* 886, 933; *adj* 886
fay *n* 979
fealty *n* 743
fear *n* 860
fear *n* 862; *v* 860
fearful *adj* 665, 830, 860, 862
fearfully *adv* 31
fearless *adj* 861
fearlessness *n* 861
feasibility *n* 470, 705
feasible *adj* 470, 705
feast on *v* 298, 377
feat *n* 680
feather one's own nest *v* 943
feathery *adj* 320

feature *n* 56, 79, 448, 550, 780
features *n* 5
fecal *adj* 653
fecund *adj* 168, 365
fecundity *n* 168
feeble *adj* 32, 158, 160, 203, 337, 477, 575, 605
feeble-minded *adj* 499
feebleness *n* 575
feebleness *n* 158
feed *v* 298, 388
feel *n* 379; *v* 375, 379, 821
feel contempt for *v* 930
feel fine *v* 654
feel for *v* 914
feel good *v* 654
feeling *n* 821
feeling *n* 375, 379, 928; *adj* 821, 914
feel pain *v* 378
feeling no pain *adj* 959
feel pleasure *v* 377
feel sorry about *v* 833
feel sorry for *v* 914
fees *n* 809
feign *v* 544, 546, 680, 855
feigned *adj* 855
feigning *n* 855
felicitation *n* 896
felicitous *adj* 23, 578, 698, 850
felicity *n* 698, 827
fell *v* 162, 213, 308
fellow *n* 17, 27, 28, 373, 890; *adj* 88
fellow creature *n* 372
fellow-feeling *n* 888
fellow man *n* 372
fellowship *n* 709, 712, 888
female *n* 374; *adj* 374
female animal *n* 374
feminine *adj* 374
femininity *n* 374
fen *n* 345
fence *n* 232; *v* 277, 477
fence in *v* 229
ferment *n* 59, 171, 173, 315, 320; *v* 173, 315, 353, 397
fermentation *n* 171, 315, 353

fermented *adj* 397
ferocious *adj* 173
ferocity *n* 173
ferret out *v* 480a
fertile *adj* 168, 371
fertility *n* 168
fertilize *v* 168
fervent *adj* 382, 821, 865
fervid *adj* 382, 824
fervor *n* 382, 821, 991
fester *v* 653
festival *n* 883
festivity *n* 840, 883
fetch *v* 270, 812
fetid *adj* 401, 653
fetidness *n* 401
fetishism *n* 991
fetishistic *adj* 991
fetor *n* 401
fetter *v* 43
feud *n* 713, 720; *v* 713
fever *n* 382, 825
feverish *adj* 824, 825
few *n* 100; *adj* 32, 103, 137
few and far between *adj* 103
fewness *n* 103
fewness *n* 32
fiasco *n* 732
fiat *n* 741
fib *n* 544, 546; *v* 544, 546
fiber *n* 205
fibrous *adj* 205
fickle *adj* 149, 605, 608
fickleness *n* 605
fiction *n* 515, 544, 546, 598
fictional *adj* 598
fictitious *adj* 546
fidelity *n* 543, 772
fidget *v* 825
fidgetiness *n* 149, 682
fidgety *adj* 149, 682, 825
field *n* 344
field of battle *n* 728
fields *n* 344
fiend *n* 980
fiendish *adj* 980
fierce *adj* 173, 825
fiery *adj* 382, 684, 825
fiery furnace *n* 386
fifty *n* 98
fifty-fifty chance *n* 156

fifty-fifty split *n* 91
fight *n* 680; *v* 606, 720, 722
fighter *n* 726
fighting *n* 173, 722
figment *n* 515
figuration *n* 554
figurative *adj* 521, 554
figure *n* 84, 550, 812; *v* 240, 448, 554, 557
figured on *adj* 871
figure of speech *n* 521
figure of speech *n* 566
figures of beauty *n* 521
filament *n* 205
filch *v* 791
filcher *n* 792
file *n* 69, 86, 266, 330; *v* 38, 60, 69, 195, 255, 330
file a claim *v* 969
filial *adj* 167
filiation *n* 11
filigree *n* 219
filing *n* 330
fill *v* 52, 186, 190, 224
filled in *adj* 527
fill in *v* 52
filling *n* 224
fill out *v* 194, 549
fill up *v* 52, 261
fill up the time *v* 106
film *n* 204, 427
filminess *n* 426
filmy *adj* 204, 329, 426
filth *n* 653
filthy *adj* 653
final *adj* 67
finale *n* 65, 67, 360, 729
final gasp *n* 360
finality *n* 67
finalize *v* 729
finally *adv* 67, 151
final stage *n* 67
final touch *n* 729
finance *n* 800, 811
financial *adj* 800
financier *n* 801, 811
find *n* 480a, 775; *v* 151
find fulfillment *v* 731
find guilty *v* 971
find oneself *v* 186
find one's way to *v* 602
find out *v* 480a, 527
find refuge *v* 666

find safety *v* 666
find the means *v* 632
find the right words *v* 566
find vent *v* 295
fine *n* 974; *v* 974; *adj* 32, 203, 322, 329, 578, 648, 845
fine art *n* 556
fine gentleman *n* 854
fineness *n* 329
fine powder *n* 330
finery *n* 847, 851
fine speaking *n* 577
finesse *n* 698, 702; *v* 702
fine writing *n* 577
finger *n* 379
fingering *n* 379
finical *adj* 459
finicky *adj* 868
finish *n* 65, 67, 142, 242, 729; *v* 52, 67, 142, 650, 729
finished *adj* 242, 698
finishing stroke *n* 361
fire *n* 171, 382, 423, 574; *v* 384, 388, 420, 824
fired *adj* 384
fire off *v* 284
fire place *n* 386
fireproof *adj* 385
firewood *n* 388
firing *n* 388, 406
firm *adj* 43, 150, 323, 604, 606
firmament *n* 318
firmly *adv* 43
firmness *n* 150, 323, 604, 606
first *adj* 66; *adv* 66
first and foremost *adv* 66
first blush *n* 125
first cause *n* 153, 976
first-class *adj* 648
first come first served *n* 607, 609a
first move *n* 66
first rank *n* 234
first-rate *adj* 33, 648, 698
first step *n* 66
firth *n* 343
fiscal *adj* 800

fluctuating adj 149
fluctuation n 149, 314, 605
flue n 351
fluency n 333
fluent adj 333, 348, 578, 584
fluffy adj 256
fluid n 337; adj 333, 337
fluidity n 333
fluke n 156, 621
flukey adj 156
flunkey n 935
flunkeyism n 933
flurry n 682, 684
flush n 382, 420; v 382, 434
flushed adj 434, 824, 838
flush out v 480a
fluster v 824
flute v 259
fluted adj 259
flutter n 315; v 315, 422
flux n 109, 144, 264, 348
flux and reflux n 314
fly v 109, 111, 267, 287, 328, 671
fly back v 277
fly from v 623
flying n 274, 267; adj 111, 267, 959
fly over v 267
fly to pieces v 328
foam n 353; v 173, 315, 353, 825
foaming n 353
foamy adj 353
focal adj 222
focus n 74
focus v 74
focus on v 222
fodder n 362
foe n 708, 710, 726, 891
fog n 353, 424
fogginess n 422, 475
foggy adj 422, 426, 353
foil n 14
foiled adj 732
fold n 258
fold n 232, 997; v 258
folded adj 258
foliage n 367

foliation n 367
folk n 372
folk music n 415
follow v 19, 63, 281, 518, 622, 743
follow after v 117
follower n 117, 541, 746
follow in a line v 69
following n 63, 117, 281; adj 63, 117, 281
follow in the steps of v 281
follow in the wake of v 281
follow the rules v 82
folly n 499
fond adj 897
fondle v 379
fondling n 379
fondness n 897
font n 153
food n 298, 637
food for thought n 454
food for worms n 362
fool n 501
fool n 493, 547, 844, 857; v 545
foolhardiness n 863
foolhardy adj 684, 863
foolish adj 477, 497, 499
foolishness n 497, 499
foot n 211
footing n 8, 71, 183, 215
fop n 854
foppery n 855
for adv 155
for a long time adv 110
for a time adv 111
foray n 716
forbear v 678, 953
forbearance n 623, 678, 740, 826
forbears n 122
forbid v 761
force n 157, 159, 170, 171, 173, 574, 739, 744; v 157, 744
forced adj 10, 579
forceful adj 157, 159, 171, 574
forcefulness n 600
force of will n 600
for certain adv 474

forcible adj 171, 574, 744
forcibly adv 744
ford v 302
fore adj 234
forebode v 909
foreboding n 512, 909; adj 909
forecast n 510, 511, 673; v 507, 511, 626
forefather n 130
forefront n 234
foregoing adj 62, 116, 122
foregone adj 611
foregone conclusion n 611
foreground n 234
foreign adj 10, 57, 220
foreign body n 57
foreign parts n 196
foreign substance n 57
fore-knowledge n 510
foreman n 694
foremost adj 33, 66, 234, 642
forenoon n 125
foreordain v 152
forerun v 62, 116, 280
forerunner n 64, 116, 534
foresee v 121, 507, 510, 511, 871
foreseen adj 507, 871
foreshadow v 909
foreshadowing adj 909
foresight n 510
forestall v 132
forestry n 371
foretell v 511
forethought n 510, 864
foretoken n 511; v 511
forever adv 16, 112
forewarn v 510, 668
foreword n 64
forfeit n 974; v 776
forfeiture n 776
for form's sake adv 82
forge n 386, 691
forge ahead v 282
forgery n 19, 21, 546
forget v 506
forgetful adj 506
forgetfulness n 506
forgive v 918
forgiveness n 918

F

forgiving *adj* 918
forgo *v* 624, 757, 782
for good *adv* 106, 141
for good and all *adv* 141
forgotten *adj* 122, 506
fork *n* 244; *v* 91, 244, 291
forked *adj* 244
for keeps *adv* 106
forking *n* 91, 291
fork out *v* 784
forlorn *adj* 859
form *n* 240
form *n* 7, 21, 54, 80, 329, 448, 569, 697, 998; *v* 54, 56, 60, 144, 161, 240, 557, 852
formal *adj* 80, 82, 240, 242, 383, 579
formal features *n* 567
formality *n* 240, 579
formal speech *n* 586
form an opinion *v* 480
formation *n* 161, 240
formative *adj* 127, 153, 161
formative years *n* 127
form a whole *v* 50
formed *adj* 820
former *adj* 62, 116, 122
formerly *adv* 122
former times *n* 122
formidable *adj* 704
form into a sphere *v* 249
formless *adj* 241
formlessness *n* 241
form part of *v* 56
forms *n* 567
formula *n* 80, 240, 626, 697
formulaic *adj* 80, 626
formulate *v* 963
forsake *v* 624, 732, 782
for sale *adj* 763, 794, 796
forswear *v* 624, 782
forsworn *adj* 782
forte n 698
forth *adv* 282
forthcoming *adj* 152
for the moment *adv* 111
for the most part *adv* 613

for the sake of conformity *adv* 82
for the time being *adv* 106
forthright *adj* 246, 946
forthwith *adv* 132
fortification *n* 717
fortify *v* 159, 717
fortitude *n* 826, 861
fortress *n* 666
fortuitous *adj* 134, 156, 621
fortunate *adj* 134, 734
fortune *n* 152, 156, 621, 734, 803
fortune-teller *n* 513
forum *n* 966
forward *adj* 234; *adv* 282
fossil fuel *n* 388
foster *v* 658
foul *adj* 401, 649, 653
foulness *n* 401
foul play *n* 619
foul smell *n* 401
found *v* 153, 215
foundation *n* 153, 211, 215, 673
founded on *adj* 211
founder *n* 164; *v* 732
foundling *n* 893
found wanting *adj* 651
fount *n* 153
fountain *n* 153
four *n* 95; *adj* 95, 96
four-flusher *n* 548
fourfold *adj* 95, 96
fourfold division *n* 97
fourth *adj* 96
fourthly *adv* 96
fourth part *n* 97
four times *adv* 96
fowls of the air *n* 366
foxy *adj* 702
fracas *n* 59
fraction *n* 100a
fraction *n* 32, 51, 84
fractional *adj* 51, 84
fractional part *n* 100a
fractious *adj* 713, 742
fracture *n* 44, 70
fragile *adj* 160, 203, 328
fragility *n* 160, 328
fragment *n* 32, 51
fragmentary *adj* 51

fragments *n* 596
fragrance *n* 400
fragrant *adj* 377, 400
frail *adj* 158, 160, 203, 328, 605, 651
frailty *n* 158, 160, 328, 575, 605
frame *n* 7, 231, 240, 329; *v* 161, 626, 852
frame of mind *n* 602
framework *n* 329
franchise *n* 748, 760; *v* 760
franchisement *n* 748
frangible *adj* 328
frank *adj* 246, 525, 543, 703
frankness *n* 543, 748
frantic *adj* 173, 503, 824
fraternal *adj* 712, 714
fraternity *n* 11, 709, 888
fraternize *v* 709, 714, 892
fratricide *n* 361
fraud *n* 545, 548, 791
fraudulent *adj* 544
fraught *adj* 52
fraught with danger *adj* 665
fray *v* 331
freak *n* 156; *v* 608, 872
freaked *adj* 173
freakish *adj* 608
freckled *adj* 440, 848
free *v* 672, 705, 748, 750, 927a; *adj* 44, 600, 685, 748, 816
freed *adj* 748, 750, 927a
freedom *n* 748
freedom *n* 600, 672, 738, 760, 927a
freely *adv* 602, 748
free space *n* 180
free spirit *n* 268
free swinging *n* 214
freethinker *n* 989
freethinking *n* 989; *adj* 989
free time *n* 685
free will *n* 600
freeze *v* 376, 383, 385
freezer *n* 387
freezing *adj* 383
freight *n* 190

F

freighter n 271, 273
frenzied adj 173, 503
frenzy n 503, 825
frequency n 136
frequent adj 104, 136, 613
frequently adv 136
fresh adj 123, 428, 435, 505
freshen v 338, 689
freshness n 123
fresh wind n 349
fret n 828; v 378, 832
fretful adj 684
fretwork n 219
friability n 330
friction n 331
friction n 179, 719
fridge n 387
friend n 890
friend n 711, 912, 977
friendliness n 888, 897
friendly adj 707, 714, 721, 888, 892
friendship n 888
friendship n 714
fright n 860
frighten v 909
frightened adj 860
frightening adj 909
frightful adj 830
frightfully adv 31
frightfulness n 846
frigid adj 158, 383
frigidaire n 387
frigidity n 383
frills n 847
fringe n 231
frippery n 643, 851
frisk n 309; v 309
frisky adj 309, 682
fritter away time v 683
fritter one's money v 818
frivolity n 4, 209, 499
frivolous adj 4, 477, 499, 608, 643
frizz v 248
frizzle v 248, 258
from all points of the compass adv 180
from bad to worse adv 835
from beginning to end adv 52
from first to last adv 52

from head to foot adv 52
from pole to pole adv 180
from side to side adv 314
from the beginning adv 66
from the bottom of one's heart adv 821
from the four corners of the world adv 180
from this time adv 121
from time to time adv 136
from top to bottom adv 52
front n 234
front n 719; v 234; adj 234
frontage n 234
frontal adj 234
frontier n 233
fronting adj 237
frontispiece n 64, 234
front rank n 234
frost-bitten adj 383
frosted adj 426, 430
frostiness n 430
frosty adj 383
froth n 353; v 353
frothy adj 353
frown v 837, 900, 901a
frown upon v 932
frozen adj 381, 383, 385
fructification n 161
fructify v 168, 658, 734
frugal adj 817, 953
frugality n 817
fruit n 154, 367
fruitful adj 168
fruitfulness n 168
fruition n 161
fruitless adj 158, 645, 732
frustrate v 706
frustrated adj 732
frustration n 509
fry v 384
fuel n 388
fuel v 388
fuel oil n 388
fugitive n 268, 623; adj 623
fulfill v 52, 161, 168,

729, 772, 926
fulfilled adj 52
fulfillment n 161, 729, 731, 772
fulfill oneself v 731
full adj 31, 50, 52, 52, 404, 729
full-blown adj 194
full circle n 311
full-flavored adj 392, 394
full grown adj 131, 192, 194
fullness n 31, 52, 131
full of incident adj 151
full turn n 311
fully adv 31, 52
fulminate v 404
fulsome adj 401
fumble v 61, 699
fumbler n 701
fume n 398, 401; v 173, 382, 825, 900
fumigate v 652
fuming adj 434, 824
fun n 842
function n 170, 625, 926, 998; v 680, 746
functional adj 625, 644
functionary n 694, 758
fund n 636
fundamental adj 5, 211, 215
fundamentally adv 31
fundamental part n 211
funds n 800
funeral n 363; adj 363
funeral rites n 363
funereal adj 363
fungus n 663
funish v 784
funnel n 350, 351
funny adj 853
funnyman n 844
fur n 223
furcation n 291
furious adj 173, 382, 825
furiously adv 31
furnace n 386
furnish v 637, 673
furor n 825
furrow n 259
furrow v 259
furrowed adj 259
further adv 37

gobble *v* 412
gobble up *v* 957
go before *v* 116, 280
go beserk *v* 173
go-between *n* 534, 631, 724
go beyond *v* 303
go boating *v* 267
go by *v* 109
go by the rules *v* 82
god *n* 976, 979
goddess *n* 979
godhead *n* 976
godless *adj* 989
godliness *n* 987
godly *adj* 976, 987
go down *v* 306, 659
go downhill *v* 659, 735
godsend *n* 618
go forth *v* 293
go for the bait *v* 547
goggle-eyed *adj* 443
goggle eyes *n* 443
goggles *n* 445
go half way *v* 628
go halves *v* 91; *v* 778
go hand in hand with *v* 178
go hard with *v* 732
going *n* 264
going back *n* 145
going hungry *n* 956
going on *adj* 53, 151
go into hysterics *v* 825
gold *adj* 435, 439
golden *adj* 435, 734
golden dreams *n* 515
golden mean *n* 29, 628, 736
golden opportunity *n* 134
golden rule *n* 697
golden years *n* 128
go mad *v* 503, 825
gone *adj* 2, 122, 360
gone bad *adj* 397, 653
gone by *adj* 122, 124
gone to waste *adj* 638
good *n* 618
good *adj* 52, 394, 618, 648, 922, 931, 944, 977
good behavior *n* 894
goodbye *n* 293
good chance *n* 472
good fellowship *n* 892
good fortune *n* 618,

731
good head *n* 502
good health *n* 654
good luck *n* 618, 621, 731
goodly *adj* 31
good man *n* 948
good manners *n* 894
goodness *n* 648
goodness *n* 618, 829, 922, 944
goods *n* 780, 798
good samaritan *n* 906
good taste *n* 578, 850
good will *n* 602, 888
gooey *adj* 396
go off *v* 173
go on *v* 106, 143
go on forever *v* 104, 112
go on vacation *v* 687
go out *v* 142
go over *v* 218
go over again *v* 104
go over the same ground *v* 104
go pit-a-pat *v* 315
gore *v* 260
gorge *n* 198; *v* 641, 869, 957
gorged *adj* 869
gorgeous *adj* 428, 845
gorgeousness *n* 845
gormandizing *n* 957; *adj* 957
go round about *v* 629
gory *adj* 361, 653
gossamer *n* 205
gossamery *adj* 329
gossip *n* 455, 532, 588; *v* 588
gossipy *adj* 588
go straight *v* 246, 628
go the way of all flesh *v* 360
go through *v* 151, 302
go to *v* 278
go to bed *v* 687
go to press *v* 591
go to seed *v* 659
go to sleep *v* 687
go to the dogs *v* 162, 735, 804
go to the law *v* 969
go to waste *v* 659

go to wrack and ruin *v* 162
gouge *n* 262; *v* 252
go up *v* 305
govern *v* 693, 737
governess *n* 753
government *n* 693
governor *n* 694, 753
go wild *v* 173
gown *n* 999
go wrong *v* 732
grab *v* 379
grace *n* 242, 578, 845, 850, 918, 987
graceful *adj* 578, 845
gracefulness *n* 242, 578, 845
graceless *adj* 579
gracious *adj* 894
graciously *adv* 602
graciousness *n* 894
gradation *n* 26, 58, 69
grade *n* 26, 58, 71, 217, 305, 306
grade crossing *n* 219
gradual *adj* 26, 69, 275, 685
gradually *adv* 26, 69, 275
graduate *v* 60, 69
graduation *n* 60
graft *v* 184, 300
grain *n* 5, 256, 329, 330
graininess *n* 330
grammar *n* 567
grammar *n* 542
grammar book *n* 567
grammarian *n* 567
grammatical *adj* 567
grand *adj* 574, 642, 882
grandchildren *n* 167
grandeur *n* 875
grandfather *n* 130, 166
grandiloquence *n* 577
grandiloquent *adj* 577
grandiose *adj* 577
grandmother *n* 130, 166
grandsire *n* 130, 166
grant *n* 784; *v* 529, 760, 762, 783, 784
grantee *n* 785
granter *n* 784
granular *adj* 330
granularity *n* 330
granulate *v* 330
granulation *n* 330

granule *n* 32
graphic *adj* 518
grapple with *v* 719
grasp *v* 518
grass *n* 367
grassland *n* 344
grassy *adj* 435
grate *v* 330, 378, 410, 414
grateful *adj* 916
grater *n* 330
gratification *n* 827
gratify *v* 829, 831
grating *n* 219, 410; *adj* 410, 414
gratitude *n* 916
gratuity *n* 784
grave *n* 363; *v* 558; *adj* 642, 739, 830
grave clothes *n* 363
gravestone *n* 363
graveyard *n* 363
gravitate *v* 306, 319
gravitate toward *v* 176
gravitation *n* 319
gravitational *adj* 288
gravity *n* 319
gravity *n* 288, 574, 642, 739
gray *n* 432
gray *n* 422; *adj* 128, 422, 428, 429, 432
graybeard *n* 130
gray hairs *n* 128
grayish *adj* 432
grayness *n* 422, 432
graze *v* 199
graze over *v* 379
grazing over *n* 379
grease *n* 355, 356; *v* 255, 332, 355
greasiness *n* 355
greasing *n* 332
greasy *adj* 355
great *adj* 31, 192
greaten *v* 35
greater *adj* 33
greatest *adj* 33
greatly *adv* 31
greatness *n* 31
greatness *n* 33, 192, 873
great waters *n* 341
greed *n* 957
greediness *n* 957
greedy *adj* 789, 819, 957

green *n* 435
green *adj* 123, 127, 435, 674
greenbacks *n* 800
greenhorn *n* 547, 701
greenish *adj* 435
greenish blue *adj* 438
greenness *n* 123, 435
greens *n* 367
gregarious *adj* 892
gregariousness *n* 892
gridiron *n* 219
grief *n* 833
grievance *n* 830
grieve *v* 828, 839
grieve at *v* 833
grievous *adj* 649, 830
grievously *adv* 31
grill *v* 384
grille *n* 219
grim *adj* 830
grimace *v* 243
grime *n* 653
grimy *adj* 653
grin *n* 838; *v* 838
grind *v* 195, 253, 330, 331, 410, 539
grinder *n* 330
grinding *n* 410
grindstone *n* 330
grip *n* 378
gripe *n* 378; *v* 378
grist *n* 637
gristly *adj* 327
grit *n* 327, 330
gritty *adj* 330, 604
grizzled *adj* 432
grizzly *adj* 432
groan *n* 839; *v* 411
groove *n* 259, 613; *v* 259
grope in the dark *v* 442
gross *adj* 653, 846, 961
grossness *n* 961
grouch *v* 900
ground *n* 181, 211, 215, 342, 467, 615; *v* 215
grounded on *adj* 211
groundless *adj* 4
grounds *n* 342, 344, 467
groundswell *n* 315
groundwork *n* 60, 64, 153, 211, 673
group *n* 72, 372, 416,

417, 712; *v* 60, 72
groupings *n* 60
grove *n* 252
grovel *v* 207, 275
groveling *n* 886; *adj* 207, 435, 886
grow *v* 35, 144, 194, 282, 367, 734
grow dim *v* 422
grow from *v* 154
growing *adj* 35
grow into *v* 144
growl *v* 412, 900
growling *n* 412
grown up *adj* 131
growth *n* 35, 144, 161, 194, 250, 282, 365
grow up *v* 131
grudge *n* 907, 921; *v* 819
grudgingly *adv* 603
gruesome *adj* 846
gruff *adj* 254, 410
grumble *v* 407, 411, 832
grumbling *n* 407
grumpy *adj* 901a
grunt *v* 412
guarantee *n* 768, 771; *v* 768, 771
guard *n* 717, 753; *v* 664, 670, 717
guard against *v* 717
guarded *adj* 459, 585, 864
guardian *n* 664, 753, 977
guardian angel *n* 977
guardianship *n* 717
guarding *n* 670
guerilla *n* 361
guess *n* 514; *v* 514
guesswork *n* 514
guffaw *n* 838
guidance *n* 537, 692, 693, 695
guide *n* 524, 527, 540, 694; *v* 537, 692, 693
guidebook *n* 527
guiding *adj* 693
guile *n* 544, 702
guileless *adj* 703, 946
guilelessness *n* 946
guiling *n* 545
guillotine *v* 361

guilt *n* 947
guilt *n* 649, 961
guiltiness *n* 947
guiltless *adj* 946
guiltlessness *n* 946, 960
guilty *adj* 947, 961
guilty verdict *n* 971
guise *n* 448
gulf *n* 343
gulf *n* 198, 343
gull *n* 486, 547; *v* 545
gulley *n* 259
gullibility *n* 486
gullible *adj* 486, 547
gully *n* 350
gulosity *n* 957
gulp *v* 298
gulp down *v* 298
gum *n* 356a
gummy *adj* 327, 352, 356a
gun down *v* 361
gunshot *n* 197
gurgle *v* 348, 353, 408
gurgling *n* 353
guru *n* 994
gush *n* 295, 348; *v* 295, 348, 584
gush out *v* 295
gust *n* 349; *v* 349
gusto *n* 390
gut *v* 162
guts *n* 221, 861
gutsy *adj* 861
gutter *n* 259, 350
guttural *adj* 410
guzzle *v* 957, 959
gymnasium *n* 728
gypsy *n* 268
gyration *n* 312

H

habit *n* 613
habit *n* 5, 820
habitat *n* 189
habitation *n* 189
habitation *n* 189
habitual *adj* 82, 104, 136, 613
habitually *adv* 136, 613
habituate *v* 613
hack *v* 44
hackneyed *adj* 598
hack up *v* 201

Hades *n* 982
haggard *adj* 203, 688
haggle *v* 794
hagiography *n* 983
hagiological *adj* 983
hail *v* 586
hair *n* 205
hair's breadth *n* 197
hairy *adj* 256
halcyon *adj* 721
hale *adj* 654
half a dozen *n* 98
half a hundred *n* 98
half and half *adj* 27, 41
half measures *n* 628
half-moon *n* 245
half-starved *adj* 956
halfway *adj* 68; *adv* 68
half-witted *adj* 499
hallowed *adj* 976
halo *n* 420
halt *n* 142, 685, 687; *v* 142, 160, 265, 275
halve *v* 91
halved *adj* 91
halving *n* 91
hammer *v* 104
hammered instruments *n* 417
hamper *v* 706
hamstring *v* 158
hand *n* 236, 372, 590, 590, 631; *v* 784
handbook *n* 527, 593
handful *n* 25, 32
handicap *v* 706
hand in hand *adv* 88
handle *n* 564; *v* 379, 677
handling *n* 379
hand of death *n* 360
hand over *v* 270, 783
hands *n* 269
handsome *adj* 845
handwriting *n* 590
handy *adj* 197, 673, 698
hang *v* 214, 361
hang a turn *v* 140
hang back *v* 683
hang by a thread *v* 665
hanging *n* 361; *adj* 214
hanging down *n* 214
hang in there *v* 604a
hang it up *v* 624
hangman *n* 975

hang over *v* 152
hang together *v* 46, 178
hap *n* 156; *v* 156
haphazard *adj* 139, 156
haphazardness *n* 139
hapless *adj* 735
happen *v* 1, 151
happening *n* 8, 151; *adj* 151
happily *adv* 827
happiness *n* 618, 827
happy *adj* 23, 134, 827, 836
happy-go-lucky *adj* 674
harangue *n* 537, 582; *v* 582
harass *v* 830
harbinger *n* 64, 512, 534
hard *adj* 159, 323, 376, 397, 704, 739, 830
hard and fast law *n* 80
hard as a rock *adj* 323
hard as nails *adj* 323
hard by *adv* 197
hard cash *n* 800
hard coal *n* 388
harden *v* 48, 159, 321, 323, 613
hardening *n* 321, 385
hard-featured *adj* 846
hard-hearted *adj* 914a
hard-heartedness *n* 914a
hardihood *n* 861
hardiness *n* 159
hardly *adv* 32, 137
hardly ever *adv* 137
hardness *n* 323
hardness of hearing *n* 419
hardness of heart *n* 951
hard of hearing *adj* 419
hardship *n* 735
hard task *n* 704
hard times *n* 735
hard to please *adj* 868
hard up *adj* 804
hardy *adj* 159, 654
harlequin *n* 501
harlot *n* 962

harm n 619; v 619,
649, 659, 828, 923
harmful adj 619, 649,
657, 663
harmfulness n 649
harmless adj 158
harmonious adj 23,
242, 413, 416, 428,
714
harmoniousness n 413
harmonious sounds n
- 415
harmonize v 23, 82,
413
harmonize with v 714
harmony n 23, 58, 242,
413, 415, 709, 714,
721, 888
harness v 43, 225
harping n 104; adj 104
harp on v 104
harpy n 980
harrow v 371, 830
harsh adj 410, 414,
579, 739, 830, 955
harshness n 410, 414,
739
hart n 373
harvest n 154, 618, 775
harvest time n 126
hash n 59
haste n 684
haste n 132, 863; v 274,
684
hasten v 132, 274, 310,
682, 684
hastily adv 132
hasty adj 684, 863
hatch n 260; v 161,
558, 626
hatchet man n 936
hate n 898
hate n 907; v 867, 898
hateful adj 649, 830,
898, 907
hating adj 898
hatred n 867, 889, 898,
907
hatred of mankind n
911
haughtiness n 878, 885
haughty adj 878, 885
haul n 190; v 190, 285
hauling n 285
haunt n 74, 189
haunted adj 980
haunt one's thoughts v

505
have v 777
have a bad name v 874
have a bad smell v 401
have a defect v 651
have affection for v
897
have a hand in v 153,
682, 709
have a knack for v 698
have an acquaintance
with v 888
have an odor v 398
have a perfume v 400
have a say v 175
have a short memory v
506
have a soft spot in
one's heart v 822
have a temper v 901
have a true ring v 494
have charge of v 693
have confidence in v 484
have done with v 678
have enough v 639
have faith v 987
have faith in v 484, 858
have free play v 170
have had its day v 124
have in common v 778
have in hand v 777
have input v 175
have in sight v 441
have in store for v 152
have its seat in v 183
have leisure v 685
have no bearing upon
v 10
have no chance v 471
have no connection
with v 10
have no curiosity v
456
have no heart for v 866
have no idea v 491
have no interest in v
823
have no limits v 104
have no motive v 615a
have no odor v 399
have no pity for v 914a
have no preference v
609a
have no relation to v
10
have no taste for v 867

have nothing to do
with v 10
have occasion for v
630
have one's act
together v 502
have one's head in the
clouds v 827
have precedence v 62
have priority v 280
have pull adj 288
have qualms v 485
have recourse to v 677
have scope v 748
have seen its day v 124
have the advantage v
28
have the lead v 208
have the means v 632
have the right v 924
have the virtue of v
944
have to do with v 9
have too high an
opinion of oneself v
889
have to oneself v 777
have two meanings v
520
have words with v 713
having a right to adj
924
having no right to adj
925
havoc n 162
hawk v 763, 796
hawker n 797
hazard n 156, 665; v
621, 665
hazard a suggestion v
514
hazardous adj 665
haze n 353, 422
hazel adj 433
haziness n 422, 426,
447, 475
hazy adj 353, 422, 426
head n 66, 353, 372,
450, 564, 694, 745; v
62, 66, 280; adj 210
head for the hills v 623
heading n 64, 66, 75,
280, 564
headland n 250
headlines n 532
headlong adj 684, 863

head of the column *n* 234

headquarters *n* 74

heads or tails *n* 156

headstone *n* 363

headstrong *adj* 606

headway *n* 282

heal *v* 660, 662

healing *n* 660

health *n* 654

health *n* 159

healthful *adj* 654, 656

healthfulness *n* 656

healthiness *n* 656

healthy *adj* 654, 656

heap *n* 31, 72, 192

hear *v* 418

hear a cause *v* 967

hearer *n* 418

hearing *n* 418

hearing *adj* 418

hearsay *n* 532

hearse *n* 363

heart *n* 5, 68, 208, 221, 222, 372, 574, 820

heart and soul *adv* 821

heart-felt *adj* 821

hearth *n* 386

heartless *adj* 383

heartsick *adj* 837

hearty *adj* 654, 836

heat *n* 382

heat *v* 382, 384

heated *adj* 382, 384

heater *n* 386

heath *n* 344

heathen *n* 984, 989

heating *n* 384

heave *v* 276, 284, 307

heaven *n* 981

heavenly *adj* 318, 829, 976, 981

heavenly bodies *n* 318

heavenly kingdom *n* 981

heavenly spirit *n* 977

heavens *n* 180, 318

heaviness *n* 202, 319, 837, 843

heavy *n* 202; *adj* 172, 194, 319, 683

heavy as lead *adj* 319

heavy heart *n* 837

heavy news *n* 830

hebetude *n* 499

heckle *v* 830

hedge *n* 232

hedge in *v* 229

hedonist *n* 954a

heed *n* 457, 459, 864; *v* 418, 457, 928

heedful *adj* 451, 457, 459, 864

heedfulness *n* 864

heeding *n* 418; *adj* 928

heedless *adj* 460, 506, 863

heedlessness *n* 458, 460, 863

heel *n* 211; *v* 279

height *n* 206

height *n* 26, 125, 210, 307

heighten *v* 35, 206, 307, 549, 835

heightening *n* 835

heinous *adj* 846

heir *n* 167

heirs *n* 121, 167

helicopter *n* 273

hell *n* 982

hellish *adj* 978, 982

helmsman *n* 269, 694

help *n* 644, 662, 707, 746, 784, 834; *v* 215, 644, 707, 746, 784, 834

helper *n* 707, 711, 746, 977

helpful *adj* 644, 707, 888

helpfulness *n* 644, 910

helpless *adj* 158

helplessness *n* 158

help onself to *v* 789

helter skelter *adv* 59

hem *n* 231; *v* 43, 231, 258

hem and haw *v* 149, 583

hemi- *adj* 91

hem in *v* 227

hemisphere *n* 181

hemorrhage *n* 299

hen *n* 374

hence *adv* 155

henceforth *adv* 121

henchman *n* 746

her *n* 374

herald *n* 64, 534; *v* 116, 280

herb *n* 367

herbaceous *adj* 367

herbage *n* 367

herbal *adj* 367, 369

Herculean *adj* 159

herculean *adj* 686

herculean task *n* 704

herd *n* 876; *v* 72

here *adv* 186

hereabouts *adv* 183

hereafter *n* 121, 152; *adv* 121

here and there *adv* 182, 183

here below *adv* 318

hereditary *adj* 5, 154

heredity *n* 167

heresy *n* 984

heretic *n* 487, 984

heretical *adj* 984

heretofore *adv* 122

herewith *adv* 88, 632

heritage *n* 11, 121, 122

hermetically sealed *adj* 261

hermit *n* 893, 955

hero *n* 948

heroic *adj* 861

heroism *n* 861

hero worship *n* 991

hesitancy *n* 485, 605

hesitant *adj* 485, 583, 603, 605

hesitate *v* 475, 485, 583, 603, 605

hesitating *adj* 485

hesitation *n* 485, 583, 603, 605

heterodox *adj* 984

heterodoxy *n* 984

heterogeneity *n* 10, 16a, 291

heterogeneous *adj* 10, 15, 41, 81

hew *v* 44, 240, 557

hiatus *n* 198

hiburnal *adj* 383

hidden *adj* 447, 526, 528, 533, 571

hidden meaning *n* 526

hide *n* 223; *v* 442, 447, 528, 862, 893

hideous *adj* 830, 846

hiding *n* 528, 893

hiding place *n* 189, 530, 666

hie *v* 264, 274

176

hierarchical *adj* 995
hierarchy *n* 995
hieroglyph *n* 561
high *adj* 206, 410, 838, 959
high birth *n* 875
high-born *adj* 875
high caliber *n* 33
higher *adj* 33
highest *adj* 210
high-flown *adj* 577
high living *n* 954
highly seasoned *adj* 392
high-minded *adj* 878
highmindedness *n* 875
high note *n* 409
high price *n* 814
high-principled *adj* 939
high relief *n* 250
high seas *n* 341
high sounding *adj* 577, 882
high spirits *n* 836
high-strung *adj* 825
high time *n* 134
hike *n* 266
hill *n* 217, 250, 305, 306
hinder *v* 179, 233, 261, 275, 647, 704, 706, 708, 751, 761
hindmost *adj* 235
hindquarters *n* 235
hindrance *n* 706
hindrance *n* 177, 179
hinge *n* 43, 153
hinge upon *v* 154
hint *n* 505, 527, 550; *v* 505, 527
hinterland *n* 235
hip *adj* 563
hire *n* 812; *v* 788
hirsute *adj* 256
hiss *v* 409, 412
hissing *n* 409; *adj* 409
historian *n* 553
historiographer *n* 553
history *n* 122, 551
histrionic *adj* 599
hit *n* 276
hitch *n* 706; *v* 43, 315
hither *adv* 278
hitherto *adv* 122
hit on *v* 612

hit the bottle *v* 959
hit the road *v* 264, 266
hit upon *v* 480a
hive *n* 189, 691
hoard *n* 636
hoard away *v* 636
hoarse *adj* 405, 410
hoarseness *n* 405
hoary *adj* 124, 432
hoax *n* 545
hobble *n* 706; *v* 275
hobgoblin *n* 980
hobo *n* 268
hocus-pocus *n* 993
hodgepodge *n* 59
hoe *v* 371
hog *n* 957; *v* 957
hoist *v* 307
hold *n* 215; *v* 46, 54, 142, 151, 215, 265, 484, 751, 777, 781, 873
hold a conversation *v* 588
hold a course for *v* 278
hold back *v* 616, 623, 636, 819
holder *n* 191, 779
hold fast *v* 781
hold forth *v* 537
hold in disrespect *v* 929
holding *n* 777, 781
holding back *n* 603
hold on *v* 143
hold one's tongue *v* 403, 585
hold out *v* 763
hold to *v* 602
hold up *v* 143, 215, 235, 707
hole *n* 182, 189, 260, 351, 530
hole puncher *n* 262
holiday *n* 685, 687
holiness *n* 987
holler *v* 404, 411
hollow *n* 208, 252; *v* 208, 252; *adj* 4, 252, 880
hollowed out *adj* 252
hollowness *n* 4, 880
hollows *n* 221
holm *n* 346
holocaust *n* 361
holy *adj* 976, 987

homage *n* 743, 926, 928, 990
home *n* 189; *adj* 221
homeless *adj* 185
homeliness *n* 576, 846, 849
homely *adj* 576, 846, 849, 876
homespun *adj* 329, 576
homestead *n* 189
homework *n* 673
homey *adj* 576
homicidal *adj* 361
homicide *n* 361
homily *n* 537
homogeneity *n* 9, 16, 42
homogeneous *adj* 16, 42
honest *adj* 246, 543, 703, 922, 939, 946, 960
honesty *n* 543, 703, 939, 946, 960
honey *n* 899
honeyed *adj* 396
honey-mouthed *adj* 933
honor *n* 733, 873, 877, 922, 928, 990; *v* 883, 928, 931
honorable *adj* 246, 543, 772, 875, 878, 939
honored *adj* 873
honorific *adj* 883, 990
honoring *adj* 990
hoodwink *v* 447, 545
hook *n* 245; *v* 43, 789
hooked *adj* 244, 245
hoop *n* 247; *v* 411
hoot *v* 411
hop *n* 309; *v* 309
hope *n* 858
hope *n* 507; *v* 858
hope for *v* 507, 858
hopeful *adj* 472, 858
hopeless *adj* 645, 704, 859
hopelessness *n* 859
hopelessness *n* 471, 645, 837
horde *n* 72
horizon *n* 196, 213
horizontal *adj* 213, 251, 308
horizontality *n* 213

identical adj 13, 17
identically adv 13
identity n 13
identity n 17, 27
idiocy n 499
idiom n 521, 566
idiomatic adj 79, 521
idiosyncrasies n 5
idiosyncracy n 820
idiosyncrasy n 79, 83, 176
idiosyncratic adj 5
idiot n 493, 501, 501
idiotic adj 499
idle v 683; adj 681, 683
idleness n 681, 683
idler n 683
idle talk n 588
idol n 897, 899, 991
idolatrize v 991
idolatrous adj 991
idolatrousness n 991
idolatry n 991
idolatry n 897, 990
idolism n 991
idolization n 991
idolize v 897, 990, 991
idolizing n 990
idol-worship n 991
idol-worshiping adj 991
if adv 8
iffy adj 156
if it so happen adv 8
if so adv 8
if worst comes to worst adv 735
ignite v 384
ignoble adj 207, 851, 876
ignominious adj 874
ignominy n 874
ignoramus n 493
ignoramus n 501
ignorance n 491
ignorance n 442
ignorant adj 435, 442, 491
ignore v 460, 773
ill n 619; adj 649, 655
ill-advised adj 499
ill-behaved adj 895
ill-bred adj 851, 895
ill-breeding n 851, 895
ill-conceived adj 499
illegal adj 964
illegality n 964

illegitimacy n 925, 964
illegitimate adj 925, 964
ill-fashioned adj 243
ill-flavored adj 395
ill health n 655
ill-humored adj 901a
illiberal adj 32, 943
illiberality n 819, 943
illicit adj 964
illicitness n 964
illiteracy n 491
illiterate n 493; adj 491
ill-judged adj 499
ill-judging adj 481
ill-made adj 243
ill-mannered adj 851, 895
ill-natured adj 907
illness n 655
illogical adj 47, 477
illogically adv 477
ill-proportioned adj 243
ill-qualified adj 699
ill repute n 874
ill-tempered adj 945
ill-timed adj 135
ill-treat v 739
ill-treatment n 649
illuminate v 420, 423, 428
illumination n 420
illumine v 420
ill-use v 739
illusion n 4, 443, 515, 545
illusory adj 4, 515, 545
illustrate v 82, 554
illustration n 82, 554
illustrative adj 82, 518, 554
illustrious adj 883
ill will n 889, 907
ill wind n 649
image n 17, 21, 448, 521, 556, 991; v 521
imagery n 521, 554
imaginable adj 470, 515
imaginary adj 4, 979
imagination n 515
imaginative adj 2, 515
imaginativeness n 515
imaginative writing n 598
imagine v 515

imagined adj 515
imagistic adj 521
imbalance n 15, 28, 503
imbalanced adj 28
imbecile n 493, 501; adj 499
imbecilic adj 499
imbecility n 499
imbecility n 450a, 497, 499
imbibe v 296, 959
imbibition n 298
imbue v 41, 300, 537
imbued adj 820
imitate v 19, 680, 788
imitation n 19
imitation n 21, 554, 556; adj 19
imitative adj 17, 19, 554
immaculate adj 650, 652, 946, 960
immaterial adj 4, 317, 643
immateriality n 317
immateriality n 643
immature adj 53, 123, 127, 435, 651, 674
immaturity n 53, 123, 651
immeasurability n 105
immeasurably adv 31
immediate adj 132
immediately adv 113, 132
immemorial adj 124
immense adj 31, 104, 192
immensity n 31, 192
immerse v 300, 310, 337
immersed in adj 229
immersion n 300, 310
immigrant n 268
immigrate v 266
immigration n 266
imminent adj 152, 286
immobile adj 172
immobility n 141, 150, 172, 265
immobilize v 265
immoderately adv 31
immodest adj 961
immodesty n 961
immoral adj 923, 940, 945

179

I

independent adj 10, 748

in despair adj 828

in detail adv 51, 79

indeterminate adj 156, 475, 520, 605

indeterminateness n 520

indetermination n 605

index n 86, 550; v 60, 562

indicate v 467, 516, 525, 550, 909

indication n 550

indication n 467, 525, 909

indicative adj 467, 550

indicator n 550

indicatory adj 550

indict v 938, 969

indictment n 938

indifference n 866

indifference n 456, 603, 609a, 643, 736, 989

indifferent adj 34, 383, 456, 460, 603, 609a, 651, 736, 823, 866, 989

indigence n 804

indigenous adj 5, 188

indigent adj 804

indignant adj 900

indignation n 900

indirect adj 279, 629

indirectly adv 629

indiscreet adj 684, 863

indiscretion n 699, 863

indiscriminate adj 41, 59, 81, 465a

indiscrimination n 465a

in disguise adj 528

indispensable adj 630

indispose v 616

indisposed adj 655

indisposition n 603, 655

indisputable adj 474

in disrepair adj 674

indissoluble adj 43, 50, 321

indistinct adj 405, 447, 475

indistinction n 465a

indistinctness n 447, 465a, 571

indistinguishable adj 13, 447

individual n 372; adj 79, 87, 372

individuality n 79, 83, 87

individualize v 79

indivisibility n 50

indivisible adj 50, 321

indoctrinate v 537

indolence n 172, 275, 683

indolent adj 275, 683

indomitable adj 159, 604, 604a, 719

indoors adv 221

in dribs and drabs adv 51

in drips and snatches adv 51

indubitable adj 474

induce v 153, 161, 175, 476, 615

inducement n 615

induct v 296, 755

induction n 296, 476

inductive adj 476

in due course adv 109

in due season adv 109

in due time adv 106, 109, 134

indulge v 740, 760, 954

indulge in v 827

indulgence n 740, 760, 918, 954

indulgent adj 740, 760, 954

induration n 323

industrious adj 539, 682

industry n 682

in earnest adv 604

inebriate n 959

inebriated adj 959

inebriety n 959

in ecstasy adv 377

inedible adj 395

ineffability n 317

ineffable adj 2, 317, 519

in effect adv 5

ineffective adj 158

ineffectual adj 158, 645, 732

inefficacy n 158, 645

inefficiency n 158, 645

inefficient adj 158, 732

inelastic adj 326

inelasticity n 326

inelegance n 579

inelegance n 846

inelegant adj 579

ineluctable adj 601, 744

inept adj 158, 499, 699

ineptitude n 158, 499, 645, 699

inequality n 28

inequality n 15, 24

inequity n 15, 24, 923

ineradicable adj 5

in error adj 481, 495

inert adj 172, 683

inertia n 172

inertness n 172

inertness n 683

inescapable adj 246, 744

inestimable adj 648

in every respect adv 52

inevitability n 474, 601

inevitable adj 474, 601

inevitableness n 601

inexact adj 571

inexactness n 495, 571

in exchange adv 148

inexcitability n 826

inexcitability n 172

inexcitable adj 826

inexhaustibility n 105

inexhaustible adj 104

inexistence n 2

inexistent adj 2

inexorable adj 601, 739, 744, 914a

inexpedience n 647

inexpediency n 647

inexpedient adj 499, 647

inexpensive adj 815

inexperience n 491, 703

inexperienced adj 435

inexpert adj 699

inexpertness n 699

in explanation adv 522

inexplicable adj 519

inexposure n 703

inexpressible adj 519

inexpressive adj 517

inextension n 180a

inextinguishable adj 159

inextravagant *adj* 881
inextricable *adj* 46
in fact *adv* 1
infallibility *n* 474
infallible *adj* 474
infamous *adj* 874
infamy *n* 874
infancy *n* 127
infant *n* 129
infanticide *n* 361
infantile *adj* 129, 499
infantlike *adj* 129
infatuated *adj* 486
infatuation *n* 486, 606
in fault *adj* 947
in favour *adj* 931
infect *v* 659, 824
infection *n* 824
infelicitous *adj* 828
infer *v* 476
inference *n* 65, 476, 480
inferential *adj* 467, 476
inferior *adj* 28, 34, 651, 736
inferiority *n* 34
inferiority *n* 28, 736
infernal *adj* 649, 978, 982
inferno *n* 982
infertile *adj* 169
infertility *n* 169
infidel *n* 989
infidelity *n* 989
infiltrate *v* 41, 294
infiltration *n* 41, 294, 302
infinite *adj* 31, 102, 104, 180
infinitely *adv* 31, 104
infiniteness *n* 105
infinitesimal *adj* 32, 193
infinitude *n* 105
infinity *n* 105
infinity *n* 112, 180
infirm *adj* 158, 160, 655
infirmity *n* 158, 160, 655
in fits *adv* 315
inflame *v* 171, 173, 384, 824
inflamed *adj* 434
in flames *adj* 382

inflammable *adj* 385
inflate *v* 194, 322, 349, 573, 880
inflated *adj* 482, 577, 880
inflation *n* 322, 577
inflect *v* 245
inflection *n* 567
inflexibility *n* 141, 246, 323, 606
inflexible *adj* 323, 604, 606
inflict *v* 680, 739
inflict pain *v* 378
inflict punishment *v* 972
in flight *adj* 267
influence *n* 175
influence *n* 153, 170, 615, 737; *v* 62, 153, 170, 176, 615
influential *adj* 157, 175, 176, 737
influx *n* 294
in force *adj* 170
inform *v* 527, 537, 668
informality *n* 83
informant *n* 527, 534
information *n* 527
information *n* 467, 490, 498, 532
informed *adj* 527
informer *n* 527, 532, 938
infraction *n* 83, 303, 742, 773, 927
infrequency *n* 137
infrequency *n* 103
infrequent *adj* 103, 137
infrequently *adv* 137
infringe *v* 303, 742, 773
infringement *n* 303
infringement *n* 83, 742, 773
in front *adv* 234, 280
in front of one's nose *adj* 446
in full sight *adj* 446
in full view *adj* 446
infuriate *v* 173
infuse *v* 41, 300, 537
infusion *n* 41, 300
in future *adv* 121
ingathering *n* 72
ingenious *adj* 698, 702

ingenuity *n* 698
ingenuous *adj* 703, 946
ingenuousness *n* 946
ingest *v* 296, 539
ingestion *n* 296, 298
in good taste *adj* 850
in good time *adv* 152
ingraft *v* 300
ingrained *adj* 5, 221, 820
ingrate *n* 917
ingratitude *n* 917
ingredient *n* 51, 56, 211
ingress *n* 294
ingress *n* 302
inhabit *v* 184, 186, 188, 189
inhabitant *n* 188
inhabiting *adj* 186
inhale *v* 398
in hand *adj* 777
inharmonious *adj* 24, 414
inharmoniousness *n* 414
in harmony with *adj* 23
in harness *adj* 749
in health *adj* 654
inherence *n* 5
inherent *adj* 5, 221
inherited *adj* 5
in hiding *adj* 528
in high esteem *adj* 931
in honor of *adv* 883
inhumation *n* 363
inimical *adj* 708, 889
inimitable *adj* 20, 33, 648, 650
iniquitous *adj* 923, 945
iniquity *n* 923, 945
initial *adj* 66
initiate *v* 66, 296
initiation *n* 66, 296
initiative *n* 66
in its infancy *adv* 66
in its own sweet time *adv* 152
in its turn *adv* 58
inject *v* 300
injection *n* 296, 300
injudicious *adj* 499
injunction *n* 630, 695, 741, 761, 864
injur *v* 848
injure *v* 619, 649, 659,

828, 923

injured *adj* 659, 848

injurious *adj* 619, 649

injury *n* 173, 619, 649, 659, 665, 776

injustice *n* 173, 923

ink *n* 431

in keeping with *adj* 23; *adv* 82

inkling *n* 514, 527

inky *adj* 431

inlaid *adj* 221, 440

inlands *n* 342

inlay *v* 440

in league *adj* 709

inlet *n* 260, 343

in lieu of *adv* 147

inmate *n* 188

in moderation *adv* 174

inmost *adj* 221

in motion *adj* 264

in mourning *adj* 839

innate *adj* 5, 221

inner *adj* 221

inner coating *n* 224

inner man *n* 820

innermost *adj* 221

innermost recesses *n* 221

inner part *n* 221

innocence *n* 946

innocence *n* 703, 944, 960

innocent *adj* 435, 703, 946, 960

in no respect *adv* 32

in no time *adv* 113

innovate *v* 140

innovation *n* 20a, 123, 140

innovative *adj* 140

innuendo *n* 527

in obedience to *adv* 743

inoculate *v* 300

inoculation *n* 300

inodorousness *n* 399

in one's birthday suit *adj* 226

in one's debt *adj* 916

in operation *adj* 170, 680

inoperative *adj* 158, 645

inopportune *adj* 135, 647

inopportuneness *n* 135

in opposition *adj* 708

in order *adj* 58; *adv* 58

inordinate *adj* 31, 641, 954

inordinately *adv* 31

inordinateness *n* 954

inorganic *adj* 358

inorganic matter *n* 358

in part *adv* 32, 51

in particular *adv* 79

in perfect condition *adj* 650

in place of *adv* 147

in plain English *adv* 576, 703

in plain sight *adv* 525

in plain terms *adv* 576

in play *adj* 170

in poor health *adj* 655

in possession of *adj* 777

in preparation *adj* 53

in presence of *adv* 186

in print *adj* 531, 532

in prison *adj* 754

in private *adv* 528

in progress *adj* 53

in prospect *adj* 121, 152, 620

in proximity *adj* 186

in pursuit of *adj* 622

input *n* 175

in question *adv* 454

in quest of *adj* 622

inquietude *n* 828

inquire *v* 461

inquirer *n* 461

inquiring *n* 461; *adj* 455, 461

inquiring mind *n* 455

inquiry *n* 461

inquiry *n* 539

inquisitive *adj* 455, 461

inquisitiveness *n* 455

inquisitor *n* 461, 739

inquisitorial *adj* 461, 739, 965

in rapport *adj* 413

in readiness *adj* 507

in reality *adv* 1

in relief *adj* 250

in reserve *adj* 636

in retaliation *adv* 718

inroad *n* 294

in rotation *adv* 138

insalubrious *adj* 657

insalubrity *n* 657

insane *adj* 173, 503

insanity *n* 503

inscrutable *adj* 519

in secret *adj* 528; *adv* 528

insect *n* 366

insecure *adj* 475, 665

insecurity *n* 475, 665

insensate *adj* 499

insensibility *n* 376, 823

insensibility *n* 866

insensible *adj* 376, 381, 506

insensitive *adj* 376, 823, 866

insensitiveness *n* 823, 866

inseparability *n* 46

inseparable *adj* 43, 46

insert *v* 221, 228, 300

insertion *n* 300

insertion *n* 37, 228, 294, 296

in short *adv* 572

inside *n* 221; *adj* 221

inside out *adj* 218

insidious *adj* 545, 702

insight *n* 477, 498; *adj* 507

insightful *adj* 842

insigne *n* 550

insignificance *n* 32, 643, 736

insignificant *adj* 4, 32, 517, 643, 736

in simple words *adv* 703

insincere *adj* 544

insincerity *n* 544

insinuate *v* 527

insinuate oneself *v* 294

insinuation *n* 228, 294, 300, 527

insipid *adj* 337, 391, 575

insipidity *n* 391

insist upon *v* 604, 770

in snatches *adv* 70

insobriety *n* 959

insolence *n* 885

insolence *n* 715, 878

insolent *adj* 715, 885

insoluble *adj* 321, 519

insolvency *n* 732, 808

insolvent *adj* 804

in some degree adv 26
in some place adv 182
inspect v 441
inspector n 694; 461
inspiration n 477, 515, 612, 824
inspire v 615, 824
inspiring adj 836
inspirit v 836
inspiriting adj 858
in spite adv 708
in spite of prep 179
instability n 149, 475, 605, 665
install v 184, 755
installation n 184
installment n 807
instance n 82
instant n 113; adj 113, 118, 630
instantaneous adj 111, 113, 132
instantaneously adv 113, 132
instantaneousness n 113
instead adv 147
instigate v 615
instigation n 170, 615
instill v 41, 300, 537
instinct n 477, 601
instinctive adj 5, 477, 601
instinctual adj 5, 477
in stir adj 754
institute n 542; v 153, 161
in store adj 152, 636
instruct v 537, 693, 695, 741
instructed adj 490
instruction n 537, 693, 695, 697, 741
instructive adj 537, 985
instructor n 540
instrument n 633
instrument adj 415
instrumental adj 176, 416, 631, 632, 633, 677
instrumentalist n 416
instrumentality n 631
instrumentality n 170
instrumental music n 415
insubordinate adj 715,

742
insubordination n 715, 742
insubstantiality n 2, 317
in succession adv 69
in such and such a place adv 183
in such wise adv 8
insufferable adj 830
insufficiency n 640
insufficiency n 53, 304, 651, 732
insufficient adj 28, 32, 304, 640, 651, 732
insufficiently adv 32
insular adj 10, 44, 87, 346
insularity n 44
insulate v 44, 87
insulation n 44
insult n 830; v 830, 929
insulting adj 885, 929
insurgence n 719
insurgent n 742; adj 742
insurrection n 719
insusceptibility n 376
in suspense adv 172
intact adj 50, 52, 141, 650, 670, 729
intactness n 52
intaglio n 22
intangible adj 2, 4, 317
in tears adj 828
integer n 84
integral adj 50
integral part n 56
integrate v 50
integrity n 50, 922, 939, 944
intellect n 450
intellect n 498, 842
intellectual n 492; adj 450, 498
intellectual giant n 872
intellectualize v 450
intelligence n 498
intelligence n 480, 498, 527, 532, 698, 842
intelligencer n 527, 534
intelligent adj 498, 698, 842
intelligibility n 518
intelligibility n 570
intelligible adj 518,

522, 570
intemperance n 954
intemperance n 959
intemperate adj 954
intend v 451, 516, 620
intense adj 31, 171, 382, 428
intensely adv 31
intensification n 835
intensified adj 835
intensify v 35, 171, 835
intensity n 26, 31, 171, 173, 382
intent n 451, 516, 600, 620
intention n 620
intention n 278, 451, 516, 611, 615
intentional adj 600, 620
intentionally adv 600, 611, 620
intentiveness n 457
intentness n 682
inter v 363
interact v 12
intercalation n 228
intercede v 724
intercession n 724, 766
interchange n 148
interchange n 12, 219, 783; v 12, 147, 148, 783
interchangeability n 148
interchangeable adj 12, 148, 794
intercourse n 148
interdepend v 12
interdependence n 12
interdict v 761
interdiction n 761
interest n 455, 618, 642, 707; v 288, 824, 829, 840
interested adj 455
interfere v 228, 708, 724
interference n 179, 228, 706, 719
interfere with v 179
interim n 106, 198
interior n 221, 342; adj 221
interiority n 221
interjacence n 228
interjacent adj 228

interject *v* 228
interjection *n* 228
interlace *v* 41, 43, 219
interlaced *adj* 219
interlard *v* 41
interlarding *n* 41
interlineation *n* 228
interlink *v* 219
interlocation *n* 228
interlocution *n* 588
interlude *n* 106, 198, 685
intermediary *n* 534, 631; *adj* 631
intermediate *adj* 29, 68, 631
intermedium *n* 631
interment *n* 363
interminable *adj* 104, 112, 200
intermission *n* 70, 106
intermittence *n* 138
intermittent *adj* 70, 138
intermittently *adv* 138
intern *v* 221
internal *adj* 5, 221
internally *adv* 221
interpenetrate *v* 228
interpenetration *n* 228
interpolate *v* 41, 228
interpolation *n* 41, 228, 300
interpose *v* 70, 228, 724
interposition *n* 37, 228, 724
interpret *v* 462, 522, 537
interpretable *adj* 522
interpretation *n* 522
interpretation *n* 155, 516
interpretative *adj* 522
interpreter *n* 524
interpreter *n* 513
interpretive *adj* 522
interregnum *n* 106, 142, 198
interrogate *v* 461
interrogation *n* 461
interrogative *adj* 461
interrupt *v* 70, 142, 198, 706
interrupted *adj* 70
interruption *n* 61, 70, 142, 198, 706

intersect *v* 219
intersection *n* 219
interspace *n* 198, 221
intersperse *v* 228
interspersion *n* 228
interstice *n* 198
intertwine *v* 41, 43, 219
intertwined *adj* 219
interval *n* 198
interval *n* 53, 70, 106, 196
intervene *v* 70, 198, 228, 631, 724
intervening *adj* 228
intervention *n* 228, 631, 724
interview *n* 588
interweave *v* 41, 43, 219
in the altogether *adj* 226
in the background *adv* 235
in the blood *adj* 5
in the bud *adv* 66
in the buff *adj* 226
in the cards *adj* 152
in the course of *adv* 106
in the course of things *adv* 151
in the event of *adv* 8
in the face of *adv* 715
in the first place *adv* 66
in the foreground *adv* 234
in the fourth place *adv* 96
in the genes *adj* 5
in the headlines *adj* 532
in the interim *adv* 106
in the lead *adv* 234
in the long run *adv* 29, 152
in the main *adv* 50
in the matter of *adv* 9
in the meantime *adv* 106
in the middle *adv* 68
in the midst of *adv* 41
in the news *adj* 532
in the nick of time *adv* 134

in the open air *adv* 338
in the open market *adj* 763
in the rear *adv* 235, 281
in the same category *adj* 9
in the thick of *adv* 228
in the third place *adv* 93
in the vanguard *adv* 280
in the wide open spaces *adv* 338
in the wind *adj* 152
intimacy *n* 888
intimate *n* 890; *v* 527; *adj* 197, 221, 888
intimately *adv* 43
in time *adv* 109, 152
intimidate *v* 909
intimidating *adj* 909
intimidation *n* 909
intolerable *adj* 830
intolerance *n* 606, 825
intolerant *adj* 606, 825
intonation *n* 402, 580
intone *v* 580
in top shape *adj* 654
in touch with *adj* 592
in tow *adj* 285
intoxicate *v* 824
intoxicated *adj* 959
intoxication *n* 824, 959
intractable *adj* 606, 704
intractability *n* 606
in trade *adj* 794
intrepid *adj* 861
intrepidity *n* 861
intricate *adj* 248, 704
intrigue *n* 626, 702; *v* 702
intriguer 626
intrinsic *adj* 5, 221
intrinsicality *n* 5
intrinsically *adv* 5
in triumph *adv* 731
introduce *v* 62, 228, 280, 296, 300
introduction *n* 64, 66, 296, 300
introductory *adj* 62, 64, 66, 116
intrude *v* 135, 228, 294
intrusion *n* 57, 135,

I

228, 294
intrusive *adj* 228, 706
intuit *v* 477
intuition *n* 477
intuition *n* 477
intuitive *adj* 477
intuitively *adv* 477
in turn *adv* 58, 138
intwine *v* 219
inundate *v* 337, 348, 641
inundation *n* 348
in unison *adj* 413
inure *v* 613
inutile *adj* 645
inutility *n* 645
invade *v* 294, 716
invader *n* 716
in vain *adv* 732
invalidate *v* 158, 479, 536, 756
invalidation *n* 479, 536, 756
invaluable *adj* 648
invariability *n* 16, 141
invariable *adj* 5, 16, 110, 141, 150
invariably *adv* 16, 82
in various places *adv* 182
invasion *n* 294, 716
invent *v* 515, 626
invented *adj* 546
invention *n* 515, 546, 698
inventive *adj* 515, 698
inventiveness *n* 168, 698
inventor *n* 164
inventory *n* 86, 596, 811; *v* 596
inverse *n* 237; *adj* 218. 237
inversely *adv* 218
inversion *n* 218
inversion *n* 14, 140, 145
invert *v* 14, 61, 218
inverted *adj* 59, 218
invest *v* 157, 755, 784
invested *adj* 225
investigate *v* 461
investigation *n* 461, 463, 595

investigator *n* 461
investiture *n* 784
investment *n* 787
inveterate *adj* 124
invidious *adj* 830, 898
in view *adj* 507, 620
invigorate *v* 159, 171
invigorating *adj* 171, 656
invigoration *n* 159
invincible *adj* 159
inviolate *adj* 141
in violation *adj* 927
invisibility *n* 447
invisible *adj* 193, 447
invisibleness *n* 447
invite *v* 288, 615, 763, 829
invocation *n* 586
in vogue *adj* 852
invoice *n* 812
invoke *v* 72, 586, 990
involuntary *adj* 601
involution *n* 248, 571
involve *v* 516, 938
involved *adj* 59, 248, 571
invulnerability *n* 664
invulnerable *adj* 664
inward *adj* 221; *adv* 221
in what manner *adv* 627
in what way *adv* 627
in writing *adj* 590
iota *n* 32
irascibility *n* 901
irascible *adj* 382, 684, 901
irate *adj* 900
iridescence *n* 440
iridescent *adj* 420, 440
irk *v* 830
irksome *adj* 704, 830, 841
iron *v* 255
iron-gray *adj* 432
ironic *adj* 856
ironical *adj* 856
irons *n* 752
irony *n* 856
irradiate *v* 420
irrational *adj* 497, 499
irrationality *n* 499
irreclaimable *adj* 951
irreconcilability *n* 10

irreconcilable *adj* 24
irrecoverable *adj* 122
irrefutable *adj* 246, 474
irregular *adj* 16a, 59, 70, 81, 83, 139, 243, 256, 475
irregularity *n* 139
irregularity *n* 16a, 59, 83, 256, 475
irregularly *adv* 59, 139
irrelation *n* 10
irrelevancy *n* 175a
irrelevant *adj* 10
irreligion *n* 989
irreligion *n* 988
irreligious *adj* 989
irremediable *adj* 859
irrepentance *n* 951
irrepressible *adj* 173, 748, 825
irresistibility *n* 601
irresistible *adj* 159, 601, 744
irresolute *adj* 149, 485, 605, 607, 609a, 683
irresolution *n* 605
irresolution *n* 149, 172, 314, 485, 609a
irrespective *adj* 10
irresponsibility *n* 773
irresponsible *adj* 773
irretrievable *adj* 776
irreverence *n* 929, 988
irreverent *adj* 929
irrevocable *adj* 604
irrigate *v* 348
irrigation *n* 348
irritability *n* 825, 901
irritable *adj* 684, 825, 901
irritate *v* 173, 289, 688, 824, 828, 830
irritated *adj* 835
irritation *n* 824, 828, 835
irruption *n* 294
island *n* 346
isle *n* 346
islet *n* 346
isolate *v* 44, 79, 87, 893, 905
isolated *adj* 10, 44, 87, 893
isolation *n* 44, 893, 905
issuance *n* 531

issue n 154, 167, 295; v 73, 151, 295, 531, 591
issue from v 154
issues n 151
itch v 380
itching n 380; adj 380
itchy adj 380
items n 79
iterate v 104
iteration n 90, 104, 136
iterative adj 104
itinerant n 268; adj 266

J

jabber n 517, 584; v 517, 584
jackanapes n 854
jaded adj 961
jag v 257
jagged adj 244
jail n 752; v 972
jailbird n 754
jailer n 753; 975
jailhouse n 752
jangle v 410
jar n 315; v 24, 410, 414, 713
jargon n 497, 517, 560
jarring adj 410, 414
jaundice n 435, 436
jaundiced adj 435
jaunt n 266
jaw v 584
jazz n 415
jealous adj 435, 900, 920, 921
jealousy n 920
jealousy n 900, 921
jeopardize v 665
jeer v 929
jeer at v 856
jeers n 856
jeopardy n 665
jerk n 285, 315, 493; v 285, 315
jerky adj 315
jest v 842
jester n 501, 844
jesuitry n 477
jet n 273, 348; v 267, 348
jet-black adj 431
jet-setter n 268
jetting adj 267
jettison v 610

jetty n 250
jewel n 648, 899
jibe v 23
jilt v 509
jingle v 408
jinx n 621; n 993
job n 676
jocularity n 836
jog n 315; v 276
joggle v 315
jog on v 736
join v 37, 41, 43, 45, 72, 87, 88, 199, 290, 712
joined adj 43
join forces v 709
join hands with v 709
joining n 37, 43, 290
joint n 43; adj 43, 88, 178, 778
jointly adv 43
joint tenancy n 778
joke v 842
joker n 844
jolly adj 836, 840
jolt n 315; v 276, 315
jostle v 179, 276, 315
jot n 32
jounce v 315
journal n 114, 551
journalist n 553
journey n 266
journey n 302; v 266
journeyer n 268
journeying adj 266
jovial adj 840
joviality n 836
jowl n 236
joy n 377, 827; v 827
joyful adj 377, 827, 836
joyous adj 836
jubilant adj 838, 884
jubilation n 838
judge n 967
judge v 480, 737, 965; v 451, 480, 850, 965, 967
judgment n 480
judgment n 450, 451, 453, 465, 490, 498, 972
judgmental adj 480
judgment seat n 966
judicator n 965, 967
judicatory adj 967
judicature n 965
judicial adj 480, 965,

967
judiciary n 967
judicious adj 174, 480, 498, 868, 967
judiciousness n 174, 868
juice v 354
juiced adj 959
juiceless adj 340
juicer n 959
juicy adj 333, 337, 339
jumble n 41, 59; v 41, 59, 61
jumbo jet n 273
jump n 305, 309; v 309, 310
junction n 43
junction n 41, 45, 48
juncture n 8, 43, 134
jungle n 59
junior adj 127
juridical adj 967
jurisdiction n 965
jurisdiction n 737
jurisdictive adj 965, 967
jurist n 967
juristic adj 967
juror n 967
just adj 246, 922
just as adv 17
just do v 639
justice n 922, 967
justification n 717, 737, 937
justified adj 937
justify v 717, 737, 937
just in time adv 134
justly adv 922
just now adv 123
jut out v 250
juvenile adj 127
juvenility n 123, 127
juxtapose v 464

K

kaleidoscope n 445
kaleidoscopic adj 440
kaput adj 503
karma n 152
keen adj 171, 253, 375, 868
keen blast n 349
keenness n 868
keep n 298; v 141, 143, 670, 751, 781, 883
keep accounts v 811

KL

lake n 343
lake n 343
lamb n 129
lame adj 53, 160, 651, 655
lame excuse n 617
lament n 411, 839; v 411, 833, 839, 915
lamentable adj 649, 830, 833, 839
lamentably adv 31
lamentation n 839
lamentation n 833, 915
lamenting adj 839
lamp n 423
lampoon v 856
lampooner n 844
lance v 260
lancet n 262
land n 342
land n 780; v 292, 342
landed adj 342
landing n 292
lands n 342
landscape n 448; v 371
landscaping n 371
language n 560
languid adj 160, 172, 275, 405, 575, 683, 685
languish v 36, 160, 655, 683
languor n 160, 172, 275, 683, 688
lankness n 203
lanky adj 200, 203
lantern n 423
lap n 221, 311
lap of luxury n 377
lapse n 661, 776; v 109, 122, 144, 659, 661
lapsed adj 122
lard n 356
large adj 31, 192, 202
largeness n 192
larger adj 194
largesse n 784
lash n 975; v 43, 173, 972
lass n 129
lassitude n 688, 841
last v 1, 106, 110, 141, 604a; adj 67, 122
last breath n 360
last forever v 112
lasting adj 106, 110, 141, 150

lastingness n 110
last resort n 666
last stage n 67
last word n 67
late adj 122, 123, 133, 275, 360; adv 133
lately adv 122, 123
latency n 526
latency n 172, 447
lateness n 133
latent adj 172, 526
latentness n 526
later adj 117; adv 117
lateral adj 236
laterality n 236
laterally adv 236
lather n 353; v 332, 353
lathering n 332
latitude n 180, 181, 202, 748
latitude and longitude n 183
latter adj 122
lattice n 219
laud v 883, 990
laudatory adj 931
laugh v 838
laughable adj 853
laughing adj 838
laughing-stock n 857
laughingstock n 547
laughter n 838
launch n 273; v 66, 284
launch into v 676
launder v 652
laureate n 597
laurel n 733
lavation n 652
lavender adj 437
lavish v 641, 784, 818; adj 641, 818
lavishness n 818
law n 80, 697, 963
lawful adj 246, 760, 922, 963
lawfully adv 922
lawfulness n 922, 963
lawless adj 964
lawlessness n 964
lawsuit n 969
lawyer n 968
lax adj 47, 738, 773
laxative n 652
laxity n 738
laxity n 47, 495, 748, 773, 989

laxness n 738, 773
lay n 413; v 184; adj 997
lay aside v 55
lay away v 636
lay bare v 260
lay claim to v 741
layer n 204
layer v 204
layered adj 204
lay groundwork v 626
lay in v 637
lay in a stock v 637
lay in a store v 637
lay in the grave v 363
lay in the ground v 363
lay it on thick v 933
layman n 997
lay oneself open to v 177, 665
lay on thick v 641
lay open v 226, 260, 529
lay out v 363, 809
lay over v 133
lay siege v 716
lay stress on v 642
lay the foundations v 673
lay the groundwork v 60
lay to rest v 363
lay up v 678
lay waste v 162
laziness n 683
lazy adj 275, 683
lazy eye n 443
lead n 234; v 116, 176, 615, 692, 693
lead astray v 545
leaden adj 422
leader n 64, 694, 745
leadership n 692, 693
leading n 280; adj 66
lead the way v 62, 66, 280
leaf n 204
leafage n 367
league n 712
leak n 198; v 295
leakage n 295
lean v 176, 217; adj 203
leaning n 176, 217, 602; adj 176
leanness n 203
lean on v 858

L

libertine n 954a
liberty n 685, 737, 748,
    760, 760
librarian n 593
libretto n 593
licence n 738
license n 748, 760, 924;
    v 760
licensed adj 924
licit adj 246, 963
lick the boots of v 886
lid n 223, 261, 263
lie n 544, 546; v 183,
    213, 538, 544, 546
lie around v 220
lie down v 213, 687
lie flat v 207, 213
lie idle v 681
lie in v 1
lie in wait for v 530
lie low v 207
lien n 771
lie still v 265
life n 359
life n 151, 171, 682
lifeblood n 5, 359
life-giving adj 168
lifeless adj 172, 360
lifelessness n 172
lifelike adj 17, 21
lifetime n 108
lift n 307; v 235, 307
lift up v 235, 307
light n 420
light n 7; v 292, 384,
    420, 423; adj 320,
    322, 420, 430, 643
light bulb n 423
light-colored adj 429
lighten v 320, 420, 705
lightening n 470
light-fingered adj 791
light-footed adj 274
lightness n 320
light of day n 420
light on v 156
light up v 824
like v 394, 827, 897,
    990; adj 17, 216
like a shot adv 113
like a ton of bricks adj
    319
likelihood n 470, 472
likeliness n 472
likely adj 176, 177, 472
likeness n 17, 21, 216,
    556

likening n 464
like two peas in a pod
    n 17
likewise adv 37
liking n 602, 897
lilac adj 437
lily-liver n 862
lily-livered adj 435,
    862
limb n 51
limber adj 324
limbo n 982
limit n 233
limit n 67, 71; v 195,
    229, 233, 469, 761
limitation n 229, 469,
    751
limited adj 103, 203,
    233
limitless adj 104, 180
limitlessness n 105
limn v 556, 594
limp v 160, 275; adj 53,
    158, 160, 324, 326
limpid adj 425
limpidity n 425
limpness n 326
line n 69, 278; v 224
lineage n 11, 69, 122,
    166
lineal adj 166, 200
linear adj 69, 200, 246
lined adj 224, 440
line of march n 278
liner n 273
lines n 230, 448
linger v 133, 275
lingering adj 110
lingo n 560
lingual adj 560
linguist n 560
linguistic adj 560
liniment n 356
lining n 224
link n 45
link n 9, 43; v 9, 43, 45,
    219
linkage n 43
link up v 43, 219
linseed oil n 356
lip n 231
lip-service n 933
liquefaction n 335
liquefaction n 333, 384
liquefy v 333, 335, 384
liquefying n 335
liquid n 337; adj 333,

337
liquidate v 807
liquidation n 807
liquid containers n
    191
liquidity n 333
list n 86
list n 217, 596; v 551,
    596
listen v 418
listener n 418
listening n 418
listing n 86
listless adj 683, 866
listlessness n 866
lists n 728
literal adj 561, 562
literally adv 19
literary adj 560
literature n 560, 590
litigant n 726, 969
litigation n 969
litigious adj 969
litter n 167; v 61
little adj 32, 193
little by little adv 26,
    275
littleness n 193
littleness n 32, 201
little one n 129
live n 374; v 1, 141,
    186, 188, 359; adj
    359
live from hand to
    mouth v 804
livelihood n 803
liveliness n 515, 682,
    829, 836
lively adj 309, 359,
    375, 515, 574, 682,
    829, 836
live off v 298
live on v 298
livery n 225
livestock n 366
live through v 151
livid adj 431, 435
lividness n 431
living being n 364
living beings n 357
living thing n 366
load n 190, 319, 828; v
    52, 190, 319, 641
loaf v 683
loafer n 683
loan n 787; v 787
loath adj 603, 867

loathe v 867, 898
loathing n 867, 898
loathsome adj 395, 830, 867, 898
local adj 183
locale n 182, 183
locality n 182, 183
locate v 183, 184
located adj 183, 184
locate oneself v 184
location n 184
location n 183
loch n 343
lock n 350; v 43
lock-up n 752
locomotion n 264
locomotive n 271
locution n 582
lodge v 184, 186
lodger n 188
lodging n 189
loft v 235
loftiness n 206, 574, 875
lofty adj 206, 574
log n 114, 388, 551
logic n 23, 476
logical adj 23, 476, 502
logician n 476
loiter v 133, 275, 683
loitering n 133
loll v 683
lone adj 87
long adj 200; adv 110
long ago adv 110, 122
long dozen n 98
longevity n 110, 128
long expected adj 507
long for v 858, 865
longhand n 590
longing n 858, 865
longitude n 200
longitudinal adj 200
longitudinally adv 200
long lost adj 776
long shot n 137
longstanding adj 110
long-winded adj 573
long-windedness n 573
look n 441, 448; v 441, 448, 457
look after oneself v 943
look ahead v 510
look askance v 443
look beyond v 510
look danger in the face

v 861
looker-on n 444
look for v 461, 507
look forward v 121
look forward to v 507, 510
looking back adj 122
looking glass n 445
look into the future v 510
look like v 17
look on v 186, 444
lookout n 448
look out for v 507
look sharp v 682
look upon v 451
loom v 152, 446
looming adj 152
loon n 501
loop n 245, 247, 629
loophole n 671
loose v 44, 750; adj 44, 47, 279, 573, 575, 738, 748, 773
loosen v 47
looseness n 47, 573, 738, 748
loosening n 47, 738
loot n 793
lop v 371
loquacious adj 584
loquaciousness n 584
loquacity n 584
lord n 745, 875, 976
lore n 490, 537
lorgnette n 445
lose v 776
lose an opportunity v 135
lose color v 429
lose ground v 283
lose heart v 837
lose it v 503
lose no time v 682
lose one's senses v 503
lose one's temper v 825
lose patience v 825
lose sight of v 506
loss n 776
loss n 40a, 449, 619, 638, 659, 732
loss of life n 360
lost adj 2, 449, 458, 732, 776
lost in thought adj 451
lost in wonder adj 870

lot n 25, 152, 621, 786
lottery n 156
loud adj 404
loudly adv 404
loudness n 404
loud noise n 404
lough n 343
lounge v 683
lounger n 683
lout n 501
lovable adj 897
love n 897
love n 897
love n 865, 897, 899, 977; v 827, 928, 990
loveliness n 829, 845
lovely adj 242, 377, 597, 829, 845, 977
lover n 897
lovesick adj 991
love token n 902
loving adj 897
low v 412; adj 32, 207, 405, 438, 649, 874, 876, 879, 930
low-born adj 876
lower v 207, 308, 879; adj 34
lowering n 308
lowland n 344
lowlands n 207
lowliness n 879
lowly adj 207, 879
low-lying adj 207
lowness n 207
low price n 815
low quality n 34
low relief n 250
low repute n 874
loyal adj 743
loyalty n 743
lubricate v 255, 332, 355
lubrication n 332
lubrication n 255, 355
lubricity n 255, 355
lucent adj 420
lucid adj 425, 502, 518, 570, 849
lucidity n 420, 425, 502, 518, 570, 578
Lucifer n 978
luck n 152, 156, 621, 731
lucky adj 134, 621, 734
ludicrous adj 853
lug v 285
lugubrious adj 837

lukewarm adj 382, 823, 866
lull n 142, 265, 403, 683, 685; v 174, 265
lull to sleep v 265
lumber v 275
luminary n 423
luminary n 500
luminosity n 420
luminous adj 420, 518
lump n 50, 51, 72, 192, 321
lumpish adj 192, 319
lump together v 72
lunacy n 503
lunar adj 245, 318
lunatic n 504; adj 503
lunch v 298
lunge n 276
lurch n 306; v 306
lure v 288
lurid adj 421, 422
lurk v 526
lurking adj 526
lurking place n 530
luscious adj 394, 396, 829
lush n 959; v 959; adj 337, 365, 396
lust n 865
luster n 420
lust for v 865
lustful adj 865
lustihood n 159
lustrous adj 420
luxuriate v 377
luxuriate in v 827
luxurious adj 377, 829
luxuriousness n 377
luxury n 377, 827
lying n 544; adj 544
lying down n 213
lymph n 337

M

ma n 166
ma'am n 374
Machiavellian adj 702
machinery n 633
macrocosm n 318
mad adj 173, 503, 824, 825
madam n 374
madame n 374
mad as a hatter adj 503
madden v 173
madman n 504

madness n 503, 825
maelstrom n 312, 348, 667
magenta adj 437
magic n 992; adj 992
magical adj 992
magician n 994
magisterial adj 737
magistracy n 965
magistrate n 967
magnetic adj 288
magnetism n 288
magnetize v 288
magnificence n 845
magnificent adj 192, 845
magnify v 35, 194, 482, 549, 990
magnifying glass n 445
magniloquence n 577
magniloquent adj 549, 577
magnitude n 25, 31, 192
mahogany adj 433
maiden n 129, 904; adj 66
maim v 158, 659
main n 341, 350
mainly adv 31
mainspring n 153, 615
mainstay n 666
maintain v 141, 143, 170, 215, 535, 670, 717, 720, 781, 937
maintain course v 143
maintenance n 141, 143, 170, 670, 781, 803
majestic adj 882
majesty n 875
major adj 33
majority n 33, 100, 131
make n 240; v 54, 56, 144, 161, 744, 852
make a choice v 609
make a circuit v 629
make a clean sweep of v 652
make a complete circle v 311
make a compromise v 628
make acquainted with v 527
make a fool of oneself v 853

make a fresh start v 66
make a generalization v 78
make allowance for v 469
make amends v 30, 952
make a mess of v 732
make a motion v 763
make an addition to v 37
make an end of v 67
make an exception v 469
make a noise v 402
make a pig of oneself v 957
make a place for v 184
make a point of v 604
make a pretext of v 617
make a resolution v 604
make a sign v 550
make a U-turn v 311
make believe v 546
make faces v 243
make for v 278
make free with v 789
make friends with v 888
make fun of v 856
make good v 660, 790
make grave v 835
make haste v 132, 682, 684
make headlines v 532
make headway v 282
make known v 525, 527, 529, 531
make light of v 483, 643
make little of v 483
make loose v 47
make manifest v 525
make merry v 840
make music v 415, 416
make news v 532
make nothing of v 871
make obeisance v 308
make one sick v 395
make one's way v 734
make out v 441
make over v 783
make payment v 807
make peace v 721, 723
make preparations v

LM

673
make productive v 168
make progress v 282, 682
make provision v 637
make provision for v 673
make public v 531
make pungent v 392
maker n 164
make ready v 673
make sail v 267
make serious v 835
makeshift n 147, 617
make solid v 150
make strides v 282
make sure v 150, 474
make terms v 769
make the best of v 826
make the mind a blank v 452
make time v 132
make-up n 54
make up for v 30
make use of v 677
make verses v 597
making verses n 597
maladroit adj 699
maladroitness n 699
malady n 655
malaise n 378, 828
malapropism n 565
malarkey n 477
malcontent adj 832
male n 373; adj 373
male animal n 373, 374
malediction n 908
malevolence n 907
malevolence n 649, 889
malevolent adj 649, 739, 907, 919, 945
malformation n 243
malformed adj 243
malice n 907
malicious adj 898, 907, 919, 945
maliciousness n 907
malign v 934; adj 649
malignant adj 919, 945
malignity n 649
mall n 799
malleability n 149, 324
malleable adj 82, 149, 324

maltreat v 649, 739, 830, 923
mamma n 166
mammal n 366
mammoth n 192; adj 31
man n 373
man n 372
man about town n 854
man after one's own heart n 899
manage v 58, 692, 693
manageable adj 705
management n 692, 693, 698
manager n 694
managerial adj 692
managing adj 693
mandate n 630, 741
maneuver v 702
manfully adv 604
mangle v 659
mangy adj 655
man-hater n 911
manhood n 131, 373
mania n 503
maniac n 504
maniacal adj 503
manifest adj 446, 525
manifestation n 525
manifestation n 446, 448
manifested adj 525
manifestly adv 525
manifold adj 15, 81, 102
manipulate v 379, 677, 702
manipulation n 379
mankind n 372
mankind n 372
manliness n 604
manly adj 131, 373
manner n 569, 613, 627
mannered adj 579, 855
mannerism n 79, 83, 579
mannerisms n 855
manner of speaking n 521
manners n 692, 852
man of learning n 500
mantle n 424
manual n 527
manufacture n 161; v

161
manuscript n 590
many adj 100, 102
many-colored adj 440
many-sided adj 81
map n 183, 527, 626
mar v 659, 848
marble n 249
marbled adj 440
march n 266
marches n 233
marching band n 417
march of time n 109
mare n 374
margin n 231
marine adj 341
marine blue adj 438
mariner n 269
mariner n 269
marital separation n 905
maritime adj 267, 341
mark n 26, 71, 550, 569, 590, 620; v 450, 550, 642
marked adj 79
market n 799
market v 795
marketable adj 794, 796
marketplace n 799
market price n 812
mark the time v 114
mark time v 114, 265
maroon adj 434
marquee n 223
marriage n 903
marriage n 43
marriageable adj 131
married adj 903
married man n 903
married woman n 903
marrow n 5, 221
marry v 43, 48, 903
marsh n 345
marshal v 60
marshy adj 339, 345
mart n 799
martial adj 722
martyr n 955
marvel n 870, 872; v 870
marvelous adj 31, 870
marvelously adv 31
masculine adj 373
masculinity n 373

M

melodious adj 377,
  413, 580
melodiousness n 413
melody n 413
melody n 415
melt v 111, 144, 335,
  384, 449
melt away v 4, 449
melting n 335, 384
member n 51, 56
membrane n 204
membranous adj 204
memento n 505
memento mori n 363
memorable adj 505
memorandum n 551
memorial n 505
memorialist n 553
memorialization n 883
memorize v 505, 539
memory n 505
memory n 122
menace n 667, 909; v
  668, 909
menacing adj 909
menagerie n 72
mend v 658
mendacious adj 544
mendicant n 767
menial n 746
mental adj 450
mental balance n 502
mental cultivation n
  539
mental excitation n
  824
mental image n 515
mental suffering n 619
mention v 527
mentor n 540, 695
mephitic adj 401
mercantile adj 794
mercantilism n 796
mercenary adj 819
merchandise n 798
merchandise v 763,
  796, 798
merchant n 797
merchant n 796
merchant ship n 273
merciful adj 740
merciless adj 914a
mercurial adj 149, 264
mercury n 389
mercy n 740, 914
mere n 343; adj 643
merely adv 32

merge v 48, 300
merge in v 56
merge into v 144
meridian n 125, 181
merit n 648, 944, 973
merit attention v 642
meritorious adj 931
mermaid n 979
merriment n 836
merry adj 829
merrymaking n 838
mesh n 219
mesmerist n 994
mesmerize v 992
mess n 59, 61, 162, 732
messenger n 534
messenger n 271, 527,
  758
mess up v 59
messy adj 59
metallurgy n 358
metamorphose v 140
metamorphosis n 140
metaphor n 521
metaphorical adj 464
mete v 786
meteors n 318
mete out v 784
meter n 413
method n 627
method n 58, 60, 569,
  626, 632, 692
methodical adj 58, 60,
  692
methodically adv 58
methodological adj
  626
methodology n 58
meticulous adj 459,
  868
metrical adj 597
metrics n 597
mettle n 861
mew v 412
miasmic adj 401
microcosm n 193
microscope n 445
microscopic adj 32,
  193
mid adj 68
mid-course n 628
midcourse n 68
midday n 125
middle n 68
middle n 29, 208, 222;
  adj 29, 68, 222; adv
  222

middle class adj 29
middle course n 628
middle ground n 68,
  174
middlemost adj 222
middle of the road n
  174
middle way n 628
middling adj 32, 651
midmost adj 68
midnight n 126
midnight n 421
mid-point n 29, 68
midriff n 68
midst n 68, 208, 222;
  · adv 222
midsummer 125
midway adj 628; adv
  68
mien n 448, 692
might n 31, 157, 159,
  173
mightily adv 31
mighty adj 31, 157,
  159, 192, 192
migrate v 266
migration n 266
migratory adj 266
mild adj 174, 382, 391,
  721, 740
mildew n 653, 663
mildewed adj 659
mildness n 174, 740
militant adj 722
militarist n 726
military adj 722
military band n 417
milkiness n 427, 430
milk-white adj 430
milky adj 352, 427, 430
mill n 330, 691
millennium n 108, 121
millions n 372
mimic v 19, 554
mimicry n 19
mince v 275
mince steps v 275
mind n 450, 498, 842; v
  602
mindblower n 137
mindful adj 451, 457
mindfulness n 457
mindful (of) adj 505
mindless adj 499
mine n 636; v 252, 260,
  659

M

mitigate v 174, 469, 834

mitigating adj 469

mitigation n 174, 469, 834

mix n 41, 48; v 41, 48, 61

mixed adj 41

mixture n 41

mixture n 48

moan n 839; v 411

moaning n 411, 839

moat n 259, 350

mob n 72, 102

mobile adj 149, 264

mobility n 149, 264

mobilization n 264

mobilize v 264

mock v 19, 856, 929; adj 17, 19

mockery n 856

mocking adj 19; adj 856

mode n 7, 569, 613, 852

model n 21, 22, 80, 240, 650, 948; v 144, 240, 557; adj 650

modeled after adj 19

modeled on adj 19

modeling n 557

model oneself on v 19

mode of expression n 569

moderate v 174, 275, 723; adj 174, 275, 628, 736, 815, 881, 953

moderately adv 174

moderation n 174

moderation n 275, 736, 740, 826, 881, 953

moderator n 724, 967

modern adj 123

modernism n 123

modernity n 123

modernize v 123

modest adj 483, 879, 881, 960

modestly adv 881

modesty n 881

modesty n 483, 879, 960

modicum n 32

modification n 20a, 140, 469

modified adj 15, 20a

modify v 15, 20a, 140, 469

modish adj 852, 855

modulate v 140

modulation n 140, 413

module n 22, 273

moist adj 337, 339

moisten v 337, 339

moisture n 339

mold n 7, 21, 22, 240, 329, 557, 653; v 144, 240, 557, 653, 852

moldable adj 324

molded adj 820

molder v 659

moldering adj 659

moldy adj 653, 659

molecule n 32

molest v 649, 716

molestation n 649

mollification n 324

mollify v 174, 324, 723

mollusk n 366

molten adj 384

mom n 166

moment n 113, 642

momentary adj 111, 113

momentous adj 642

momentousness n 642

monetary adj 800

money n 800

money n 803

moneybag n 802

money matters n 811

mongrel n 41; adj 41

moniker n 564

monochrome n 429

monocle n 445

monody n 839

monogram n 561

monolog n 589

monomania n 606

monomaniacal adj 606

monosyllable n 561

monotheism n 983

monotonous adj 16, 27, 104, 841

monotony n 16, 27, 104, 841

monsoon n 349

monster n 192, 949, 980

monstrosity n 192, 243, 872

monstrous adj 31, 192, 846

monstrously adv 31

monument n 363, 551

moo v 412

mood n 7, 176, 602, 820

moodiness n 901a

moods n 5

moody adj 901a

moon n 420, 423

moonbeam n 420

moor n 344; v 43

moored adj 184, 186

mooring n 184

mope v 837

moper n 683

moral adj 922, 944

moral imperative n 926

morality n 922, 944

moralize v 537

morals n 922

moral sensibility n 822

morass n 345

moratorium n 133

morbid adj 655

more adv 33, 37

more or less adj 25

moreover adv 37

more than one adj 100

morgue n 363

morn n 125

morning n 125

morning n 125

morningtide n 125

moron n 493, 501

morose adj 901a

moroseness n 901a

morphology n 368

morrow n 121

morsel n 32, 390

mortal n 372; adj 111, 361, 372

mortal coil n 362

mortality n 111, 360, 372

mortal remains n 362

mortar and pestle n 330

mortgage n 771, 787; v 771

mortification n 828, 830

mortify v 828, 830, 879

mortuary n 363; adj 363

mosaic adj 81, 440

moss n 345
most adv 31
most likely adv 472
mote n 32, 451
moth-eaten adj 653, 659
mother n 166, 192
mother earth n 342
motherhood n 166
motherland n 189
motion n 264
motion n 550
motionless adj 172, 265, 683
motivate v 615, 744
motivation n 615
motive n 615
motive power n 264
mot juste n 496
motley adj 16a, 41, 81
motorboat n 273
motorcar n 272
motorcycle n 272
motoring n 266
motorscooter n 272
mottled adj 440
motto n 496, 566
mound n 192
mount v 206, 305
mountain n 192, 250
mourn for v 833
mournful adj 830, 839, 901a
mourn over v 839
mouth n 231, 343
mouthful n 25, 32
mouthpiece n 582
movable adj 264, 270
movableness n 264
move n 264, 270; v 175, 264, 266, 270, 302, 615, 763, 824
move away from v 287
move back v 287
moved adj 821, 914
movement n 264, 680, 682
move off v 293
move out v 293
move quickly v 274
mover n 164
move slowly v 275
move to the center v 29
move towards v 286
moving n 266, 680; adj

264
mow v 371
Mr. n 373
Ms. n 374
much adj 641; adv 31
much ado about nothing n 549
much the same adj 17, 27
muck n 653
muckraking n 529
mud n 345, 653
muddle n 59; v 61
muddle-headed adj 499
muddy adj 339, 345, 352, 519
muffle v 403, 408a, 590
muffled adj 405, 408a
muffled drums n 408a
muffler n 408a
muggy adj 339
mulish adj 606
mulishness n 606
mulling around n 681
multi-colored adj 440
multifarious adj 16a, 81
multifold adj 81
multiformity n 81
multiple adj 102
multiplication n 168
multiplicity n 102
multiply v 35, 85, 102, 163, 168
multiply by four v 96
multiplying by four n 96
multi-purpose adj 148
multitude n 102
multitude n 31, 72, 100, 876
multitudes n 372
multitudinous adj 102; adj 102
mum n 166; adj 581, 585
mumble v 583
mumbling n 583
mumbo-jumbo n 993
mummify v 363
mummy n 166
munch v 298
mundane adj 318
munificence n 816, 910

munificent adj 816, 910
munitions n 727
murder n 361; v 361
murderer n 361
murderous adj 361
murk n 421
murkiness n 421
murky adj 421, 422, 426, 431
murmur n 405; v 348, 405
murmured adj 405
muscular adj 159
muse v 451
mushiness n 326
mushy adj 324, 339
music n 415
musical adj 413, 415, 416, 597
musical instruments n 417
musicalness n 413
musician n 416
musing n 451
muster n 72; v 72, 85
mustiness n 401
musty adj 401, 653
mutability n 149
mutable adj 149
mutation n 140
mute n 408a; v 408a, adj 403, 581, 585
muted adj 405, 408a
muteness n 581
muteness n 403, 585
mutilate v 38, 241, 361, 659
mutilation n 38, 241
mutineer n 742
mutinous adj 742
mutinousness n 742
mutiny n 146, 742; v 742
mutter v 405, 583
muttering n 583
mutual adj 12, 148
mutuality n 12
muzzle v 158, 403, 581
myopia n 443
myopic adj 443
mysterious adj 208, 447, 519, 528, 533
mystery n 447, 533
mystify v 519

M

N

nab v 789
nacreous adj 427, 440
nadir n 211
naiad n 979
naive adj 435, 703, 946
naivete n 703, 946
naked adj 226
nakedness n 226
name n 13, 562, 564,
  569, 873, 877; v 564,
  755
namely adv 522
namesake n 564
naming n 564
nannygoat n 374
nap n 256
naphtha n 356
napping adj 458
narrate v 594
narration n 594
narrative prose n 598
narrow v 195, 203,
  469; adj 32, 203
narrow escape n 671
narrowing n 469
narrow-minded adj 32,
  499
narrow-mindedness n
  32
narrowness n 203
narrowness n 203
nascent adj 66
nasty adj 395, 653
natal adj 66
nation n 188
national adj 372
native n 188; adj 188
nativity n 66
natural n 501; adj 82,
  494, 578, 703, 849
natural causes n 360
natural gas n 388
natural harbor n 343
natural history n 357
naturalist n 357
natural light n 423
natural philosophy n
  316
natural world n 357
nature n 5, 80, 176,
  318, 357, 820
naught n 4, 101
nauseate v 395, 830,
  867

nauseating adj 401,
  867, 898
nauseous adj 395, 401,
  830
nautical adj 267
naval adj 267
navel n 222
navigable adj 267
navigate v 267
navigation n 267
navigator n 269
navy n 273; adj 438
near v 286; adj 17, 121,
  152, 186, 197, 199;
  adv 197
nearly adv 32
near miss n 671
nearness n 197
nearness n 9, 186, 286
near side n 239
nearsighted adj 443
nearsightedness n 443
near the mark adv 32
neat adj 58, 576, 578,
  652, 849
neaten v 652
neatness n 652
nebbish n 547
nebula n 353
nebulosity n 353, 422
nebulous adj 422, 519
necessarily adv 154,
  601
necessary adj 601, 630,
  744
necessitate v 601, 630,
  744
necessity n 601
necessity n 630, 744
neck and neck race n
  27
necklace n 247
necromancer n 513,
  994
necromancy n 992
need n 630, 684, 804,
  865; v 630, 640
needful adj 601, 630
neediness n 804
needle n 253, 262
needless adj 641
needy adj 804
negate v 536
negation n 536
negation n 468
negative n 22; adj 14,
  84, 489, 536

neglect n 460
neglect n 730, 732,
  773, 927; v 53, 460,
  678, 730, 773, 927
neglected adj 460
neglectful adj 460
neglecting adj 460
negligence n 460, 773
negligent adj 460, 738,
  773, 927
negotiate v 724, 769,
  794
negotiation n 724, 769,
  774, 794
negotiator n 724
neigh v 412
neighbor v 197
neighborhood n 197,
  227
neighboring adj 197
neighborly adj 707,
  888, 892
nemesis n 919
neologic adj 563
neological adj 563
neologism n 563
neologist n 563
neology n 563
neophyte n 541
nereid n 979
nerve n 159, 861; v 159
nervous adj 574, 825
nescient adj 491
ness n 250
nest n 189
nestle v 186
net n 219; v 219
nethermost adj 211
netting n 219
nettle n 663
network n 219
neutral adj 29, 609a,
  628
neutrality n 609a
neutrality n 29, 609a,
  628
neutralization n 179
neutralize v 30, 179
neutral tint n 429, 432
never adv 107
never-ending adj 104,
  112
nevermore adv 107
nevertheless adv 30
never to be forgotten
  adj 505
new adj 18, 123, 146,

N

435
new birth *n* 660
newborn *adj* 129
newfangled *adj* 83,
  123, 140
new-fangled
  expression *n* 563
newfangledness *n* 123
newly *adv* 123
newness *n* 123
news *n* 532
news *n* 498, 527
newsmonger *n* 527,
  532, 534
newsstory *n* 532
New Testament *n* 986
next *adj* 63; *adv* 117
next generation *n* 127
next world *n* 152
nibble *v* 298
nice *adj* 394, 829, 868
nice distinction *n* 15
nicety *n* 465, 868
niche *n* 182, 221, 244
nick *n* 257; *v* 257
nickname *n* 564, 565;
  v 564
nick of time *n* 134
niggard *n* 819
niggardly *adj* 819
niggling *adj* 643
nigh *adj* 197; *adv* 197
night *n* 421
nightfall *n* 126
nihilist *n* 165
nil *n* 4
nimble *adj* 274, 498,
  842
nincompoop *n* 501
nine *n* 98
ninny *n* 501
nip *n* 392; *v* 385
nip in the bud *v* 361
nipping *adj* 383
nipple *n* 250
nippy *adj* 392
nirvana *n* 981
nit-picking *adj* 477
nixie *n* 979
nobility *n* 875
nobility *n* 33
noble *adj* 31, 875, 878
nobody *n* 101
no choice *n* 609a
nocturnal *adj* 421
node *n* 250
no doubt *adv* 474

nodular *adj* 250
nodulation *n* 256
nodule *n* 250
noise *n* 402, 404, 414
noiseless *adj* 403
noisily *adv* 404
noisome *adj* 401, 657
noisy *adj* 404
nomad *n* 268
nomadic *adj* 264, 266
nomadism *n* 266
nom de guerre *n* 565
nom de plume *n* 565
nomenclature *n* 564
nominal *adj* 564
nominate *v* 755
nomination *n* 755
nominee *n* 758
no more *adj* 360
no more than *adv* 32
nonadhesion *n* 47
nonadhesive *adj* 47
nonappearance *n* 187
nonattendance *n* 187
nonbeliever *n* 485,
  487, 989
noncohesive *adj* 47
noncompletion *n* 730
noncompletion *n* 53,
  304
noncompliance *n* 742,
  773
noncompliant *adj* 764
nonconforming *adj*
  984
nonconformist *n* 489,
  984; *adj* 489, 984
nonconformity *n* 16a,
  24, 79, 83, 489, 984
none *n* 101
nonentity *n* 2
nonessential *adj* 57,
  643
nonetheless *adv* 30
nonexistence *n* 2
nonexistent *adj* 2, 187
nonexpectant *adj* 508
nonexpectation *n* 508
nonextension *n* 180a
nonfulfillment *n* 730
nonfunctional *adj* 674
nonimitation *n* 20
noninterference *n* 748
nonlinear *adj* 245
nonobservance *n* 773
nonobservance *n* 83,

742, 927
nonobservant *adj* 773
nonpayment *n* 808
nonperformance *n*
  730, 732, 927
nonplus *v* 704
nonpreparation *n* 674
nonrational *adj* 450a
non-relation *n* 10
nonresidence *n* 187
nonresistance *n* 725
nonresonance *n* 408a
nonresonant *adj* 408a
nonsense *n* 497, 517
nonsensical *adj* 477,
  497, 499, 517, 853
non sequitur *n* 497
nontranslucent *adj*
  426
nontransparency *n*
  426
nontransparent *adj*
  426
noodle *n* 450
nook *n* 182, 221, 244
noon *n* 125
noon *n* 125
noonday *n* 125
noontide *n* 125
noontime *n* 125
normal *adj* 5, 29, 82,
  736
normalcy *n* 80
normality *n* 502
normal state *n* 80
nose *n* 250
not a bit *adv* 32
notable *adj* 31, 642
notably *adv* 31
not act *v* 681
not a jot *adv* 32
notary *n* 553
not at all *adv* 32
not a whit *adv* 32
not bad *adj* 651
not beat around the
  bush *v* 576
not be good for *v* 657
not be surprised *v* 871
not care *v* 823
notch *n* 257
notch *n* 244; *v* 257
notched *adj* 257
not come up to *v* 28,
  34

N

not come up to snuff *v* 28

not complete *v* 730

not conversant *adj* 699

not curved *adj* 246

not cut it *v* 640

not discriminate *v* 465a

not do *v* 640, 681

note *n* 550, 551, 592, 596; *v* 450, 550, 596

not enough *adj* 640

notes *n* 802

noteworthy *adj* 31

not exist *v* 2

not expect *v* 508

not germane *adj* 57

not get involved *v* 623

not give an inch *v* 604

not have *v* 777a

not have much of a chance *v* 473

not hear *v* 419

not here *adj* 187

nothing *n* 4, 101, 643

nothingness *n* 2, 4

notice *n* 457, 668; *v* 450, 457, 480a, 928

notification *n* 527

notify *v* 668

no time *n* 107

not in *adj* 187

not included in *adj* 55

not in sight *adj* 447

not in the least *adv* 32

not in use *adj* 678

notion *n* 451, 453, 515

not licensed *adj* 925

not many *adj* 103

not matter *v* 643

not often *adv* 137

not pass muster *v* 34, 651

not pay *v* 808

not pertinent *adj* 10

not possible *adj* 471

not present *adj* 187, 187

not quite *adv* 32

not reach *v* 304

not see *v* 442

not smell *v* 399

not sorry *adj* 951

not straight *adj* 243

not suffice *v* 640

not the same *adj* 15

not think *v* 452

not true *adj* 243

not use *v* 678

not well *adj* 655

not with it *adj* 246

notwithstanding *adv* 30

nourishment *n* 298, 359

novel *n* 593; *adj* 18, 123

novelty *n* 18, 123

novice *n* 541, 701

now *adv* 118

nowadays *adv* 118

now and then *adv* 136

no way *adj* 471

noway *adv* 32

nowhere *adv* 187

nowise *adv* 32

now or never *adv* 134

noxious *adj* 649, 657

nozzle *n* 250

nuance *n* 15

nub *n* 68, 222

nubile *adj* 131

nuclear power *n* 388

nucleus *n* 68, 153, 222

nude *adj* 226

nudity *n* 226

nuisance *n* 619, 663, 830, 975

null and void *adj* 756

nullification *n* 536, 756

nullify *v* 2, 30, 179, 536, 756

nullity *n* 4

numb *v* 376; *adj* 376, 381

number *n* 84

number *v* 85

number among *v* 76

numbering *n* 85

numberless *adj* 104

numbers *n* 102

numbing *adj* 383

numbness *n* 381

numbness *n* 376

numerable *adj* 85

numeral *n* 84; *adj* 84, 85

numeration *n* 85

numerical *adj* 85

numerous *adj* 100, 102

numskull *n* 493, 501

nuptials *n* 903

nurse *n* 753; *v* 662

nursery *n* 127

nursling *n* 129

nurture *v* 235, 673

nut *n* 504

nutbrown *adj* 433

nutriment *n* 298, 359

nutrition *n* 298

nutritious *adj* 299, 656

nutritive *adj* 299

nuts *adj* 503

nutshell *n* 32

O

oaf *n* 501

oath *n* 535, 768

obduracy *n* 606, 951

obdurate *adj* 600, 951

obedience *n* 743

obedience *n* 725, 749, 772

obedient *adj* 725, 743, 772, 926

obediently *adv* 743

obeisance *n* 308

obese *adj* 192, 194

obesity *n* 192

obey *v* 725, 743, 772

obey the rules *v* 82

obfuscate *v* 528

obfuscation *n* 528

object *n* 3, 316, 453, 516, 620

objection *n* 704

objectionable *adj* 846

objective *n* 453; *adj* 6

object to *v* 932

obligate *v* 630

obligation *n* 177, 601, 768, 806, 926, 963

obligations *n* 770

obligatory *adj* 744, 926

oblige *v* 707, 744, 770

obliged *adj* 177, 916, 926

obliging *adj* 894, 906

oblique *adj* 217

obliquely *adv* 217

obliquity *n* 217

obliquity *n* 243

obliterate *v* 2, 552

obliterated *adj* 552

obliteration *n* 552

obliteration *n* 2

obliteration of the past *n* 506

O

oil lamp *n* 423
oily *adj* 255, 355
oink *v* 412
ointment *n* 355, 356, 662
old *adj* 124, 128, 130
old age *n* 124, 128
older *adj* 128
old-fashioned *adj* 124
old hand *n* 700
old lady *n* 166, 903
old maid *n* 904
old man *n* 130, 166, 903
oldness *n* 124
old soldier *n* 700
Old Testament *n* 986
old woman *n* 130
oleaginous *adj* 355
olive *adj* 435
olive oil *n* 356
omen *n* 512
omen *n* 668
ominous *adj* 665, 668, 909
omission *n* 53, 55, 460, 732, 773, 893
omit *v* 55, 460, 773
omitted *adj* 893
omnipotence *n* 157, 976
omnipotent *adj* 104, 157
omnipresence *n* 186, 976
omnipresent *adj* 186
on *adv* 125, 282
on a bed of roses *adv* 377
on account of *adv* 155
on a large scale *adv* 31
on a level with *adj* 27
on a line with *adv* 278
on all sides *adv* 227
on a moment's notice *adv* 113
on an equal footing with *adj* 27
on a par with *adj* 27
on bended knee *adv* 879
once and for all *adv* 67
once more *adv* 90, 104
on compulsion *adv* 744
on condition *adv* 770
on dry land *adv* 342

one *n* 372; *adj* 13, 52, 87, 729
one and the same *adj* 27
one by one *adv* 44
on edge *adv* 507
one in a million *n* 648
on end *adv* 212
oneness *n* 87
one of a kind *adj* 20
onerous *adj* 649, 706, 830
oneself *n* 13
one's own *n* 11
one's own flesh and blood *n* 11
one step at a time *adv* 275
on every side *adv* 227
one way or another *adv* 627
on fire *adj* 382
on foot *adj* 170
ongoing *adj* 53
on land *adv* 342
onlooker *n* 444
only *adv* 32
only just *adv* 32
only so far *adv* 233
on no account *adv* 32
on no occasion *adv* 107
on one's back *adv* 213
on one's honor *adj* 768
on one side *adv* 217, 236
on one's own time *adv* 133
on one's toes *adj* 507
on purpose *adv* 620
onset *n* 66, 716
on sight *adv* 441
onslaught *n* 716
on target *adj* 494
on tenterhooks *adj* 507
on that occasion *adv* 119
on the average *adv* 29
on the ball *adj* 498
on the brink of *adv* 121
on the dot *adv* 132
on the eve of *adv* 121
on the face of it *adv* 448
on the face of the earth

adv 180, 318
on the go *adv* 264
on the horizon *adj* 152, 507
on the horns of a dilemma *n* 476
on the instant *adv* 132
on the march *adv* 264
on the move *adv* 264
on the offensive *adv* 716
on the other hand *adv* 30
on the point of *adv* 121
on the road *adj* 264, 266
on the road to *adv* 278
on the safe side *adj* 664
on the sly *adv* 528
on the spot *adv* 132, 134
on the spur of the moment *adv* 113, 132, 134
on the wagon *adj* 958
on the wane *adj* 36
on the watch *adj* 457; *adv* 507
on the whole *adv* 50
on time *adj* 132; *adv* 132
ontology *n* 1
on trial *adv* 675
onus *n* 926
onward *adv* 282
ooze *v* 295, 348
oozing *n* 295
oozy *adj* 352
opacity *n* 426
opacity *n* 353
opalescence *n* 427
opalescent *adj* 427
opaline *adj* 430, 440
opaque *adj* 422, 426
opaqueness *n* 426
ope *v* 260
open *v* 66, 194, 198, 260, 525; *adj* 177, 260, 338, 525, 543, 665, 703
open air *n* 338
open-eyed *adj* 507
open field *n* 134
opening *n* 260
opening *n* 66, 198, 260
open into *v* 348
openly *adv* 525

O

308; *v* 162, 308
overture *n* 763
overturn *n* 146, 218, 308; *v* 162, 218, 308, 479
overvaluation *n* 482
overweening *adj* 641, 880
overwhelm *v* 641
overwhelming *adj* 824
overwork *v* 679
overwrought *adj* 549, 824
overzealous *adj* 825
ovoid *adj* 249
owing to *adj* 154, 155
own *v* 488, 777
owner *n* 779
ownership *n* 777, 780
own in common *v* 778
own up *v* 529

P

P.M. *n* 126
pace *n* 264; *v* 106
pacific *adj* 174, 721, 723
pacification *n* 723
pacification *n* 174
pacify *v* 174, 723
pack *n* 72
pack it up *v* 293
pact *n* 23, 769
pad *n* 189; *v* 194, 224
padding *n* 224, 263
paddle *v* 267
paddock *n* 232
paean *n* 838
pagan *n* 984; *adj* 991
pagan deity *n* 991
pageant *n* 448
pageantry *n* 882
pain *n* 378, 828
pain *n* 619, 663, 686, 974, 982; *v* 649, 830
painful *adj* 378, 649, 830, 982
painfully *adv* 31, 830
painfulness *n* 830
painfulness *n* 649
pain in the neck *n* 663
pains *n* 459, 974
painstaking *adj* 459
paint *n* 428; *v* 428, 556
painter *n* 559
painting *n* 556

pair *n* 17, 89; *v* 89
pair off *v* 89
pal *n* 890
palatability *n* 394
palatable *adj* 377, 390, 394
palaver *n* 588
pale *n* 232, 233; *v* 422, 429; *adj* 422, 429, 430, 435
paleness *n* 422, 429
paleontology *n* 368
paling *n* 232
pall *n* 363; *v* 376, 395
palliative *adj* 174, 662, 834
pallid *adj* 429, 430
pallor *n* 429
palm *n* 733
palmer *n* 268
palpability *n* 379
palpable *adj* 3, 316, 379, 446, 525
palpitate *v* 315
palpitation *n* 315
palsied *adj* 160
paltriness *n* 32, 643, 736
paltry *adj* 32, 34, 643, 736
panacea *n* 662
pandemonium *n* 59, 982
pander to *v* 933
pang *n* 378, 828
panhandler *n* 767
panic *n* 860
panic-stricken *adj* 860
pant *v* 349, 382, 688
pap *n* 250
papa *n* 166
paper *v* 223
par *n* 27
parabola *n* 245
parade *v* 882
paradigm *n* 22
paradisaic *adj* 981
paradise *n* 981
paradisical *adj* 981
paradox *n* 497
paradoxical *adj* 497
paragon *n* 650, 948
paralipsis *n* 476
parallel *n* 17; *v* 9, 17, 19, 216; *adj* 17, 216, 242
parallelism *n* 216

parallelism *n* 13, 17, 23, 242
paralysis *n* 158, 376
paralytic *adj* 158, 376
paralyze *v* 158, 376
paralyzed *adj* 158
paramount *adj* 33, 642, 737
paramour *n* 897
paraphrase *n* 19, 21
parasitic *adj* 789
parasol *n* 223, 424
parboil *v* 384
parcel out *v* 60, 786
parch *v* 340, 382, 384
parched *adj* 340
pardon *n* 918, 970; *v* 918, 970
pare *v* 38, 195, 204
pared back *adj* 103
pare down *v* 38, 201
parentage *n* 166
parentage *n* 11
parental *adj* 166
parenthesis *n* 70
parenthetical *adj* 10, 228
parenthetically *adv* 10, 228
pariah *n* 893
parishioner *n* 997
parity *n* 27
parlance *n* 582
parley *n* 582, 588, 724
parody *n* 19, 21; *v* 19
paroxysm *n* 173, 825
parricide *n* 361
parry *v* 717
parsimonious *adj* 817, 819, 943
parsimony *n* 819
parsimony *n* 817, 943
parson *n* 996
part *n* 51
part *n* 56, 100a, 625; *v* 44, 51, 291
partake *v* 778
part company *v* 44
partial *adj* 28
partially *adv* 32, 51
participant *n* 690, 778
participate *v* 56, 709, 778
participation *n* 778
participation *n* 709

OP

P

peeping adj 455
peep of day n 125
peep up v 446
peer n 27; v 441
peevish adj 684, 901a
peg n 250
pellet n 249
pellucid adj 425, 570
pelt v 276
pen n 232, 752; v 590
penalize v 972, 974
penalized v 974; adj 972
penalizing adj 972
penalty n 974
penalty n 972
penance n 974
penchant n 177, 602
pencil n 556
pendant n 214
pendent adj 214
pendulous adj 214
pendulum n 214
penetrate v 294, 302
penetrating adj 480, 498
penetration n 294, 302, 441, 480, 498
penitence n 950
penitence n 833
penitent n 950; adj 833, 950
penitential adj 950
penitentiary n 752
penmanship n 590
pen name n 565
penniless adj 804
pennywise adj 819
pensioner n 785
pensive adj 451
pent up adj 751
penumbra n 421
penurious adj 819
penury n 804
people n 188, 372, 997; v 102
people the world v 163
pep n 171
pepper n 393; v 392
peppery adj 392
peradventure adv 470
perambulate v 264
perambulation n 266
perceivability n 446
perceivable adj 446

perceive v 375, 441, 490
perceptibility n 446
perceptible adj 446
perception n 418, 441, 453, 490
perceptive adj 375, 465, 490, 842
perch n 189; v 184, 186
perchance adv 156, 470
percolation n 295
percussion n 417
perdition n 162
peregrination n 266
peremptory adj 737, 739
perennial adj 69
perfect v 650, 729; adj 31, 52, 104, 648, 650, 729, 960
perfection n 650
perfection n 52, 648, 729, 960
perfectly adv 729
perfidious adj 544
perforate v 260
perforated adj 260
perforation n 260
perforator n 262
perform v 161, 170, 415, 416, 599, 644, 680, 772, 926
performable adj 470
performance n 161, 599, 680, 729, 772
perform a rite v 998
performer n 416, 599, 690
performing n 680
perfume n 400; v 400
perfumed adj 400
perfunctory adj 53, 640
perhaps adv 470
peril n 665
perilous adj 475, 665
perimeter n 230
period n 108
period n 71, 106, 138, 198, 200
periodic adj 70, 138
periodical adj 138
periodically adv 138
periodicity n 138
peripatetic adj 266
periphery n 230

perish v 2, 162, 360, 659
perishable adj 111
permanence n 141
permanence n 16, 110, 150
permanent adj 106, 110, 141, 150, 613
permanently adv 141
permeable adj 260
permeate v 186, 228, 302
permeation n 186, 228, 302
permissible adj 760
permission n 760
permission n 737, 762
permissive adj 760
permit n 737, 755, 760; v 737, 748, 760, 762
permitted adj 760
permutation n 140, 148
pernicious adj 649, 663
perpendicular adj 212, 246
perpendicularity n 212
perpetrate v 680
perpetrator n 690
perpetual adj 104, 110, 112, 136, 143, 150
perpetually adv 112, 136
perpetuate v 112, 143
perpetuation n 143
perpetuity n 112
perpetuity n 105
perplex v 475, 519, 704, 830
perplexed adj 59
perplexity n 59
persecute v 649, 830
persecution n 649
perseverance n 604a
perseverance n 143, 150, 604, 682
persevere v 604a, 682
persevering adj 604a
persicuity n 518
persist v 106, 110, 141, 143, 604a, 606, 682
persistence n 110, 141, 143, 604a, 606
persistent adj 141, 143, 604a, 606
person n 3, 372

personage n 372
personal adj 5, 79, 372
personality n 5, 13, 79
personate v 19, 554, 599
personify v 554
personnel n 56
persons n 372
perspective n 183, 441, 448
perspicacious adj 480, 498, 868
perspicacity n 441, 480, 868
perspicuity n 570
perspicuous adj 570
perspiration n 299, 339
perspire v 299, 339
persuade v 175, 615, 695
persuasion n 175, 484, 695
persuasive adj 615, 695
pertain to v 9
pertinacious adj 150, 606
pertinacity n 150, 606
pertinent adj 23
perturb v 61, 824
perturbation n 61, 315, 824
peruse v 539
pervade v 186
pervasion n 186
pervasive adj 186
pervasiveness n 186
perverse adj 606, 704, 901a
perversion n 477, 523, 538
perversity n 606
pervert v 477, 523, 538
pessimism n 483, 859
pessimist n 165
pessimistic adj 483, 837
pest n 975
pester v 830
pestilence n 649
pestilential adj 657
pet n 899
petite adj 32
petition n 765, 990; v

765, 990
petitioner n 767
petrification n 321, 323
petrify v 321, 323
petroleum n 356, 388
pettifogging adj 477
pettiness n 32
petty adj 32, 643
petulant adj 684, 901
phantasm n 443, 515
phantom n 4
phase n 7, 8, 71, 448
phenomenon n 151, 448, 872
philanthropic adj 784, 906, 910
philanthropist n 910
philanthropy n 910
philanthropy n 784, 906
philology n 562
philosopher n 500
phonetic adj 561
phonetics n 402, 561
phonology n 402
phony n 548; adj 19, 544
phosphorescence n 423
phosphorescent adj 420, 423
photoengraving n 558
photography n 420
phrase n 566
phrase n 521; v 566
phraseology n 560, 566, 569
physical adj 3, 173, 316
physical elements n 316
physical gratification n 377
physical insensibility n 381
physicality n 316
physical science n 316
physician n 662
physicist n 316
physics n 316
physiognomy n 448
physiology n 357
physique n 364
phytology n 369
pick n 609, 648; v 609

picket v 43
pickings n 793
pickle n 7; v 392, 670
pick of the litter n 648
pickup n 274
picky adj 465
pictorial adj 556
pictorialization n 556
picture n 448, 556; v 554, 594
picture gallery n 556
picturesque adj 556, 845
piddle v 683
piddling adj 643
piebald adj 440
piece n 51
piecemeal adv 51
pieces n 596
piece together v 43
pied adj 440
pierce v 260, 378, 385, 649
piercer n 262
pierce the ears v 404
piercing adj 404, 410, 498
pietist n 987
pietistic adj 987
piety n 987
pig n 957
pigeon n 547
pigeonhole n 182
piggish adj 957
piggishness n 957
pig-headed adj 606
pigment n 428
pigmy adj 193
pile n 72, 256
pile on v 641
pile up v 37
pilfer v 791
pilferer n 792
pilgrim n 268
pilgrimage n 266, 676
pill n 249
pilot n 269, 694; v 693
pimple n 250
pin n 253, 262, 263; v 43, 45
pince-nez n 445
pinch n 8, 704; v 195, 378, 385, 819
pinched adj 203
pinch hit v 147
pine v 655

P

861; v 789
plucked instruments n 417
pluck out v 301
plug n 261, 263; v 261
plugging n 261
plug up one's ears v 419
plumb adj 212
plum-colored adj 437
plump adj 192
plumpness n 192
plunder n 793
plunge n 310
plunge v 300; v 208, 300, 310, 337, 863
plunge into v 676
plural adj 100
plurality n 100
plus adv 37
ply n 258; v 677
pock n 250
pocket v 789
poesy n 597
poet n 597
poetaster n 597
poetic adj 521, 597
poetical adj 597
poetic device n 521
poeticize v 597
poetics n 521, 597
poetry n 597
poetry n 590
poignancy n 392
poignant adj 516
point n 8, 26, 32, 71, 180a, 182, 253, 620; v 253, 278
point-blank adj 703; adv 278, 576
pointed adj 201, 253, 516, 518
pointedly adv 31, 620
pointedness n 253
pointer n 550
point of departure n 293
point of view n 441
point out v 525
points of the compass n 278
point to v 155, 472, 516, 938
point toward v 278
poison v 659, 663
poisonous adj 649, 657, 663

polar adj 210, 383
polarity n 89, 179, 218, 237
pole n 222
polemic n 726
polemicist n 476
poles apart adv 237
policy n 626, 692
polish n 255, 578, 850; v 255, 331
polished adj 255, 578, 850, 852
polite adj 383, 457, 852, 879, 894, 928
politeness n 457, 894
polite society n 852
politic adj 498, 702
poll n 85; v 85
poltroon n 862
poltroonery n 862
polyglot adj 560
polyp n 250
polyphony n 413
polysyllable n 561
pommel n 249
pomp n 882
pompous adj 482, 577, 882
pompousness n 882
pond n 343
ponder v 451, 870
pondering n 451
ponderous adj 319, 579
pool n 343, 709; v 709
poor adj 34, 477, 575, 640, 643, 736, 804, 828, 879
poorer adj 34
poorly adj 655
poorly timed adj 135
poorness n 34, 640
poor substitute adj 651
pop n 166, 406
pop music n 415
pop off v 360
populace n 72, 876
popular music n 415
populate v 102
population n 188, 372
populous adj 72, 102
pop up v 446
porch n 231, 260
pore over v 539
porous adj 260
port n 239

portable adj 270
portal n 231, 260
portend v 511, 668, 909
portent n 511, 512, 668, 909
portentous adj 511, 668
porter n 271; 532
portion n 51, 100a, 786
portion out v 786
portly adj 192
portrait n 21
portraiture n 554
portray v 554, 594
portrayal n 594
pose n 183; v 475, 704, 855
position n 8, 71, 183, 625
positive adj 1, 31, 84, 246, 474, 484, 535
possess v 777
possessed adj 503
possessed of adj 777
possessing adj 777
possession n 777
possession n 780
possessions n 780
possessive adj 777
possess oneself of v 789
possessor n 779
possess the means v 632
possibility n 470
possibility n 2, 156
possible adj 2, 177, 470, 515
possibly adv 470
post n 183; v 184, 274, 811
post bail v 771
post card n 592
postdate v 115
posterior n 235; adj 117, 235
posteriority n 117
posteriority n 63
posterity n 167
posterity n 117
posthaste adv 274
posthumous adj 117
postman n 271
post meridian n 126
post mortem examination n 363

P

P

535
proof n 463, 467, 478, 591
proofreader n 591
prop n 215; v 707
propagandist n 540
propagate v 161, 531
propagation n 168, 531
propane n 356, 388
propel v 264, 284
propensity n 176, 177, 602, 820
proper adj 79, 494, 578, 646, 868, 881, 922
proper name n 564
proper time n 134
property n 780
prophecy n 511
prophesy v 511
prophet n 513
prophetess n 513
prophetic adj 511
propinquity n 197
propitiate v 723, 826, 952
propitiating adj 952
propitiation n 952
propitiatory adj 952
propitious adj 134, 648, 734, 858, 888
proportion n 9, 242, 786
proportionate adj 413
proportions n 180, 192
proposal n 620, 763
propose v 476, 514, 620, 763
proposition n 476, 514, 763
propound v 514
proprietor n 779
proprietorship n 777
proprietress n 779
propriety n 578, 646, 852, 881
propulsion n 284
propulsion n 276
propulsive adj 284
propulsive force n 284
prop up v 215
prosaic adj 575, 598, 841, 843
pros and cons n 476
proscenium n 234

proscribe v 971
proscribed adj 964
proscription n 971
proscriptive adj 761
prose n 598
prosecute v 622, 680, 969
prosecuting attorney n 968
prosecution n 969
prosecutor n 938, 968
prospect n 121, 448, 472, 507, 510
prospective adj 507, 510
prospectively adv 121
prospects n 152
prospectus n 596
prosper v 731, 734
prosperity n 734
prosperity n 618, 731
prosperous adj 731, 734
prostitute n 962; v 679
prostitution n 679
prostrate v 213, 308; adj 207, 213, 308
prostration n 158, 207, 213, 308, 828
prosy adj 575, 598
protect v 664, 670, 717
protected adj 223
protection n 175, 664, 670, 717
protective adj 717
protector n 664, 753, 977
protest n 489, 764, 766, 808; v 489, 766
protester n 489
protoplasm n 357
prototype n 22
prototype n 80
protract v 110, 133, 200
protracted adj 110, 200, 573
protraction n 110, 133, 143
protrude v 250
protrusion n 250
protuberance n 250
protuberant adj 250
proud adj 878, 880
prove v 151, 463, 478
proved adj 478
proven adj 478

provender n 298, 637
proverb n 496
proverbial adj 496
provide v 637, 673, 746, 770
provide against v 673
provided adj 469; adv 8
provided that adj 469
providence n 976
provident adj 510, 673, 864
providential adj 134
providing n 637
province n 75, 181
provincial adj 181, 246
provision n 637
provision n 673, 803; v 637
provisional adj 8, 111, 673, 770
provisionally adv 8, 770
provisions n 298, 632, 770
proviso n 469
provisos n 770
provocation n 824
provocative adj 615
provoke v 153, 824, 830
prowl v 266
proximate adj 63, 197
proximation n 197
proximity n 186, 197, 199
proxy n 634, 759
prudence n 459, 480, 498, 510, 864
prudent adj 451, 459, 498, 510, 864
prudery n 881
prudish adj 881
prudishness n 881
prune v 38, 201
prurience n 961
prurient adj 961
pry v 441, 455
prying n 455; adj 455
pseudo adj 17
pseudonym n 565
psychical adj 317
puberty n 127, 131
pubescence n 131
pubescent adj 131
public n 372; adj 260,

rain in torrents v 348
rainy adj 348
raise v 35, 161, 235, 250, 307, 370
raised adj 250
raise one's voice v 411
raise spirits v 992
raise to a fervor v 824
raise up v 206
raising n 307, 370
rake n 962; v 371
rake out v 301
rally v 660
rallying point n 74
rally round v 709
ram n 373
ramble v 266, 279, 499, 573
rambler n 268
rambling adj 47, 266, 279
ramification n 51, 291
ramify v 291
ram in v 300
rammer n 263
rampage v 173
rampant adj 173, 175, 307, 748
ramrod n 263
ramshackle adj 124
ranch v 370
ranching n 370
rancid adj 397, 401, 653
rancidity n 401
rancor n 907
rancorous adj 907
random adj 156, 621
range n 26, 69, 180, 196, 200, 278, 386, 965; v 60, 196, 266
rank n 26, 58, 69, 71, 875; v 58, 60, 480; adj 365, 401, 649
rank and file n 876
rankle v 653, 659
rankness n 401
rant n 517, 549, 577; v 503, 517, 582, 825
ranter n 584
rap n 276, 406, 588; v 276, 406, 588
rapacious adj 789, 819
rapacity n 819
rapid adj 274, 684
rapidity n 274, 684,

819
rapids n 348
rapture n 827, 897, 993
rapturous adj 821, 829, 977
rare adj 20, 83, 103, 137, 322, 648
rarefaction n 322
rarefy v 322
rarely adv 137
rare occurrence n 137
rarity n 137, 322
rascal n 941
rash n 72; adj 499, 684, 863
rashness n 863
rashness n 499
rasp n 330; v 330, 331
rasping n 410; adj 410
ratatat n 407
rate n 26, 264, 812; v 466, 480
rather adv 32
ratification n 535, 762
ratify v 535
ratio n 9, 26, 786
ratiocination n 476
ration n 786
rational adj 450, 498, 502
rationale n 155, 462
rationalism n 476
rationalist n 476
rationalistic adj 476
rationality n 450, 502
rations n 298
rattle v 407
raucousness n 410
ravage v 162, 659
ravager n 165
rave v 503
ravel v 219
raveled adj 59
raveling n 59
ravenous adj 789
raver n 504
ravine n 198, 259
raving n 503; adj 173, 824
ravish v 829
ravishment n 824, 827
raw adj 378, 383, 435, 674, 699
raw materials n 635
ray n 420
raze v 162
razor edge n 253

razor sharp adj 253
reach n 26, 196, 200; v 27, 270
reach a point v 292
reaching n 292
reach to v 196, 200
react v 179, 277, 287
reaction n 145, 179, 276, 277, 287, 718
reactionary adj 179, 277
reactive adj 718
read v 539
readable adj 578
reader n 542, 591
readily adv 705
readiness n 132, 602, 673, 698
read the law v 968
ready adj 507, 602, 673, 682
ready for battle v 727
real adj 1, 494
real estate n 342, 780
realism n 646
reality n 1, 494
realize v 450, 484, 490
realm n 181
reanimate v 163, 359, 660, 689
reanimation n 163
reap v 371, 789
reappear v 104
reappearance n 104, 163
reappearing adj 163
rear n 235
rear n 235; v 161, 235, 307; adj 235
rearguard n 235
rear rank n 235
rearward adv 235
reason n 450, 498, 502, 615; v 450, 498
reasonable adj 174, 472, 498, 502, 736, 815
reasonable chance n 472
reasonableness n 174; 498
reasoner n 476
reason falsely v 477
reasoning n 476
reasoning adj 476
reasons n 476

R

R

738
relaxation n 47, 160,
    174, 687, 738, 840
relaxed adj 47, 160,
    174
relaxing adj 840
release n 360, 671, 672,
    750, 777a, 783, 807;
    v 672, 750, 777a,
    927a, 970
released adj 970
relegate v 55, 270
relegation n 270
relent v 324
relentless adj 604, 739,
    914a
relentlessness n 739
relevant adj 9
reliability n 150, 474
reliable adj 150, 246,
    474, 664
reliance n 484, 507,
    858
relic n 40, 124, 551
relics n 362
relied on adj 871
relief n 834
relief n 250, 660, 662,
    689, 707
relieve v 707, 834
religion n 983
religious adj 983, 987
religious garments n
    999
religious persuasion n
    983
religious truth n 983a
religious writings n
    986
relinquish v 624, 678,
    757, 782
relinquishment n 624,
    782
relinquishment n 678,
    757
relish n 377, 390, 393,
    394; v 377, 394, 827
relocate v 184
reluctance n 603, 704,
    719
reluctant adj 603, 764
rely on v 484, 507, 858
remain v 1, 40, 106,
    110, 141, 186, 265
remainder n 40
remaining adj 40
remains n 40, 362, 551

remake v 144
remark v 457
remarkable adj 31, 870
remarkably adv 31
remediable adj 660
remedial adj 660, 662
remediless adj 859
remedy n 662
remedy v 660, 662, 834
remember v 451, 505
remembrance n 505
remind v 505
reminder n 505
reminisce v 505
reminiscence n 505
reminiscent (of) adj
    505
remiss adj 460, 674,
    683, 738
remission n 756, 918
remissness n 460, 683
remit v 790
remittance n 807
remnant n 40
remodel v 140, 144,
    146
remonstrance n 616,
    766
remonstrate v 616, 766
remonstrative adj 766
remorse n 833, 950
remorseful adj 950
remorseless adj 951
remote adj 10, 196
remote cause n 153
remoteness n 196
remote past n 122
removable adj 38
removal n 38, 185, 270,
    287, 293, 301
remove n 196; v 2, 38,
    185, 270, 301, 662
removed adj 196
remunerate v 30, 807,
    973
remuneration n 973
remunerative adj 775,
    810, 973
renaissance n 660
renascence n 660
renascent adj 163, 660
rend v 44
render v 144, 784, 790
render blunt v 254
render certain v 474
render concave v 252

render curved v 245
render few v 103
render general v 78
render horizontal v
    213
render insensible v
    376
render intelligible v
    518
render invisible v 447
render oblique v 217
render powerless v
    158
render sensible v 375
render straight v 246
render uncertain v 475
render unintelligible v
    519
render violent v 173
rendezvous n 74
renegade n 607
renew v 90, 123, 163,
    660, 689
renewal n 90, 163, 660
renounce v 536, 607,
    610, 624, 757, 764,
    782
renovate v 123, 163,
    660
renovated adj 123
renovation n 123, 163,
    660
renown n 31, 873
renowned adj 873, 883
rent n 44, 198, 260; v
    788
renunciation n 607,
    610, 624, 757, 764,
    782
reorganize v 144, 660
repair n 658, 660, 689;
    v 658, 660, 662, 689,
    790, 952
reparation n 30, 660,
    790, 952, 973
reparatory adj 973
repartee n 842
repay v 718
repeal n 756; v 756
repeat v 90, 104, 136
repeated adj 104
repeatedly adv 104,
    136
repel v 289, 610, 616,
    717, 719, 764, 830,
    867
repellant adj 830

repellent *adj* 289, 719, 867
repelling *adj* 289
repent *v* 833, 950, 952
repentance *n* 833, 950
repentant *adj* 950
repenting *adj* 950
repercussion *n* 145
repetition *n* 104
repetition *n* 17, 90, 136, 143, 641
repetitious *adj* 104, 641
repetitive *adj* 104
repine *v* 832
replace *v* 63, 147, 660
replacement *n* 147, 634, 660
replenish *v* 52, 637
replete *adj* 52, 641
repletion *n* 641, 869
replica *n* 13, 19, 21
reply *n* 462; *v* 467
report *n* 532, 594, 873; *v* 527
reported *adj* 527
reporter *n* 527, 532, 534
repose *n* 687
repose *n* 265, 681; *v* 265, 685, 687
reposing *adj* 687
repository *n* 191
reprehensible *adj* 649, 923, 945
represent *v* 147, 550, 554, 556, 594, 759
representation *n* 554
representation *n* 17, 19, 21, 550, 556, 594, 599, 626
representative *n* 147, 524, 534, 690, 758, 759; *adj* 17, 550, 554
representing *adj* 17
repress *v* 179, 751, 826
repression *n* 179, 751
repressive *adj* 751
reprieve *n* 133, 671, 672, 918; *v* 672, 918
reprint *n* 21
reprisal *n* 148, 718, 789, 919
reproach *v* 932
reproachful *adj* 932
reproduce *v* 19, 104,

163, 168, 660
reproduction *n* 163
reproduction *n* 13, 19, 21, 104, 660
reproductive *adj* 163
reproof *n* 972
reprove *v* 932, 972
reprover *n* 936
reptile *n* 366
repudiate *v* 55, 489, 536, 610, 764
repudiation *n* 55, 536, 610, 764, 808
repugnance *n* 867, 898
repugnant *adj* 867, 898
repulse *n* 145, 277, 289, 764; *v* 289, 719, 764
repulsed *adj* 893
repulsion *n* 289
repulsion *n* 719
repulsive *adj* 289, 395, 719, 830, 846, 867, 898
reputable *adj* 246, 873
reputation *n* 873
repute *n* 873
reputed *adj* 873
request *n* 765
request *n* 741, 865; *v* 630, 765, 865
require *v* 601, 630, 640, 741, 744, 765, 812
requirement *n* 630
requirement *n* 601, 741
requisite *n* 601, 630; *adj* 601, 630
requisition *n* 630, 741
requital *n* 30, 148, 718, 919, 973
requite *v* 148, 718, 919, 973
rescind *v* 44, 756, 764
rescue *n* 672, 707; *v* 660, 670, 672, 707
research *n* 461, 463
resemblance *n* 13, 17, 216
resemble *v* 17, 197
resembling *adj* 17
resent *v* 900, 921
resentful *adj* 900, 907, 919, 920
resentment *n* 900

resentment *n* 907, 920
reservation *n* 528
reserve *n* 528, 585, 636; *v* 636, 678, 781
reserved *adj* 383, 528, 585, 901a
reservoir *n* 191, 343, 636
reside *v* 188
residence *n* 189
resident *n* 188; *adj* 186
residual *adj* 40
residue *n* 40
residuum *n* 40
resign *v* 624, 725, 757, 782
resignation *n* 757
resignation *n* 624, 725, 782, 826, 831
resigned *adj* 826, 831
resign oneself to *v* 826
resilience *n* 325
resiliency *n* 325
resilient *adj* 325
resin *n* 356a
resin *v* 356a
resinous *adj* 356a
resist *v* 179, 708, 715, 719, 742, 764
resistance *n* 719
resistance *n* 179, 708, 715, 742
resistant *adj* 323, 327, 708, 715, 719
resisting *n* 708
resolute *adj* 150, 604, 604a, 606, 861
resolutely *adv* 604
resoluteness *n* 150, 600, 604
resolution *n* 604
resolution *n* 144, 150, 600, 604a, 606, 620
resolve *n* 604, 611, 620; *v* 604
resolve beforehand *v* 611
resolved *adj* 604
resolve into *v* 144
resolve into its elements *v* 49
resonance *n* 408
resonance *n* 277, 402, 404
resonant *adj* 402, 408
resort *n* 677

R

revelatory adj 985
revel in v 377
reveling n 838
revenge n 919
revenge n 718; v 718, 919
revengeful adj 718, 919
reverberant adj 104, 408
reverberate v 277, 408
reverberating adj 104, 408
reverberation n 104, 277, 407, 408
revere v 860, 897, 928, 987
reverence n 860, 926, 928, 987, 990; v 860, 928
reverend n 996
reverent adj 987
reverential adj 926, 987, 990
revering adj 990
reversal n 14, 140, 218, 287, 607
reverse n 235, 237; v 145, 218; adj 14, 218, 237
reversion n 145
reversion n 218
revert v 14, 104, 145, 283, 287
reverting n 145
review n 595
reviewer n 480, 595
revile v 988
reviler n 936
revise v 658
revision n 658
revival n 163, 660, 689
revive v 163, 359, 660, 689
revivification n 163, 660
revivify v 159, 163, 660
revocation n 607, 756
revoke v 536, 607, 756, 764
revolt n 146; v 146, 289, 719, 742, 830
revolting adj 846, 898
revolution n 146
revolution n 138, 140, 218, 312
revolutionary adj 146,

742
revolutionize v 146
revolve v 138, 312
revolving adj 312
revulsion n 145, 146, 218, 277
reward n 973
reward n 733; v 973
rewarded adj 973
rewarding adj 973
rhapsodic adj 497
rhapsodist n 504, 597
rhapsody n 497
rhetoric n 517, 577, 582
rhetorical adj 577
rhetorical flourish n 577
rhetorician n 582
rheumy adj 337
rhyme v 597
rhymeless adj 598
rhymer n 597
rhymes n 597
rhyme with v 17
rhyming n 597
rhythm n 104, 138, 413
rhythm n 413
rhythmic adj 104, 138, 597
rhythmical adj 138
rib n 215
ribald adj 961
ribaldry n 961
ribbed adj 259
rich adj 394, 413, 428, 577, 734, 803
riches n 803
richly adv 31
richness n 573
rickety adj 160
ricochet n 145, 277; v 277
riddle n 520; v 260
ride n 226
rider n 39, 268
ride roughshod over v 885
ride the waves v 267
ridge n 250, 346
ridicule n 856
ridicule v 856, 929
ridiculous adj 497, 499
ridiculousness n 853
rid of adj 776
rife adj 78, 175
rifler n 792

rift n 44, 198, 260
rig n 272
rigging n 225
right n 238, 922
right n 780, 924, 965; v 246, 658, 662; adj 494, 922, 944
right ahead adv 234
right and left adv 180, 227
right angle n 244
righteous adj 944, 977
righteously adv 922
righteous man n 987
rightful adj 494, 922
rightfully adv 922
right hand n 238
right-handed adj 238
rightly adv 922
right now n 118
right on adj 494
right side n 238
rigid adj 82, 150, 240, 323, 704, 739, 955
rigidity n 141, 323, 739
rigmarole n 517
rigor mortis n 360
rigorous adj 739, 955
rigorousness n 739
rig out v 225
rill n 348
rim n 231
rimple n 258; v 258
rind n 223
ring n 247, 408, 712, 728; v 408
ringing n 408; adj 413
ring in the ear v 408
ring in the ears v 404
riot n 59, 173; v 173
rioter n 742
riotous adj 59, 173, 742
ripe adj 128, 673
ripe age n 128
ripen v 144, 650, 658, 673
ripeness n 124, 131, 673
ripen into v 144
ripe old age n 128
rip open v 260
rip out v 301
ripple n 258, 314, 315, 348; v 258, 314
rise n 35, 217, 282,

R

305; v 35, 146, 305,
734
rise above v 31
rise from v 154
rise up v 146, 206, 719
rising n 146, 305; adj
217, 305
rising ground n 217
risk n 665; v 621, 665
risky adj 665
rite n 998
rites n 990
ritualistic adj 998
ritualize v 883
rival n 710, 726; v 648,
720
rivalry n 720
rive v 44
river n 348
river n 348
rivet v 43, 824
rivulet n 348
road n 278, 302, 627
road to ruin n 162
roam v 266
roan adj 433
roar n 404, 408, 411; v
173, 404, 411, 412,
838
roaring n 404
roast v 384
rob v 791
robber n 792
robbery n 791
robe n 999; v 225
robust adj 159, 654,
836
robust health n 654
rock n 342, 415
rock and roll band n
416
rocks n 667
rod n 215, 975
roe n 374
rogue n 941
role n 625
roll n 407
roll n 86, 248, 249, 312,
408; v 248, 255, 264,
314, 348, 407
roll call n 85
roller n 249
rolling pin n 249
rolling seas n 348
roll into a ball v 249
roll on v 264
romance n 515

romantic n 504; adj
515
romp v 173
roof n 223
rookie n 701
room n 180
roomy adj 180
roost n 189; v 186
root n 153; v 184
rooted adj 124, 184
root out v 301
ropy adj 205
rosin n 356a; v 356a
rosy adj 434
rot n 49, 653; v 49, 653,
659
rotary adj 312
rotate v 312
rotating adj 312
rotation n 312
rotation n 138, 145
rotten adj 160, 401,
649, 653, 659
rottenness n 659
rotund adj 249
rotundity n 249
rotundity n 247
roué n 962
rough adj 16a, 173,
241, 254, 256, 329,
397, 410, 674
roughen v 256
rough-hewn adj 256
rough it v 686
roughness n 256
roughness n 254
rough seas n 348
rough up v 256
round n 69, 138; v 245,
247, 249; adj 247,
249, 254
roundabout adj 279,
311, 573, 629; adv
279
roundabout way n 629
round and round adv
138, 248
rounded adj 245, 247,
254
rounded inward adj
252
roundness n 247, 249
round number n 84
round the edge v 254
rouse v 175, 615, 824
rouse oneself v 682
rousing adj 171

route n 302, 627
routine n 16, 58, 80,
138, 613; adj 16, 138
rout out v 652
rove v 266, 279
rover n 268
roving n 266; adj 266
row n 59, 69; v 267
rowdy n 887
royalty n 875
rpm n 138
rub v 255, 331, 379
rubadub n 407
rubbery adj 325
rubbing n 331, 379
rubbish n 643
rub out v 331, 552
rubric n 697
ruby adj 434
ruckus n 59
ruddy adj 434
rude adj 173, 241, 579,
851, 885, 895, 929
rudeness n 885, 895,
929
rudimental adj 66, 674
rudiments n 66
rue v 833, 950
rueful adj 830, 833
ruffian n 887
ruffle n 258; v 59, 256,
258, 824
rugged adj 241, 256
ruin n 162, 619, 638; v
162, 619
ruinous adj 162, 619,
663, 830
ruins n 40
rule n 80, 157, 175,
240, 466, 537, 613,
693, 737, 741; v 157,
480, 693, 737, 749
rulebook n 567
ruler n 737, 745
rules of language n 567
ruling passion n 820
rumble n 408; v 59,
407
rumbling n 407
ruminate v 450, 451
rumor n 532
rump n 235
rumple v 256, 258
rumpus n 59
run n 264; v 109, 264,
274, 333, 348
run abreast v 27

run against v 276
run amuck v 173
runaway n 623
run away v 287, 671
run counter to v 179
run down v 649, 934; adj 124
run for one's life v 623
run headlong v 173
run into v 276
run into trouble v 665
run its course v 67, 109, 122
runner n 271, 534
running water n 348
run off at the mouth v 584
run of the mill adj 29, 736
run on and on v 573
run out v 67
run over v 641
run parallel v 178
run riot v 173, 641
run smoothly v 705
run the eye over v 441
run the fingers over v 379
run the risk of v 177
run through v 186, 361
run up against v 179
run up bills v 808
run wild v 173, 825
rupture n 44, 713, 720; v 44
ruse n 545
rush n 72, 274, 310, 348, 684; v 173, 274, 310, 684
russet adj 433
rust v 659; adj 433
rustic adj 876
rustle v 409
rusty adj 659, 683, 699
rut n 259, 613
ruthless adj 739, 914a

S

Sabbath n 687
sable adj 431
saboteur n 361
saccharine adj 396
saccharinity n 396
sacred adj 976, 987
sacrilege n 988
sacrilegist n 988
sacrosanct adj 976

sad adj 649, 837
sadden v 830
sadly adv 31
sadness n 837
safe n 802; adj 664, 670
safe and sound adj 664
safecracker n 792
safeguard n 664, 666, 670, 717; v 670, 717
safekeeping n 664, 670
safety n 664
safety valve n 435
saffron adj 435
sag v 245
sagacious adj 498, 842, 868
sagacity n 480, 498, 698, 842
sage n 500
sage n 492, 872; adj 498
sall n 267; v 267
sailboat n 273
sailing n 267; adj 267
sailor n 269
saint n 948
saintly adj 987
salable adj 796
salad oil n 356
sale n 796
sale n 783, 813
salesman n 797
saleswoman n 797
salient adj 250, 642
sallow adj 429, 430, 435
sally n 716; v 293
salmon adj 434
salt n 393; v 392
salt and pepper n 432; adj 440
salt of the earth n 648, 948
salt water n 341
salty adj 392
salubrious adj 656
salubrity n 656
salutary adj 644, 648, 656
salutation n 896
salute n 896; v 586, 836, 896
salvation n 670, 672
salve n 356
salvo n 406
sameness n 13, 16, 17, 104

sample n 82
sanctify v 987
sanctimoniousness n 988
sanctimony n 988
sanction n 737, 760, 924, 931; v 737, 760, 931
sanctioned adj 924
sanctity n 987
sanctuary n 666
sand n 330, 667; v 255
sand bar n 209
sanded adj 255
sandiness n 330
sandpaper v 255
sandy adj 330
sane adj 246, 502
sanguine adj 831, 858
sanitary adj 656
sanity n 502
sans adv 187
sap n 5, 501; v 162, 659
sapience n 498
sapient adj 498
sapless adj 340
sapphire adj 438
sappy adj 333, 499
sarcastic adj 856
sarcophagous n 363
sash n 247
Satan n 978
satanic adj 978, 982
satanism n 978
sate v 869
satiate v 376, 829, 869
satiated adj 869
satiety n 869
satire n 856
satirist n 844, 936
satirize v 856
satisfaction n 772, 807, 827, 831, 952
satisfactory adj 639
satisfied adj 474, 484, 831
satisfy v 462, 639, 746, 772, 807, 829, 831, 952
saturate v 52, 339, 869
saturated adj 52
saturation n 869
satyr n 980
sauce n 393
saunter n 266; v 266, 275

RS

229

sauté v 384
savage adj 173
savant n 492
save v 672, 817; adv 38, 83
saving n 817
savoir faire n 698; n 852
savor n 390; v 390, 394
savoriness n 394
savory adj 390, 394
saw n 257; v 44
say n 175; v 535, 560, 582
saying n 496
say nothing v 517, 585
say what comes to mind v 612
scabrous adj 256
scaffolding n 673
scald v 384
scale n 69, 71, 204, 466; v 305
scale the heights v 305
scallop n 257; v 257
scalpel n 262
scaly adj 204
scamper v 274
scan v 441
scant adj 32, 137, 640
scantiness n 103, 203
scanty adj 32, 103
scarce adj 32, 103, 137, 640
scarcely adv 32, 137
scarcity n 32, 103, 640
scared adj 862
scarify v 257
scarlet adj 434
scatter v 61, 73, 291
scattered adj 73
scene n 448
scenery n 448
scent n 398, 550; v 398, 400
scented adj 400
scentless adj 399
scepter n 747
schedule n 86
scheme n 626; v 626
schemer n 626
schism n 713, 984
schismatic adj 984
scholar n 492
scholar n 541
scholarly adj 539

scholarship n 490, 539
scholastic adj 537, 539, 542
school n 542
school v 537
schoolbook n 542
schoolboy n 129
schooled adj 498
schoolgirl n 129
schooling n 537
schoolmaster n 540
schooner n 273
science n 490
science of existence n 1
science of light n 420
science of living beings n 357
science of matter n 316
science of sound n 402
science of the mineral kingdom n 358
scintilla n 32, 420
scintillate v 420
scintillating adj 842
scintillation n 420
scion n 167
scoff v 929, 988
scoff at v 856
scoffer n 988
scoffing n 856, 988
scold v 972
scoop n 262; v 252
scoop out v 252
scope n 26, 180, 748
scorch v 384
scorched adj 384
score n 98, 259, 805, 806, 811; v 259
scores n 102
scorn n 930; v 715, 929, 930
scornful adj 929, 930
scotch v 659
scot free adj 748
scoundrel n 941, 949
scour v 331, 652
scourge n 975
scourge v 663, 972
scour the country v 266
scout n 664, 668
scowl v 900, 901a
scraggly adj 256
scramble n 59, 684; v 684
scrap n 32

scrape n 704, 732; v 38, 195, 255, 330, 331
scratch n 257, 259; v 257, 331, 380, 590, 649
scratching n 380; adj 410
scratchy adj 380
scrawl v 590
scrawny adj 203
scream n 411, 669; v 404, 410, 411, 839
screech v 411, 412
screeching n 412; adj 414
screen n 223, 424, 530, 717; v 424, 442, 528, 664, 717
screening n 528
screw n 243; v 43, 243
screw up the eyes v 443
scribble v 590
scribe n 553, 590
scrimp v 819
script n 590, 593
scriptural adj 983a
Scriptures n 985, 986
scrivener n 590
Scrooge n 819
scrub v 331, 652
scruple n 485
scrupulous adj 246, 459, 543, 603, 772, 868, 939
scrupulousness n 603
scrutinize v 457
scrutinizing adj 461
scrutiny n 457, 461
scull n 267
sculpt v 557
sculptor n 559
sculpture n 557
scum of the earth n 949
scurrilous adj 934
scurry v 684
scuttle v 162
scuttlebutt n 532
sea n 341
sea dog n 269
seafaring adj 267
seafaring man n 269
sea-girt adj 346
seagoing adj 267, 341
sea-green adj 435

S

senility n 124, 128, 158, 160, 659

seniority n 128

sensation n 375, 379, 390

sensational adj 824

sensations of touch n 380

sense n 450, 498, 502, 516, 842

senseless adj 376, 497, 499, 517

senselessness n 517

sense of duty n 926

sensibility n 375, 822

sensibility n 821

sensible adj 316, 375, 498, 502

sensical adj 450

sensitive adj 375, 597, 821, 822

sensitiveness n 375, 822

sensitivity n 821, 901

sensitize v 375

sensual adj 377, 829

sensual delight n 377

sensualist n 954a

sensualist n 962

sensuality n 377, 827

sensuous adj 375, 377

sensuousness n 377

sentence n 972

sententious adj 577

sentient adj 375

sentiment n 453, 821

sentimental adj 822

sentimentalism n 822

sentimentality n 821, 822

sentinel n 444, 664, 668

sentry n 668

separate v 44, 55, 291, 905; adj 44

separated adj 905

separately adv 44

separateness n 44

separation n 44, 55, 198, 291, 489, 905

sepia adj 433

septet n 415

septic adj 657

sepulchral adj 363

sepulchre n 363

sepulture n 363

sequel n 65

sequel n 39, 63, 117, 281

sequence n 63, 281

sequence n 58, 117, 281

sequential adj 63, 281

sequester v 893, 974

sequestered adj 893

sequestration n 893, 974

seraph n 977

seraphic adj 977

serene adj 265, 721

serenity n 265, 826, 831

serfdom n 749

serial adj 69, 138

serially adv 138

series n 58, 63, 69

serious adj 642, 739

seriousness n 642, 739

sermon n 537, 582

sermonize v 537, 582

serous adj 333

serpent n 248, 548, 978

serpentine adj 248

serrated adj 244, 257

serum n 337

servant n 746

servant n 690, 707

serve v 618, 644, 707, 743, 746, 749, 969

serve with a writ v 969

service n 618, 644, 677, 707, 749, 990, 998

serviceable adj 631, 644, 648

servile adj 886, 933

servility n 886

servitude n 749

session n 696

set n 7, 240, 278, 712; v 150, 184, 306, 321; adj 43, 240, 613

set about v 676

set against adj 898

set an example v 22

set apart v 44, 465

set a price v 812

set aside v 55, 185, 678

set at ease v 831

set at naught v 773

set a trap for v 530

set at rest v 462

set down v 551, 590

set fire to v 384

set foot on dry land v

342

set forth v 293, 594

set forward v 293

set free v 44, 672, 748, 750, 970; adj 970

set going v 276

set in motion v 66, 284, 677

set in one's ways adj 5

set loose v 750

setoff n 30

set one's sights on v 278

set on fire v 384

set out v 60, 66, 293

set phrase n 566

set right v 662

set sail v 293

set store by v 642

set the fashion v 62

setting side by side n 464

settle v 60, 150, 184, 265, 306, 769, 774, 807

settled adj 67, 184, 474

settle down v 184, 265

settled purpose n 620

settlement n 23, 184, 762, 807

settle up v 790

settle upon v 784

set too high a value on v 482

set to rights v 660

set to work v 677

set up v 153, 161, 307

set upon v 716

seven n 98

sever v 44, 291

several n 100; adj 100, 102

severally adv 44, 79

severance n 44, 291

severe adj 242, 576, 739, 830, 849, 955

severely adv 31, 739

severity n 739

severity n 173, 576, 849

sew v 43

sewer n 350

sex n 377

sextet n 415

sexual adj 377

sexual abstinence n 904

sexual failure n 158
sexuality n 377
shabby adj 34, 643, 659, 851
shade n 424
shade n 15, 26, 223, 362, 421, 422, 428, 530, 980; v 421, 422, 424
shading off adj 26
shadow n 4, 21, 281, 421, 424, 515, 980; v 281, 353, 421, 422
shadowiness n 422
shadowy adj 4, 421, 422, 424, 447
shady adj 421, 424, 426, 874
shaft n 208, 351
shaggy adj 256
shaggy dog story n 549
shake n 315; v 160, 314, 315, 383, 404, 407, 616, 659
shake one's sides v 838
shake the foundations of v 659
shake up v 315
shaking adj 315
shaky adj 160, 315, 665
shallow n 209; adj 209, 491, 499, 643
shallow excuse n 617
shallowness n 209
shallowness n 499
shallows n 667
sham n 544, 545, 855, 880; v 546; adj 544
shaman n 994
shamble v 275, 315
shame n 874, 930; v 874, 879
shameful adj 874, 930
shape n 448; v 240, 557, 852
shapeless adj 241
shapelessness n 241
shapeliness n 242
shapely adj 242
share n 786; v 709, 778, 786
shareholder n 778
share in v 56, 778
sharer n 778
sharp adj 171, 173, 217, 253, 375, 392,

397, 404, 410, 416; adj 490, 498, 682, 698, 702, 842, 868
sharp edged adj 253
sharpen v 171, 173, 253, 375, 824
sharpness n 253
sharpness n 392, 397, 410, 698
sharp outline n 446
shatter v 44, 158, 162, 328
shattered adj 160
shave v 195, 201, 204, 255
she n 374
shear v 195, 201
sheathe v 225
shed n 223; v 73
shed light on v 522
shed light upon v 420
sheen n 420
sheeny adj 420
sheepish adj 881
sheer v 52, 425
sheerness n 425
sheet n 204, 223, 811
shelf n 215
shell n 363
shellac n 356a; v 356a
shellfish n 366
shelter n 666, 670, 717; v 528, 664, 670, 717
sheltering n 528
shelve v 133, 678
shepherd n 996
shield n 223, 717; v 670, 717
shift n 140, 147, 270; v 140, 144, 264, 270, 279
shifting n 144; adj 264
shiftless adj 674
shilly-shally v 133, 605
shimmer n 420; v 420
shine v 420
shiny adj 255, 420
ship n 273
ship n 271; v 190
shipment n 190
ship out v 293
shipping n 267
shipshape adj 58
shirk v 623, 742
shirker n 623
shiver v 315, 328, 383
shivering adj 383

shoal n 209
shoals n 667
shock n 276, 315, 508, 713; v 824, 830
shockingly adv 31
shoot n 378; v 194, 274, 284, 361, 367, 378
shoot ahead of v 303
shooting n 361, 378
shoot up v 250, 367
shop v 795
shopkeeper n 797
shopper n 795
shopping center n 799
shore n 231, 342
shore up v 215
short adj 28, 53, 201, 572, 640, 739
shortcoming n 304
shortcoming n 28, 34, 53, 640, 651, 730
short distance n 197
shorten v 36, 38, 201, 596
shortened adj 201
shortening n 36, 38, 201
shorthand n 590
short-lived adj 111
shortly adv 132
short memory n 506
shortness n 201
short of adj 53; adv 32, 34, 38
short-tempered adj 901
shot n 284
shot in the dark n 621
shoulder n 236; v 215, 276
shoulder to shoulder adv 709
shout n 411, 838; v 404, 411, 836, 838
shout at the top of one's lungs v 411
shove n 276; v 276, 284
shove in v 300
shovel v 270
shove off v 267, 293
show n 448, 855, 882; v 448, 467, 478, 525, 529
shower n 348
shower down v 348
showery adj 348

233

S

234

small talk *n* 588
smart *n* 378, 828; *v* 378; *adj* 682, 698
smarts *n* 450, 498
smash *v* 162
smatch *n* 390; *v* 390
smear *v* 653
smell *n* 398, 400; *v* 398, 401
smell bad *v* 401
smell of *v* 398
smell rotten *v* 401
smell sweet *v* 400
smelly *adj* 398
smile *n* 838; *v* 838
smirch *v* 431, 653
smirk *n* 838; *v* 838
smite *v* 649
smitten *adj* 897
smoggy *adj* 426
smoke *v* 382, 392
smoking *adj* 382
smoky *adj* 426
smolder *v* 382, 526
smoldering *adj* 172
smooth *v* 16. 174, 255, 705, 723; *adj* 174, 213, 251, 255, 705
smoothly *adv* 705
smoothness *n* 255
smoothness *n* 251, 705
smooth-tongued *adj* 933
smother *v* 361, 581
smudge *v* 653
smug *adj* 878
smut *n* 653, 961; *v* 431
smutch *v* 431
smutty *adj* 653, 961
snag *n* 667
snaggy *adj* 253
snake *n* 248
snake in the grass *n* 548, 649, 667
snaky *adj* 248
snap *n* 406
snap *n* 277; *v* 44, 328, 406
snap back *v* 277
snappish *adj* 901
snap up *v* 789
snare *n* 530, 545, 667
snarl *v* 412, 900
snatch *n* 32; *v* 789
sneak *n* 941; *v* 275, 623, 862, 886

sneak off *v* 623
sneer *n* 856; *v* 929
sneer at *v* 856
sneeze *v* 409
sniff *v* 398
snip *v* 44
snippet *n* 32
sniveling *adj* 886
snobbish *adj* 878
snort *v* 412
snout *n* 250
snow-white *adj* 430
snowy *adj* 430
snuff *v* 398
snuff out *v* 421
snug *adj* 261, 664
soak *v* 337, 339, 959
soak up *v* 340
soap *n* 356
soar *v* 31, 206, 267, 303, 305
sob *n* 839; *v* 411, 839
sobbing *n* 411
sober *v* 174; *adj* 174, 246, 502, 826, 953, 958
sobriety *n* 958
sobriety *n* 502, 953
sobriquet *n* 565
so-called *adi* 565
sociability *n* 894
sociable *adj* 892
sociableness *n* 892
social *adj* 372, 892
social interaction *n* 892
social intercourse *n* 892
social sm *n* 778
social ist *n* 778; *adj* 778
socia istic *adj* 778
socia ility *n* 892
society *n* 188, 372, 852
society of men *n* 372
sodden *v* 339; *adj* 337
soft *adj* 255, 324, 345, 403, 405, 413, 499
soft as butter *adj* 324
soft coal *n* 388
soften *v* 174, 324
softening *n* 324
softness *n* 324
softness *n* 160, 326
soggy *adj* 337, 339
soi-disant adj 565
soil *n* 181, 342; *v* 653
soiled *adj* 653

sojourn *v* 186
solace *n* 834
solar *adj* 318
solar energy *n* 388
solar system *n* 180, 318
solder *v* 43, 46
soldier *n* 726, 948
sole *n* 211; *adj* 87
solecism *n* 568
solecism *n* 579
solecize *v* 568
solemn *adj* 403, 642, 882
solemnity *n* 642
solemnization *n* 883
solemnize *v* 883
solicit *v* 765, 865
solicitation *n* 411, 765
solicitor *n* 767, 968
solicitous *adj* 411, 765, 860, 920
solicitude *n* 459, 828, 860
solid *adj* 16, 52, 150, 202, 321, 323
solidarity *n* 52
solid body *n* 321
solidification *n* 321, 385
solidify *v* 46, 48, 321
solidity *n* 150, 321
solidness *n* 321
soliloquize *v* 582, 589
soliloquy *n* 589
solipsism *n* 943
solipsistic *adj* 943
solitary *adj* 87, 893
solitude *n* 893
solo *n* 415; *adj* 87; *v* 416
soloist *n* 416
solubility *n* 333
soluble *adj* 333, 335, 462, 662
solubleness *n* 335
solution *n* 462, 522, 662
solve *v* 462, 662
solvency *n* 803
solvent *adj* 335, 807
somatic *adj* 316
somber *adj* 431, 901a
some *adj* 25, 100; *adv* 32
somebody *n* 372
someone *n* 372

somersault *n* 218
something like *adj* 17
some time ago *adv* 122
sometimes *adv* 136
somewhere *adv* 182
somewhere about *adv* 32
son *n* 167
sonata *n* 415
song *n* 413, 415
sonneteer *n* 597
sonority *n* 402
sonorous *adj* 402, 404, 577
sonorousness *n* 402, 408
soon *adv* 111, 121, 132
sooner or later *adv* 121
soothe *v* 723, 834
soothing *adj* 834
soothsayer *n* 513, 994
soothsaying *n* 511
sooty *adj* 431, 653
sop *v* 339
sophism *n* 477
sophist *n* 477, 548
sophistical *adj* 477
sophistry *n* 477
sophistry *n* 538
soporific *adj* 683
sorcerer *n* 994
sorcerer *n* 513
sorcery *n* 992
sordid *adj* 32, 207, 435
sordidness *n* 32
sore *n* 378, 830; *adj* 378, 830
sorely *adv* 31
soreness *n* 378
sore subject *n* 830
sorority *n* 11
sorrel *adj* 433
sorrow *n* 833
sorrowful *adj* 828, 839
sorrow over *v* 839
sorry *adj* 643, 828, 833, 950
sorry sight *n* 830
sort *n* 75; *v* 60
sortie *n* 716
sorting *n* 60
SOS *n* 669
so-so *adj* 32, 643, 651
sot *n* 959; *v* 959
so to speak *adv* 17
sotted *adj* 959

sough *n* 350
soul *n* 5, 359, 372, 820
soul-stirring *adj* 821, 824
sound *n* 402
sound *n* 343; *v* 208, 402; *adj* 50, 150, 246, 498, 650, 654, 664, 670, 983a
sound dead *v* 408a
sounding *adj* 402
soundings *n* 208
soundless *adj* 208, 403
soundness *n* 150, 502, 654, 983a
sound the alarm *v* 669
sound vibrations *n* 402
soupçon *n* 32
sour *v* 397; *adj* 392, 395, 397, 410, 901a
sourness *n* 397
sourness *n* 392, 395
souse *v* 310, 337
souvenir *n* 505
sovereign *n* 737; *adj* 737
sovereignty *n* 157
sow *n* 374; *v* 73, 371
sow the seeds of *v* 153
space *n* 180
space *n* 106, 198, 318
space heater *n* 386
spaceman *n* 269
spaceship *n* 273
space station *n* 273
spacious *adj* 180, 192
span *n* 106, 180, 196, 200; *v* 43, 45
spare *v* 678, 784; *adj* 40, 636, 641, 685
spare no effort *v* 686
spare no expense *v* 816
spare time *n* 685
sparing *adj* 953
spark *n* 382, 420, 423
sparkle *v* 420
sparkling *adj* 574, 836, 842
sparse *adj* 32, 73, 103, 640
sparseness *n* 32, 103
spasm *n* 146, 173, 315, 378
spasmodic *adj* 70, 139, 173
speak *v* 580, 582

speak directly *v* 576
speaker *n* 524, 582
speaking of *adv* 134
speak in low tones *v* 405
speak one's mind *v* 703
speak plainly *v* 576
speak prettily *v* 521
speak softly *v* 405
speak the truth *v* 543
speak to *v* 586
spear *n* 262; *v* 260, 361
special *n* 79; *adj* 20, 79, 474
special committee *n* 755
specialist *n* 700
speciality *n* 79
specialize *v* 79
specially *adv* 79
specialty *n* 79
species *n* 75
specific *n* 662; *adj* 79
specify *v* 79, 564
specimen *n* 82
specious *adj* 477, 545
speciousness *n* 477
speck *n* 32, 848
speckle *v* 440
speckled *adj* 440
spectacle *n* 448, 872
spectacles *n* 445
spectator *n* 444
specter *n* 980; 443
spectral *adj* 2, 4, 980
spectroscope *n* 428
spectrum *n* 428
speculate *v* 155, 514, 621, 675, 870
speculation *n* 156, 451, 514, 621, 675
speculative *adj* 514, 621, 675
speech *n* 582
speech *n* 560, 586
speech impediment *n* 583
speechless *adj* 403, 581, 583
speechlessness *n* 403, 590
speed *n* 264, 274, 684; *v* 274, 682, 684
speedily *adv* 132
speediness *n* 132

squeak v 411, 412

squeal v 411

squeeze v 195, 348, 354

squeeze out v 301

squeezing n 195, 301

squelch v 162

squint n 443; v 443

squirt n 348

squishy adj 324

stab v 260, 361, 649

stability n 150

stability n 16, 110, 141

stabilization n 150

stabilize v 150

stable adj 110, 141, 150, 265

staff n 215, 696, 747

staff of life n 359

stag n 373

stage n 26, 71, 106, 204, 728

stage business n 399

stage name n 565

stage-play n 599

stagey adj 855

stagger v 275, 314, 315, 508, 824, 870

stagnant adj 265, 901a

stagnate v 265

stagnation n 265

stagy adj 599

staid adj 826

stain n 428, 874; v 428, 653, 848, 874

stained adj 961

stainless adj 652

stake n 621, 771; v 621

stale adj 124, 659

stalk n 215

stalk v 133

stall v 133

stallion n 373

stalwart adj 192

stamina n 159, 604a

stammer v 583

stammering n 583

stamp n 7, 22; v 240, 550

stamp out v 162, 385

stand n 71, 211, 719; v 106, 110, 141, 719

stand a chance v 177, 470

stand aloof v 681

standard n 22, 26, 80, 466, 650; adj 29, 82, 650

standardization n 16

standardize v 58

stand as an example v 82

stand as opposites v 237

stand at the head v 66

stand by v 186

stand condemned v 971

stand convicted v 754

stand erect v 212

stand fast v 141, 265

stand firm v 150, 265, 604

stand for v 147, 550, 759, 771

stand immobile v 265

stand-in n 634

stand in front v 234

standing n 8, 26, 71, 110, 183, 873

stand next to v 197

stand one in good stead v 644

stand out v 250

standpoint n 183, 441

stand still v 265

stand straight and tall v 212

stand the test v 648

stand to reason v 474

stand up v 719

stand upright v 212

stand up straight v 212

staple commodity n 798

staples n 635

starboard n 238

starchy adj 352

stare n 441; v 455, 870

stark adj 31

stark-naked adj 226

stars n 423

start n 66, 293; v 66, 151, 276, 284, 293, 309, 870

start again v 66

start fresh v 652

starting point n 66, 293

startle v 508, 824, 870

startled adj 870

startling adj 508, 870

start over v 66

start up v 250, 446

starvation n 956

starve v 385, 804, 819, 955, 956

starved adj 956

starving adj 956

starving oneself n 956

stash n 636; v 636

state n 7

state n 188; v 516, 535

stated adj 474

stateliness n 875

stately adj 875, 878

statement n 535, 594, 811

station n 26, 71, 183; v 184

stationary adj 265

statistical adj 85

statistics n 85

statuary n 557

statue n 557, 963, 991

statuette n 557

stature n 206

status n 7, 8, 71

statute n 697; 963

staunch adj 150, 604a

stave in v 252

stay n 133, 215, 685; v 1, 133, 141, 142, 186, 265

stay away v 187

stay in the background v 881

stay together v 46

stead n 644

steadfast adj 150, 604, 604a

steadfastness n 150, 604a

steadiness n 138, 150

steady adj 80, 138, 150, 604a

steal v 275, 789, 791

steal a march on v 132

steal away v 623, 671

steal from v 788

stealing n 791

stealing n 788

stealthily adv 528

stealthy adj 528, 702

steam n 353; v 267, 336, 353

steamer n 273

steaming n 336

steam press v 255

steam up v 353

steamy adj 353

steel v 159

steep v 337; adj 217, 306

steepness n 217

steer n 373; v 693

steerage n 693

steer a middle course v 628

steer clear of v 279, 623

steer for v 278

steersman n 269

stench n 401

stencil n 21

stenography n 590

stentorian adj 404, 411

step n 71, 264

step by step adv 26, 58, 69, 275

step in v 724

steppe n 344

stereoscope n 445

sterile adj 158, 169

sterility n 169

stern adj 604, 739, 955

sternness n 739

stew v 382, 384

steward n 801; v 693

stewardship n 693

stewed adj 959

stewed to the gills adj 959

stick n 215, 975; v 46, 260

stick fast v 150, 265

stick in v 300

stickiness n 46, 352, 396

stick it out v 604a

stick out v 250

stick to v 143

stick to an idea v 606

stick up v 250

sticky adj 46, 327, 352, 396

stiff adj 240, 579, 739

stiff breeze n 349

stiffen v 323

stiffness n 246, 579

stifle v 361, 403

stifled adj 405

stifling adj 382

stiletto n 262

still v 174, 403, 723; adj 174, 265, 403; adv 30

still-born adj 732

stillness n 265, 403

stilted adj 307, 577, 855

stilts n 215

stimulate v 171, 173, 382, 615, 689, 824, 829

stimulating adj 171

stimulation n 824

stimulus n 615

sting v 378, 380, 663

stinginess n 819, 943

stinging n 380; adj 392

stingy adj 819, 943

stink n 401; v 401, 653

stinking adj 401

stinky adj 401

stint v 819

stipple v 558

stipulate v 769, 770

stipulations n 770

stir n 264, 315, 682, 752; v 264, 315, 375, 382, 824

stir about v 682

stirring adj 151, 505

stir up v 173, 824

stitch n 43, 378, 828; v 43

stock n 11, 25, 635, 636, 637, 798; v 637; adj 598, 613

stocks n 802

stock-still adj 265

stockyard n 232

stoical adj 383, 826

stoicism n 826

stoke v 388

stolen away adj 671

stolen goods n 793

stolid adj 499, 843

stolidity n 499

stomach v 826

stone-blind adj 442

stone-deaf adj 419

stone's throw n 197

stony adj 914a

stoop v 217, 306, 886

stop n 133, 142, 360; v 67, 70, 142, 261, 265, 403

stopcock n 263

stopgap n 147

stoppage n 142, 261, 706

stop payment v 808

stopper n 263

stopper n 261

stopping n 142, 263, 706

stop short v 142, 265

stop up v 261

stopwatch n 114

storage n 636

storage areas n 191

store n 636

store n 31, 637, 798, 799; v 72, 636, 637, 670

store up v 636

storing n 636

storm n 173, 315, 348, 349; v 173, 349, 716

stormy adj 173, 349

story n 204, 546, 593

storyteller n 548

stout adj 159, 192

stout-hearted adj 861

stoutness n 159

stove n 386

stow away v 528

strabismus n 443

straggle v 279

straggler n 268

straggling adj 59

straight n 857; adj 212, 246, 278, 807, 958; adv 132, 278

straighten v 246

straighten out v 60

straightforward adj 543, 703, 849; adv 278

straight line n 246

straightness n 246

straightway adv 132

strain n 402, 413, 415, 686; v 42, 686, 688

strait n 704

strait-laced adj 739

straitness n 203

straits n 343, 804

strand n 205, 205

strange adj 10, 83, 519, 870

strangely adv 31

strangle v 158, 361

strangulation n 361

strap n 975; v 43

strapper n 192

strapping adj 159

stratagem n 545, 626, 702

strategic adj 626

strategical adj 692
strategist 626
strategy n 692, 722
stratified adj 204
stratosphere n 338
stratum n 204, 213
straw-colored adj 435
stray v 279; adj 73, 279
streak n 259, 420; v 440
streaked adj 440
streakiness n 440
stream n 347
stream n 264, 347, 348, 420; v 72, 264, 333, 348, 349
streamy adj 348
street-walker n 962
strength n 159
strength n 25, 26, 31, 157, 171, 327, 364, 739
strengthen v 157, 159, 171, 689
strengthening n 159
strength of mind n 604
strenuous adj 686
stress n 580, 642, 686
stretch n 180; v 194, 200, 325
stretch out v 200
stretch the meaning v 523
stretch to v 196, 200
strew v 73
strewn adj 73
striate v 440; adj 440
striated adj 259
striation n 440
stricken adj 828
strict adj 82, 739, 955, 983a
strictness n 739, 983a
stricture n 706
stride n 264
stride forward v 282
stridency n 410
strident adj 410
strife n 713, 720
strike v 170, 276
strike a balance v 27
strike dumb v 581
strike out v 552
strike up v 416
strike while the iron is hot v 134
strikingly adv 31

string n 69; v 43
stringency n 739
stringent adj 739
strings n 417
string together v 69
stringy adj 200, 205, 327
strip v 226, 789
stripe v 440
striped adj 440
stripling n 129
strip to essentials v 849
strive v 675, 686, 720
stroke n 276, 731; v 379
stroking n 379
stroll n 266; v 264
strong adj 31, 150, 157, 159, 171, 323, 327, 392, 401, 654
strongbox n 802
stronghold n 666, 802
strong language n 574
strongly adv 159
strong smelling adj 398, 401
strop v 253
structural adj 329
structure n 329
structure n 7
struggle n 675, 686, 713, 720; v 720
struggling n 720
strumpet n 962
strut v 884
stubble n 40
stubborn adj 150, 327, 606, 704, 719, 742
stubbornness n 606
stubbornness n 150, 327, 704, 742
stubby adj 201
stud n 250
studded adj 253, 440
student n 492, 541
studio n 556, 691
studious adj 539
study n 457, 461, 539, 595; v 457, 461, 539
stuff n 3, 635; v 190, 194, 224, 376, 869
stuffed adj 869
stuff in v 300
stuffing n 190, 224, 263
stuff oneself v 957
stuff up v 261

stumble n 495; v 306, 315, 699
stumble on v 156
stumble onto v 480a
stumbling block n 706
stump n 40; v 582
stumpy adj 201
stun v 376, 404, 419, 508
stunned adj 419
stunted adj 193, 195, 201
stupefaction n 870
stupefy v 376, 870
stupendous adj 31, 192
stupendously adv 31
stupid adj 275, 486, 491, 497, 499, 843
stupidity n 491, 497, 499, 843
stupor n 683
sturdy adj 150, 159
stuttering n 583
stygian adj 982
style n 569
style n 7, 560, 564, 567, 852; v 564, 569
stylish adj 123, 852
stylishness n 123
stylistic adj 569
styptic adj 397
suasive adj 615, 695
sub n 634; v 147, 634
subdivide v 44
subdivision n 44, 51, 75, 100a
subdue v 744, 879
subdued adj 826
subject n 454, 746; v 601, 744, 749; adj 177, 749
subjection n 749
subjection n 34, 601
subjective adj 5
subject-matter n 454, 516
subjoin v 37
subjugate v 749
subjugation n 749
sublimation n 307
sublime adj 206, 574
sublimity n 206, 574, 845
sublunary adj 318
submerge v 310, 337
submerged adj 208

sunshine n 420

sunup n 125

sup v 298

superabound v 641

superabundance n 641

superabundant adj 641

superannuation n 124, 128

supercilious adj 878

superciliousness n 878

superficial adj 209, 220, 491

superficiality n 209

superficies n 220

superfluity n 40, 641

superfluous adj 40, 57, 641

superfluousness n 57

superhuman adj 976

superimpose v 223

superintendent n 694

superior adj 33, 642, 648

superiority n 33

superiority n 28, 62, 648, 650

superlative adj 33, 648

superlatively adv 31, 33

supernal adj 210, 981

supernatural adj 976, 980

supersaturate v 641

supersede v 147, 678

superstition n 486

superstitious adj 486

supervise v 692, 693

supervision n 693

supervisor n 694

supervisory adj 693

supination n 213

supine adj 207, 213, 683

supping n 298

supplant v 147

supplanting n 147

supple adj 324

supplement n 37, 39, 65; v 37

supplemental adj 37

supplementary adj 37

suppliant n 767, 990

supplicant n 767

supplicate v 765, 990

supplication n 765, 990

supplies n 635, 800

supply n 636, 637; v 637, 784

supplying n 637

support n 215

support n 153, 666, 670, 707, 937; v 170, 215, 670, 707, 737, 834, 937

supported adj 215, 937

supporter n 215, 707, 890, 912

supporting adj 215

supportive adj 707

suppose v 451, 514

supposing adj 469

supposition n 514

supposition v 453, 515

suppress v 581, 751

suppressed adj 528

suppression n 162, 528, 751

suppressive adj 751

supremacy n 33, 737

supreme adj 31, 33, 210, 737

supreme being n 976

supremely adv 31, 33

sure adj 246, 474, 484, 664

sure enough adv 474

surety n 664, 771

surf n 348, 353

surface n 220, 329

surfeit n 641; 869; v 869

surfeited adj 869

surge n 348; v 72

surgeon n 662

surly adj 901a

surmise v 510, 514

surmount v 206, 303, 305, 731

surname n 564

surpass v 33, 303

surpassingly adv 33

surplice n 999

surplus n 40, 641

surprise n 137, 508, 870; v 508, 702

surprised adj 508, 870

surprisingly adv 31

surrender n 624, 725, 782; v 624, 725, 782

surreptitious adj 528

surrogate n 759

surround v 227, 229

surrounding adj 227

surroundings n 7, 227

survey n 441, 466, 596; v 441, 466, 596

surveyor n 694

survival n 110

survive v 1, 40, 110, 141

surviving adj 40

susceptibility n 176, 177, 821, 822

susceptible adj 375, 822

suspect v 485, 487, 514

suspend v 133, 142, 214

suspended adj 214

suspense n 485, 507

suspension n 214

suspension n 133, 142

suspension of hostilities n 723

suspicion n 485, 487, 514, 860, 920

suspicious adj 485, 487, 860, 920

sustain v 143, 159, 170, 215, 670, 707

sustenance n 298, 670

swab v 340

swaddle v 225

swagger n 878, 884, 885

swaggerer n 887

swaggering n 884

swain n 373

swallow v 298, 486, 547, 826

swamp n 345; v 162

swampy adj 345

swap n 148; v 148, 794

swarm n 72; v 72, 102, 641

swarming adj 72

swarm with v 102

swarthiness n 431

swarthy adj 431

swash v 348

swathe v 225

sway n 157, 175, 737, 741; v 175, 217, 315, 615, 737

swear n 908; v 535, 768, 908, 988

S

swearing n 535
sweat n 299; v 299,
  382, 686
sweep n 180, 245; v
  245, 274
sweep along v 264
sweep away v 162
sweeping adj 52, 76
sweep out v 652
sweet adj 377, 396,
  413, 428, 652, 829
sweeten v 396
sweetened adj 396
sweetheart n 897, 899
sweetness n 396
sweet scent n 400
sweet scented adj 400
sweet smell n 400
sweet smelling adj 400
sweet-sounding adj
  413
sweet sounds n 413,
  415
swell n 348, 404; v 194,
  367, 404
swelling n 194, 250;
  adj 250, 577
swell up v 250
swelter v 382
sweltering adj 382
swerve v 140, 279, 291,
  603
swerving n 279
swift adj 274, 684
swiftly adv 274
swiftness n 111, 274,
  684
swill v 959
swim v 320
swim in v 377
swindle v 791
swindler n 548
swindling n 791
swing n 180, 415; v
  214, 314
swinging adj 214
swinish adj 957
swivel v 312
swivel eye n 443
swollen adj 194, 250
swoon v 158, 688
swoop down v 306
sworn adj 768
sybarite n 954a
sybaritism n 954
sycophancy n 886, 933
sycophant n 886, 935

sycophantic adj 886,
  933
syllabic adj 561
syllable n 561
syllabus n 596
syllogistic adj 476
syllogistic reasoning n
  476
sylph n 979
sylphic adj 979
symbol n 84, 512, 550,
  561, 562, 747, 991
symbolic adj 550, 554
symbolical adj 550
symbolism n 550
symbolize v 550, 554
symmetrical adj 27,
  58, 242, 413
symmetry n 242
symmetry n 27, 58
sympathetic adj 714,
  740, 821, 914
sympathize v 915
sympathizer n 890,
  906
sympathize with v
  714, 888, 914
sympathy n 714, 820,
  821, 888, 914, 915
symphonic adj 415
symphonic music n
  415
symphonious adj 413
symphonize v 413
symphony n 413
symphony orchestra n
  416
symptom n 550
synagogue n 1000
synchronism n 120
synchronize v 120
synchronized adj 413
syncopation n 413
syndicate n 696
synonymous adj 27
synopsis n 596
synoptic adj 596
syntactic adj 567
syntactical adj 567
syntax n 567
synthesis n 48, 54, 476
synthesize v 476
synthesizer n 417
synthetic adj 476
syrupiness n 396
syrupy adj 396
system n 58, 626

systematic adj 58, 60,
  626
systematically adv 58
systematization n 60

T

table n 86, 251; v 133
tableau n 448
tablet n 204, 251
table talk n 588
tabula rasa n 2
tabulate v 60, 69
taciturn adj 403, 583,
  585
taciturnity n 585
taciturnity n 403, 583
tack n 278, 627; v 140
tackle v 676
tack on v 37
tacky adj 851
tact n 698
tactful adj 459, 698
tactical adj 692
tactics n 692, 722
tactile adj 379
tactility n 379
tactlessness n 895
tactual adj 379
tag n 65
tag phrase n 566
tail n 214
taint n 651, 653, 848,
  874; v 653, 659, 848,
  874
tainted adj 659, 874,
  961
take v 785, 789, 791,
  810
take a breather v 70,
  687
take account v 85
take a decisive step v
  604
take advantage of v
  698
take a fancy to v 827
take after v 17, 19
take a holiday v 687
take aim v 278
take a nap v 687
take an assumed name
  v 565
take an interest in v
  455, 906
take apart v 162
take a peep v 441
take a shine to v 827
take a trip v 266

take a turn v 140
take away v 2, 38, 789
take away from v 789
take back again v 790
take care v 459, 864
take care of v 664
take cognizance of v 450
take counsel v 695
take down v 308
take effect v 170
take fire v 384
take flight v 623
take for granted v 514
take from v 38, 789
take heart v 861
take hold v 46
take ill v 655
take in v 54, 518, 545, 785
take in hand v 676
take into account v 469
take into consideration v 469
take in tow v 285
take it easy v 683
take its course v 151
take liberties v 885
take no interest in v 456, 866
take no note of time v 115
take oar v 267
take off v 19, 226, 267, 293, 813
take offense v 900
take off like a shot v 274
take off the point v 254
take one's chances v 156
take one's leave v 293
take one's time v 685
take orders v 996
take out v 301
take over v 775
take pains v 686
take pen in hand v 590
take place v 1, 151, 151
take pleasure in v 827
take possession of v 775
take precautions v 664
take precedence v 33, 62, 280
take refuge v 666

take root v 184, 613
take shelter v 666
take sick v 655
take soundings v 208
take steps v 673
take the average v 29
take the bull by the horns v 861
take the first step v 66
take the initiative v 66
take the lead v 66, 280
take the place of v 147
take the pledge v 958
take time v 133
take to the altar v 903
take to the skies v 267
take up v 307, 676, 677
take up one's abode v 189
take upon oneself v 676
take up quarters v 184
take up the pen v 590
take what's offered v 607
take wing v 266, 267
taking n 789
taking nourishment n 298
tale n 546, 549
talebearer n 532
talent n 79, 698
talents n 698
talismanic adj 992
talk n 582, 588; v 582
talk a mile a minute v 584
talkative adj 582, 584
talkativeness n 584
talk big v 577, 884
talker n 584
talk fancy v 577
talk it over v 588
talk nonsense v 497
talk together v 588
talk to oneself v 589
tall adj 200, 206
tallness n 206
tallow n 356
tall tale n 546
tally n 86, 805; v 23, 85
tallying n 85
tame v 174, 370, 749; adj 172, 370, 575, 725
taming n 370
tamper with v 140
tan adj 433

tang n 390, 392, 394
tangerine adj 439
tangibility n 3
tangible adj 3, 316
tangle v 61, 219
tangled adj 59
tanked adj 959
tanker n 273
tantalize v 509
tantamount adj 27
tap n 263, 276; v 260, 276, 406
taper n 423; v 203
tapering adj 253
taper to a point v 253
tapping n 407
tar n 356a
tardiness n 133, 275
tardy adj 133, 275
target n 620
tarn n 343
tarnish n 874; v 429, 653, 848, 874
tarnished adj 874
tarpaulin n 223
tarry v 110, 133
tarrying n 133
tart adj 397
tartness n 397
task n 676, 704; v 677, 688
taskmaster n 694, 739
taste n 390, 850
taste n 394, 465, 480, 578; v 298, 390, 394
taste bad v 395
tasteful adj 465, 578, 850
tastefully adv 850
taste good v 394
taste great v 394
tasteless adj 337, 391, 395, 579
tastelessness n 391
tastelessness n 395, 579
tastiness n 394
tasty adj 377, 390, 394
tattle v 588
tattler n 532
tattoo v 440
taunt v 856
taunts n 856
taut adj 43
tautological adj 104
tautology n 104
tawdriness n 851

tawdry *adj* 643, 851
tawny *adj* 433, 435
tax *v* 677, 688
teach *v* 537, 673
teacher *n* 540
teacher *n* 753
teaching *n* 537
team-work *n* 709
tear *v* 44, 173, 274
tearful *adj* 839
tear out *v* 301
tears *n* 411
tear to pieces *v* 44
tear up *v* 162
teasing *n* 377
teat *n* 250
technicality *n* 697
technique *n* 627
tedious *adj* 275, 841, 843
tedium *n* 688, 841
teem *v* 168
teeming *adj* 72, 102, 168
teem with *v* 102
teenage *adj* 131
teenage years *n* 131
teeter *v* 160, 275, 315
teetering *adj* 160
teetotaler *n* 953, 958
teetotalism *n* 958
telescope *n* 445
telethermometer *n* 389
tell *v* 85, 467, 527, 529, 594
teller *n* 801
telling *n* 594; *adj* 642
temper *n* 5, 7, 323, 820; *v* 174, 323, 324
temperament *n* 5, 176, 820
temperamental *adj* 901
temperance *n* 953
temperance *n* 174
temperate *adj* 174, 736, 953
temperateness *n* 174
temperature *n* 382
tempered *adj* 820
tempest *n* 173, 315, 349, 825
tempest in a teacup *n* 549
tempestuous *adj* 349
temple *n* 1000
temporal *adj* 111, 997

temporarily *adv* i 11
temporary *adj* 111
tempt *v* 615, 675
temptation *n* 615
tempter *n* 978
tempt fate *v* 621
tempt fortune *v* 675
ten *n* 98
tenable *adj* 664
tenacious *adj* 46, 150, 327, 604, 604a
tenacity *n* 327
tenacity *n* 150, 604, 604a
tenancy *n* 777
tenant *n* 188, 779; *v* 186
tend *v* 176, 278, 472
tendencies *n* 5
tendency *n* 176
tendency *n* 177, 278, 472, 613
tender *n* 763; *v* 763; *adj* 324, 378, 428, 597, 740 821, 822, 897, 906
tender age *n* 127
tender-hearted *adj* 906
tenderness *n* 378, 821, 822, 897, 906
tender years *n* 127
tending *adj* 176
tendril *n* 205, 248
tend toward *v* 278
tenet *n* 451, 484, 537, 983
tenor *n* 7, 26, 278, 516
tensile *adj* 325
tension *n* 159
tent *n* 223
tentative *adj* 675
tenuity *n* 322
tenuous *adj* 322
tenure *n* 777
tepid *adj* 382
tergiversation *n* 607
term *n* 71
term *n* 106, 108, 198, 200, 233, 562; *v* 564
terminal *adj* 67, 233
terminate *v* 67, 142, 729
termination *n* 67, 142, 233, 261, 729
terminology *n* 560, 562

terminus *n* 233
terms *n* 476, 770
terrain *n* 342
terrestrial *adj* 318, 342
terrible *adj* 846, 860
terribly *adv* 31
terrified *adj* 860
territorial *adj* 181, 342
territory *n* 181, 965
terror *n* 860
terror-stricken *adj* 860
terse *adj* 572
terseness *n* 572
tertiary *adj* 92
test *n* 463; *v* 463
testify *v* 467, 535
testimony *n* 467
testy *adj* 684, 901
tête-à-tête *n* 588
tether *v* 43
tetrad *n* 95
text *n* 22, 542, 591
textbook *n* 542
texture *n* 256, 329
textured *adj* 256
thank *v* 916
thankful *adj* 916
thankfulness *n* 916
thankless *adj* 917
thanklessness *n* 917
thanks *n* 916
that being the case *adv* 8
thatch *n* 223
that is to say *adv* 522
thaw *v* 335, 382, 384
thawing *n* 335
the all-merciful *n* 976
the all-powerful *n* 976
the almighty *n* 976
theater *n* 599, 728
theatrical *adj* 599, 855, 882
theatricals *n* 599
the cloth *n* 996
the common people *n* 876
the converse *n* 14
the drama *n* 599
the eternal *n* 976
theft *n* 788, 789, 791
the future *n* 121
the infinite *n* 976
the inverse *n* 14
theism *n* 983
the latest thing *n* 123

T

T

transgression *n* 303, 773, 927
transience *n* 111
transient *adj* 111, 264
transit *n* 144, 270
transition *n* 144, 270
transitional *adj* 264
transitoriness *n* 111
transitory *adj* 111
translate *v* 522
translation *n* 522
translator *n* 524
translucent *adj* 425
translucence *n* 425
transmissible *adj* 270
transmission *n* 270, 302, 783
transmissive *adj* 783
transmit *v* 270, 783
transmit light *v* 425
transmittable *adj* 270
transmutable *adj* 144
transmutation *n* 140, 144
transmute *v* 140
transparence *n* 425
transparency *n* 425
transparent *adj* 337, 425, 518
transpire *v* 532
transplant *v* 270
transplantation *n* 270
transport *n* 270, 827; *v* 270, 829
transportable *adj* 270
transportation *n* 272
transporter *n* 271
transporting *adj* 977
transposal *n* 218
transpose *v* 148, 185, 218, 270
transposition *n* 140, 148, 185, 218, 270
transverse *adj* 217, 219
trap *n* 530, 545, 667
trappings *n* 225
trash *n* 643
trashy *adj* 209, 575, 643
travail *n* 686
travel *n* 266; *v* 266
traveler *n* 268
traveling *n* 266; *adj* 264, 266
traverse *v* 266, 302
travesty *n* 21, 523; *v* 19, 523

trawler *n* 273
treacherous *adj* 544
treachery *n* 545
tread *n* 264
tread down *v* 749
tread upon *v* 649
treasure *n* 648; *v* 991
treasurer *n* 801
treasury *n* 802
treat *v* 595, 829
treatise *n* 593, 595
treatment *n* 662
treat well *v* 906
treaty *n* 23, 721, 769
treble *v* 93; *adj* 93
trebly *adv* 93
tree *n* 367
trellis *n* 219
tremble *v* 149, 160, 315, 383
tremendously *adv* 31
tremor *n* 315
tremulous *adj* 149, 315
trench *n* 259
trenchant *adj* 171, 253, 572, 574, 642
trend *n* 176, 278, 516
trendiness *n* 123
trendy *adj* 123
trepidation *n* 860
trespass *n* 303; *v* 303, 945
trestle *n* 215
triad *n* 92
trial *n* 463, 675, 686, 828, 830, 969
triality *n* 92
tribe *n* 72, 75
tribunal *n* 966
tributary *n* 348; *adj* 784
trice *n* 113
trick *n* 545; *v* 545
trickle *n* 348; *v* 295, 348
trickly *adj* 348
tricky *adj* 545, 702
trifle *n* 32, 451, 643; *v* 499
trifling *n* 499, 643; *adj* 4, 32, 477, 499, 643, 880
triform *adj* 92
trill *v* 407
trim *n* 231, 240; *v* 27, 231; *adj* 652
trimming *n* 231

trinity *n* 92
trio *n* 92, 415, 416
trip *n* 266, 302, 306; *v* 306, 309
tripartition *n* 94
triple *v* 93; *adj* 93
triplet *n* 92
triplicate *adj* 93
triplication *n* 93
triplicity *n* 93
tripling *n* 93
triply *adv* 93
trip the light fantastic toe *v* 309
trip up *v* 495
trisect *v* 94
trisection *n* 94
trite *adj* 496, 598, 613
triumph *n* 731, 733, 838; *v* 731, 838
triumphant *adj* 731, 838, 884
trivial *adj* 32, 209, 499, 517, 643, 880
triviality *n* 32, 209, 643, 736, 880
troll *n* 980
trollop *n* 962
troop *n* 72
trophy *n* 733
tropical *adj* 382
troubadour *n* 597
trouble *n* 59, 686, 704, 735, 828, 830; *v* 61, 828, 830
troublemaker *n* 913
trouble oneself about *v* 682
troublesome *adj* 59, 704, 830
trough *n* 252, 259, 350
trove *n* 480a
truant *n* 623
truce *n* 142, 721, 723
truck *n* 271, 272; *v* 264
trudge *v* 275
true *adj* 1, 17, 246, 246, 494, 543, 648, 772, 922, 604
true faith *n* 983a
truelove *n* 897
true to life *adj* 17
truism *n* 496
truistic *adj* 496
truly *adv* 31
trump card *n* 731

TU

U

ungodly *adj* 989
ungovernable *adj* 173, 825
ungoverned *adj* 748
ungraceful *adj* 579
ungracious *adj* 895
ungrammatical *adj* 568
ungrammatical usage *n* 568
ungrateful *adj* 917
ungrounded *adj* 4
unguarded *adj* 460
unguent *n* 356
unhallowed *adj* 989
unhandy *adj* 699
unhappy *adj* 828, 837
unharmonious *adj* 410
unhealthiness *n* 657
unhealthy *adj* 655, 657
unheard of *adj* 137, 508
unheeded *adj* 460
unheedful *adj* 452
unheeding *adj* 419, 458
unhewn *adj* 674
unhindered *adj* 748
unhinge *v* 61
unhinged *adj* 173, 503
unhip *adj* 246
unholy *adj* 989
unhoused *adj* 185
unhurried *adj* 275
unhurt *adj* 670
unification *n* 48, 87
unified *adj* 46, 48
uniform *v* 225; *adj* 16, 42, 58, 80, 242
uniformity *n* 16
uniformity *n* 17, 23, 58, 80, 87, 150, 242
uniformly *adv* 16, 82
uniforms *n* 225
unimaginable *adj* 471
unimaginative *adj* 598, 843
unimitated *adj* 20
unimpaired *adj* 50, 670
unimpeachable *adj* 474
unimportance *n* 643
unimportance *n* 32, 175a
unimportant *adj* 32, 34, 643, 736
unimpressionable *adj* 823

unimproved *adj* 659
uninfluential *adj* 175a
uninformed *adj* 491
uninjured *adj* 670
uninquiring *adj* 456
uninquisitive *adj* 456
uninstructed *adj* 491
unintellectual *adj* 450a
unintelligent *adj* 450a
unintelligibility *n* 519
unintelligibility *n* 533, 571
unintelligible *adj* 519, 571
unintentional *adj* 621
unintentionally *adv* 621
uninterested *adj* 456, 841
uninteresting *adj* 843
uninterrupted *adj* 69, 112, 143
unintoxicated *adj* 958
union *n* 23, 43, 46, 48, 178, 709, 714, 903
unique *adj* 18, 20, 79, 83, 87, 870
uniqueness *n* 18, 20, 123
unison *n* 87, 714
unite *v* 41, 43, 48, 72, 87, 178, 290, 709, 712
united *adj* 46, 903
uniting *n* 37
unity *n* 87
unity *n* 13, 23, 50, 52, 714
universal *adj* 78
universality *n* 78
universalize *v* 78
universe *n* 180, 318
university *n* 542
unjust *adj* 923
unkempt *adj* 653
unknown *n* 233; *adj* 533
unlawful *adj* 964
unlawfulness *n* 923, 964
unlearn *v* 506
unlearnedness *n* 491
unless *adv* 8, 83
unlettered *adj* 491
unlicensed *adj* 964
unlike *adj* 15, 18

unlikelihood *n* 473
unlikely *adj* 473
unlikeness *n* 18
unlimited *adj* 31, 104, 180, 748
unlimited space *n* 180
unload *v* 185
unlooked for *adj* 508
unlovely *adj* 846
unlucky *adj* 135, 735
unmake *v* 145
unman *v* 158
unmanageable *adj* 704
unmarked *adj* 447
unmarried *adj* 904
unmarried man *n* 904
unmarried woman *n* 904
unmask *v* 529, 529
unmatched *adj* 15, 18, 20
unmeaningness *n* 517
unmelodious *adj* 414
unmerciful *adj* 914a
unmindful *adj* 452, 458, 460, 917
unmindfulness *n* 458
unmistakable *adj* 525
unmitigated *adj* 52
unmixed *adj* 42, 960
unmoved *adj* 265, 823
unmoving *adj* 172
unmusical *adj* 410, 414
unmuzzled *adj* 748
unnatural *adj* 83, 855
unnaturalness *n* 855
unnecessary *adj* 641
unnerve *v* 158, 160
unnerved *adj* 160
unnoticed *adj* 460
unobservant *adj* 458
unobserved *adj* 460
unobstructed *adj* 748
unobtainable *adj* 471
unobtrusive *adj* 881
unoccupied *adj* 452
unopened *adj* 261
unorthodox *adj* 984
unorthodoxy *n* 984
unostentatious *adj* 881
unpaid *adj* 806
unpalatable *adj* 395, 830
unparalleled *adj* 20, 33
unperceptive *adj* 376
unperformable *adj* 471
unpersuasive *adj* 175a

U

U

255

vampire n 980
van n 280
vanguard n 234, 280
vanish v 4, 111, 360, 449
vanished adj 449
vanishing point n 193
vanity n 880
vanity n 878
vantage ground n 175
vapid adj 337, 391, 575, 843
vapor n 353
vaporization n 336
vaporize v 336
vaporous adj 334, 336
vaporousness n 334
vapory adj 336
variability n 475
variable adj 140, 149, 475
variance n 15, 24, 291, 713
variant adj 15
variation n 20a
variation n 15, 83, 140
varied adj 15, 16a, 20a
variegate v 440
variegated adj 41, 440
variegation n 440
variety n 75, 81
various adj 15, 102
varnish n 223, 356a; v 356a
vary v 15, 18, 20a, 140, 149, 291, 314
vast adj 31, 104, 180, 192
vastness n 31, 105
vault n 245, 309, 318, 363, 802; v 309
vaulted adj 245
vaunt v 884
veer v 140, 279
vegetable n 367
vegetable adj 367
vegetable kingdom n 367
vegetable life n 365
vegetable oil n 356
vegetable physiology n 369
vegetal adj 367
vegetarian n 953
vegetate v 367
vegetation n 365
vegetative adj 365, 367

vehemence n 173, 825
vehement adj 173, 382, 574, 825
vehicle n 272
vehicle n 271, 631
veil n 424, 530; v 424, 528
veiled adj 447, 526
veiling n 528
vein n 176, 205, 602
veined adj 440
velocity n 274
velocity n 264
velvety adj 255, 256
venal adj 211, 819
venality n 819
vend v 796
vendible adj 796
vendition n 796
vendor n 796
veneer n 223; v 204, 223
venerable adj 124, 128, 928
venerate v 860, 928, 987
veneration n 860, 928, 987
vengeance n 718, 919
vengeful adj 718, 919
vengefulness n 919
venom n 663, 907
venomous adj 649, 657, 663, 907
vent n 260, 351
ventilate v 338, 349, 652
ventilation n 338
venture n 621, 675, 676; v 621, 665, 675, 861
venturesome adj 621, 675
veracious adj 494, 543
veracity n 543
veracity n 494
verbal adj 562
verbal interchange n 588
verbiage n 573
verbose adj 573, 584, 641
verbosity n 573, 584, 641
verdant adj 367, 435
verdict n 480, 969

verdure n 367, 435
verdurous adj 435
verge n 231, 233; v 176, 278
verification n 478
verify v 478
veritable adj 494
verity n 494
vermilion adj 434
vernacular n 560; adj 560
versatile adj 149
versatility n 149
verse n 590, 597
versification n 597
versifier n 597
versify v 597
versus adv 708
vertex n 210
vertical adj 212, 246
verticality n 212
vertically adv 212
verve n 159, 515, 574
very adv 31
very best adj 648
very much adv 31
vespers n 126
vessel n 191, 273
vestal virgin n 960
vestige n 551
vestments n 999
veteran n 130
veteran n 700
veterinary science n 370
veto v 761
vex v 828, 830
vexation n 828, 830, 835
vexatious adj 830, 901a
vibes n 314
vibrate v 314
vibration n 138, 314, 408
vibrato n 408
vice n 945
vice n 649, 923
vice versa adv 148
vicinity n 186, 197
vicious adj 907, 945
vicissitude n 111, 149
victimize v 649
victorious adj 731
victory n 731
vie v 648, 720

view n 441, 448, 453, 484, 620; v 441
viewpoint n 441
vigilance n 459, 682, 864, 920
vigilant adj 459, 507, 682, 864, 920
viginal adj 960
vignette n 594
vigor n 574
vigor n 157, 159, 171, 359, 364, 604, 654, 682
vigorous adj 159, 171, 359, 574, 654
vile adj 207, 211, 395, 649, 830, 846, 874, 898, 930
vilification n 934
vilify v 934
vilifying adj 934
villager n 188
villain n 941, 949
villainous adj 649
vinculum n 45
vindicate v 717, 919, 937
vindicated adj 937
vindicating adj 937
vindication n 937
vindication n 717
vindicator n 919, 937
vindictive adj 919
vindictiveness n 919
vinegariness n 397
vinegary adj 397
vintage adj 124
violate v 742, 773, 927
violate the law v 964
violation n 773, 927
violation of custom n 83
violence n 173
violence n 825
violent adj 59, 173, 382, 825
violently adv 31, 173
violet adj 437
virgin n 904, 960; adj 66, 123
virginal adj 123, 946
virginity n 960
virility n 159
virtually adv 5
virtue n 944
virtue n 648, 922, 939, 946, 960

virtuous adj 881, 939, 944, 946, 960
virtuousness n 944, 946
virulence n 649
virulent adj 649, 657
virus n 663
visage n 448
viscid adj 352
viscosity n 352 .
viscous adj 327, 352
visibility n 446
visible adj 446, 525
vision n 441
vision n 443, 515, 980
visionary n 504; adj 2, 4, 441, 515
visit often v 136
visor n 530
vista n 448
visual adj 441
vital adj 359, 642
vital flame n 359
vitality n 159, 359, 364, 654
vitalize v 359
vital spark n 359
vitiate v 659
vivacious adj 359, 515, 682, 829, 836
vivacity n 359, 515, 682, 836
vivid adj 171, 375, 420, 428, 505
vivify v 159, 359
vocabulary 562
vocal adj 415, 416, 580
vocal group n 416
vocalist n 416
vocality n 580
vocalization n 580
vocalize v 416, 566, 580
vocal music n 415
vocation n 625
vociferate v 411
vociferation n 411
vociferous adj 404, 411
vociferousness n 404
vogue n 613, 852
voice n 580
voice n 402; v 566, 580, 582
voiceless adj 581, 583
void n 2, 4, 187; v 2, 297, 756; adj 2, 187
volatile adj 149, 320,

336
volatility n 149, 320, 334
volcanic adj 173, 384, 825
volition n 600
volitional adj 600
volubility n 584
voluble adj 334, 584
volume n 25, 31, 102, 192, 590, 593
voluminous adj 192
voluntarily adv 600
voluntary adj 600
volunteer v 676
voluptuary n 954a, 962
voluptuous adj 377, 829
voluptuousness n 827
vomit v 297
voodoo n 993
voracious adj 957
voracity n 957
vortex n 312, 315, 348
voucher n 807
vow n 768
vowel n 561
voyage n 267, 302
voyager n 268
V-shaped adj 244
vulgar adj 579, 851, 876, 895
vulgarity n 851
vulgarity n 579, 895
vulgarize v 851
vulnerability n 177

W

wad v 224
wadding n 224, 263
waddle v 275
wade through v 539
waft v 320, 349
wag n 844
wager n 621; v 621
wages n 775, 812
wage war v 722
waggle v 315
wagon n 272
waif n 268
wail n 411, 839; v 411
wailing n 411, 839
wait v 133, 265, 681
wait for v 507
waiting n 507, 946
wait on v 88, 746
waive v 624, 678, 782,

W

W

W